Criminal Justice in Canada

Criminal Justice in Canada

An Introduction

Colin Goff

University of Winnipeg

ITP Nelson

an International Thomson Publishing company

Toronto • Albany • Bonn • Boston • Cincinnati • Detroit • London • Madrid • Melbourne
Mexico City • New York • Pacific Grove • Paris • San Francisco • Singapore • Tokyo • Washington

I(T)P™
International Thomson Publishing
The ITP logo is a trademark under licence

Published in 1997 by
I(T)P Nelson
A division of Thomson Canada Limited
1120 Birchmount Road
Scarborough, Ontario M1K 5G4

Visit our Web site at **http://www.nelson.com/nelson.html**

Cover art, cover design, and interior design: Steve MacEachern

---

Canadian Cataloguing in Publication Data

Goff, Colin H., 1949–
    Criminal justice in Canada : an introduction

Includes bibliographical references and index.
ISBN 0-17-604873-1

    1. Criminal justice, Administration of
—Canada.   I. Title.

HV9960.C2G63   1997   364.971   C96-990005-8

Publisher and Team Leader	Michael Young
Acquisitions Editor	Charlotte Forbes
Senior Production Editor	Bob Kohlmeier
Projects Editor	Evan Turner
Assistant Art Director	Sylvia Vander Schee
Senior Composition Analyst	Zenaida Diores
Project Coordinator	Brad Horning
Photo Researcher	Ann Ludbrook

Send your comments by e-mail to the production team for this book: college_arts_hum@nelson.com

Printed and bound in Canada

5 6 7 8 9 10 TCP 5 4 3 2 1 0 9

Dedication

To Sarah, Buddy, and Robley

Contents

Field Practice

Exhibits

Preface

Over the past two decades, public interest in the operation of the Canadian criminal justice system reached an all-time high. This surge in interest is not surprising, considering the attention currently given to issues such as crimes of violence and the ability of police to adequately control crime. Many citizens are demanding increased rights for victims, an increase in the number of police officers, and harsher penalties for convicted offenders. Not surprisingly, more students are demanding more post-secondary courses in criminal justice, with the result that colleges and universities today are graduating large numbers of graduates who will be employed in our criminal justice system.

This increasing interest led me to introduce more information about our criminal justice system in criminology courses. The popularity of this approach made apparent the great need for a comprehensive introductory course about criminal justice. *Criminal Justice in Canada* was written to fill that need—to provide a concise and accurate account of the basic features of our criminal justice system.

This text describes the formal processes of our criminal justice system and shows how these processes reflect the basic structural and procedural aspects of our system. This approach entails discussion of the major criminal justice agencies and the way those agencies operate to identify, apprehend, process, and control offenders. The book covers what most experts consider to be the central facets of our criminal justice system. It does not aim to describe every feature and nuance of every criminal justice agency but rather to spotlight only those legal cases that have shaped the operation of the various agencies in fundamental ways. Criminological research studies are included also, and so are federal and provincial government evaluations and policy efforts. In addition, some of the most recent developments and controversial areas of our system are included: community policing, intermediate punishments (such as electronic monitoring), and specialized courts (such as domestic violence courts).

The system of justice has undergone many changes over the past 15 years, especially since the introduction of the Charter of Rights and Freedoms. Many of those changes are noted here, including some of the most important recent legal decisions that have influenced the day-to-day operation of our justice system. The results of many recent studies and evaluations of the operation of our system are included also.

Equally important to an understanding of the criminal justice system is an appreciation of the manner in which the various criminal justice agencies develop informal systems of operation. These informal systems—which help agencies cope with day-to-day operations as well as help them reach their goals—are crucial aspects of the criminal justice agencies, and they can be just as important to an understanding of the operation of our justice system as the formal procedures. This informal aspects of our criminal justice system are discussed where applicable.

The text is divided into chapters that reflect the structure and operation of our justice system. The first four chapters give students a basic overview of the criminal justice system, the scope of the crime problem, the law, and different ways of conceptualizing the justice system. Chapter 1 introduces students to the formal structure of our criminal justice system. The informal justice system is reviewed also, and so is the importance of discretion at all stages of the system. Chapter 2 provides a discussion of our criminal law as well as its importance to our criminal justice system. A feature of this chapter is a discussion of the law in context—that is, why and how criminal laws are introduced in this country. Chapter 3 gives students information about the trends and patterns of crime in Canada. This chapter also discusses how crime statistics are collected, and considers some of the strengths and weaknesses of the various ways crime is measured in Canada. Chapter 4 introduces students to the four guiding models that underpin the operation of our criminal justice system. Each model is discussed as it would operate in an ideal manner, without influence from any other model. This chapter also discussed aboriginal justice systems, and ends with a brief discussion about the relevance of these models to criminological theory.

Chapters 5 and 6 give students an overview of the police. Some attention is given to the history of the police in Canada, but Chapter 5 discusses the functions and changing operations of the police in our society. Chapter 6 examines the major issues facing the police today: the recruitment of minorities, the practice of discretion, and police misconduct.

Chapters 7–10 look at the trial process, from pre-trial procedures to sentencing. Chapter 7 explains the basic components of pre-trial procedure as it applies to the police and the earliest stages of the operation of our justice system, including the legal rights of the defendant to legal counsel and the rules that govern the use of warrants by the police. Chapter 8 considers the basic features of trial procedure, particularly as it applies to criminal trials. It also reviews the different levels of the courts in Canada and the functions of prosecutors and defence lawyers. Chapter 10 focuses on sentencing—different types of sentences, disparity in sentencing, and healing circles.

Chapters 11 and 12 are devoted to our correctional system, particularly the federal system. The differences between the federal and provincial correctional systems are discussed, as is probation and the effectiveness of the various forms of conditional release. The traditional manner of operating our correctional system is discussed first, and this is followed by an extensive discussion of alternatives, in particular intermediate punishments.

Instructor's Support Material

Available to instructors is a test bank that includes multiple-choice, true-or-false, and short-answer questions. The test bank ISBN is 0-17-604925-8.

Also available is a video that includes film clips from CTV that illustrate the issues and concepts discussed in each chapter of the textbook. The video ISBN is 0-17-606973-9.

Acknowledgments

Any project of this scope is never the work of one person only, and the planning, writing, and editing of this text absorbed the time and energy of a small group of dedicated individuals. Cindy Jarigen deserves special recognition. Her contributions cannot be measured easily. Her work as editorial and research assistant, library researcher, manuscript reviewer, and critic was unfailingly top quality, and her constant support and insights made it all easier. Ann Champion provided software expertise, and her suggestions greatly added to the overall quality of the final manuscript. Her encouragement gave me reason to believe in "a light at the end of the tunnel." Bob Bangs and Kevin Harrison provided expert advice based on their many years of experience working within the criminal justice system. Their observations and opinions contributed significantly to the quality of the manuscript. Two special mentors—Gil Geis, Professor Emeritus at the University of California, Irvine, and Frank Cullen, Professor of Criminal Justice at the University of Cincinnati—provided much emotional and intellectual support.

Many criminal justice practitioners across Canada shared their insights into the criminal justice system and gave important assistance. Special thanks goes to all of them for responding to my questions and my requests for interviews. Other individuals who contributed include Colleen Dell, the librarians at the University of Winnipeg, Walter DeKeseredy, and Leslie Murphy.

Many thanks go also to key individuals at ITP Nelson. Cathryn Cranston, a representative of ITP Nelson, was the first to see the potential of this project. The enthusiasm, direction, and foresight of Charlotte Forbes, Acquisitions Editor, helped at all stages of the project, particularly the latter ones. Other individuals at ITP Nelson gave an enormous amount of time and energy. Heather Martin worked hard on the development of the manuscript, and her contributions are reflected throughout the final product. Bob Kohlmeier assisted with the manuscript toward the end of the project, giving insight into the final stages. Special recognition goes to Evan Turner, who joined the editorial team in the latter stages of the project and gave much encouragement and saw that everything was done on time.

Finally, the reviewers of the manuscript provided important suggestions. Among those reviewers were Jim Anderson, John Abbott College; W.R. Anderson, Durham College; Gina Antonacci, Humber College; Rick Linden, University of Manitoba; David MacAlister, Kwantlen University College; Chris

McCormick, Acadia University; Scott Nicholls, Humber College; Julian V. Roberts, University of Ottawa; T.A. Rudolph, Lethbridge Community College; K.R. Spencer, University of Alberta; and Brian Young, Camosun College.

An Overview of the Criminal Justice System in Canada

The criminal justice system in Canada comprises the operation of three major agencies: the police, the courts, and the correctional system. Though great differences exist among these agencies, they are generally viewed as operating together in a formal manner, following the procedures developed to guide their actions. This system works informally as well; each agency operates according to its goals and mandates, sometimes to the detriment of other agencies. This chapter begins by identifying the major components of the Canadian criminal justice system and the cost of operating them. It then considers the formal and informal operations of the criminal justice system.

On the night of May 28, 1971, two groups of two men met in Wentworth Park, in Sydney, N.S. Roy Ebsary, a man in one of the groups, feared that he and his friend were about to be robbed by the two other men. Ebsary pulled a knife and lunged at the other two, stabbing one of them, Sandy

CHAPTER OBJECTIVES

- identify the major agencies of the criminal justice system
- discuss the costs of operating the various agencies of the criminal justice system
- examine how these agencies operate within the formal structure of the criminal justice system
- examine the operation of the major categories of the "crime funnel"

Seale, in the stomach and the other, Donald Marshall, in the left forearm. Seale died soon after, and Marshall, after a police investigation, was arrested and on June 5 charged with the second-degree murder of Sandy Seale. Marshall was held in the county jail until his trial was heard in early November. On the basis of statements given by witnesses, Marshall was found guilty by a jury and sentenced to life imprisonment on November 5, 1971. Later that month, the Appeal Division of the Supreme Court of Nova Scotia upheld the conviction of Marshall. However, unbeknown to Marshall, statements had been given both to police and prosecution that supported his contention that someone else had stabbed Seale.

It was not until he had served almost 12 years in various federal correctional institutions, all the while maintaining his innocence in the murder of Seale, that Marshall was informed by a friend of the identity of the individual who killed Seale. The friend told Marshall that Ebsary told *him* that he had "killed a black guy and stabbed an Indian in [Wentworth] park in 1971." Police in Sydney had until then failed to follow up on the statements made to them that implicated Ebsary. This time, the Union of Nova Scotia Indians hired a lawyer to deal with the case. The RCMP were requested to re-examine the case, and their subsequent investigation revealed that three teenagers during the original murder trial gave perjured testimony implicating Marshall as the assailant. During questioning by the RCMP, all three stated they had given false testimony under pressure from a member of the Sydney Police Force. Marshall was soon released on bail, and in December 1982 Nova Scotia's appeals court found him not guilty of the murder. In 1985, Roy Ebsary was convicted of the charge of manslaughter in the death of Sandy Seale and sentenced to one year in the Cape Breton Correctional Centre (Harris 1986; Mannette 1992).

Donald Marshall, who served nearly 12 years in prison in Nova Scotia for a crime that he did not commit, was found guilty in 1996 of illegally catching and selling eels. (Photo: Andrew Vaughn/Canadian Press)

Also in Nova Scotia, and at about the same time that Marshall was released on bail, an abused woman, Jane Stafford, shot and killed her husband as he slept, passed out, in the cab of his pickup truck. Her husband had abused her for a number of years and was well known to local residents and the RCMP for his violent behaviour. Later, Jane Stafford was interrogated by the local RCMP, and after confessing to the murder she overheard the staff sergeant telling some of his fellow police officers that she "deserved a medal . . . she probably saved a couple of our officers' lives." Jane was charged with first-degree murder, but a jury found her not guilty of that charge. Two weeks later, the Crown appealed the decision and won the right to have the case heard by the Appeal Division of the Supreme Court of Nova Scotia. In court for the second time, she pleaded guilty to the lesser charge of manslaughter.

What then became an issue was the sentence Jane Stafford should receive for her offence. The Crown prosecutor argued that she should receive a jail term "to discourage others from taking the law into their own hands," while her lawyer argued that a suspended sentence would be sufficient penalty. The appeals court judge, while agreeing that Jane had lived a "tragic life" and "was not a danger to society," stated "there must be deterrence in the law but that there must be protection of society as a whole." He sentenced her to six months in provincial jail and two years' probation (Vallee 1986).

A number of issues arise in both the Donald Marshall case and the Jane Stafford case. In the Marshall, how can someone serve 12 years for a murder he did not commit? Why did the Crown prosecutor decide not to share with his defence lawyer the information that could have acquitted Marshall? Why was Ebsary, identified by his friend as the person who killed Seale, never considered by police to be the potential murderer? As a result of these events, the Supreme Court of Canada changed the rules on disclosure of evidence in criminal courts after hearing the *Stinchcombe* case (see Exhibit 2.5).

In the Stafford case, some supporters of her actions argued she was the real victim of the case. Although her husband was well known as a local bully, although his abusive nature toward his wife was well known, the police were unable to protect her. A few years later the Supreme Court of Canada accepted the "battered woman syndrome" defence in the *Lavallee* case. Both the Marshall case and the Stafford case therefore had a significant impact on the rights of the accused within the Canadian criminal justice system.

The Criminal Justice System

Canada has developed a number of agencies designed to protect the public from individuals who violate the law. These agencies make up a vast network of organizations and facilities charged with the investigation, detection, prosecution, and correction of offenders. The direct cost of this system to provincial, territorial, and federal levels of government exceeded $9 billion in 1992–93. And this figure excludes the hidden costs of crime such as the loss of work and psychological trauma suffered by many crime victims.

The agencies involved in the investigation, court processing, and punishment of offenders are linked together in what is commonly called the criminal justice system. Viewing the operation of criminal justice as a system allows us to comprehend the "interdependency of the parts of the entire process" since "many factors influence each decision and decision-maker in the justice process" (Travis 1990:34). Conventional wisdom holds that all the parts of the criminal justice system interact with one another in a coordinated fashion.

FIGURE 1.1

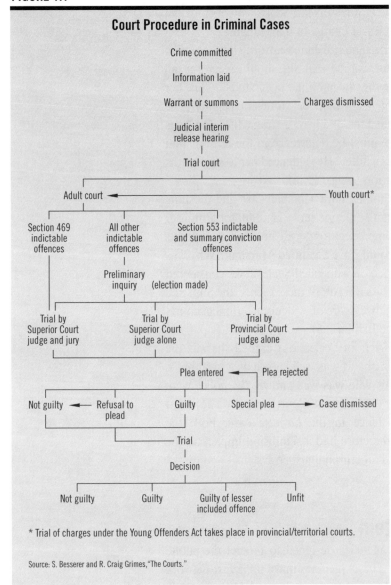

Court Procedure in Criminal Cases

Crime committed

Information laid

Warrant or summons ———————— Charges dismissed

Judicial interim release hearing

Trial court

Adult court ◄———————————————— Youth court*

Section 469 indictable offences

All other indictable offences

Section 553 indictable and summary conviction offences

Preliminary inquiry (election made)

Trial by Superior Court judge and jury

Trial by Superior Court judge alone

Trial by Provincial Court judge alone

Plea entered ◄——— Plea rejected

Not guilty ◄— Refusal to plead

Guilty

Special plea ——► Case dismissed

Trial

Decision

Not guilty — Guilty — Guilty of lesser included offence — Unfit

* Trial of charges under the Young Offenders Act takes place in provincial/territorial courts.

Source: S. Besserer and R. Craig Grimes, "The Courts."

Though the word *system* presents an image of criminal justice agencies operating in concert, the image is not completely accurate. These agencies are related in the sense of being involved with the apprehension and control of criminals, but "they have not yet become so well coordinated that they can be described as operating in unison" (Senna and Siegel 1995:11). While these agencies are formally independent of one another and have their own goals, these goals can lead to one agency's informally influencing the actions of another. For example, in Canada the formal powers of the police end when they hand over a case to the prosecutor. In reality, however, police can stay involved with the case to influence the prosecutor's decisions on charges and punishment (Wheeler 1987).

Another case of deviation from the way the system should formally operate is competition between agencies. Consider an example of interagency competition that involves the reporting procedures of a customs officer when she discovers an individual transporting a narcotic across the border. The formal policy is clear in this case: customs officials report to the federal police force any individual caught transporting narcotics into Canada. The law specifies that only this police force is to be contacted and only to this police force is the suspect handed over, since transporting narcotics into Canada is a violation of a federal statute. However, the customs officer contacts the municipal police force instead, because of poor relations between the customs agency and the federal police force. This is an example of a "real world" problem that appears and then disappears as the conflict between the agencies changes over time.

EXHIBIT 1.1

The Due Process and Crime Control Models of the Criminal Justice System

(N.B.: The following models were developed by Herbert Packer and are different from those presented in Chapter 3.)

How should we respond to individuals who violate the law? Two models have been developed to answer this question: the due process model and the crime control model. The due process model argues that rights be *natural* or *inalienable* and as such stresses the need for procedural safeguards for the accused over the rights of society. In contrast, the crime control model emphasizes the need to control criminal activity and so focuses on the preservation of the social order over the rights of the accused.

The Crime Control Model
This model is best characterized by such statements as "get tough on crime" and "the criminal justice system is weak on criminals." According to the crime control model, the most important goal of the criminal justice system is to reduce crime and to incarcerate criminals for lengthy periods of time. This reduces lawlessness and protects the rights of law-abiding citizens. To achieve this goal, the criminal justice system operates like an assembly line—it moves offenders as quickly as possible to conviction and punishment as efficiently as possible so that effective crime control is attained. Certainty of punishment is reached through mandatory sentences, longer prison terms, and the elimination of parole.

The crime control model rests on the presumption of guilt, especially as offenders are processed through the court system. That is, most individuals who are arrested are, in reality, factually guilty. Thus the model puts great trust in the decisions made by criminal justice officials, who wish to protect society. The model assumes that these individuals make few, if any, errors, since most defendants are guilty. Each stage of the criminal justice system involves a series of uniform and routine decisions made by officials. Finality is important to officials, because it means there are few problems with the system and, as a result, few challenges to the system are made. Support for the use of discretion throughout the system is a key feature of this model, since legal technicalities reduce the efficiency of punishing offenders. If the criminal justice system is allowed to run as efficiently as possible, a reduction in the crime rate results. Consequently, concerns for legal rights should not be allowed to erode the system's ability to reduce crime. Furthermore, when issues about the administration of justice come into conflict with the protection of society, the crime control model errs in favour of the protection of the rights of the law-abiding citizenry.

The Due Process Model
In contrast to the crime control model, the due process model emphasizes the protection of the legal rights of the accused who are formally involved in the criminal justice system. The most important goal of the system is not to reduce crime but to see that justice is done—specifically, by protecting the legal rights of the accused. This ensures that innocent people are not convicted. If they are, travesties of justice have been committed somewhere in the system, and they need to be corrected immediately. The best way to protect the rights of the accused is to limit the powers of criminal justice officials in order to avoid potential wrongdoing. The operation of the criminal justice system is much different from the crime control model—it's like an obstacle course.

Before people are arrested, prosecuted, and convicted, all attempts are made to ensure that the accused are treated with fairness and that justice is served. All offenders are presumed innocent, regardless of their apparent guilt. Criminal justice officials are constantly monitored, since they are likely to abuse their powers and to make errors in judgment when processing and convicting individuals. The high-profile cases of Donald Marshall and, more recently, Guy Paul Morin both involved officials who convicted innocent people. As a result of these abuses, legal controls have been introduced to make sure that officials don't abuse their powers.

It is difficult, if not impossible, for the criminal justice system to reduce crime, say the supporters of this model, because the criminal sanction is limited in its ability to stop criminal behaviour, so justice should not be sacrificed in the name of crime control that is largely beyond reach. Issues that bring the administration of justice into disrepute are of great concern to the due process model, and even if an accused is factually guilty, the fact that a member of a criminal justice agency violates the criminal procedures governing its operation means the offender is allowed to go free.

Source: Herbert Packer, *The Limits of the Criminal Sanction* (Stanford, Calif.: Stanford University Press, 1968); and Gresham M. Sykes and Francis T. Cullen, *Criminology,* 2nd ed. (Fort Worth, Tex.: Harcourt Brace Jovanovich, 1992).

The Costs of the Criminal Justice System

The Canadian criminal justice system is expensive to operate. A recent Canadian study reported that a $2500 robbery can ultimately cost in excess of $200 000 by the time the offender is caught, tried in a formal court setting, and, if found guilty, incarcerated (Hess 1995). The estimated costs of processing this robbery case through the criminal justice system, from the police investigation to the end of incarceration, include the following:

- the money lost by the victim in the robbery ($2500)
- the amount of time it took the police to solve the crime ($3665)
- the cost of prosecuting the case in court ($1300)
- the cost of providing legal aid ($790)
- judicial and related court costs ($900)

Assuming the accused is found guilty of the offence and is incarcerated for the full extent of his sentence, the final bill would be around $215 000.

This same study investigated the financial costs of other crimes and found similarities. A $3123 fraud offence costs the criminal justice system over $195 000 by the time the accused serves his sentence, while an individual found guilty of a break and enter with the theft of $2042 ends up costing taxpayers approximately $137 000.

Lengthy police investigations and criminal court cases can easily land Canadian taxpayers with bills of millions of dollars. The police investigation into Paul Bernardo and the resulting trial is reported to have cost Ontario taxpayers between $5 million and $10 million.

The costs of operating other areas of our justice system can be high. Presently it costs about $47 000 to keep an offender incarcerated for one year in a federal institution, although this cost varies by security level. Looking after one offender for one year in a maximum-security prison exceeded $70 000 in 1993. It cost about half of that ($36 227) for a year in a minimum-security institution, while a year in a community correctional centre cost $28 269 (Young 1994).

The expense of operating the criminal justice system continues

FIGURE 1.2

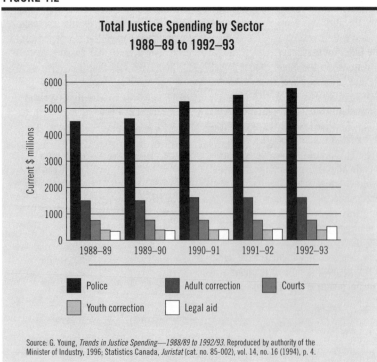

Source: G. Young, *Trends in Justice Spending—1988/89 to 1992/93.* Reproduced by authority of the Minister of Industry, 1996; Statistics Canada, *Juristat* (cat. no. 85-002), vol. 14, no. 16 (1994), p. 4.

to grow at a significant rate annually. The cost of policing in 1992–93 was $5.7 billion, a 30-percent increase from 1988–89; the cost of operating the courts cost almost $1 billion, a 35-percent increase over the same period. The adult and youth correctional systems experienced similar spending increases. Over the same five-year period, the cost of operating the youth correctional system increased by 37 percent (to almost half a billion dollars) while the adult correctional system experienced an increase in spending in excess of 28 percent (to almost $2 billion).

Large numbers of individuals are required to investigate, apprehend, process, guard, and reintegrate the large numbers of individuals processed by our justice system. In excess of 120 000 individuals work in criminal justice-related jobs. During 1992–93, almost 77 000 individuals were employed by municipal, provincial, and federal police forces, over 28 000 people full-time in both provincial and federal adult corrections, and about 12 000 persons in various roles within the court system. These large numbers are needed to operate a criminal justice system that handles as many criminal offences as Canada has. In 1993, a total of 2 568 912 adults and youths in Canada had been convicted of a crime sometime in their lives. On an average day in 1993, over 31 000 adults in both provincial and federal correctional facilities were under sentence, remand, or lockup. Another 112 000 persons were on probation and conditional release programs (Young 1994).

Significant unanticipated financial costs can be incurred by the criminal justice system as well. If an individual is falsely accused and convicted of a crime he didn't commit, the government responsible pays compensation to the individual. While the documented cases involving falsely accused and convicted individuals are few in Canada to date, governments have paid substantial amounts to individuals falsely charged, convicted, and imprisoned. The compensation package to Donald Marshall for spending 12 years in prison for a murder he didn't commit will exceed $1.3 million if he lives to the age of 65. Richard Norris—incarcerated nine months for indecent assault in 1980 and acquitted in 1991 after someone else confessed to the crime—was awarded over $507 000 by the Ontario government. And in a British Columbia case, Norman Fox received $275 000 in compensation after serving a ten-year prison term

James Lockyer, lawyer for the acquitted Guy Paul Morin, right, registers delight at the way his client handled a question about compensation at a Toronto news conference. (Photo: Tibor Kolley/*The Globe and Mail*)

as a result of having been mistakenly identified as an assailant in a series of crimes, including rape (Platiel 1995).

The victims of crime can suffer from significant financial costs too. According to the Canadian Urban Victimization Survey (1985), the total cost of all crimes to victims for a one-year period totalled $431 million. Victims of crime reported losses of $211.5 million in unrecovered property and cash, $41.9 million in damage to property, and $7 million in medical expenses and lost wages. About $170 million was reimbursed to victims by private insurance companies. And, in 1993, victim losses due to crime were estimated to be $4 billion. Assuming that it costs $1000 per day to hospitalize the victim of a violent crime, hospital costs for all victims of assaults in 1993 (not including outpatient services) were estimated to be $68 million (Howard 1996).

The Major Agencies of the Criminal Justice System

Three major agencies operate within the criminal justice system: the police, the courts, and the correctional system. While the three agencies share similar goals, significant diversity exists. A brief description of the main types of each agency appears below.

The Police

Policing is the responsibility of the federal, provincial, and municipal governments in Canada. As Young (1994) points out, each province in Canada has the responsibility to develop its own policies about municipal and provincial policing. This means that a province may require all its cities of a particular size (e.g., 10 000 population) to maintain a municipal police force.

The three main levels of police forces in Canada are municipal, provincial, and federal. In 1993 there were 579 municipal police forces across Canada. This number includes municipal forces whose police chief and sworn police personnel are hired by the municipality as well as those that contract out their policing duties to the RCMP and the OPP. Municipal police forces are found in almost every major Canadian city, including Vancouver, Calgary, Edmonton, Winnipeg, Toronto, Montreal, and Halifax. The ten regional police forces located in southern Ontario (e.g., the Halton Regional Police Force and the Peel Regional Police Force) are also classified as municipal police departments. Canada's largest municipal police department in terms of police personnel is the Metropolitan Toronto Police Force, with over 5500 sworn officers in 1993. Municipalities that contract out their policing services with the RCMP can include larger cities, such as Burnaby, B.C., and North Vancouver, but many of these contracts are found in cities with a population between 50 000 and 100 000. Yukon, the Northwest Territories, and Newfoundland and Labrador were the only locations in Canada without municipal police forces in 1993. The number of police officers involved in municipal policing (including those in the

Royal Canadian Mounted Police and the Ontario Provincial Police) accounted for 62 percent of all sworn police personnel in 1993.

The RCMP, while involved with municipal policing and enforcing the Criminal Code, are also in charge of enforcing federal statutes, carrying out executive orders of the federal government, providing protective services for visiting dignitaries, and policing airports. In addition to enforcing the Criminal Code and federal laws, the RCMP also operate forensic facilities and the Canadian Police College, an educational facility in Ottawa for all police forces. They are also responsible for the operation of the Canadian Police Information Centre (CPIC), which is an automated national computer system available to all police forces in Canada (Young 1994). The total number of police officers involved in federal policing with the RCMP totalled 4715 in 1993, or 8 percent of all police officers in Canada.

The three provincial police forces currently in existence in Canada are the Ontario Provincial Police, the Quebec Police Force (Sûreté du Québec), and the Royal Newfoundland Constabulary, which provides policing services only to the three largest municipalities in Newfoundland. Provincial police forces enforce the Criminal Code and all provincial laws. For the rest of the provinces and territories, the RCMP are responsible for provincial-level policing. In 1993, 25 percent of all police officers in Canada were involved at the provincial level.

Police forces, regardless of their size or jurisdiction, differ in the style they follow when policing their community or region. According to Wilson (1968), policing can be classified into three main styles: **legalistic** (law enforcement), **watchman** (order maintenance), and **social service**. All police forces practise all three styles, but one style is dominant over the others, depending on the jurisdiction's social class, racial and ethnic composition, and political structure, in addition to the police department's own policies and organization.

Police forces that use the legalistic approach enforce all laws to the limits of their authority. All crime-related incidents and suspects are treated in accordance with the formal dictates of the law. This means that all suspects are arrested and charged if enough evidence is found, that all traffic violators are issued tickets, and that discretion is minimal. This approach entails investigating all criminal incidents; apprehending, interrogating, and charging suspects, and protecting the constitutional rights of suspects as well, because the law states this is what police officers are supposed to do.

The police are also involved in order-maintenance activities in the community. This watchman style of policing is largely tolerant in private matters between citizens as well as in minor criminal offences. Much is left up to the citizens—if the police are called to an address for the second time, they may separate the individuals, but an arrest is unlikely unless a major incident has occurred. Order-maintenance policing therefore entails the restoration of "disruptive situations to normalcy without arresting the citizens involved" and the "management of situational tensions" (Brannigan 1984:53). In these cases, the police "move along" drunks to hostels instead of arresting them, and escort mentally ill patients back to their facilities when they wander.

The social service style is characterized by policing that follows the wishes of the community residents. The police are expected by residents to protect them from outsiders and to respond to their concerns, whether they involve criminal violations or not. Police forces are expected to direct their formal legal powers toward strangers while tolerating and/or warning local residents first. The search for order in the community has emerged as an important police function during the past decade in Canada. Some police departments—those in Edmonton and Winnipeg, for example—have changed their names from Police *Force* to Police *Service* to emphasize their main purpose is the provision of services to the community.

The Courts

All provincial court systems in Canada have three levels, though their formal titles vary by province (Russell 1987; Mewett 1996). At one level are the **lower courts,** commonly called the provincial courts in most jurisdictions, though in Ontario known as the Court of Justice and in Quebec as the Court of Quebec. The next level involves the **superior courts,** known as the Court of Queen's Bench or Supreme Courts (Trial Division). In Ontario these courts are called the Court of Justice, General Division, and in Quebec they are called the Superior Court. The highest level of criminal court in any province or territory is the **appeal court**. The court with the greatest authority in any criminal matter is the Supreme Court of Canada.

The provincial courts are the first courts most Canadians encounter when they are charged with a criminal offence. They are typically organized into specialized divisions that deal with different areas of the law. For example, a province may decide to divide its court into a criminal court, family court, small claims court, youth court, and family violence court. These courts deal with the majority of criminal cases, including violations of the Young Offenders Act, disorderly conduct, common assaults, property offences, traffic violations, municipal by-laws and provincial offences. Provincial criminal-court dockets are crowded with cases to be dealt with. The courtrooms themselves have an air of "assembly-line justice," as defendants line up to enter the courtroom, only to have their cases summarily dispatched. Defendants rarely contest their cases in front of a judge in these courts. Researchers and observers report that most defendants who enter the provincial courts plead guilty to the charges during their initial appearance or find the charges either stayed or withdrawn by a prosecutor (Ericson and Baranek 1982; Wheeler 1987; Ursel 1994; Desroches 1995). Desroches (1995:252) found that 90 percent of the 70 robbers he interviewed pleaded guilty in provincial court, quickly ending any thought of arguing over the charges in an open courtroom. Most indicated they pleaded guilty simply because they wanted to "get the thing over with." Most criminal cases in Canada end up being heard in the provincial courts, which handle the routine criminal cases. For most Canadians, this is the extent of their involvement in our court system.

For the majority of indictable offences, the accused has the right to be tried in either the provincial court or the superior court. The superior courts have to hear certain indictable offences such as first- and second-degree murder (see Chapter 2). These courts also hear appeals of the cases decided at the provincial court level. An important difference between the superior and provincial courts is that at the provincial level a judge alone always tries the case while at the superior court level the case may be heard by a judge alone or by a judge and jury, depending on the charge. If the accused elects to be tried in a superior court he has the right to a **preliminary inquiry,** which is heard by a provincial court judge. At the preliminary inquiry a judge determines whether enough evidence exists for a jury to determine that the accused is guilty or innocent of the specified offence.

The accused is present at trials heard in provincial and superior courts. A fundamental constitutional right in Canada guarantees that during all stages of a trial the legal rights of the accused are protected. These rights include the right to representation by a lawyer, the right to a speedy court trial, the right to face and cross-examine the accuser in court, as well as the opportunity for the accused to testify on his own behalf.

The highest level of court in a province or territory—the appeal court—hears appeals from the superior courts and occasionally from provincial courts. These courts do not try criminal court cases; rather, they deal with issues concerning the possibility of procedural errors and sentence lengths. Defendants rarely appear in cases heard in appeal courts. Instead, lawyers representing the Crown and the defendant argue the case before a panel of appeal court judges.

All levels of our court system ideally operate on the basis of an **adversarial system**, in which the Crown prosecutor and defence lawyer oppose one another and debate the facts of the case. The goal of the adversarial system is to search for the truth, specifically the determination of the guilt or innocence of the accused. Theoretically, this system ensures that the accused's fundamental legal rights are protected, that the trial is fair, and that the final decision is impartial. Critics of this image (Ericson and Baranek 1982; Wheeler 1987) argue it operates in theory only and that the legal protections given to the accused are ignored or plea bargained away by defence counsel and the prosecutor. As such, "legal justice" does not exist. Instead, most defendants receive what is referred to as a form of "bargain justice," where the accused are encouraged to plead guilty in return for a reduced sentence or the dropping of a number of charges. These critics argue the final result is a court system in which the vast majority of the accused plead guilty before any item is contested in the open court. This guilty plea usually involves a reduction in the number of charges or a recommendation to the judge that the sentence be reduced.

Corrections

Once an individual is found guilty he may be sentenced to a term in the federal or provincial/territorial correctional system. In Canada, the correctional system involves a vast array of facilities, agencies, and programs. The responsibility for adult corrections is divided between provincial/territorial governments and the federal government. Provincial and territorial governments are responsible for any individual serving a term of incarceration under two years and all noncustodial sentences (e.g., probation). The federal government, through Correctional Service of Canada, is responsible for any adult sentenced to a prison term of two years or more. If an individual is sentenced to a term of two years or more but decides to appeal the conviction or sentence, he will first be incarcerated in a provincial institution. Those individuals who waive their right to an appeal are sent to a federal institution to start serving their sentence.

In recent years, the number of incarcerated offenders has increased significantly. The average number of adults serving a custodial sentence in Canada on any given day in 1992–93 totalled 26 477. Of these, 14 135 (53 percent) were serving their sentence in provincial or territorial facilities while the remaining 12 342 (47 percent) were housed in federal institutions. In addition, 5232 individuals were in provincial facilities but not serving a sentence. Ninety-eight percent (or 5111) of these individuals were remanded in custody while waiting for some type of judicial action on their case, while the remaining 2 percent (or 121) individuals were on temporary detention (Foran and Reed 1996). The number of individuals incarcerated in Canada grows steadily each year. In 1992–93, the total number of individuals incarcerated in a correctional facility increased by

Serial killer Clifford Olson, shown here at a 1989 inquest into the suicide of a fellow inmate, has once again stirred public outrage by announcing his intention to seek early release under the controversial "faint hope" clause. (Photo: Canadian Press)

3266 people (12.5 percent) since 1988–89. In addition, 7370 offenders entered the Canadian correctional system, while 6803 were released during 1992–93.

To house adult inmates, there are currently 161 provincial/territorial jails and 60 federal institutions, but this number is gradually increasing. The federal government has opened four new regional institutions for women during the past few years as well as a healing lodge for aboriginal women located in Saskatchewan.

Most of the individuals in the correctional population are serving all or part of their sentence under community supervision. Community supervision comprises various types of parole, probation, statutory release, and temporary absences. An average of 116 251 offenders were on a form of community supervision in 1992–93. The majority of these offenders (100 102, or 86 percent) were sentenced to a term of probation, while the remaining 16 149 were on conditional release (e.g., parole, statutory release, or temporary absences). Since 1988–89, the total correctional population (including those both incarcerated and on probation or conditional release) has increased from 110 117 to 147 960, an increase of 34 percent (Foran and Reed 1996).

When we think of an individual serving a period of time in a Canadian correctional facility we usually think of a young male (under age 25). This is only partly true. The majority of those serving time in correctional facilities are male. During 1992–93, males accounted for 91 percent of admissions to provincial/territorial facilities and 97 percent of admissions to federal institutions. Aboriginal peoples accounted for 17 percent of those sentenced to provincial and territorial facilities and 12 percent of those sentenced to federal facilities. Adult female offenders accounted for 8 percent of individuals sentenced to a term in either a provincial or territorial facility in 1989–90 (Lipinski 1991).

However, the average age of those individuals in custody continues to increase. In 1984–85, 59 percent of those serving time in federal institutions were 25 years of age or older. This percentage increased to 73 in 1992–93. A similar trend occurred in provincial/territorial correctional facilities. In 1990–91, 40 percent of inmates in those institutions were under 25, but that percentage fell to 29 in 1992–93 (Reed 1994).

The correctional system has been criticized by the public, as well as by other criminal justice agencies

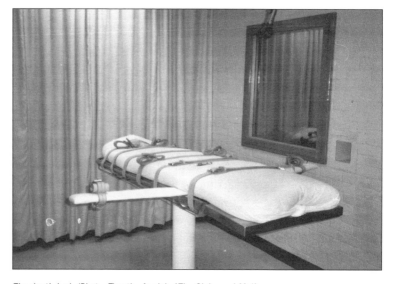

The death bed. (Photo: Timothy Appleby/*The Globe and Mail*)

for decisions that reflect an apparent disregard of public safety. Critics point to high recidivism rates as an indication of the failure of institutions to rehabilitate offenders. They also claim that correctional officials are easily fooled by inmates, and as a result some who should remain incarcerated are released, resulting in higher crime rates. Despite such criticisms, the correctional system continues to maintain an important role in the criminal justice system. It plays a multiple, and seemingly contradictory, number of roles—deterring crime, incapacitating those convicted of crimes, and rehabilitating offenders. It is a system in which competing beliefs about what to do with offenders have to be dealt with on a day-to-day basis. Despite the differences of opinion about how to deal with offenders, the correctional system reinforces society's disapproval of their actions.

The Formal Organization of the Canadian Criminal Justice System

According to the Law Reform Commission of Canada (1988a), a key function of our criminal justice system is to bring offenders to justice. At the same time, our legal system has created a number of legal rights and protections for those accused of crimes. Various fundamental principles exist that attempt to ensure that no arbitrary actions violate these principles. Our criminal justice system is supposed to presume the innocence of all defendants, and to conduct itself in a manner that is fair, efficient, accountable, participatory, and protective of the legal rights of those arrested and charged with the commission of a criminal action.

An integral part of these guarantees is found in what is known as criminal procedure. Criminal procedure is concerned with the way various criminal justice agencies operate during the interrogation of suspects, the gathering of evidence, and the processing of the accused through the courts. Criminal procedure also ensures that the agents of the state act in an impartial and fair manner in their search for truth. Our system of criminal procedure is divided into two major parts: pre-trial procedure and trial procedure.

Pre-Trial Criminal Procedure

Arrest, Appearance Notice, and Summons

The main purpose of arresting someone is to ensure the accused appears in a criminal court, in which that person's guilt or innocence is determined. Another purpose of **arrest** is to prevent the commission of a further crime. With or without a warrant, police officers can arrest a suspect for violating the law.

A **warrant** is issued after a crime is committed, and the police, during their subsequent investigation, collect enough evidence to give themselves reasonable and probable grounds to suspect that a certain person committed the offence. Once the evidence is collected, the police must go to a justice of the peace and lay an information against the suspect, indicating why they feel it is in the public interest to arrest the suspect. Once the arrest warrant is signed, the police execute the order by arresting the individual named on the warrant. Most warrants are issued only for the province in which the police investigated the crime. A Canada-wide warrant is issued after an individual fails to appear in court after being charged with a violent or serious property offence.

But even without a warrant, police can arrest an individual. This generally occurs when police officers have no chance to **lay an information,** such as when they discover a crime in progress. Section 495(1) of the Criminal Code identifies five such situations when a police officer can arrest without a warrant:

1. when an officer discovers an individual in the process of committing any criminal offence
2. when an officer knows the individual has committed an indictable offence
3. when an officer has reasonable and probable grounds that the accused has committed an indictable offence
4. when an officer has reasonable grounds to believe an indictable offence is about to be committed
5. when an officer reasonably believes that there is an outstanding warrant for the arrest of an individual (Source: Justice Canada)

Police officers need not arrest an individual when the offence in question is a summary conviction offence or is an indictable offence that does not allow the accused to choose a jury trial. Nor do police officers need to arrest a suspect (1) when they are certain the suspect will appear in court at the designated time and date, (2) when the prosecutor can proceed by way of summary or indictable offence (i.e., a hybrid offence), and (3) when the offence involves a charge of keeping a gaming or betting house, placing bets, or keeping a common bawdy-house.

Police may issue an **appearance notice** to a suspect or request a justice of the peace to issue a summons. An appearance notice is given to the suspect by a police officer at the scene of the crime. In these cases, the police officer hands the accused a form with information pertaining to the offence, as well as the time and place the accused has to appear in court to answer the charge (or charges). The police officer must then lay an information with a justice of the peace as soon as possible.

Another alternative to an arrest is a **summons.** Here, the accused or a witness is ordered to appear in court by a justice of the peace. The summons must be handed to the accused by a police officer or person granted special powers by provincial authorities. When this document is served, the accused is compelled to appear in court at a designated time and place (Barnhorst et al. 1992).

Detention

Once an individual is arrested, the police have a number of decisions to make about the suspect. In particular, they have to determine whether the person arrested should be held in custody before the trial. The law in Canada states the accused must be released unless there is a good reason for keeping him in detention. The police cannot hold an individual for an undetermined reason; Section 9 of the Charter of Rights and Freedoms states "everyone has the right not to be arbitrarily detained." In addition, Section 10(a) specifies "everyone has the right on arrest or detention to be informed promptly of the reasons thereof." If it is decided by the arresting officer that the accused be formally detained, the "officer in charge" at the police station to which the accused is taken has the discretion to release the suspect. The officer usually exercises that discretion unless the suspect is charged with a criminal offence punishable by imprisonment of five years or more, unless the suspect is felt to pose a threat to the public or unless the suspect is believed unlikely to appear in court. If the officer decides that the accused remain in custody, the accused must be taken before a justice of the peace within 24 hours or, if this is not possible, at the earliest possible time. While the accused is in detention, the police may take fingerprints and photographs if the individual is charged with an indictable offence.

Bail or Custody

The purpose of bail is to ensure that the accused appear at his trial while permitting the accused to participate in the development of his defence (Ouimet 1969). Many concerns were raised during the 1960s about the relationship between the ability of an accused to pay bail and the judicial determination of his guilt or innocence. Studies conducted in the United States, which influenced Canadian policy on the granting of bail, pointed out the ramifications of such an approach: only 18 percent of individuals jailed pending trial were acquitted, while 48 percent of those granted bail were acquitted (Vera Institute of Justice 1972). In response to these concerns about the relationship between bail and the outcome of a trial, Canada passed the Bail Reform Act (1972), which allowed an accused to be released on his own recognizance if he promised to appear in court on the date of his trial, if he was considered a good member of the community, and had not committed a serious or violent crime.

However, in a series of studies conducted within a decade of the enactment of the Bail Reform Act, Canadian researchers discovered that many accused people who were eligible for bail still weren't granted it and that their denial of bail significantly increased their chances of being convicted and receiving a longer sentence (Koza and Doob 1975; Doob and Cavoukian 1977). In addition, Hagan and Morden (1981) studied individuals held in detention while awaiting a bail hearing. They found that detention increased their chances of being found guilty and of subsequent incarceration.

In Canada today, the Criminal Code requires all individuals arrested to be brought before a justice of the peace, who then decides if the accused is to be released before his trial. This hearing, commonly referred to as the bail hearing, is formally known as the "judicial interim release hearing." The justice of the peace is expected to release the accused unless the prosecutor supplies evidence to show why the individual should not be released or why conditions should attach to the release. Those charged with first- and second-degree murder can be released on bail only by a superior court judge.

Bail is considered such an important part of Canadian legal process that Section 11(e) of the Charter of Rights and Freedoms guarantees the right of the accused "not to be denied reasonable bail without just cause." According to the Criminal Code (Section 457), bail may be denied where denial can be proved in the public interest or necessary for the protection or safety of the public, and necessary to ensure the appearance of the accused on the designated date of the trial. In certain circumstances, it is up to the accused to inform the judge why he should be released pending his trial. This occurs when

- the accused is already on bail and is charged with the commission of an indictable offence
- the accused is not a resident of Canada and has been charged with an indictable offence
- the accused failed to appear while on release for a previous offence
- the accused is charged with an offence such as drug trafficking under the Narcotics Control Act (Source: Justice Canada)

In these situations, the justice of the peace will automatically detain the accused unless the accused can persuade the court that he shouldn't be detained.

Whether the accused is granted bail or is held until the trial, almost all criminal prosecutions in Canada start with an information. As Mewett (1996) points out, an information serves two important purposes in the Canadian legal system. First, it compels the accused to appear at court on a specific date and at a designated time. Second, it forms the written basis for the charge that the accused faces in court.

Trial Procedure

The First Court Appearance
During the first court appearance (or **arraignment**, as it is sometimes called), the accused is brought before a provincially appointed judge. At this time all formal charges are read by the court clerk, and then the accused (or his lawyer) makes his initial plea.

Sometimes defence counsel or the prosecutor indicates to the judge that he or she is not ready to proceed. This usually happens with cases involving complex issues and more time is needed to prepare the defence or prosecution. In such cases the presiding judge agrees to set aside the case until a later date. During such a postponement, the conditions that governed the accused individual before his initial appearance will apply. Because the Charter guarantees the right to a trial within a reasonable period of time, the accused may be asked to sign a waiver of this right before the court proceeds any further (see Chapter 8).

If a plea of not guilty is entered, a trial date is specified. However, if the accused decides to enter a plea of guilty, the judge sets a sentencing date and decides whether the accused is to be held in custody until sentencing. If a plea of not guilty is entered, an indictment is drafted; but before the actual trial takes place, the accused may have the right to a preliminary inquiry.

The Indictment and Preliminary Inquiry

In cases where the charge involves an election indictable offence, an estimated 80 percent of the accused in Canada give up their right to a preliminary inquiry and go directly to trial. And approximately 80 percent of these cases end with the accused pleading guilty on first appearance in court. However, a preliminary inquiry is a right of the accused and is supposed to be held prior to the formal trial of a case in court. Preliminary inquiries are heard by a provincial court judge. Summary conviction offences proceed differently from indictable offences in our court system and they don't involve a preliminary inquiry.

The function of a preliminary inquiry is not to determine the guilt or innocence of the individual charged with a crime but rather to determine if there is enough evidence to send the accused to trial. During a preliminary inquiry, a prosecutor attempts to show the judge that enough evidence exists for a criminal trial. The prosecution has the power to call as few or as many witnesses as it feels necessary to prove to the judge that a case merits a trial. Once a witness testifies for the prosecution, defence counsel has the right of cross-examination.

The defence too has the right to call witnesses to support its claim of innocence. If the defence proves to the judge that the prosecution doesn't have a good case, there won't be a trial. Thus, a good defence during the preliminary inquiry can lead to the discharge of the accused. Another reason why the defence may call witnesses is to get their testimony on record, especially if they are sick or about to leave the country. The evidence provided by witnesses may be used during the trial. Most preliminary inquiries last less than a day, and only rarely does a preliminary inquiry end in a judicial decision to discharge the accused or withdraw the charges. An inquiry is important to the defendant because it reveals much of the evidence that the prosecution will use against him during the trial. He may then decide to plead guilty. In a study by the Law Reform Commission of Canada (1984b), 71 percent of preliminary inquiries resulted in a plea of guilty once the case reached the actual court trial.

When the judge decides enough evidence exists to proceed to a trial, the offence for which the accused is to stand trial is then written in the form of an indictment. The indictment replaces the information, and it forms the basis of the prosecution. It is a formally written allegation that states that the accused has committed a particular offence.

However, even if the judge decides to discharge the accused, a discharge does not mean that the accused is acquitted. It simply means that there is insufficient evidence at this time to proceed to trial. As Mewett (1996:82) points out, a discharge means "the accused cannot be tried on that information and that proceedings on that information are terminated." If, at a future date, new evidence is produced and strongly indicates the accused was involved in the crime, the prosecution usually proceeds by way of a direct indictment instead of requesting another preliminary inquiry. Whatever the avenue chosen, the Attorney General or a senior official in the provincial Justice department is required to give personal approval of the Crown's actions.

The Trial

For most indictable offences the accused can elect trial by judge alone or by judge and **jury**. Some exceptions apply, such as first- and second-degree murder charges, where the accused must be tried by judge and jury unless both the defendant and the Attorney General of the province agree to proceed by way of judge alone. Some indictable offences are considered so minor (e.g., gaming offences) that in almost every circumstance they are heard by a judge alone.

In Canada, the accused has the right to change his mind about the type of trial he wants, although certain restrictions apply. In a re-election, as this process is called, an accused who initially selected trial by a provincial court judge has 14 days to change his mind and request a trial by a judge and jury. And if he originally selected trial by judge and jury, the accused has 15 days after the completion of the preliminary inquiry to change his mind and select a trial heard by a provincial court judge alone.

Once the indictment is read to the accused in court, he has to plead to the charge (or charges) by entering a plea of either guilty or not guilty. If the accused pleads not guilty, the prosecution has to prove the defendant is guilty of the specified offence beyond a reasonable doubt. In this situation, no reasonable amount of doubt concerning the guilt or innocence of the accused can be left unresolved. If there is reasonable doubt, the accused is acquitted of all charges.

Sentencing

If the accused is found guilty, the judge has numerous sentencing options available. The sentences most commonly used in Canada include **probation, incarceration, suspended sentence,** and **fines**. A judge may also decide to combine two of these sentences, such as a period of incarceration with a fine. The sentence depends in large part on the charges that the individual was found guilty of and the prior record of the offender. In a few instances a judge has no choice in setting the penalty. For example, if the judge finds an offender guilty of a charge of first- or second-degree murder he or she must sentence the accused to life imprisonment.

In many instances, a judge also relies on a **pre-sentence report** compiled by a probation officer to assist in the determination of the sentence. This report may evaluate such things as the employment record of the offender as well as any family support. Other sources of information that a judge may use to determine a sentence include a victim impact statement, information given about the accused at the sentence hearing by the Crown prosecutor or the defence lawyer, as well as any mitigating or aggravating circumstances surrounding the commission of the crime. These can be significant factors in the sentencing.

Incarceration

If the sentence involves a period of incarceration, the offender is sent either to a provincial jail or a federal institution. If he is sentenced to a federal institution, the offender can apply for day parole six months before he is eligible to make an application for full parole. Full parole is possible for most offenders after they complete one-third of the sentence or serve seven years, whichever period is shortest. Most offenders in Canada do not serve the full term of their sentence because if they don't receive full parole, they automatically receive statutory release after serving two-thirds of their sentence. While they are incarcerated, offenders can receive some form of rehabilitation or treatment. Though the amount of treatment given to offenders varies, programs are designed to help offenders reintegrate into society. After their release, offenders on parole must contact their parole officer on a regular basis. They may be required to spend some time in a halfway house or under some other form of community supervision.

The Criminal Justice 'Funnel'

The criminal justice system is best thought of as a process. This view emphasizes the key decision points that cases pass. Each decision point is, in effect, a screening stage that involves a series of routinized operations and whose success is gauged primarily by its efficiency in passing the case to the next stage and a successful conclusion. The police, for example, have the function of collecting sufficient evidence to lay charges, thereby allowing the case to pass into the hands of a Crown prosecutor. Of course, Crown prosecutors can't try a case if the police don't collect enough evidence to lay a charge. Similarly, at the parole stage, a decision is made by parole board members about whether to release an inmate directly into society, to place him in a community facility, or to keep him institutionalized. Each decision is crucial—if an error is made, members of the public may be placed at risk or an innocent person may be incarcerated for a crime he didn't commit.

All members of criminal justice agencies involved with the detection, prosecution, and sentencing of offenders may use their discretion in many professional matters. The police, for example, have the powers of arrest, but they may decide to enforce the law selectively—for example, when a police patrol officer decides not to arrest an individual involved in a domestic dispute despite an official police department policy of mandatory arrest in such cases. Plainclothes police officers on a stake-out may decide to ignore a drug deal because their shift is almost over and they don't want to spend the next few hours writing up a report. Similarly, Crown prosecutors may decide to plea bargain with a defendant's lawyer by reducing a substantial number of charges in return for a plea of guilty, or information concerning another crime, or the location of a criminal who has eluded the police for some time. A judge too may exercise discretion; he or she may decide to give a long sentence to someone just convicted because that offender was not employed; if he were employed, the judge would have selected a period of probation. Discretionary judgments are found throughout the criminal justice system, and they can heavily influence the flow of the accused's case through each stage of the criminal justice process. Whether such discretion is exercised consistently and used to favour some groups over others remains a topic of debate.

The criminal justice system does not successfully prosecute all who are charged with a crime and tried in court. At each stage in the system, the number of accused persons is reduced, sometimes because they plead guilty or because charges are dropped on account of insufficient evidence. Figure 1.3 illustrates the operation of the Winnipeg Family Violence Court for the years 1990–91 and 1991–92 (Ursel 1994). Notice the reduction in the number of cases at each stage. Of 4080 family violence cases during this two-year span, the minority— 1098 (27 percent)—were stayed. The majority of the cases proceeding to trial didn't involve a determination of guilt by a judge and/or jury, since defendants pleaded guilty in 2182 (74 percent of the total cases) of the remaining cases. Eight hundred cases (26 percent) involved a court trial. Two hundred and sixty-one of the cases (33 percent) tried in court resulted in a determination of guilt by the courts. The remaining 539 cases (67 percent) resulted in dismissals, discharges, or findings of not guilty. In summary, of the 4080 original cases that entered the Winnipeg Family Violence Court, 2443 (60 percent) ended in the determination of guilt. Of these cases, only 548 (14 percent) of the cases ended with the defendant sentenced to a period of incarceration.

To explain the flow of cases through the courts, the term criminal justice "funnel" is sometimes used. When a crime is committed it enters the big end of the funnel; the case passes through the funnel and exits the small end when an offender is either acquitted of all charges or is found guilty and sentenced. Between the beginning and end of this funnel are key decision-making points, each one a stage where the case load might be reduced. Some cases are eliminated due to procedural errors, others because of a lack of evidence, still others because the defendants are acquitted of all charges by a judge or jury.

FIGURE 1.3

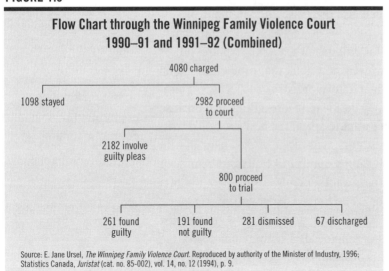

Flow Chart through the Winnipeg Family Violence Court 1990–91 and 1991–92 (Combined)

Source: E. Jane Ursel, *The Winnipeg Family Violence Court.* Reproduced by authority of the Minister of Industry, 1996; Statistics Canada, *Juristat* (cat. no. 85-002), vol. 14, no. 12 (1994), p. 9.

Figure 1.5 illustrates how many cases and charges disappear at each stage of the criminal justice system but for the offence of homicide. Homicide consists of four different offences: first-degree murder, second-degree murder, manslaughter, and infanticide. As indicated by Figure 1.5, 576 homicides were reported in 1988. Of these, 85 were not solved at the time of the study. Of the 491 solved homicides, 530 individuals were identified: 477 were charged, 45 committed suicide immediately following the commission of the offence, and 8 cases were cleared otherwise (three of the suspects were under the age of 12, and 5 were cleared for other reasons, e.g., the accused was killed or died before being charged). There were 477 individuals charged in relation to 431 offences: 228 were charged with first-degree murder, 211 with second-degree murder, 35 with manslaughter, and 3 with infanticide. Figure 1.4 illustrates what happened to the 228 persons charged with first-degree murder. Of the 195 adults sent to trial, only 40 (20 percent) were convicted of first-degree murder while 71 (35 percent) were convicted of second-degree murder.

FIGURE 1.4

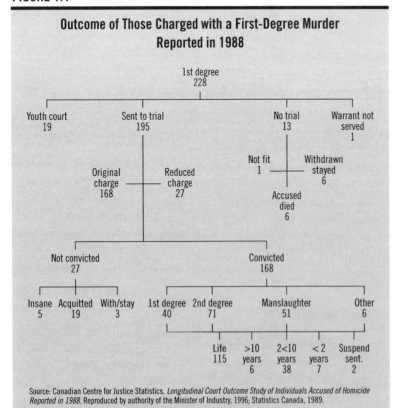

Outcome of Those Charged with a First-Degree Murder Reported in 1988

Source: Canadian Centre for Justice Statistics, *Longitudinal Court Outcome Study of Individuals Accused of Homicide Reported in 1988.* Reproduced by authority of the Minister of Industry, 1996; Statistics Canada, 1989.

Reporting the Crime

Some people who have been victimized in a crime may not realize they have been victimized; other people who have been victimized realize what has happened but don't report the crime to the police. They may decide, not to report a property crime, for example, because they feel it isn't worth the effort. Police forces themselves may refuse to investigate a property crime or fraud case when they feel it is too minor or when they stand only a minimal chance of discovering the perpetrator. It may not be feasible for the police to investigate a stolen bicycle, though it is worth a few hundred dollars, or a bad cheque under $100, because of the amount of time required to investigate the crime and the low probability of solving the case. But if the police accept the complaint, an occurrence report is recorded.

Recent victimization studies in Canada reveal that substantial numbers of victims of violent crimes do not report these crimes to the police. In the Canadian Urban Victimization Survey, the four most common reasons given to researchers by victims about their reasons for not reporting an incident to police were, in order of priority, "too minor," "the police couldn't do anything," "inconvenience," and "nothing taken" (Solicitor General 1985). Researchers discovered victims didn't report to the police 11 000 (62 percent) sexual assaults, 27 000 (55 percent) robberies, and 185 000 (66 percent) assaults committed against them.

In 1993, Statistics Canada conducted a national Violence Against Women survey. Twelve thousand three hundred women were interviewed about their experiences with physical and sexual violence since their sixteenth birthday. Only 6 percent of the women who were sexually assaulted reported the incident to the police (Statistics Canada 1994). Those that indicated they didn't report these incidents to the police were asked to give the reasons for their nonreporting (see Table 1.1). Some respondents gave many reasons for not reporting to the authorities, including their feeling that the offence was "too minor" and that they "didn't think the police could do anything about it." The high rates of nonreporting in Table 1.1 can significantly reduce the number of cases that reach the next stage of the crime funnel—the reporting of the incident as a criminal offence by the police.

FIGURE 1.5

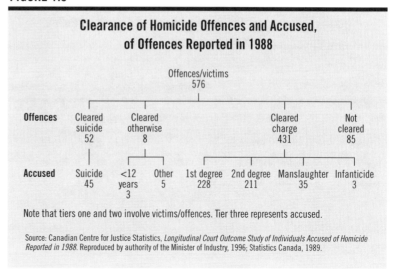

Clearance of Homicide Offences and Accused, of Offences Reported in 1988

Note that tiers one and two involve victims/offences. Tier three represents accused.

Source: Canadian Centre for Justice Statistics, *Longitudinal Court Outcome Study of Individuals Accused of Homicide Reported in 1988.* Reproduced by authority of the Minister of Industry, 1996; Statistics Canada, 1989.

Recording of the Crime by the Police

Even if the police are contacted about a possible criminal act, they may decide after an investigation that an official report and the laying of formal criminal charges is not required. Such cases are categorized as "unfounded," which means that, after a preliminary investigation into the incident, the police decide a crime was neither attempted nor actually committed.

TABLE 1.1

Victims' Reasons for Not Reporting Sexual Assault to Police, Percent Distribution, 1993

Reasons Sexual Assault	Total Sexual Assault	Sexual Attack	Unwanted Sexual Touching
Too minor	44	28	53
Didn't think the police could do anything	12	14	11
Wanted to keep the incident private	12	17	8
Dealt with though other channels	12	15	12
Shame or embarrassment	9	15	6
Didn't want involvement with police or court	9	12	7
Wouldn't be believed	5	8	5
Fear of the perpetrator	3	6	2
Didn't want him arrested or jailed	3	3	2
Didn't want or need help	2	—*	3

*not statistically reliable

Note: Columns do not total 100% because more than one reason could be given.

Source: J.V. Roberts, *Criminal Justice Processing of Sexual Assault Cases*. Reproduced by authority of the Minister of Industry, 1996; Statistics Canada, *Juristat* (cat. no. 85-002), vol. 14, no. 7 (1994), p. 6.

There are many reasons why an incident may be classified as "unfounded." Ericson (1982), in his study of policing in the Toronto region, discovered that patrol officers used many tactics to record an incident as "unfounded." Often they did not "officially record an incident because, in spite of their efforts, they are frustrated by the complexities and the lack of citizen assistance in sorting them out." In addition, Ericson found it rare for a minor complaint, such as a traffic accident involving damage under $200, to be recorded as a crime.

Patrol officers reacted quite differently when they were contacted by victim-complainants about one or more of four different types of complaints considered "major"—interpersonal incidents, property disputes, automobile disputes, and "other" disputes, according to Ericson. When one of these complaints was reported, the police officially recorded the event as a crime in slightly more than half (52 percent) of their investigations. Official reports were more likely to be made in incidents where property damage or loss occurred. Incidents were also more likely to be recorded as crimes when no personal injury to the victim was involved. Interpersonal disputes, however, were often not officially recorded as crimes. The reason for this was that "a prior relationship between a victim and a suspect substantially decreases the probability that the suspect will be convicted if charged" and "there are usually greater problems in sustaining a charge for assault arising out of interpersonal conflicts" (Ericson 1982:119). As a result, officers "routinely dealt with interpersonal troubles by informal means, while property-related troubles were more routinely processed as officially-determined crimes."

But if a crime is committed, the police hope to arrest a suspect. Different crimes have different rates of clearance, and these can change over time. Between 1983 and 1992, for example, largely due to changes in reporting laws and the laws protecting victims, the clearance rates for sexual assault in Canada increased with the seriousness of the crime. Why this is so is not clear, but the nature of the harm involved with the most serious sexual assault incidents may mean that "physical evidence is more readily available, a suspect more readily identifiable, and that a higher priority is given to the case by police, all which increase the likelihood that a charge will be laid against a suspect" (Roberts 1994:12).

Laying a Charge

Once a suspect is identified and there is sufficient evidence to lay an information, the incident is considered to be "cleared by charge" (see Figure 1.6). Incidents may also be classified as "cleared otherwise" in cases where the complainant declines to proceed with the charges or when the suspect dies before a charge can be laid. If a suspect is present at the scene when the police arrive, and the officer decides the complaint has merit, one would think that a strong possibility exists the individual would be arrested, taken to the police station, interrogated, and subsequently charged with a criminal offence. According to Ericson (1982), however, patrol officers did not always arrest an identifiable suspect even when they decided a complaint was, in fact, a crime. Of the 392 individuals formally classified as "criminal suspects," Ericson found that no further formal action or report was taken against 137 of them. Official reports were made on 40 other suspects, but again no further action was taken against them for a variety of reasons. This means that almost half of the individuals classified as "criminal suspects" were not processed to the next stage of the criminal justice system. Only 107 (or 27 percent) of the criminal suspects were arrested and subsequently formally prosecuted.

If a victim-complainant identified a suspect who left the crime scene, an occurrence report was usually written up by a patrol officer, who then handed it over to a detective for further investigation. In his study of detectives, Ericson discovered they cleared very few of the cases forwarded to them. They were able to solve only 50 of 235 cases (21 percent) by laying a criminal charge, while 47 cases (20 percent) were classified as "cleared otherwise." The remaining 138 cases (59 percent) were ultimately written off as "investigation exhausted" and

FIGURE 1.6

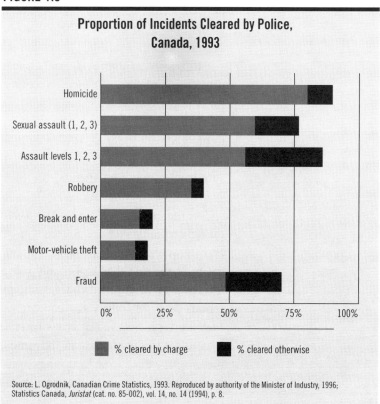

Proportion of Incidents Cleared by Police, Canada, 1993

- Homicide
- Sexual assault (1, 2, 3)
- Assault levels 1, 2, 3
- Robbery
- Break and enter
- Motor-vehicle theft
- Fraud

0%   25%   50%   75%   100%

■ % cleared by charge   ■ % cleared otherwise

Source: L. Ogrodnik, Canadian Crime Statistics, 1993. Reproduced by authority of the Minister of Industry, 1996; Statistics Canada, *Juristat* (cat. no. 85-002), vol. 14, no. 14 (1994), p. 8.

filed without clearance. Ericson also reported detectives were under no significant pressure from the police department to clear a high rate of crimes. Quality, rather than the quantity of charges, was emphasized.

However, in his study of robbers, Desroches (1995) discovered detectives usually assumed that the robber had committed multiple robberies—an assumption he found to be correct in most instances. Detectives correctly laid multiple charges by studying incidents to see if any similarities exist. When similarities are detected suspects are questioned, and if they admit to the crimes a higher clearance rate results. However, if robbers change their tactics, they were rarely if ever questioned about other robberies, with the result that these "cases, presumably, are never cleared from the books even though the offender is in custody on other charges" (Desroches 1995).

Prosecution

Research has consistently revealed that the greatest amount of attrition of major or indictable cases within our criminal justice system occurs between the time the police lay a criminal charge and the time that a prosecutor decides to accept the case and take it into court. The common assumption holds that prosecutors accept any case in which the police decide there are "reasonable and probable grounds" that a crime was committed and the individual charged did in fact commit it. But prosecutors review most, if not all, of the cases involving serious crimes handed to them in order to assess the quality of the evidence before they proceed to the courtroom. And concerns about the quality of evidence collected by the police often lead prosecutors to stay the charges or to drop them altogether (Petersilia et al. 1990).

Factors other than evidentiary issues may have a significant impact on the prosecution of cases. In their interviews with crown prosecutors in Manitoba, for example, Gunn and Minch (1988) discovered that approximately 10 percent of cases were not prosecuted because the victim of a sexual assault decided not to proceed with the trial. The decision not to proceed, according to the prosecutors, came from the fear of having to testify in court, a fear of revenge, pressure from family and friends, the prior relationship with the offender, and sympathy for the offender.

At the prosecution stage, one assumes, the Crown prosecutor takes over the file and the police are no longer involved in any way. This is not always the case, however. Charges involving minor offences can follow a procedure different from the one that is formally recognized. Unlike what happens in cases involving major criminal charges, the police can take on an active role in less serious cases. In some Canadian cities, for example, Crown prosecutors don't even keep a file on minor cases or review them before they appear in court. Such cases usually remain in the hands of the police, generally until the days they are scheduled to be heard in provincial court. What the police tell the prosecutor about a case can therefore have a significant impact on any decision made about proceeding with the case (Wheeler 1987). The police have also been found to engage in striking deals with offenders in order to gain information about other crimes and criminals. Here again, the police can have considerable impact on the decision a Crown prosecutor makes about the charges or sentence for any particular case. Defence lawyers, usually without their clients, often negotiate with the police for their clients, and after an agreement has been reached the police confirm the agreement by discussing it with the Crown prosecutor (Klein 1976; Ericson and Baranek 1982). As a result, criticisms have been aimed at the control that police have over many of the minor court cases. It also means that prosecutions of these type of cases "are not as subject to checks and balances as formal legal procedures would have it. In only a tiny fraction of cases does the accused actually have a trial. In the vast majority, the 'trial' is the plea bargaining session and the accused is not allowed to attend" (Wheeler 1987).

Sentencing

As noted previously, most accused persons in Canada plead guilty when they enter the provincial courts, thus eliminating the opportunity to argue the facts of the case with the prosecution. In Desroches' (1995) study of robbers, the reasons given for pleading guilty were numerous. Some people simply wanted to "get the thing over with," while others had already given to police a statement admitting their guilt. Other people believed that the police had enough evidence to convict them anyway or that a trial might actually lead to a longer sentence. Still others agreed to a guilty plea prior to the court case in the hope they would receive a lenient sentence. Whatever their hopes, most considered their sentence too harsh. As one convicted robber said, "You can molest children or kill somebody in this country and get a slap on the wrist. But don't you dare steal our money or we'll put you in prison and throw away the key" (Desroches 1995:253).

This inmate was referring to discrimination in the sentences given to offenders. Certainly, it would seem logical to expect the perpetrators of the most serious crimes to receive the harshest sentences, but this is not always the case. Extra-legal factors such as race, gender, age, and social class may become significant when sentencing decisions are made by the judge. These variables can have various impacts at the sentencing stage. Research results may differ in various parts of Canada, but studies have found that race is a significant factor in the type and length of sentencing of offenders. For example, Correctional Service of Canada statistics consistently reveal that an aboriginal is more likely to be sent to federal prison than a white with a similar criminal record and prior record (Moyer et al. 1985). The Ontario Commission on Systematic Racism came to a similar conclusion in 1995 when it compared sentences among black and white offenders in that province. Other studies

EXHIBIT 1.2

The 'Wedding Cake' Model of Criminal Justice

Both the formal and informal approaches described above can operate at the same time within our criminal justice system. Criminal cases that proceed through the criminal justice system can be handled with a significant degree of consistency. What varies is the type of case being processed. If it involves a murder charge, a wealthy defendant can hire an expensive lawyer and have the finer points of the law argued in the court, while someone who is homeless probably ends up being processed without much legal assistance and might end up pleading guilty on first appearance in court. Walker, in developing what he calls the "wedding cake" model of criminal justice, identifies four levels of the justice system (Walker 1989).

Level I of this model involves the most highly publicized cases of our criminal justice system—the Paul Bernardo, Susan Nelles, and Henry Bauxbaum cases, for example. For these trials some of the best defence lawyers in the Canadian legal system were hired by the accused, and their actions during the trials were covered meticulously by the press. As a result, the public is informed about the testimony of expert witnesses and the arguments over seemingly minor legal points. Since these cases were so well publicized—books were written about them and movies may yet be made about them—the public considers them to be representative of the everyday world of the court system for all Canadians. But this is not the case.

Level II of the criminal justice system includes crimes considered to be the most serious indictable offences, notably crimes involving violence and crimes committed by repeat offenders. Most murder trials are included in this category, and so are those cases involving major drug dealers, the most serious cases of sexual assault and robberies among strangers. These trials are often decided by a jury, and the accused, if convicted, can expect a lengthy term of incarceration. The Donald Marshall and Jane Stafford cases are good examples of this layer of the wedding-cake model.

Level III of the model includes indictable offences, usually violent crimes viewed as "nonserious" or property crimes involving very little damage, and usually committed by first-time offenders. The cases are disposed of quickly when they enter the criminal justice system. Most of these offenders do not retain private legal counsel but are represented by, at best, legal aid lawyers. The accused plead guilty at their initial appearance in court, and the Crown prosecutor usually recommends a light sentence, such as probation, a fine, or a short period of incarceration in a provincial facility.

Level IV of the wedding-cake model is where the bulk of the offences are processed through the court system. These cases involve summary conviction offences only. Most of these cases involve a plea of guilty when the accused enters a plea, as in Level III cases, but the punishments are less harsh. Generally they involve such sanctions as fines or court orders to stay away from certain people or places. Rarely does a sentence at this level include a period of incarceration.

have discovered the poor may not be able to afford quality legal representation and as a result receive harsher sentences (Ericson and Baranek 1982).

Summary

During the past 30 years the study of criminal justice developed into a major field of study. It combines different disciplines—such as criminology, law, psychology, political science, and social welfare—in an attempt to gain better understanding of the crime problem, of how to improve the operation of the various criminal justice agencies, and of the most effective way in which to punish criminals. Much effort has gone into improving our knowledge of crime and determining how our agencies should fight crime, but the enterprise is extremely costly, and the costs rise each year.

Criminal justice can be viewed as a system as well as a "funnel." As a system it functions in a formal and highly visible manner, with all the major agencies working together as a coordinated unit. In its actual operation, the criminal justice system resembles a funnel, in the sense that many crimes are committed but relatively few individuals are convicted. The highest-profile cases are representative of the formal operation of the criminal justice system, with lawyers debating the facts and an impartial judge ensuring that the rules of legal procedure are followed. Most individuals don't enjoy the luxury of a formal trial, however. Their cases are resolved during their initial appearance in court or, if a trial is conducted, in a matter of hours or days. Thus, two opposing models of the criminal justice system emerge.

According to the crime control model, criminal law establishes an important difference between the law-abiding and the law-breakers. Those who support the crime control model say the focus should be on the capture, processing, and control of individuals who break the law. In contrast, the due process model emphasizes the legal rights of individuals. This model's adherents believe that the legal system is in fact an obstacle course and place emphasis on the rights of the accused. Even if the accused is factually guilty, the prosecution must prove the legal guilt before the accused can be convicted and punished. In the due process model, the operation of all agencies in the criminal justice system are open to investigation and questions about their actions.

Discussion Questions

1. Should we spend more money on the courts? If so, what impact would that have on crime?
2. Discuss the relative strengths and weaknesses of the crime control model.
3. Discuss the relative strengths and weaknesses of the due process model.
4. Discuss the efforts made to reduce crime in our society. What stops us from attaining a crime-free society? Is a high crime rate the price that our society must pay to have legal rights?
5. What is a good way to reduce the costs of the operation of our criminal justice system? Is there a way to reduce costs but to gain effectiveness in reducing the crime rate?
6. What should be the predominant function of the police in contemporary society?
7. Should we try to control the discretion of our criminal justice agencies? If we do, and succeed, what would the impact be?
8. Why don't victims report their crimes to the police? Have you or members of your family ever witnessed or been a victim of a crime and not reported it? If so, why was the crime not reported?

9. Give an example of a crime for each layer of the criminal justice "wedding cake."

Suggested Readings

Boydell, C., and I.A. Connidis, eds. *The Canadian Criminal Justice System.* Toronto: Holt, Rinehart, and Winston, 1982.

Brannigan, A. *Crimes, Courts, and Corrections: An Introduction to Crime and Social Control in Canada.* Toronto: Holt, Rinehart, and Winston, 1984.

Desroches, F.J. *Robbery and Fear: Robbery in Canada.* Scarborough, Ont.: Nelson Canada, 1995.

Ericson, R.V., and P.M. Baranek. *The Ordering of Justice: A Study of Accused Persons as Dependants in the Criminal Justice Process.* Toronto: University of Toronto Press, 1982.

Harris, M. *Justice Denied: The Law versus Donald Marshall.* Toronto: Totem Books, 1986.

Kennedy, L.W., and V.F. Sacco, eds. *Crime Counts: A Criminal Event Analysis.* Scarborough, Ont.: Nelson Canada, 1996.

Vallee, B. *Life with Billy.* Toronto: Seal Books, 1986.

Wilson, James Q. *Varieties of Police Behavior.* Cambridge, Mass.: Harvard University Press, 1977.

CHAPTER 2

Criminal Law and Criminal Justice in Canada

The criminal justice system is, in reality, a system concerned with the enforcement of the law, the processing of accused law violators, and the punishment of individuals convicted of violating the law. But what are the legal aspects of determining whether an individual has broken the law? What are the technical grounds for assessing such activities? How do we make laws in Canada? What are the legal protections given to the accused as they progress through the criminal justice system? It is crucial to know something about the source, nature, purpose, and content of law in our society, as well as differences between types of laws.

Is it possible for the law to make someone responsible for another's criminal actions? It is, and most laws in this respect are found in the area of youthful offences. Indeed, the law has long recognized the family to be a central factor in delinquency. Since

CHAPTER OBJECTIVES

- understand the ways criminal law can be established, including the common law, case law, and statute law

- understand what offences are included in the three main categories of crime

- understand the difference between substantive and procedural laws

- recognize the basic principles used by legislatures and the courts in developing and interpreting substantive laws

- understand what protections are given to the accused by the Charter of Rights

An arrest in Edmonton. (Photo: Rick MacWilliam/*The Edmonton Journal*)

parental discipline and control are assumed to be closely associated with youth crime, some American jurisdictions are now making parents responsible for their child's criminal behaviour. In Canada, Manitoba Justice Minister Rosemary Vodrey has called for similar laws to be enacted by the federal government.

These laws are not without precedent, since variants of them have existed in one form or another in both Canada and the United States throughout the twentieth century. The first parental-responsibility laws penalized parents for "contributing to the delinquency of a minor." These laws allow the courts to punish parents in juvenile courts for behaviours associated with or suspected of encouraging their child's delinquency.

Another approach was to make parents civilly responsible for the actions of their children. Parents whose children break the law may be required to pay for the damages caused by those children. In the United States, all states with the exception of New Hampshire have parental-liability laws in their statutes, although there are limits on how much money can be paid out. The average amount of money parents are responsible for is currently $2500. Vermont has the lowest rate, at $250, while Texas, with a maximum if $15 000, has the highest.

Some U.S. jurisdictions are now making parents responsible for the criminal actions of their children. In 18 cases reported since 1990 parents were ordered to serve time in jail because their children had broken the law. California in 1988 passed an antigang law that allows judges to sentence parents to a year's imprisonment and a maximum fine of $2500 if they fail to exercise due care to prevent their children from participating in delinquency. This law was upheld by the California Supreme Court in July 1993, at which time it was ruled the law sets a standard of behaviour that a reasonable parent can understand. Perhaps the most widely reported case took place in Elgin, Ill., when in May 1992 a judge sentenced a mother to 30 days in jail for failing to keep her Grade 2 daughter in school. Other parents have been ordered to serve time in classrooms with their chronically truant children. After analyzing these and other cases, Geis and Binder (1991) came to the conclusion that laws making parents responsible for the criminal actions of their children are "nasty and vicious."

Most of what was presented in Chapter 1 dealt with the procedural law—how the various agencies formally and informally enforce substantive law. Much of this chapter is concerned with substantive criminal law in Canada, as well as procedural safeguards found in the Charter of Rights and Freedoms.

Substantive and Procedural Laws

On August 26, 1987, an information was sworn against an individual in Ontario for allegedly committing a sexual assault against a 4-year-old girl. In September 1987, the accused appeared in provincial court and pleaded not guilty to the charge. Since the charge involved an election indictable offence, the accused elected to be tried by judge alone in the Ontario Provincial Court. The trial date was set for April 8, 1988, the earliest possible date the case could be heard.

Between September 1987 and April 1988, however, Bill C-15, which introduced legislation on child sexual assault, was enacted in Canada. The implications of this new law were far-reaching, and one section of it would have a tremendous impact on the accused. At the time the offence was committed, Section 586 of the Criminal Code stated that "(n)o person shall be convicted of an offence upon the unsworn evidence of a child unless the evidence of the child is corroborated in a material particular by evidence that implicates the accused." This section was removed from the Criminal Code by Bill C-15 and replaced by Section 274, which specifies that corroboration in sexual assault and child sexual abuse offences is no longer required.

As a result, when the accused entered the courtroom in early April 1988, the law no longer required that the unsworn evidence of a child be corroborated. However, the judge ruled that since the alleged offence occurred prior to the enactment of Bill C-15, any evidence given in court by the young girl needed corroboration. Since no other evidence against the accused was provided by the prosecution, the defendant was acquitted of all charges.

This seemed to be a reasonable decision, but on January 18, 1989, the Ontario Court of Appeal agreed to hear an appeal of the lower court ruling. The Crown's position was based on the argument that the trial judge made his decision on an incorrect application of the distinction between substantive and procedural law.

Substantive law defines crimes in our society. It is concerned with certain acts, mental states, and accompanying circumstances or consequences, all of which are necessary features of crimes. Substantive law identifies some behaviour as wrong and prescribes punishments to be imposed for such conduct. References made to laws found in the Criminal Code are actually references to the substantive criminal law. Substantive laws can include references to procedural law, specifically if the law directs the procedure of law enforcement officers in any given situation.

Procedural laws are the rules that instruct law-enforcement officers in the enforcement of substantive law. These laws specify the approach that police, prosecution, and correctional personnel must take when proceeding against a suspect. For example, laws instructing police officers in how to properly conduct searches and any subsequent seizure of goods are procedural. These laws are "a set of rules governing the balance of the conflicting governmental functions of maintaining law and order while at the same time protecting the rights of individual citizens" (Territo et al. 1995:53). As a general rule, any change to a law that is procedural in nature applies to the date of the trial, regardless of when the alleged offence happened.

It is easy to see how the prosecution and defence counsel differed in their opinions about this case. In April 1988, before the Ontario Court of Appeal, the defence argued that Bill C-15 was, in fact, substantive law. And since the accused's act occurred prior to the introduction of the amendments introduced to the Criminal Code and the Canada Evidence Act, no new trial should take place. The Crown argued that changes introduced by Bill C-15 were procedural in nature, and therefore the Court of Appeal should rule that the trial judge had erred in his judgment and that a new trial should be ordered.

The Ontario Court of Appeal ruled in favour of the prosecution: "the repeal of the statutory provisions requiring corroboration did not constitute a change in the substantive law and the learned judge erred in law holding that the amendments could not operate retrospectively." Therefore, the acquittal was set aside and a new trial ordered.

The Legal Definition of Crime

Canada practises a federal system of criminal law, which means that all criminal law is passed by the federal government. Only Parliament has the authority to enact criminal laws. In order to understand what the criminal law involves, two levels of legal definitions—the general and the legal—have developed to explain what a crime is. According to the general level, a crime can be defined as any action

1. that is harmful
2. that is prohibited by the criminal law
3. that can be prosecuted by the state
4. in a formal court environment
5. for which a punishment can be imposed (Senna and Siegel 1995)

The legal definition of crime involves both a mental and a physical element. It also specifies that certain aspects of the criminal act in question must be proven in a court of law. Our criminal law is based on seven principles traditionally determined and followed by legislators and the courts. Our system of criminal law is based on the existence of these essential features in every criminal act. These principles are summarized by the term *corpus delecti,* which means literally "the body of the crime." In order to convict someone, it is the duty of the state in most cases to prove each of the following seven elements:

1. legality
2. mens rea
3. actus reus
4. concurrence of mens rea and actus reus
5. harm
6. causation
7. punishment

As Jerome Hall (1947:17), a famous American jurist, noted, the "harm forbidden in penal law must be imputed to any normal adult who voluntarily commits it with criminal intent, and such a person must be subjected to the legally prescribed punishment."

Legality

Legally, a crime is defined as "an intentional act or omission in violation of the criminal law, committed without defense or justification and sanctioned by the state . . . " (Tappan 1966:10). This means that an act, to be considered criminal, must be "forbidden in a penal law" (Brannigan 1984:25). The idea is that there can be no crime unless a law forbids the act in question. This is embodied in the phrase *nullum crimen sine lege,* or "no crime without a law."

Mens Rea

An assumption found in the Criminal Code is that the act of becoming involved in a criminal act results from a guilty mind. This is referred to as **mens rea,** or the mental element of a crime. Mens rea is commonly defined as the "guilty mind," although it is commonly referred to as intent. It rests on the idea that a person has the capacity to control his or her behaviour and has the ability to choose between alternative types of action. Many people may fantasize about committing "the perfect crime," but no crime is committed until some action is taken to realize this fantasy. In addition, a person is not culpable (i.e., blameworthy) unless he or she intends to commit an act prohibited by law or to avoid doing something that the law requires him or her to do. Police officers and judges are often asked for forgiveness by an accused on the grounds that the accused, in committing a harmful act, "didn't mean to do it."

Intent is commonly confused with "motive," although the two concepts are distinct. Intent refers to an individual's mental resolve to commit a criminal offence; motive refers to the reason for committing the actual illegal act. While motive is distinct from mens rea, Barnhorst et al. (1992:40–41) claim it is relevant to the criminal justice system in two ways. First, motive provides evidence of intent by establishing a reason why a person committed a crime (e.g., out of greed or jealousy). Second, motive may assist a judge in sentencing the accused in the same way—by giving a reason why the person committed the crime. According to Barnhorst et al. (1992:41) the accused may receive a lighter sentence if there was a good reason for committing the crime (e.g., mercy killing, as opposed to killing someone out of greed for an inheritance).

The intent to commit a crime may take either of two forms, each of which requires a different amount of proof. Some offences require only general intent, which means that mens rea is inferred from the action or inaction of the accused. In these crimes (e.g., homicide) there is no need for the prosecution to prove, through an independent investigation, the state of the defendant's mind at the time of the offence. It is necessary for the prosecution only "to prove that the accused committed the prohibited act intentionally and with the necessary knowledge of the material circumstances" (Verdun-Jones 1989:120). For example, the intent to commit a homicide is inferred from the fact that the accused pointed a weapon at the victim and discharged it. The offence of homicide is found in Section 222 of the Criminal Code:

> 222. (1) A person commits homicide when, directly or indirectly, by any
> means, he causes the death of a human being.
> (5) A person commits culpable homicide when he causes the death
> of a human being
> (a) by means of an unlawful act . . . (Source: Justice Canada)

Therefore, the elements of culpable homicide are (1) the unlawful death (2) of a human being (3) by another human being.

Specific intent requires that the prosecution prove beyond a reasonable doubt the intent specified in the statute's definition of the elements of a crime. These offences are identified by phrases such as "with intent" or "for the purpose of . . . (Barnhorst et al. 1992). In these cases the prosecution must prove "not only an intention to commit an actus reus of the crime in question but also the 'intention' to produce some further consequence beyond the actus reus" (Verdun-Jones 1989:121). For the offence of breaking and entering, the element of intent to commit an indictable offence typically must be established separately from the act of breaking and entering. According to Section 348 (1)(a) of the Criminal Code, the prosecution must prove that an individual not only intended to commit the offence of break and enter but he did so "with the specific intent to commit an indictable offence such as theft," although "it is not necessary to show that the person actually committed an indictable offence" (Barnhorst et al. 1992:39).

348. (1) Every one who
    (a) breaks and enters a place with intent to commit an
indictable offence therein
    (b) breaks and enters a place and commits an indictable
offence therein . . .
is guilty of an indictable offence . . . (Source: Justice
Canada)

In the case of breaking and entering, therefore, the elements of the crime are (1) the breaking (2) and entry (3) of a dwelling house (4) of another (5) with the intent to commit an indictable offence therein.

In addition to the concepts of general and specific intent, there are three distinct levels or degrees of mens rea, varying along a continuum from the most to the least culpable states of mind—intent, knowledge, and recklessness. The highest level of culpability is purposefully or intentionally causing harm, and such offences are identified with the word "intent." These offences are indicated in the Criminal Code by words such as "intentional" and "wilful" and refer to those actions that purposefully or intentionally cause harm. For example, a person commits theft when he takes or converts anything with the intent of depriving the owner or person who has a special interest in it.

322. (1) Every one commits theft who fraudulently . . . converts to his
use or to the use of another person, anything whether animate
or inanimate, with intent . . . (Source: Justice Canada)

Knowledge is used to indicate that the accused possessed an awareness of a particular circumstance. For example, if someone utters a threat to another individual, the question is whether the accused knowingly stated the threat. According to Section 264.1 of the Criminal Code,

264.1 (1) Every one commits an offence who, in any manner, knowingly utters, conveys or causes any person to receive a threat
    (a) to cause death or serious bodily harm to any person
    (b) to burn, destroy or damage real or personal property, or
    (c) to kill, poison or injure an animal or bird that is the
property of any person (Source: Justice Canada)

Recklessness refers to a situation in which an individual violates a law simply by lacking the appropriate care and attention about something he is doing. For example, if an individual decides to practise shooting a weapon in a crowded schoolyard during the lunch break and kills a child, he may argue that he did not have the intention to harm anyone. Yet he would probably be charged with the criminal offence of manslaughter because he was acting with reckless disregard for the safety of those around them. Recklessness is a requirement for the offence of criminal negligence.

219. (1) Every one is criminally negligent who
    (a) in doing anything, or

(b) in omitting to do anything that it is his duty to do, shows wanton or reckless disregard for the lives or safety of other persons. (Source: Justice Canada)

Some defences in court can be made on the basis that the mens rea element does not apply. The issue here is the notion of criminal responsibility, and Canadian law allows certain persons to be unable to form the mental state necessary to commit a crime. This means that an individual might be excused for committing an action that would normally be classed as criminal. For example, children under 12 years of age cannot be charged with a criminal offence in Canada. Mens rea is also lacking when people commit a crime in self-defence or while under duress.

Actus Reus

Another criterion that has to be met before a criminal charge can be laid against a suspect involves an action known as **actus reus.** This is the physical or action element of a crime and it is generally referred to as the "guilty act" or "evil act." In the Criminal Code actus reus usually refers to the physical act performed by the accused—a punch, shove, or similar type of action directed against another individual. The actor, and the actor alone, is responsible for his actions. In other words, a person cannot blame someone else for his criminal act. However, an attempt is being made to modify this idea, as some legislators and crime control officials argue that parents who are in control of their children should be subject to criminal prosecution for the illegal acts committed by the children over whom they have control, as described at the beginning of this chapter.

While actus reus usually involves the commission of an illegal act, it refers also to the failure to do something—in other words, an omission of an act when the Criminal Code specifies there is a duty to act. Sections 219 and 220 of the Criminal Code, for example, refer to the offences of criminal negligence and criminal negligence causing death:

219. (1) Every one is criminally negligent who
     (a) in doing anything, or
     (b) in omitting to anything that it is his duty to do, shows wanton or reckless disregard for the lives or safety of other persons.
 (2) For the purposes of this section, "duty" means a duty imposed by law.

220. Every one who by criminal negligence causes the death of another person is guilty of an indictable offence and is liable to imprisonment for life. (Source: Justice Canada)

For some criminal offences a person doesn't have to become physically involved in an action, as would be commonly thought. The Criminal Code also specifies, in certain circumstances, that the mere act of talking (or speech) can be interpreted as a physical act. In fact, a crime can be committed by speech (as opposed to thoughts) in our legal system. For example, Section 465 of the Criminal Code specifies it is illegal for two or more persons to agree to commit a crime. If both individuals are in agreement about the plan, the act of criminal conspiracy has transpired. In addition, Section 131 of the Criminal Code specifies an individual is guilty of a criminal offence when he commits perjury, and Section 225 states any individual who causes the death of another individual through threats, fear of violence, or deception is guilty of a crime.

Concurrence between Mens Rea and Actus Reus

While not an "official" element of a crime, **concurrence** requires that "intent both precede and be related to the specific prohibited action or inaction that was or was not taken" (Brown et al. 1991:68). Concurrence is usually not considered a controversial issue, since in most instances the connection between act and intent is obvious.

Harm

An important element in our legal system is the belief that conduct can be criminal only if it is harmful. This ideal is "reflected in the notion of due process, which holds that a criminal statute is unconstitutional if it bears no reasonable relationship to the matter of injury to the public" (Territo et al. 1995:33–34). This means there has to be a victim for the action to be harmful. Others argue that if the offence is a **"victimless" crime**—e.g., gambling, abortion, prostitution—it is "not the law's business" (Geis 1974). The basis for this view is that victimless crimes violate morality, not the law, and that making them illegal doesn't contribute to the good of society.

Criminal harm may result in physical injury, but such harm is by no means restricted to physical injury. Physical injury is not inflicted when perjury is committed, for example, though perjury is still considered harmful. This is because the criminal law has to deal with intangibles, such as harm to public institutions as well as the harm that occurs as a result of feelings of concern about one's well-being. For example, Canada's antistalking law is concerned with protecting citizens from criminal harassment (see Exhibit 2.1). In addition, Canada has developed "hate" laws. These are usually attached as an additional punishment to acts of violence or a crime against property if they are "committed because of the victim's race, gender, or sexual preference" (Territo et al. 1995:34).

Causation

Causation refers to crimes that require that the conduct of the accused produce a specific result. In other words, as long as the act (or omission) of the accused started a series of events that led to harm, causation has occurred. Important

EXHIBIT 2.1

Harm and Criminal Harassment

In the early 1990s, a number of well-publicized incidents of men stalking and harassing women with whom they once had relationships led to tragic results. Terri-Lynn Babb, for example, was killed in broad daylight in Winnipeg by a man who was once a patient at the hospital where she was employed. Her death, and others like it, led to demands that the federal government create a new statute that would outlaw stalking, formally known as criminal harassment. This legislation was passed by Parliament in August 1993.

The federal minister of Justice at the time, Pierre Blais, informed the House of Commons that the new criminal harassment legislation was intended to correct this situation. Blais (House of Commons *Debates* 1993) pointed out it was now against the law to "repeatedly follow someone; spend extended periods of time watching someone's home or place or work; make repeated phone calls to someone or her friends, make contact with someone's neighbors or co-workers; and contact and possibly threaten someone's new companion, spouse or children." According to Johnson (1996:199), the intention of this law is not to punish criminal conduct that "hasn't yet occurred, but to punish harm that has already been perpetrated by virtue of the psychological harm of the threat of violence and injury, and fear of what the person might be capable of doing."

The law on criminal harassment, found in Section 264 of the Criminal Code, states:

(1) No person shall, without lawful authority and knowing that another person is harassed or recklessly as to whether the other person is harassed, engage in conduct referred to in subsection (2) that causes that other person reasonably, in all the circumstances, to fear for their safety or the safety of anyone known to them.

(2) The conduct mentioned in subsection (1) consists of:
(a) repeatedly following from place to place the other person or anyone known to them;
(b) repeatedly communicating with, either directly or indirectly, the other person or anyone known to them;
(c) besetting or watching the dwelling-house, or place where the other person, or anyone known to them, resides, works, carries on business or happens to be; or
(d) engaging in threatening conduct directed at the other person or any member of their family. (Source: Justice Canada)

In addition, Section 515 of the Criminal Code, which deals with the conditions for bail, was revised. Any person charged with criminal harassment can be prohibited from possessing a firearm or ammunition. Criminal harassment is a hybrid offence, allowing the Crown prosecutor the discretion to proceed by way of either summary conviction or indictment. The maximum punishment is five years imprisonment and/or a fine of $2000.

According to Hendrick (1995), three out of four victims of criminal harassment during 1994 were women. For female victims, the greatest threat came from casual acquaintances (28 percent) and ex-spouses (27 percent), followed by close friends, a category that includes both intimate and ex-intimate relationships (18 percent), strangers (10 percent), spouses (8 percent), other family members (5 percent), and business acquaintances (4 percent). For males, the greatest threat came from casual acquaintances (44 percent), followed by strangers (20 percent), business acquaintances (12 percent), other family members (10 percent), ex-spouses (8 percent), close friends (5 percent), and spouses (2 percent).

concerns have been raised about causation when the mens rea and the actus reus are separated over a lengthy period of time. In some cases it is easy to see the harm that results from an act, but it is not easy to establish the mens rea element. This is particularly true for those actions generally referred to as corporate crime. Take, for example, an employee of a corporation who is told that because spraying a particular chemical mixture is "safe," the employee is therefore not required to wear safety equipment. If the individual dies immediately after applying the chemical, concurrence could easily be determined. But what if the worker suffers no ill health for 15 years but then suddenly dies from a rare blood disease that is associated with exposure to the chemical mixture? The lack of concurrence would make it extremely difficult to prove that a crime was committed. This situation may be further complicated by the fact that many other workers applied the spray at the same time without contracting a terminal disease, or that some suffered from seemingly unrelated illnesses.

Punishment

The law must state the sanctions for every crime in order that everyone be aware of the possible consequences of his actions. The Criminal Code therefore specifies the sanctions for every crime. In Canada, there are sanctions for two types of offences: indictable and summary conviction offences. These are discussed in detail later in this chapter.

Sources of the Criminal Law in Canada

The Common Law

The **common law** is an important source of our criminal law and is an important component of the substantive law in Canada. Common law originated under King Henry II (who reigned 1154–1189), as a result of his desire to establish a strong central government. Part of his vision included a court system that would try cases on the basis of laws passed by the government and that would apply to all citizens. To achieve this, he appointed judges to a specific territory (or circuit) to hear cases in order to ensure that the "King's Law" was administered and enforced. Over time, judges exchanged information about their legal decisions and this growing body of knowledge slowly began to replace laws based on local customs. In the traditional system, serious crimes such as murder, rape, and assault were viewed as wrongs between private citizens. Judges began to redefine these as wrongs against the state, i.e., as criminal offences.

A system gradually developed where judges decided cases on the basis of previous judgments in similar cases. Crimes had general meanings attached to them, and most people knew what was meant by murder or other criminal offences. This shared knowledge resulted in a practice that continues today in our system of criminal law: deciding trials on the basis of *precedent* that would be followed, even if it were not necessarily binding, in future decisions. This practice evolved into a principle or rule, called *stare decisis* ("based upon situations of similar facts"), that requires the judiciary to follow previous decisions in similar cases. Today, judges in Canada still follow precedent. This generally means that the lower courts must follow the decisions of higher courts and the courts of equal rank should try to follow one another's decisions if possible. Thus, by process of making decisions in case after case, and guided by the rule of precedent, these early English judges created a body of law that applied to all the people of England. This law was then common to all.

Case Law

Every time a judge in Canada makes a decision in a court case, he or she has the discretion to interpret the relevant statutes. Statutes may need to be interpreted because they are stated only in general terms while the court case may call for a specific meaning. For example, a judge may decide all previous decisions are problematic because they are outdated or too vague, given the facts of the case currently before the court. As a result, the law may be redefined to make it reflect the specifics of the case at hand. Once a judge makes a decision that changes the traditional legal definitions, an appeal is usually made to the respective provincial court of appeal. Following *that* decision, there is a strong likelihood that it too is appealed, to the Supreme Court of Canada. If the Supreme Court refuses to hear the case, the ruling made by the provincial court of appeal stands. However, if the Supreme Court decides to hear the case, that ultimate decision becomes law.

Statute Law

Most common-law offences have been updated to include more detailed definitions of crime. In order to change the common law, governments have to modify existing laws or introduce new laws by enacting statutes. **Statute law** is today considered to be the most important source of law in Canada, and it is through the use of statutes that criminal law is created, changed, or eliminated.

The power to enact statute law in Canada is divided among the federal government (i.e., Parliament), the provinces, and the municipalities. However, only Parliament has the power to enact criminal law. Statute law always overrules case law, except in conflicts over the Canadian Charter of Rights and Freedoms. The Charter allows citizens the right to possess certain rights and freedoms "that cannot be infringed upon by the government" and so "limits the legislative authority of the government" (Barnhorst et al. 1992:7–8). In Canada, all statutes are changed approximately every ten years when Parliament repeals the existing statutes and replaces them with revised versions.

The Classification of Criminal Offences

In Canada today, the decision on how to classify a crime is made by the federal government. An important element of this classification is the determination of the penalties attached to each offence. In Canada, two major classifications of crimes are used, and both involve legal and general definitions. Legal classifications include indictable offences, summary conviction offences, and hybrid offences, while general classifications refer to offences used by police and other criminal justice agencies to classify criminal offences, such as violence or property crimes.

EXHIBIT 2.2

Changing a Statute: Rape to Sexual Assault

Prior to 1983, the offences of sexual aggression were dealt with in Sections 139–154 of the Criminal Code. These offences were found in Section VI of the Criminal Code, which dealt with "Offences against the Person and Reputation." Four principal offences were used by the courts against offences related to rape. The key provision of the Criminal Code dealing with rape was found in Section 143. It stated that before a person could be found guilty of rape, the following general conditions would have to be established:

1. the complainant had to be female
2. the accused had to be male
3. the complainant and accused were not married to each other
4. sexual intercourse occurred
5. the act of intercourse occurred without the consent of the woman

The other three principal offences in Section VI were attempted rape (Section 145), indecent assault against a female (Section 149), and indecent assault against a male (Section 156). The penalties for these four offences were life, 10 years, five years, and 10 years, respectively.

Many criticisms were raised against these laws over the decades, including the argument that they reflected "the gender dichotomy and cultural perceptions of gender relations that were functional to the male status maintenance" (Los 1994). As a result, Canada enacted new legislation (referred to as Bill C-127) on January 1, 1983. Bill C-127 reflected a number of significant changes. Sexual assault was reclassified and placed in Section VI of the Criminal Code ("Offences against the Person and Reputation"), which emphasizes that "sexual assault involves physical violence against another person." In addition, the legislation was changed to recognize that victims may be either male or female and that spouses can be charged with a sexual assault. It also established protections for women against cross-examination on their past sexual history. The four principal offences under old legislation were replaced by three new sexual assault sections: Section 271 (sexual assault), Section 272 (sexual assault with a weapon, threats to a third party, or caus-ing bodily harm), and Section 273 (aggravated sexual assault). Section 271, known as "Sexual Assault I," has a maximum penalty of 10 years; Section 272 ("Sexual Assault II") has a maximum penalty of 14 years; and Section 273 ("Sexual Assault III") has a maximum penalty of life imprisonment.

This law was amended in 1991, the result of a ruling by the Supreme Court of Canada in *Seaboyer* and *Gayme* (1991). In this case, the two accused successfully challenged the constitutionality of the Criminal Code restrictions on the admissibility of evidence concerning the past sexual history of women who were sexually assaulted. As a result, Parliament introduced a new test relating to a complainant's prior sexual history as well as a new definition of "consent" for sexual assault offences.

Source: M. Los, "The Struggle to Redefine Rape in the Early 1980s," in J.V. Roberts and R.M. Mohr, eds., *Confronting Sexual Assault: A Decade of Legal and Social Change* (Toronto: University of Toronto Press, 1994); D. Majury, "*Seaboyer* and *Gayme*: A Study InEquality," in Roberts and Mohr, *Confronting Sexual Assault*; J.V. Roberts and R.M. Mohr, "Sexual Assault in Canada: Recent Developments," in Roberts and Mohr, *Confronting Sexual Assault*.

Summary Conviction, Indictable and Hybrid Offences

Summary conviction offences are generally punished by a period of incarceration not exceeding six months and a maximum fine of $2000. Summary conviction trials are always heard by a provincial court judge. In addition, court proceedings for summary conviction offences have to start within six months of the commission of the offence. If a period of imprisonment is part of the sentence, the offender serves the sentence in a provincial facility.

In contrast, there are three methods of trial for **indictable offences.** The less serious indictable offences (e.g., theft under $5000) are also known as **absolute jurisdiction indictable offences.** The accused has to be tried by a provincial court judge. The most serious crimes (e.g., first- and second-degree murder) are referred to as **supreme court exclusive indictable offences.** They must be tried by a federally appointed judge and a jury in a provincial superior court. In some cases, the accused may request that the case be heard by judge alone, but this request has to be permitted by the provincial attorney general or minister of Justice). For all other indictable offences the accused can choose to have the trial by a provincially appointed judge without a jury, by a federally appointed judge with or without a jury, by judge alone, or by judge and jury. These offences, which make up the majority of indictable offences in Canada, are known as **election indictable offences.** If convicted of an indictable offence, the accused may receive a variety of sentences. For some offences (e.g., homicide) there are life sentences, while for others (e.g., sexual assault) punishments vary according to the degree of harm inflicted on the victim. Few minimum punishments are stipulated by the Criminal Code, so it is up to the judge to select the appropriate sentence up to the severest allowable by law.

Hybrid offences give prosecutors the discretion to decide if they wish to proceed with a case as a summary conviction offence or an indictable offence. The prosecutor's decision is formally based on such factors as the previous record of the offender as well as any mitigating factors (e.g., the social status of the offender) or aggravating factors (e.g., crimes involving violence) associated with the crime. In reality, the prosecutor's decision can be influenced by police officers. In Ericson's study of detectives in Peel Region, he found they were able to "fundamentally affect the outcome of a case both in terms of what the accused is convicted of and in terms of sentencing" (Ericson, in Wheeler 1987:27). However the final decision is reached, it has a significant impact on most of the procedures that will apply to the accused. For example, the decision determines:

1. possible appeals

2. the maximum length of the sentence

3. whether a fine may be imposed in addition to imprisonment

Crimes of Violence, Property, and 'Other' Criminal Code Offences

Crimes can also be grouped on the basis of certain shared traits. The police and other justice system agencies use three major crime categories—violent, property, and "other"—when collecting and reporting criminal offences. Each category consists of numerous criminal offences, but people usually refer to the crime rate for each category rather than specific crimes within. This makes it easier to compare categories of crimes on an annual basis. Each year, when the federal government releases its crime statistics, great attention is placed on whether a particular crime category has increased from the previous year. The crimes reported in each category are "police-reported crimes" and do not reflect crimes that don't come to their attention.

Violent crimes, or crimes against the person, include robbery, homicide, attempted murder, sexual assault, and assault causing harm. During 1994,

A Vancouver drug seizure in 1995 netted heroin from China worth $11 million. (Photo: Customs Border Service, Canada)

77 percent of violent crimes recorded by the police in Canada were nonserious assaults (i.e., assaults not involving a weapon or serious physical injury), while the next largest category was sexual assault, which accounted for 12.5 percent of the crimes in this category. Less than 1 percent of violent crimes involved murder and attempted murder (see Figure 2.1). Violent crimes accounted for approximately 11 percent of all Criminal Code offences in 1994, a slight decrease (3.0 percent) from 1993. This was the first decrease in the rate of violent crimes in Canada since 1977. Significantly, murders decreased to 596 from 630, a 14-percent reduction. Robberies also decreased 5 percent, attempted murder decline 8 percent, and abductions by 7 percent.

Property crimes include fraud, theft, breaking and entering, and the possession of stolen goods. The most common property crime recorded was theft under $1000, which accounted for almost 60 percent of the offences in this category; breaking and entering was the next-highest offence in the category, with 26 percent (see Figure 2.2).

FIGURE 2.1

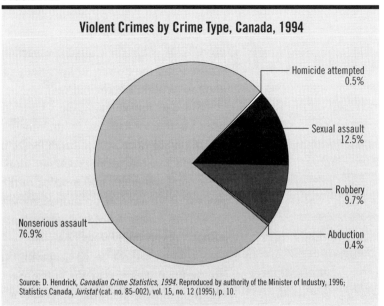

Violent Crimes by Crime Type, Canada, 1994

- Homicide attempted 0.5%
- Sexual assault 12.5%
- Robbery 9.7%
- Abduction 0.4%
- Nonserious assault 76.9%

Source: D. Hendrick, *Canadian Crime Statistics, 1994.* Reproduced by authority of the Minister of Industry, 1996; Statistics Canada, *Juristat* (cat. no. 85-002), vol. 15, no. 12 (1995), p. 10.

FIGURE 2.2

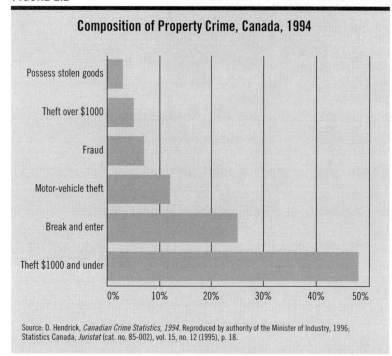

Composition of Property Crime, Canada, 1994

- Possess stolen goods
- Theft over $1000
- Fraud
- Motor-vehicle theft
- Break and enter
- Theft $1000 and under

0%   10%   20%   30%   40%   50%

Source: D. Hendrick, *Canadian Crime Statistics, 1994*. Reproduced by authority of the Minister of Industry, 1996; Statistics Canada, *Juristat* (cat. no. 85-002), vol. 15, no. 12 (1995), p. 18.

Property crimes decreased by 6 percent from 1993 to 1994. The greatest decrease was recorded for the offence of theft under $1000, which dropped 7 percent over the same period.

The third major crime category is referred to as "other" Criminal Code. Crimes in this category include mischief, vandalism, disturbing the peace, bail violations, and possession of offensive weapons. The most common criminal charge in this category during 1993 and 1994 was mischief. In 1993, it accounted for 52 percent of all crimes in this category, but this figure dropped to 48 percent in 1994.

The Canadian Charter of Rights and Freedoms

One of the most important additions to our Canadian legal system has been the Charter of Rights and Freedoms, enacted on April 17, 1982. The Charter differs from common law and statute law because it applies mostly to the protection of the legal rights of criminal suspects and convicted persons, the powers of the various criminal justice agencies, and criminal procedure during a trial. It is a complex piece of legislation and only parts of it deal with issues relevant to the criminal justice system. However, the sections concerned with the operation of the justice system have had a tremendous impact on criminal procedural issues in Canada, especially as they apply to the rights of the accused and the powers of criminal justice agencies involved in the detection and prosecution of criminals.

Since its introduction, the Charter has played an important role in establishing and enforcing certain fundamental principles related to the operation of the criminal justice system, such as the protection of due process rights, a fair trial, and freedom from cruel and unusual punishment. The Charter divides these legal principles into a series of different sections. Section 7 is the most general; it guarantees no individual will be denied his or her basic rights in Canadian society "except in accordance with the principles of fundamental justice" as specified by Section 1 of the Charter.

Sections 8 through 10 deal with the rights of individuals when they are arrested and detained by the police. Section 8 gives individuals the right to be secure against unreasonable search or seizure. Section 9 ensures no one is

EXHIBIT 2.3

Robbery: Violent Crime or Property Crime?

Seldom in Canada does one government organization define a crime in a way that differs from the way another organization defines the same offence. But this is the case with the offence of robbery. This offence is defined in Section 343 of the Criminal Code—a section that relates to offences committed against the rights of *property*.

343. Every one commits robbery who
(a) steals, and for the purpose of extorting whatever is stolen or to prevent or overcome resistance to the stealing, uses violence or threats of violence to a person or property;
(b) steals from any person, and, at the time he steals or immediately before or immediately thereafter, wounds, beats, strikes, or uses any personal violence to that person;
(c) assaults any person with intent to steal from him; or
(d) steals from any person while armed with an offensive weapon or imitation thereof. (Source: Justice Canada)

The punishment of robbery is found in Section 344:

344. Every one who commits robbery is guilty of an indictable offence and liable to imprisonment for life. (Source: Justice Canada)

However, as Desroches (1995) discusses in his study of bank robbers in Canada, robbery is an offence punishable by life imprisonment because of the possibility of the threat of or use of violence. As a result, the National Parole Board defines robbery as a violent offence. Statistics Canada too defines it as a violent crime when it categorizes crimes, since robbery can result in physical injury to the victim (or victims). Statistics Canada actually divides robbery into three categories: (1) robberies involving the use of firearms, (2) holdups committed with the use of other offensive weapons, and (3) robberies committed without weapons. In addition, many criminologists (e.g., Normandeau 1968) view robbery as a violent crime because a victim is confronted by the offender, who often threatens the victim with the use of force.

Desroches (1995:10–11) points out many robbers never intend to use force in their crimes. Some are unarmed and simply pass a note asking for money, threatening no one, and leave the bank if a teller refuses to give money. Should such an act be defined as a violent crime or a property crime?

Source: F.J. Desroches, *Force and Fear: Robbery in Canada* (Scarborough, Ont.: Nelson Canada, 1995); and A. Normandeau, *Trends and Patterns in Crimes of Robbery* (Philadelphia: University of Pennsylvania, 1968).

Rarely is assistance given to people recovering from the shock of being a crime victim. (Photo: Canada Wide Photo Service)

EXHIBIT 2.4

The Charter of Rights and Freedoms: Legal Rights and the Canadian Criminal Justice System

Legal Rights

7. Everyone has the right to life, liberty and security of the person and the right not to be deprived thereof except in accordance with the principles of fundamental justice.

8. Everyone has the right to be secure against unreasonable search or seizure.

9. Everyone has the right not to be arbitrarily detained or imprisoned.

10. Everyone has the right on arrest or detention
    (a) to be informed promptly of the reasons therefor;
    (b) to retain and instruct counsel without delay and to be informed of that right; and
    (c) to have the validity of the detection determined by way of habeas corpus and to be released if the detention is not lawful.

11. Any person charged with an offence has the right
    (a) to be informed without unreasonable delay of the specific offence;
    (b) to be tried within a reasonable time;
    (c) not to be compelled to be a witness in proceedings against that person in respect of the offence;
    (d) to be presumed innocent until proven guilty according to law in a fair and public hearing by an independent and impartial tribunal;
    (e) not to be denied reasonable bail without just cause;
    (f) except in the case of an offence under military law tried before a military tribunal, to the benefit of trial by jury where the maximum punishment for the offence is imprisonment for five years or a more severe punishment;
    (g) not to be found guilty on account of any act or omission unless, at the time of the act or omission, it is constituted an offence under Canadian or international law or was criminal according to the general principles of law recognized by the community of nations;
    (h) if finally acquitted of the offence, not to be tried for it again and, if finally found guilty and punished for the offence, not to be tried or punished for it again; and
    (i) if found guilty of the offence and if the punishment for the offence has been varied between the time of the commission and the time of sentencing, to the benefit of the lesser punishment.

12. Everyone has the right not to be subjected to any cruel and unusual treatment or punishment.

13. A witness who testifies in any proceedings has the right not to have any incriminating evidence so given used to incriminate that witness in any other proceedings, except in a prosecution for perjury or for the giving of contradictory evidence.

14. A party or witness in any proceedings who does not understand or speak the language in which the proceedings are conducted or who is deaf has the right to the assistance of an interpreter.

Equality Rights

15. (1) Every individual is equal before and under the law and has the right to the equal protection and equal benefit of the law without discrimination and, in particular, without discrimination based on race, national or ethnic origin, colour, religion, sex, age or mental or physical disability.
    (2) Subsection (1) does not preclude any law, program or activity that has as its object the amelioration of conditions of disadvantaged individuals or groups including those that are disadvantaged because of race, national or ethnic origin, colour, religion, sex, age or mental or physical disability.

Enforcement

24. (1) Anyone whose rights or freedoms, as guaranteed by this Charter, have been infringed or denied may apply to a court of competent jurisdiction to obtain such remedy as the court considers appropriate and just in the circumstances.
    (2) Where, in proceedings under subsection (1), a court concludes that evidence was obtained in a manner that infringed or denied any rights or freedoms guaranteed by this Charter, the evidence shall be excluded if it is established that, having regard to all the circumstances, the admission of it in the proceedings would bring the administration of justice into disrepute. (Source: Justice Canada)

arbitrarily arrested and detained. Section 10 deals with the rights of individuals detained by the police.

For example, Section 10(b) of the Charter states "everyone has the right on arrest or detention to retain and instruct counsel without delay and to be informed of that right." According to the ruling in *R. v. Therens* (1985), the Supreme Court of Canada ruled that evidence obtained by the police without first informing the suspect of his right to a lawyer could not be used. This interpretation was expanded in *R. v. Manninen* (1987), when the right to legal counsel was extended to anyone detained by the police. In addition, the police were instructed they had to inform anyone in their custody how that person could exercise this right before being questioned. In *R. v. Ross* (1989), the Supreme Court ruled that the rights set out in this section of the Charter are not absolute, pointing out that a suspect's right to retain and instruct counsel must be exercised diligently by the suspect. This means that a suspect cannot refuse the chance to contact legal counsel, be questioned by the police, and then complain about having said things he or she shouldn't have because no lawyer was present. Finally, in the case of *Brydges v. The Queen* (1990), the Supreme Court extended the police duty to advise individuals about their right to legal counsel, ruling that police must give any accused or detained individual a reasonable opportunity to retain and instruct counsel. In addition, the police now have to refrain from questioning any suspect until a reasonable opportunity exists to exercise that right.

Section 11 of the Charter outlines the rights of individuals charged with a criminal offence as they proceed through a criminal court case. Section 11 is divided into nine components and deals with issues concerned with the presumption of innocence, court delays, and the right not to be denied reasonable bail. Section 11(d), for example, deals with the "presumption of innocence." In *R. v. Oakes* (1986), the Supreme Court struck down a section of the Narcotic Control Act because it violated the presumption of innocence of the accused, since the accused had to prove to the court he did not possess a narcotic for the reason of trafficking. Section 12 protects individuals from any form of cruel and unusual punishment. Sections 13 and 14 deal with the rights of witnesses within, during, and after a criminal trial, as well as the right against self-incrimination.

Equality rights are the concern of Sections 15(1) and 15(2), and they specify the need for the equal protection of all persons within our system of justice as well as equality before and under the law. Section 28 guarantees that rights of equality extend to both women and men.

Section 24(1) deals with remedies in the event of any violation of the above rights. Section 24(2) outlines a test to determine whether the rights of the accused have been infringed upon and the justice system brought into disrepute because of illegal evidence. In general, this section protects the accused by excluding evidence illegally collected by the police and used during the trial. However, there is no hard rule for the police to operate with under Section

24(2). The Canadian system is different from the one developed in the United States. There, a strict law known as the exclusionary rule makes it illegal to use evidence collected in an improper manner. The closest the Supreme Court has come to establishing a test to determine the admissibility of evidence is found in *Collins v. The Queen* (1987). The Supreme Court adopted the "reasonable-person test," which asks the question "Would the admission of the evidence bring the administration of justice into disrepute in the eyes of a reasonable man, dispassionate and fully apprised of the circumstances of the case?" (Stuart 1994:82). The Supreme Court summarized the specifics of this test the next year in *R. v. Jacoy* (1988):

> First, the Court must consider whether the admission of evidence will affect the fairness of the trial. If this inquiry is answered affirmatively, "the admission of evidence would tend to bring the administration of justice into disrepute and, subject to a consideration of other factors, the evidence generally should be excluded" . . . One of the factors relevant to this determination is the nature of the evidence; if the evidence is real evidence that existed irrespective of the Charter violation, its admission will rarely render the trial unfair.

In Canada, it is up to the courts to decide, on a case-by-case basis, what evidence can be admitted or excluded in a case. In *Stinchcombe v. R.* (1991), the Supreme Court ruled that all relevant evidence, with certain exceptions, be given by the police and prosecution to defence counsel (see Exhibit 2.5).

Criminal Law Reform

During the past decades, the federal government has revised various **substantive laws** and **procedural laws** to reflect current concerns. At the same time, new ideas have been introduced into the social sciences that change the way we have traditionally granted legal rights in our society. The result is that a particular action that was perfectly legal 25 years ago is now a criminal offence. For example, can a 4- or 5-year-old child be allowed to give uncorroborated testimony in court against someone who allegedly sexually assaulted him or her? If so, how can we determine if the child knows the difference between true and false statements? In other areas of the law, the authorities are beginning to enact legislation that gives them more powers to forfeit material possessions, especially drugs, purchased with money made through illegal activities. These are just two of the legal changes introduced by the federal government in the past decade.

Child Sexual Assault

An increasing awareness of the special legal protections needed by children led to the passage of a new Canadian statute in 1988. To understand the nature of childhood victimization and the legal protections children need, the federal

EXHIBIT 2.5

The Charter in Action:
Stinchcombe v. The Queen (1991)

Disclosure is one of the most important features of our criminal justice system. According to the Law Reform Commission of Canada, disclosure of relevant information among all the parties involved in a court case is an important factor in the fairness and efficiency in the administration of the Canadian justice system. According to the Law Reform Commission of Canada (1974b:1):

> Fairness and efficiency in the administration of justice depend in large measure upon the quality of information available to litigating parties. In Canadian law pre-trial disclosure and discovery are commonplaces of civil procedure, designed to expedite the resolution of a dispute by refining the issues to be debated at trial and minimizing the risk of surprise. Our rules of criminal procedure, however, do not provide for such disclosure, although the preliminary inquiry is commonly used by defence counsel as an opportunity to discover the strength and the scope of the Crown's case.

However, clear-cut guidelines concerning the exact nature of how disclosure should operate were never developed. The lack of any principles governing disclosure was one of the most important legal issues that emerged from the investigation into the wrongful conviction of Donald Marshall. One of the problems of the original court case was the lack of disclosure between all the parties involved during both the pre-trial actions

and subsequent trial (Brucker 1992). The investigation following the release of Donald Marshall found that the police and the prosecution had withheld information from the defence. That withholding, together with the failure of the defence counsel to seek disclosure from the Crown, was a major contributing factor in the wrongful conviction. According to the final report on the wrongful conviction of Donald Marshall, if "the police are not candid in their dealing with Crown prosecutors, the whole policy on disclosure may go for naught. It is trite to say that a dishonest cop who wishes to subvert the system may do so, and rules are not likely to completely contain such abuse" (House of Commons *Debates*, 1966). As a result, recommendations were made in the hope that guidelines on disclosure would emerge and that the authorities would comply with them in order to achieve the "sound administration of criminal justice . . ." One of the problems with this case was the lack of clear directives concerning the role of disclosure during the prosecution.

The guidelines for disclosure emerged from the decision reached by the Supreme Court of Canada in the case of *Stinchcombe v. The Queen* (1991). This case involved an Alberta lawyer who was convicted in the Alberta Provincial Court of misappropriating funds from a client. Stinchcombe argued the client had actually made him a business partner and, as a result, he had done nothing wrong. Stinchcombe appealed his conviction to the Alberta Court of Appeal, but the appeal was dismissed. The Supreme Court of Canada decided to hear the case, however, perhaps because it saw the opportunity to create clear directives concerning disclosure in criminal trials.

The key issue concerned certain information given to the police after the preliminary inquiry but before the actual

trial. This information concerned a taped statement given to the RCMP by Stinchcombe's secretary. The tape supported the claim that Stinchcombe was innocent. The Crown prosecutor informed the defence of this taped statement but declined to inform them about the exact nature of its contents. In addition, the secretary refused all offers to be interviewed by the defence. During the trial, defence counsel discovered that the secretary was not going to be called as a witness by the Crown. As a result, the defence requested that the judge make the Crown disclose the contents of the taped statement. The judge refused, since there was no obligation on the part of the Crown either to put the witness on the stand or disclose her statements.

The Supreme Court of Canada overturned the decision made by the lower court. In a unanimous 7–0 vote favouring Stinchcombe, it ruled that Crown prosecutors must disclose to the defence any information in serious criminal matters that is capable of affecting the accused's ability to prepare a defence— and to do so early enough to allow the accused time to prepare that defence. However, this rule is not absolute and is subject to judicial interpretation. For example, the police are not required to give the names of any informant who supplies them with information relevant to a case. The Supreme Court decision is based on the fundamental right of the accused to give full answer and defence to the charges. However, the Supreme Court also ruled that "the defence has no obligation to assist the prosecution and is entitled to assume a purely adversarial role ..."

Source: The quoted extract is from "Discovery in Criminal Cases," Law Reform Commission of Canada, 1974, Justice Canada. Reproduced with the permission of the Minister of Public Works and Government Services Canada, 1976.

government appointed the Committee on Sexual Offences against Children and Youths (known as the "Badgley Committee") in 1981. This committee was to investigate and report on the nature and extent of child sexual abuse, juvenile prostitution, and child pornography across Canada. Three years later,

Lorelei and Steven Turner arrive at court in Miramichi, N.B., in 1995. They were convicted of manslaughter in the May 1994 death of their son, who died of starvation. (Photo: Canadian Press)

in its final report, the committee reported there was a significant need for the federal government to add special substantive and procedural provisions into the Criminal Code and Canada Evidence Act to give children special legal protections and privileges. The purpose of these proposals was to allow children to have greater legal rights as well as a central role in criminal proceedings.

The committee detailed a number of problems experienced by children who became involved with the criminal justice system. One problem was that young females and males were given different protections under the law. For many offences, it was discovered, the victim had to be a female and the perpetrator a male. The law was also found to be inadequate for protecting children from the vast number of offences committed against them, such as sexual exploitation. In addition, children often faced formidable obstacles when they appeared in court. For instance, it was rare for a child under the age of 12 to testify in a trial due to the restrictive nature of the Canada Evidence Act. This statute stipulated that children under 14 could not testify in court unless they were able to understand the nature of an oath. In such cases, judges had to be aware or warn the members of a jury about the unreliability of a child's testimony. As a result of these restrictions, it was rare for prosecutors to charge a suspect with a criminal offence committed against a young child unless there was corroborating evidence from experts, such as a medical doctor.

The result was the proclamation on January 1, 1988, of Bill C-15, An Act to Amend the Criminal Code and the Canada Evidence Act with Respect to Sexual Offences against Children. Three new Criminal Code offences were created by this new legislation—Section 151, "Sexual Interference"; Section 152, "Invitation to Sexual Touching"; and Section 153, "Sexual Exploitation." In addition, numerous changes were made to sections of the Criminal Code that related to child sexual abuse. These changes included the addition to the Criminal Code of offences relating to juvenile prostitution. This act also included sections that radically altered the role of children who give evidence in court, and this led to a number of changes in the Canada Evidence Act. These changes included the possibility of convicting the accused purely on the basis of a child's testimony, without the legal necessity of corroborating evidence.

Field Practice 2.1
Enforcement of Child Sexual Assault Legislation

1. One of the most fundamental rights in criminal trials is the right of the accused to face his or her accuser in court. This has traditionally been interpreted to mean that both individuals have to be present in the courtroom at the same time. However, Bill C-15, Section 442 (2.1), allowed for the use of a one-way screening device to be used if the judge felt the child witness would benefit from its use, particularly in the event that the witness felt intimidated by the presence of the accused in the court. In *R. v. A.B.* (unreported) defence counsel argued that the use of a screen in the courtroom would prevent the accused from having the full opportunity to cross-examine the complainant and would also create an inference of guilt that would violate the presumption of innocence of the accused and therefore violate Sections 7 and 11 of the Charter. While the judge agreed that Section 442 did violate those two sections of the Charter, Section 442 was upheld as a reasonable limit under Section 1 of the Charter. The trial court judge ruled that it satisfied the test that (1) "its object to obtain a 'full and candid account' is of sufficient importance to override a constitutionally provided right and freedom; and (2) the means to meet that objective are proportional to achieve this end." The judge also commented that in each case a judge "must balance the interests of society and the accused . . . Section 442.(2.1) has been carefully worded to allow the trial judge to make a decision about fairness to the accused which might vary from case to case." The judge ruled this section of Bill C-15 to be constitutional.

2. In *R. v. M.E.R.* (49 CCC (3d), 475) the Appeal Division of the Supreme Court of Nova Scotia upheld the constitutionality of using closed-circuit television in the courtroom, as specified by Section 486 (2.1) of the Criminal Code. This section, introduced by Bill C-15, allowed a child witness to testify by closed-circuit television as long as the child was present in the courthouse during the testimony. Defence counsel had argued that by virtue of a child's testifying via closed-circuit television, the fundamental right of the accused to face his accuser in court was violated. The Appeal Division of the Supreme Court of Nova Scotia upheld the constitutionality of this section of the Criminal Code, noting that "the right to face one's accusers is not, in this day and age, to be taken in the literal sense . . . [I]t is simply the right of the accused person to be present in court to hear the case against him and to make answer and defence to it."

Other changes involved abolishing the recent complaint rule, admitting a videotape of the child's disclosure of sexual abuse, and providing for the possibility of a child giving testimony outside of the court or behind a screen. In addition, the Canada Evidence Act was altered to allow younger children to testify by permitting those who demonstrate "an ability to communicate" and who promise to tell the truth to give evidence. The spouses of the accused could also be compelled to give evidence.

As discussed in the introduction to this chapter, it was not long before some of the more controversial provisions of this new legislation were challenged in court. In 1989 it was established in *R. v. Bickford* (1989) that corroboration is no longer required when a child gives unsworn testimony in court. This made it possible to convict the accused on the basis of the child's testimony alone if the trial court judge was satisfied the child understands the nature of an oath and promises to tell the truth. As a result of this decision, children as young as 4 years of age have been permitted to give testimony in court.

As a result of these procedural and evidentiary changes, significant increases in the number of child sexual abuse cases are now reported to the authorities. Police are laying more charges, prosecutors are prosecuting more cases involving young children between the ages of 4 and 9, and in courts across Canada younger complainants are allowed to testify without corroborating evidence.

Proceeds of Crime Legislation

The prolific growth of the illicit drug trade over the past three decades has led to legislation that lawmakers hope will control the illegal flow of drugs. Intelligence gathered on the Colombian drug cartels revealed that traditional enforcement techniques were extremely limited in their ability to detect cartel activity. Moreover, the cartels' hierarchical structure proved to be an effective shield against action taken by the authorities. For example, the largest and most successful of the drug cartels were divided into numerous self-contained "cells," with each cell subject to reporting procedures through a chain of command that comprises branch and regional offices. Each cell was constructed in such a way as to be isolated from all other cells. When a law enforcement agency infiltrated one cell, the remaining ones remained untouched to carry on their operations.

In 1987, in an effort to control the activities of the drug cartels in Canada, the federal government launched the National Drug Strategy, with $210 million allocated over five years. These funds were distributed in the following areas: treatment and rehabilitation (38 percent), education and prevention (32 percent), enforcement and control (20 percent), information and research (6 percent), international cooperation (3 percent), and national focus (1 percent).

The first piece of Canadian legislation related to the issue of the proceeds of crime was enacted in 1976, when Parliament amended Section 312 of the Criminal Code. This section, titled Possession of Property Obtained by Crime, was broadened to include the laundering and importation of "dirty" money into Canada (Donald 1992). Little use was made of this provision, however, until 1981, when the RCMP created their Anti-Profiteering Sections. Officers working in these units immediately became aware of the deficiencies of this provision, most importantly those related to the freezing, seizing, and ultimate forfeiture of monies obtained through crime.

George Burden's $1.5-million residence, in the posh Southlands neighbourhood of Vancouver, was raided by the RCMP in 1994. The Mounties found over $500 000 in cash buried in garbage bags. (Photo: Tim Pelling/*The Globe and Mail*)

The power of law-enforcement officers to search and seize came solely through search warrants, as set forth in Section 443 of the Criminal Code. However, these warrants were limited in the sense that they allowed seizure only of "tangible" assets that were capable of being brought before a justice (Bowie 1988b). Consequently, intangible items such as bank accounts could not be seized and therefore could be retained by the individuals holding them. The inability of authorities to freeze these accounts permitted the accused to move their assets out of the reach of the law. To the law enforcement agencies involved in the enforcement of drug legislation, it was imperative that the Canadian government strengthen these provisions.

On January 1, 1989, Bill C-61, the Proceeds of Crime Act, came into existence. This legislation added a number of amendments to the Criminal Code, the Narcotics Control Act, and the Food and Drug Act that were designed to strengthen the powers of investigators in the area of the forfeiture of monies obtained through crime. The proceeds-of-crime legislation allows the Crown to proceed against an individual and examine the liability, rights, and obligations to that specific person with respect to a particular piece of property. A prerequisite of this forfeiture action is the conviction of the individual for a criminal offence. After a conviction is secured, it is the duty of the prosecution to prove that the seized property is probably a proceed of crime—specifically, the crime under which the conviction was registered. Thus, if an individual is convicted under Section 4(2) of the Narcotic Control Act (Possession of a Narcotic for the Purpose of Trafficking), it is possible for the authorities to seize the individual's vehicle if that vehicle is thought to have been purchased with money received through the selling of drugs. This forfeiture also allows prosecutors to seize property in the absence of a criminal conviction; however, an information in relation to an offence must be sworn first. Before the court can order the vehicle forfeited, the Crown has to prove that all or part of the vehicle was, on the balance of probabilities, purchased with proceeds from the sale of narcotics. Although the burden of proof in forfeiture proceedings is less stringent than the burden of proof in criminal cases (which require the test of "beyond a reasonable doubt"), the direct connection between the asset seized and the substantive offence is not always easy to make.

Although this new piece of legislation gave criminal investigators many new powers, it failed to include a number of other legal mechanisms. Probably the most important enforcement tool left out of the new legislation was the failure to require a mandatory reporting law directed toward the Canadian banking establishment, as is required in the United States. Instead, the federal government decided to allow banks to develop their own reporting procedures (Jensen 1989).

The Seriousness of Crime

Legal Responses to Violent Crimes

Criminal statutes have punishments that reflect the seriousness of the crime committed. Some offences in the Criminal Code recognize different levels of violence together with differences in the maximum amount of punishment applicable to each. Examples of single offences with gradations of seriousness within are homicide and sexual assault.

The offence of sexual assault consists of three offences, the least serious of which is found in Section 271 of the Criminal Code. This is a hybrid offence, so if the Crown prosecutor elects to proceed by way of an indictable offence, the maximum length of punishment is 10 years. However, the Crown prosecutor also has the discretion to proceed by way of summary conviction, and the accused, if convicted, faces a maximum punishment of 18 months. For a person convicted of sexual assault of the next-highest level of seriousness— Section 272 of the Criminal Code, which addresses sexual assault with a weapon, threatening, or causing bodily harm—the maximum length of the prison term is 14 years. The most serious form of **sexual assault,** dealt with in Section 273 of the Criminal Code, involves the charge of aggravated sexual assault. An individual convicted of this offence can receive the maximum sentence of life imprisonment (Roberts and Mohr 1994).

Field Practice 2.2

Enforcement of Proceeds of Crime Legislation

1. RCMP investigating a convicted drug dealer discovered he bought a $44 000 1992 Cadillac by putting a cash down payment of $35 900. The salesperson informed the police he received 249 100-dollar bills and 555 20-dollar bills. On investigation, the police discovered that the dealer's taxable income for the year was $1, that the total income claimed on his tax returns from 1989 until 1993 was $7455, and that he registered the car in his father's name (although of 32 separate occasions his father was seen only once in the vehicle).

The prosecution went to court to permanently seize the Cadillac under the Proceeds of Crime Act. The prosecution claimed there was no evidence that the drug dealer was employed in any legitimate work. Defence counsel argued that the circumstances surrounding the case may have appeared suspicious but that this wasn't a reason to take away someone's physical possession. The judge decided in favour of the prosecution, ruling the Crown had the power to seize a physical asset.

2. An individual was charged by the RCMP for conspiracy to traffic cocaine in 1990, but he fled Canada just before the trial date. His occupation was listed as "restaurateur" and he earned a total of $33 000 between 1987 and 1990. However, the police seized $145 000 from a safety deposit box and $38 500 hidden in a neighbour's house. The federal government wanted to forfeit the money under the Proceeds of Crime Act. However, the individual's ex-wife claimed the $145 000 also, saying she had saved the money, which was accumulated through the sale of property and from cash gifts. She made no claim on the $38 500, which contained 38 marked bills that undercover police officers used in their investigation.

The Crown argued financial records showed that the couple spent $86 000 in 1990, a year in which they earned approximately $20 000. In addition, the Crown pointed out, the accused's net worth grew in excess of $380 000 in 1989 and 1990 despite that his tax returns for that period showed a total income of $12 000. In addition, police taped a conversation of his wife in which she stated that her husband marked all his money. In their search of the suspect's house, police found a list of serial numbers that corresponded to 49 1000-dollar bills found in the safety deposit box.

According to the judge who heard the case, the evidence gave "the inescapable conclusion . . . that the funds are the proceeds of crime." As a result, he ruled that the $145 000 and $38 500 had to be turned over to the federal government.

In contrast to sexual assault, **homicide** is divided into four categories in the Criminal Code. A person who commits homicide, according to Section 222, "directly or indirectly, by any means, causes the death of a human being." This section specifies that only culpable homicide is punishable. Once the police have determined that a homicide is culpable, they can lay one of the following

charges: first-degree murder, second-degree murder, manslaughter, and infanticide. **First-degree murder** is planned and deliberate. However, an individual
can be charged with first-degree murder even if the act wasn't planned and
deliberate when the victim is a police officer, a prison guard, an individual
working in a prison setting, or "is another similar person acting in the course
of duty." In addition, a charge of first-degree murder can be laid if the act was
planned or deliberate and if anyone dies during the commission of one the
following crimes: Section 76(1)—hijacking an aircraft; Section 271—sexual
assault; Section 272—sexual assault with a weapon; Section 273—aggravated
sexual assault; Section 279—kidnapping and forcible confinement; and Section
279.1—hostage taking. All murder that is not first-degree murder is **second-
degree murder** (Silverman and Kennedy 1993).

The charge of **manslaughter** can be laid if the Crown prosecutor is unable
to establish all the elements of murder. Usually a charge of manslaughter is laid
when the death in question (an accidental death) is caused either by an unlawful act, such as assault, or by criminal negligence. Manslaughter is an
indictable offence, and the maximum punishment is life imprisonment.

Infanticide is one of the rare sections of the Canadian Criminal Code that
specifies the gender of the alleged perpetrator of the crime. This charge can be
laid only against a "female person" when she "causes the death of her newly-
born child . . . " An infant, in the eyes of the law, is a person under one year of
age. The maximum punishment for the offence of infanticide is five years in
prison. This law is based on the reasoning that a woman may be "mentally
disturbed of giving birth . . . and thus less responsible for her actions. In this
situation, the law mitigates the severity of punishment for what would otherwise be murder or manslaughter."

The punishment for both first- and second-degree murder is life imprisonment. There is an important difference between the two, however, and that is
the possibility of release on parole. At the sentencing of a person convicted of
second-degree murder, the judge can state that the accused is eligible for parole
after serving a designated amount of time of the sentence. At the present time,
a judge has the right to grant an offender eligibility for full parole after serving
10 years. An individual convicted of first-degree murder must serve life imprisonment. However, the law stipulates that that individual must serve a minimum
of 25 years of the sentence before applying for full parole.

In theory, an individual convicted of first-degree murder spends the rest of
his life in prison, i.e., there is no guarantee of him ever leaving a federal correctional institution. However, since 1991, once a person convicted of first-degree
murder serves 15 years, that individual can apply for a review of his case under
Section 745 of the Criminal Code for the purpose of receiving parole (the faint-
hope clause). The jury decides whether to allow the application for reducing
the number of years before the person receives parole. If the latter decision is
reached, the National Parole Board reviews the case and agrees or refuses to
grant parole. By 1996, most individuals applying for parole under this section

of the Criminal Code received the right to apply for a reduction in their sentence length. Of the first 43 applicants under Section 745, 36 were successful in obtaining a parole board hearing, and 15 of the 36 received notification they could apply for parole immediately.

Public Perceptions of Violent Crime and Fear of Victimization

According to Hung and Bowles (1995), the crimes that the public are most concerned about are violent crimes. In fact, they found the public considered most criminal offences to be violent, although only about 11 percent of crimes recorded by the police in 1993 were violent. Fifty-eight percent of all crimes were classified as property crimes and the remaining 30 percent were "other" Criminal Code offences. Put differently, the rate of violent crime was 1079 per 100 000 population in 1993, and the corresponding rate of property crimes was over five times higher, at 5562 per 100 000 population.

Crime has consequences not only for victims but for persons who have never been victims of a serious, violent crime. This is because the thought of becoming a victim has been found to lead to fear in people, and fear of becoming a victim can lead people to change their lifestyle. Fear of crime has the potential for changing lifestyles, although the number of fearful individuals at any one time exceeds the number of actual victims. This fear may influence the activities of a larger proportion of the public than crime itself. Fear of crime is not uniformly distributed but is significantly related to age and sex. For example, woman feel more unsafe walking alone in the neighbourhood than men do (see Figure 2.4).

Information collected in the General Social Survey of 1988 indicates that women of all age groups feel more unsafe than do men in the same age groups, in urban areas and in rural areas. Men and women over age 65 had the highest concerns about personal safety. And women in

FIGURE 2.3

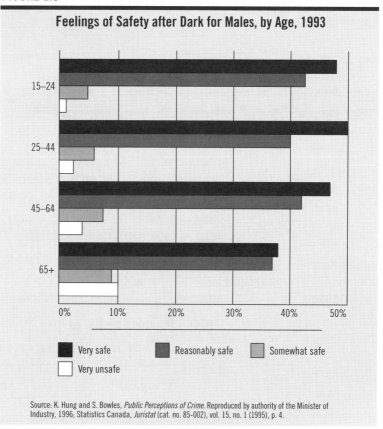

Source: K. Hung and S. Bowles, *Public Perceptions of Crime.* Reproduced by authority of the Minister of Industry, 1996; Statistics Canada, *Juristat* (cat. no. 85-002), vol. 15, no. 1 (1995), p. 4.

FIGURE 2.4

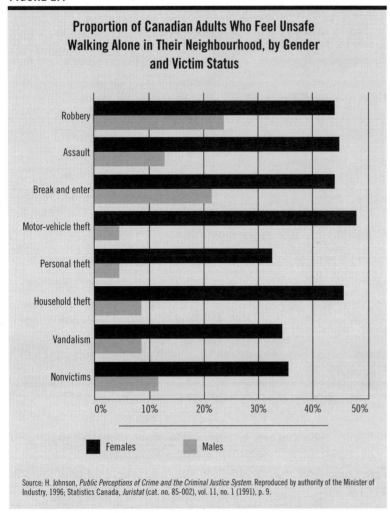

Proportion of Canadian Adults Who Feel Unsafe Walking Alone in Their Neighbourhood, by Gender and Victim Status

Source: H. Johnson, *Public Perceptions of Crime and the Criminal Justice System.* Reproduced by authority of the Minister of Industry, 1996; Statistics Canada, *Juristat* (cat. no. 85-002), vol. 11, no. 1 (1991), p. 9.

this age group displayed greater concern for their personal safety than did their male counterparts, regardless of the type of offence.

Hung and Bowles found Canadians were becoming more fearful of criminal victimization. Between 1988 and 1993, they reported, there was a slight increase in the percentage of Canadians, in both rural and urban areas, who said they felt "very unsafe" (from 9 percent to 12 percent) walking alone in their neighbourhoods after dark; at the same time there was a significant reduction in the percentage of those who said they felt "very safe" (from 40 percent to 32 percent). Women were found to have the greatest fear of crime (see Figure 2.5). Nineteen percent of all women in the study reported feeling "very unsafe" compared to just 4 percent of males. And both men and women living in rural areas felt safer than did their urban counterparts.

Wright (1993) examined personal victimization rates in relation to place of residence (rural versus urban) and sex. She reported urban residents experienced higher rates of victimization than did rural residents. The differences were consistent for all types of crimes against the person. Figure 2.6 reveals that the differences between urban and rural residents were greater for women than for men. Men living in urban areas were victimized 24 percent more often than their rural counterparts. In comparison, women residing in urban areas reported being victims of personal crimes 47 percent more than women residing in rural areas.

Public Perceptions of the Criminal Justice System

Recent years have seen a growing interest in Canadians' perceptions of crime and the effectiveness with which the criminal justice system responds to it. Because we live close to the United States and are exposed to much American news about violent crimes, Canadians' perceptions about the seriousness of crime in their own country—and the ability of the various agencies of the criminal justice system to control it—could be strongly influenced by events across the border. Throughout the 1980s, studies of Canadians' perceptions about crime confirmed this influence. Doob and Roberts (1982; 1983) discovered that Canadians substantially overestimate the amount of violent and property crime. Later, Roberts and Doob (1989) also reported that most Canadians overestimate the rate of recidivism among first-time parolees. Most respondents believed the recidivism rate to be somewhere between 30 percent and 100 percent, while the actual figure was between 13 percent and 17 percent. Still, Canadians disagreed with the introduction of lengthy sentences, because they felt it would not be a good policy to incarcerate large numbers of minor offenders.

Yet other studies found Canadians' knowledge about the operation of the criminal justice system was limited. The Canadian Sentencing Commission (1987) found that most Canadians held erroneous ideas about the sentencing practices of provincial and superior court judges. The Canadian adults sampled were found to underestimate the average length of sentences for the offences of assault, breaking and entering, and robbery. For example, over 75 percent of the respondents felt less than 60 percent of convicted robbers received prison sentences, whereas in reality the figure is closer to 90 percent. The same study discovered most Canadians did not know the maximum penalty for the offence of robbery was 10 years and break and entering a home was life imprisonment.

FIGURE 2.5

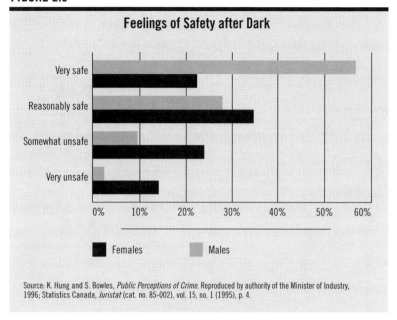

Source: K. Hung and S. Bowles, *Public Perceptions of Crime.* Reproduced by authority of the Minister of Industry, 1996; Statistics Canada, *Juristat* (cat. no. 85-002), vol. 15, no. 1 (1995), p. 4.

FIGURE 2.6

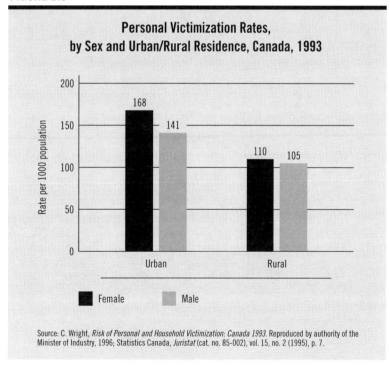

Source: C. Wright, *Risk of Personal and Household Victimization: Canada 1993.* Reproduced by authority of the Minister of Industry, 1996; Statistics Canada, *Juristat* (cat. no. 85-002), vol. 15, no. 2 (1995), p. 7.

TABLE 2.1

Population Who Perceive the Criminal Courts to Be Doing a Good Job, by Type of Victimization and by Age

	Providing justice quickly	Helping the victim	Determining guilt	Protecting the rights of the accused
Type of victimization	%	%	%	%
Total population	14	16	25	44
Victims	11	13	26	47
Violent victimizations	10	10	25	47
Property victimizations	11	13	27	47
Non-victims	15	17	25	44
Age				
Total population	14	16	25	44
15–24	18	23	30	43
25–44	12	13	25	45
45–64	12	14	24	45
65 and over	14	18	22	41

Source: H. Johnson, *Public Perceptions of Crime and the Criminal Justice System*. Reproduced by authority of the Minister of Industry, 1996; Statistics Canada, *Juristat* (cat. no. 85-002), vol. 15, no. 2 (1991), p. 12.

Johnson (1991) reported that 65 percent of her sample felt judges handed out lenient sentences, while only 2 percent felt sentences were too severe. She also found many Canadians held positive views of the police. Over 60 percent of her sample felt the police were doing a good job enforcing the law. Fifty percent felt the police were responding to calls for assistance as promptly as possible. In keeping with their feelings about judges and sentencing, Johnson also found, less than half (44 percent) of those she questioned perceived the Canadian courts to protect the rights of accused. Only 16 percent considered the courts to be doing a good job in assisting the victims of crime. Her sample viewed the court system in a similar fashion; only 14 percent believed the court system is doing a good job of providing justice quickly.

Summary

Our criminal justice system is founded on the protection of law-abiding citizens through the operation of the law. In essence, the criminal justice system develops, administers, and enforces the criminal law. What constitutes a crime is defined by the federal government, but the actual administration of justice is in the hands of provincial governments; thus, one can find variations in the operation of our legal system across Canada. Crimes are categorized as indictable or summary conviction offences, depending on their seriousness.

Our understanding of what criminal conduct is changes over time. Today the Criminal Code is a complex document, because our knowledge of criminal behaviour has increased dramatically during the past decade. In recent years Canada has passed laws designed to combat child sexual assault and the profits made from criminal activities. These legal charges can be procedural or substantive in nature. Changes in the rules of the processing of the accused through the criminal justice system reflect procedural concerns.

In our system of law, all individuals are believed to be innocent until proven guilty. To determine guilt, the accused must be shown to have possessed mens rea and committed the act in question. These facts must be proven beyond a reasonable doubt in a court by the prosecution. No matter what the standards our criminal justice has to employ in the courtroom, the perceptions held by the Canadian public toward our legal system may vary from those of our legal professionals. In general, the public consider violent actions to be more serious offences than property crimes.

Discussion Questions

1. Define the word "law."

2. What are the goals of the criminal law?

3. What is a crime? When are individuals criminally liable for their actions?

4. Discuss the various kinds of crime classifications that we use in Canada. Are there other crime classifications we should use, such as an offence index or a white-collar-crime index?

5. Can you think of any laws that should be revised and made stronger? How would this help to control the behaviour you have in mind?

6. Do you think Crown prosecutors should have the power to determine if a hybrid offence should proceed as an indictable offence or a summary conviction offence?

7. Do you think public opinion should be considered by legal officials as an important component in the development or change of crime and legal policies?

8. Should we increase the punishments associated with the Proceeds of Crime Act? Would this make this statute more effective?

9. Why do you think some people don't consider most white-collar crimes as serious offences? Can you think of any recent examples that show that white-collar crimes have serious results?

10. Do you think the punishments for summary conviction offences should be made harsher?

Suggested Readings

Barnhorst, R., S. Barnhorst, and K.L. Clarke. *Criminal Law and the Canadian Criminal Code,* 2nd ed. Toronto: McGraw-Hill Ryerson, 1992.

Boyd, N. *Criminal Law: An Introduction*. Toronto: Harcourt Brace and Company, 1995.

Gall, G.L. *The Canadian Legal System,* 3rd ed. Toronto: Carswell, 1990.

Mewett, A.W. *An Introduction to the Criminal Process in Canada,* 3rd ed. Scarborough, Ont.: Carswell, 1996.

Parker, G. *An Introduction to Criminal Law*, 3rd ed. Toronto: Methuen, 1987.

Roberts, J.V., and R.M. Mohr, eds. *Confronting Sexual Abuse: A Decade of Legal and Social Change.* Toronto: University of Toronto Press, 1994.

Verdun-Jones, S. *Criminal Law in Canada: Cases, Questions, and the Code.* Toronto: Harcourt Brace Jovanovich, 1989.

CHAPTER 3

Models of Criminal Justice

Underlying our criminal justice system are four distinct models. Two of these (deterrence and rehabilitation) have traditionally guided criminal justice. Deterrence emerged in the 18th century, while rehabilitation gained prominence in our criminal justice system in the early 20th century. During the past 25 years these two models have been joined by two others: selective incapacitation and justice. Selective incapacitation focuses primarily on those individuals labelled as "dangerous," while the justice model is probably the dominant criminal justice model today, as it forms the basis of the Canadian Charter of Rights and Freedoms. Recently, aboriginal justice systems have been proposed as an alternative to Western legal models, though there is controversy over how an aboriginal justice system should operate. Should aboriginal peoples be allowed to create a separate justice system or should they

CHAPTER OBJECTIVES

- understand the differences and similarities among the four different models of criminal justice in terms of the criminal sanction and operation of the major components of the criminal justice system

- recognize the need for an aboriginal justice system

- recognize how each of these models is connected to either the positivist or classical school of criminology

be given a role within the existing justice system, especially in the sentencing of offenders?

Supporters of the selective incapacitation model have argued for the introduction of "three strikes laws" as a method to "get tough" with chronic or habitual offenders. They believe that once the worst offenders are off the streets the overall crime rate will decrease significantly. Their strongest argument is that many of the most violent offenders will be incarcerated, thus leading to a dramatic decrease in the rate of predatory crimes.

California is one of many U.S. jurisdictions to pass such three-strikes legislation. The object of the new law is to remove habitual criminals from the street. Any individual convicted of a third felony must serve a prison term of 25 years to life. While the first two felonies must be classified as "serious," the third does not have to be either serious or violent. This means that persons convicted of a minor felony for their third offence could receive life imprisonment. For example, on March 2, 1995, Jerry Dewayne Williams, a California resident with four prior felony convictions, was sentenced to 25 years to life for stealing a slice of pizza from some children. And on October 27, 1995, Kevin Weber, 32, a parolee, was sentenced to 25 years to life for second-degree commercial robbery. Weber's crime was to crawl into a restaurant through a vent and grab some chocolate-chip cookies. He was arrested by police moments later, before heading toward the safe. His first two felony convictions were for separate burglaries at an apartment complex where, during one of the break-ins, he pulled a weapon on a tenant. For those crimes he received two years' imprisonment.

Because of the possibility of long sentences for such offences, reports of some judges defying the three-strikes laws—because they feel they are unnecessarily harsh, given the circumstances of the crime—are widespread. As a result, some prosecutors are reducing what they feel are "minor" felonies to misdemeanours.

The three-strikes laws will no doubt put some chronic offenders into correctional institutions, but can we expect them to lower the crime rate, as the selective incapacitation advocates say they will? Mark Mauer of the Sentencing Project, a U.S.-based private organization that researches justice-related issues, observes that these laws may fulfil our need to punish those we feel are the worst criminals, but they make little practical sense. First, he points out, most three-time losers are nearing the end of their criminal careers, so locking them up for extremely long periods of time probably has little effect on the crime rate. Second, despite that many chronic violent offenders are already serving lengthy sentences, this has only a limited impact on the rate of violent crimes. Third, Mauer argues, police officers may be at higher risk if two-time offenders who know they face a life sentence will start to resist arrest in high numbers. Researchers at the Rand Corp. in San Francisco agree with many of Mauer's statements. They feel a better alternative would be to guarantee for serious criminals a full but shorter prison term without a chance of parole.

Their research reveals that a guaranteed full-term incarceration policy would lead to the same benefits but at much lower cost to the state (Mauer 1994; Rand Corp. 1994).

This chapter presents two different ways of understanding the criminal justice system. In the first section, the four contemporary criminal justice models—justice, deterrence, selective incapacitation, and rehabilitation—are discussed. Each is presented in as balanced a manner as possible. While providing students with an understanding of the overall operation of each model, the second section allows them to evaluate how our criminal justice system responds to crime. For example, is it consistent to toughen up some sections of our criminal justice system and at the same time give most offenders shorter sentences?

Crime Control in Canada

One of the most common complaints made against the criminal justice system is that it is too "soft" on criminals. Critics readily point to a series of shortcomings—criminals who are granted parole and then commit more crimes, plea bargaining, lenient sentences imposed by judges, and police officers who warn offenders instead of arresting them. Left unchecked, critics argue, these factors are sources of rising crime rates. Others argue that parole boards make informed decisions concerning prisoners, that plea bargaining is beneficial to the successful conclusion of criminal cases, and that judicial discretion in sentencing is an asset. These individuals feel that extraneous social issues that can't be controlled by the criminal justice system, such as family breakdown, contribute the most to the increasing crime rate.

These opinions spill over into significant public policy debates. Should there be mandatory sentences for all convicted criminals? Should convicted violent offenders never be allowed out of prison? Should plea bargaining be banned? Should police budgets be increased dramatically to hire more police officers, who in turn investigate and apprehend more criminals? Finally, should judicial discretion be banned outright or at least closely controlled?

An armed SWAT team member stands guard as boxes of seized cocaine are transported from a Montreal police station in 1996. The seizure was part of an international police operation that led to 24 arrests. (Photo: Paul Chiasson/Canadian Press)

Many observers say it would be extremely difficult, because of the complexity of the criminal justice system today, to introduce clear policy directives that would influence that system's operation. The informal operation of the system, as well as self-interests held by the various groups who work within it, would also make improvement difficult. Despite these real-life questions, the major crime control models can be conceptualized in an ideal manner.

Models of Criminal Justice

Four major models guide the operation of our criminal justice system: **justice, deterrence, selective incapacitation,** and **rehabilitation.** Because these models are constantly being revised and updated, many people speak of "neo-deterrence" and "neo-rehabilitation" systems. While legislation uses these models to guide their policies, not one of the models exclusively guides the operation of our criminal justice system. It usually happens that two or more of these crime control models are combined. For example, when the Young Offenders Act was enacted in 1984 it was grounded almost exclusively in the strategies of the deterrence and justice models. Combining models leads to confusion about which strategy is important in a given situation, and it raises questions about the success or failure of any particular crime control initiative.

These models address different issues, although some share certain conceptual features. For example, only rehabilitation focuses on the actor, so it emphasizes the individual treatment of most convicted criminals. The other three models focus, although in different ways, on the act. The justice model focuses exclusively on the criminal act committed by the alleged perpetrators. Punishment is then based on the seriousness of the offence. The deterrence and selective incapacitation models, like the justice model, focus on the act, but with the purpose of preventing future crimes. In contrast to the justice model, however, the issue of the current criminal offence is of secondary importance.

Each of these four models can be clearly described, and though some overlap exists among some of them, they are better known for their differences. Price and Stitt (1986) developed a framework to compare the models, showing how each crime control strategy approaches crime control through criminal sanctions followed by their concomitant policy implications. The following description of the four models follows the Price and Stitt outline.

The Justice Model

History

The justice model, though a recent creation, has had a significant impact on the operation of the criminal justice system. The first major document to offer support for the justice model appeared in *Struggle for Justice* (1971), written by the American Friends Service Committee. This committee, developed as a response to an analysis of a prison riot in the New York City area, recommended the criminal justice system be guided by the ideals of justice, fairness, and the need to protect human rights and dignity. It recommended the elimination of the discretionary powers held by prosecutors, the judiciary, and parole boards. One of its most important recommendations was the need for the sentence to fit the offence, and not the offender. All individuals convicted of a certain offence must receive the same sentence, although the committee did recommend that repeat offenders be given longer sentences than first-time offenders for the same crime.

This message was repeated by Marvin Frankel, a U.S. federal judge, whose book *Criminal Sentences: Law without Order* (1972) recommended that the principles of objectivity, fairness, and consistency be the basis of the operation of the justice system. He also argued that criminal offences be ranked according to their severity and that punishments reflect the severity of the crimes.

Perhaps the most influential argument for the creation of a justice model-based criminal justice system came from the Committee for the Study of Incarceration. Its book, entitled *Doing Justice* (1975), proposed the creation of sentencing guidelines based on the seriousness of the crime and the prior record of the offender. In addition, it proposed shorter punishments for most crimes as well as the expansion of alternative sanctions.

The first criminal justice systems based on the justice model emerged in the United States during the 1970s and early 1980s. Maine enacted its new legislation in 1975, followed by California (1976), Minnesota (1981), Pennsylvania (1982), and Washington (1984). While these states varied in the particular manner in which they developed their systems, they shared a number of features, namely the elimination or control of prosecutorial discretion, the abolition of individualized sentencing practices, limited treatment programs for prisoners, as well as the termination of early-release programs such as parole (Griset 1991).

The Criminal Sanction

According to the justice model, the essential factor "is to punish offenders—fairly and with justice—through lengths of confinement proportionate to the gravity of their crimes" (Logan 1993). The punishment must fit the crime—specifically, the most serious crimes deserve the most severe punishments, in accordance with the doctrine of proportionality. In addition, the rights of the accused must be guaranteed by due process protections from arrest to incarceration (Hudson 1987).

The justice model assumes that a direct relationship exists between the seriousness of the offence and the severity of the punishment. Ideally, any personal circumstances of those individuals involved in the crime are ignored. The only thing the justice model needs to know about an offender is his prior record. This "ensures the individual is not made to suffer disproportionably for

the sake of social gain" and that "disproportionate leniency" as well as "disproportionate severity" are not allowed (von Hirsch 1976; Hudson 1987). An example of a violation of the principle of proportionality involves the use of capital punishment to punish parking violators, where the punishment far outweighs the seriousness of the offence, i.e., it is assumed that parking violators could be dissuaded by other, lighter sanctions, such as towing or fines.

In Canada, the federal government determines the proportionality between crimes and punishments. While it is easy to conclude a violent criminal should receive a more severe punishment than a parking violator, the development of a comprehensive scale of proportional punishments is a difficult task, given the wide variety of crimes found in our Criminal Code. Should a person who sexually assaults a child receive a longer sentence than a person who robs a bank at gunpoint? To create a truly proportional system of punishment would require much discussion about which offences are truly the most serious.

In order to ensure that changes in proportions could be made, the Minnesota Sentencing Commission was formed. If the commission believed the rank of a crime should be changed, it would alter the sentencing guidelines annually. As a result, the ranking of criminal offences is different today than it was when the sentencing guidelines were introduced. And since 1983, trial court judges have the right to depart from the sentencing guidelines by increasing or decreasing the sentence in cases where certain "substantial" and "compelling" factors are involved. For example, if an individual shot another person during a fight and then went over and severely kicked the wounded victim, the judge would probably lengthen the sentence due to this circumstance. All such departures from the sentencing grid have to be written down by the trial court judge and then sent to the Minnesota Court of Appeal for review (Hudson 1987).

The founders of the justice model also specified that a significant proportion of those who commit a crime be subject to what are referred to as alternative sanctions, as when, for example, a convicted person is allowed to serve the sanction outside prison. Alternative sanctions are featured in the Minnesota sentencing guidelines by their placement in the top half of the sentencing grid. This means any individual who is convicted of an offence in categories one through six (and who does not have an excessive number of prior offences) receives an alternative sentence that keeps that person in the community. The justice model approach is in strong favour of alternatives to incarceration, with community service orders and probation orders favoured for many first- and second-time property offenders. This means many offenders don't serve time in a prison facility, until of course the number of their prior convictions grows to the point where they will be incarcerated. Dangerous violent offenders, however, will always serve time in a state prison facility, even if they have no prior convictions.

In addition, the justice model guarantees due process rights for all persons accused of committing a crime. Both pre-trial and trial procedural rights are guaranteed. This means that each suspect receives protections to ensure that police do not overextend their investigatory powers. In addition, anyone under investigation or charged with an offence is presumed to be innocent. This means that although someone may admit he or she committed the crime to police investigators (i.e., factual guilt), that person's guilt nonetheless has to be established (i.e., legal guilt) in a court of law. Due process ensures that only the facts of the case are at issue, that information is collected according to the rules of evidence, and that formal hearings are held and procedural regularity is maintained. Extra-legal issues are considered to be inconsistent with the issue of fundamental justice.

The Operation of a Justice Model-Based Criminal Justice System

The main concern of the justice model is the elimination or control of discretion within the criminal justice system, particularly as discretion is exercised by prosecutors, the judiciary, and members of the parole board. Supporters of the justice model argue the major barrier to the attainment of justice is the discretion held by the major actors within the criminal justice system. Concerns about discretion lead to concerns about the protection of rights for all the accused. The solution is to operate the justice system in a fair and equitable manner. The main policy recommendations of justice model advocates are (1) to eliminate or control discretion and (2) to enhance due process protections for all who enter the criminal justice system.

The role of the police is pivotal, because their decisions affect all other groups involved in the later stages of the crime control process. According to the justice model, the police must charge the accused with *all* the crimes he committed as long as sufficient evidence exists for the charges. Thus, if an individual commits multiple offences, the police lay all the relevant charges.

Prosecutors would then have to prosecute the accused on the basis of all charges laid. This means that plea bargaining would be eliminated or strictly controlled by guidelines enacted by the legislative authorities. The desired result, in the justice model, is that plea bargaining is not normally a factor in the trial. In reality, however, plea bargaining has proved to be very difficult to ban. The state of Alaska attempted to ban all forms of plea bargaining in 1975. This policy lasted only a few years, due to a number of problems, including the fact that the ban had no influence on the disposition of cases involving serious crimes. In addition, other criminal justice agencies (notably the police) increased their discretion prior to laying any charges (Rubenstein et al. 1980). The most popular policy has been to permit some plea bargaining but to control it by developing strict guidelines to govern its use. This approach is more popular, since it allows prosecutors to bargain with the accused about his knowledge of other, more serious, crimes or gain evidence about other criminals who would otherwise not be charged.

EXHIBIT 3.1

Have Legal Rights of Individuals Gone Too Far?

There will always be a debate between supporters of the legal rights for the accused and those who argue that crime control should take precedence in judicial decisions. But can one side be taken too far? Many Canadians feel the courts have, since the introduction of the Charter of Rights and Freedoms, gone too far to protect the accused, to the detriment of law-abiding citizens and police forces. In particular, criticism has been directed toward the Supreme Court of Canada and some of their recent decisions regarding the rights of the accused. On two days at the end of September 1994, three decisions made by the Supreme Court led the supporters of crime control to argue that the members of Canada's top court are focusing too much on the principle of justice in their decisions while ignoring the reality of crime. The controversial decisions made by the Supreme Court on these two days were these:

(1) *R. v. Borden.* DNA evidence linked a repeat sex offender to the rape of a 69-year-old woman in Nova Scotia after she returned from a prayer meeting. Police requested a blood sample from the accused, but informed Mr. Borden they wanted it for another sexual assault investigation. The police didn't inform him they really wanted to use the DNA analysis in connection with the sexual assault on the senior citizen. Borden was convicted and sentenced to six years' imprisonment, based on the results of the DNA test. The Appeal Division of the Supreme Court of Nova Scotia overturned Borden's conviction on the grounds that his legal rights were violated under Section 8 of the Charter of Rights and Freedoms, which section controls unlawful search and seizures. The Crown appealed this verdict, but the Supreme Court of Canada agreed in a 7–0 ruling that the DNA evidence could not be admitted as evidence because the police did not tell Borden how the blood sample and the subsequent DNA analysis could be used against him.

(2) *R. v. Swietlinski.* A convicted murderer applying for early parole eligi-

bility was found to have been denied a fair hearing because the Crown prosecutor was found to have consistently and improperly appealed to the jury's passions. Swietlinski was convicted of the first-degree murder of Mary Francis McKenna in 1976. He had stabbed her 132 times with five different knives. Although sentenced to a minimum of 25 years in a federal correctional facility, Swietlinski applied for early parole under Section 745 of the Criminal Code. Section 745 sets out a process for those convicted of first-degree murder to apply for parole eligibility after 15 years.

Swietlinski was granted the hearing, but during the proceedings the jurors were subject to "appeals" directed at their "passions" by the Crown prosecutor. The prosecutor told the jury, among other things, not to forget the victim in their decision, saying that "she doesn't have a chance to come before a group of people to ask for a second chance." Furthermore, the minimum-security prison where Swietlinski was incarcerated was described as "too comfortable," and "his residency there was reward enough for good conduct in jail." Surprisingly, the lawyer representing

Supporters of the justice model argue that the problem with traditional sentencing approaches is the amount of discretion held by judges. This discretion led to a concern about discrimination sentencing, as some defendants received more severe punishments apparently on the basis of their group characteristics—such as race or gender—instead of their crimes. To eliminate discrimination sentencing, the justice model recommends a determinate sentencing approach. In this type of sentencing approach, all judges are required to follow the sentencing guidelines. For example, if the punishment for one charge of kidnapping is five years' imprisonment, the judge has no alternative but to send the convicted individual to prison for five years. All those convicted of the same crime and having the same number of prior convictions receive the same punishment.

The discretionary powers held by parole boards are of concern to the justice model advocates, too, since those boards can decide to release inmates prior to serving the full length of their sentence. The justice model's solution is either to eliminate the parole board altogether (by eliminating parole) or to remove it from the decision to release an inmate. In the latter case, the parole

Models of Criminal Justice

Swietlinski took no exception to these and other similar comments made by the prosecutor. Ultimately, the jury refused Swietlinski's request for the possibility of early parole.

The Supreme Court, in a 5–4 ruling, agreed with Swietlinski that he was denied his right to a fair hearing and therefore deserved another jury review. The majority ruling was based on the opinion that the Crown prosecutor's role at a review hearing is much the same as it is at criminal trials—to assist the judge and jury in making decisions that lead to "the fullest possible justice" while avoiding "any appeal to passion." The minority ruling was based in large part on the silence of Swietlinski's lawyer, a silence that the jury interpreted as agreeing that the prosecutor's comments were not unfair.

(3) *R. v. Prosper.* The Supreme Court of Canada, in a 5–4 vote, ruled that the police must "hold off" questioning suspects until those suspects have received a reasonable chance to contact a lawyer. Prosper was arrested after police stopped a person who was driving recklessly. The arresting officer informed Prosper of his rights, including the right to retain and instruct counsel without delay, to call any lawyer he wished, and to apply for free legal assistance. Asked if he wanted to first take the breathalyzer test or contact a lawyer, Prosper said he wanted to contact a legal-aid lawyer. After 15 phone calls, however, Prosper had not managed to contact one because of a work-to-rule campaign by legal-aid lawyers. Prosper said he couldn't afford private counsel, and soon thereafter he took two breath tests. Both indicated he had a blood–alcohol level that exceeded the legal limit. He was subsequently convicted.

However, Prosper appealed on the basis of Section 10(b) of the Charter of Rights and Freedoms, which states that those arrested or detained have the right to counsel without delay, and to be informed of that right. The majority of the Supreme Court agreed with Prosper's statement that while the police may not have to wait in "compelling and urgent" cases, this case was not so urgent that the suspect had to take a breath test within two hours. The police erred by not informing Prosper that they had a duty to wait until he had a reasonable chance to contact a lawyer. According to Chief Justice Lamer, the principle behind the legal right to seek counsel without delay is to ensure that criminal suspects are able to get advice on how to exercise their rights.

These rulings have led legal scholars to comment that "the administration of justice can be brought into disrepute if grossly tainted evidence can be used to convict," but that there is also a danger that the administration of justice can also be brought into disrepute "if those who have committed crimes go free."

Source: *R. v. Swietlinski* (1992), 73 C.C.C. (3d) 376; *R. v. Prosper* (1992), 75 C.C.C. (3d) 1; S. Fine, "Has the High Court Lost Touch with Reality?" *The Globe and Mail,* October 8, 1994, p. D2; S. Fine, "Murderer Denied Fair Hearing, Court Says," *The Globe and Mail,* October 1, 1994, p. A4; S. Fine, "Right to Seek Counsel Beefed Up," *The Globe and Mail,* September 30, 1994, p. A1; S. Fine, "Failure to Inform Suspect Invalidates DNA Evidence, Top Court Rules," *The Globe and Mail,* October 1, 1994, p. A8.

board is responsible only for parole supervision. It is conceivable, however, that the elimination of parole could lead to prison overcrowding, since no prisoners would be released early. To alleviate potential overcrowding, convicted criminals would serve all their sentences, but the length of the sentences would be shortened. When the justice model was instituted in Minnesota almost all sentence lengths were reduced. The exception was that for first-degree murder, which remained punishable by a mandatory life sentence. The only exceptions to these policies would be the reduction of a sentence by 15 percent in exchange for an inmate's good behaviour during incarceration. Finally, while treatment programs are offered to inmates, such programs are limited in scope and voluntary in nature.

Deterrence

History

Deterrence is the oldest of the four major criminal justice models. Its roots are in 18th-century Europe, where two reformers, one Italian (Cesare

Beccaria) and the other English (Jeremy Bentham), proposed significant reforms to the criminal justice system. They argued that the goal of the criminal justice system was the prevention of future crimes by individuals who were caught and punished for their crimes (i.e., specific deterrence) and by members of the broader society who might contemplate committing a crime (i.e., general deterrence). Faced with a system that was biased and barbaric, Beccaria wrote *On Crimes and Punishment* (1764) with the hope of achieving reforms that were equitable and eliminated favouritism. It is important to note that Beccaria's recommendations became the source of modern criminal justice systems, including those in Canada and the United States. His book became the first widely read text that demanded due process rights be placed throughout the criminal justice system, that sentences reflect the harm committed against the state and the victim, and that punishments be quick, certain, and contain a degree of deterrence. His major recommendations were as follows:

- The right of governments to punish offenders derives from a contractual obligation among its citizens not to pursue their self-interest at the expense of others.

- Punishment must be constituted by uniform and enlightened legislation.

- Imprisonment must replace torture and capital punishment as the standard form of punishment.

- The punishment must fit the crime. It must be prompt and certain, and its duration must reflect only the gravity of the offence and the social harm it caused (Beirne and Messerschmidt 1991:290)

Bentham argued that legislators need to calculate the amount of punishment needed to prevent crimes and punish criminals. This system, which he referred to as a calculus, could include both positive sanctions (rewards) and negative sanctions (punishment). In addition, he argued the criminal justice system should operate in a manner that allows it to catch suspects with certainty, process criminal cases in a speedy yet efficient manner, and to punish those convicted of a crime with an appropriate (not excessive) amount of punishment.

An important basis of this approach was the reformers' strong belief that all people are rational, that is, they possessed free will. Criminals differ from law-abiding persons only because they choose to engage in criminal as opposed to noncriminal activities. Over time, however, legislators have recognized a number of limitations to those arguments. Today most Western legal codes recognize limits to criminal responsibility, including such factors as age, duress, self-defence, and insanity.

The Criminal Sanction

Deterrence is an objective phenomenon, as it implies a behavioural result of the fear a potential offender feels because that person thinks his or her illegal act may lead to capture and punishment. Supporters of the deterrence doctrine hope any individual contemplating a crime will be deterred because of the certainty, or risk, that that individual will be caught and punished. Deterrence is also a perceptual phenomenon in the sense that potential criminals decide not to commit crimes on the basis of their perception that they may be caught and punished. According to Gibbs (1975:2), a strong advocate of this model, deterrence is defined as "the omission of an act as a response to the perceived risk and fear of punishment for contrary behavior."

The deterrence approach assumes a direct relationship between the certainty of punishment and the severity and swiftness of punishment. The severity is achieved at a level that maximizes its deterrent effect—i.e., "the pain of punishment would exceed the pleasure of the offense for a majority of potential offenders" (Price and Stitt 1986:26). The deterrence model places great emphasis on the efficient operation of the criminal justice system, namely the reduction of court delay as well as the time between arrest, preliminary inquiry, and court trial (Feeley and Simon 1992).

One of the best contemporary examples of the deterrence model is the mandatory charging of individuals who assault their wives (see Chapter 2). Individuals who perceive they will be arrested and charged for assault will not commit assault, presumably because they perceive they will be caught and punished. The deterrence model, then, operates in the hope that assaults will thus be prevented. In the area of criminal sanctions, the model recommends that the punishment (in this case, an arrest or a criminal charge) be mandatory, and so prevents such behaviour in the future.

The Operation of a Deterrence-Based Criminal Justice System

Any deterrence-based criminal justice system would introduce policies to attain the greatest certainty of capture, swiftness of prosecution, and, in cases of conviction for a crime, severity of punishment. The goal of this system is the prevention of future crime. More emphasis is given to the protection of society and the law-abiding public than to the protection of individual rights of defendants. To ensure that the justice system and its agencies work to their maximum efficiency, more money would have to be spent on all criminal justice agencies. More police officers, prosecutors, judges, and correctional personnel would be hired, and more facilities such as jails, courts, and prisons built. Further, the government would have to revise existing statute laws and pass new ones that would grant more powers to the police in the areas of investigation and apprehension, with the sole purpose of increasing the chance that suspected

criminals are caught. Essentially, the criminal justice system would operate like an assembly line, pushing offenders as efficiently as possible through conviction to punishment.

The number of police and police resources involved in crime detection within a deterrence-based criminal justice system would increase, since police are the front-line agency in the "war" on crime. Police officers would be better educated and better trained, and receive the latest technology in order to increase the certainty of capture of criminals. But not all the new resources given to the police would be involved in actual crime-fighting. Procedural laws that inhibit the police during their search for and arrest of criminals would be reduced. Emphasis would be placed on crime control and factual guilt. If, for example, a police officer accidentally violates the right of an alleged offender during an investigation, this violation would probably be overlooked, assuming the individual in question is guilty of the offence.

Not all of this increase in police resources would go to hiring more police for street-level patrols. The deterrence doctrine also supports the *prevention* of crime. As a result, more money would be given to proactive policing activities, such as the Neighbourhood Watch, Operation Identification, and Crime Stoppers programs. These programs involve members of the community in the fight against crime and would enable more police to pursue criminals, thereby increasing the probability of capture and subsequent punishment.

The deterrence approach would control all forms of plea bargaining. Price and Stitt (1986:27) point out controlling plea bargaining "could be the greatest single step to increase both certainty and severity of punishment." In addition, suspects awaiting trial would find it more difficult to receive bail, since they are presumed guilty. This means that most of the individuals arrested are guilty, particularly as they move past arrest and into the court system (Packer 1968). As was the case in the justice model, prosecutors would pursue all charges laid against the defendant by the police.

Judicial discretion would be eliminated. Governments would provide judges with a system of mandatory determinate sentences. This would lead not only to the uniformity of punishment but also to the certainty that an individual receives a designated punishment. However, in contrast to the justice model, most sentences under a deterrence approach would become longer, in order to impress on individuals contemplating a crime that, if caught and convicted, they will be punished severely.

Parole would be abolished. More prisons would be built to house those guilty of an offence and to discourage potential criminals from committing a criminal offence by making them fearful of being caught and incarcerated. Risk assessments of offenders would become normal practice. Offenders would be placed into groups based on their predicted future behaviour. All sanctions are therefore viewed in terms of their effectiveness at reducing the risk of further offences. At one extreme is secure incarceration; at the other is probation, with levels of intermediate punishments between (Morris and Tonry 1990).

Selective Incapacitation

History

Selective incapacitation emerged as a major force in the 1970s. James Q. Wilson, a prominent criminologist, gave this model strong support in his book *Thinking about Crime* (1975). He wrote that serious crimes could be reduced by about one-third if each individual convicted of a violent crime received a sentence of three years and were not paroled. Then a study conducted by the Rand Corporation, of San Francisco, entitled *Selective Incapacitation* appeared in 1982. In this study, Peter Greenwood studied 2190 prison and jail inmates in California, Texas, and Michigan. He claimed that a sentencing approach based on this model could reduce robbery by 15 percent and reduce prison populations by 5 percent. The imprisonment of an increased number of chronic offenders would be more than offset by the elimination of low-risk offenders currently in prison. This report received great attention, since it suggested that more effective crime control could be achieved at less cost. Another study, entitled *Making Confinement Decisions*, was published by the United States Justice Department in 1987. This report concluded that, assuming the average chronic offender committed 187 crimes a year, a saving of $430 million could be made annually (Walker 1994).

However, critics—e.g., Zimring and Hawkins (1988)—have argued that the reduction in crime promised by the supporters of selective incapacitation has not materialized. They claim these figures are based on estimates of the number of crimes a chronic offender remembered he committed each year. Many of the critics' harshest criticisms are based on their claim that attempts at reducing crime may be limited by a number of factors. These include problems in the identification of high-risk offenders and the possibility that one offender, if arrested, is simply replaced by another. If the offender who is incarcerated is a gang member, the gang may continue to commit the same amount of crime. While selective incapacitation would no doubt have some limited influence on the crime rate, its success would be dependent on the ability of the criminal justice system to identify chronic offenders in the early stages of their career (Visher 1995).

The Criminal Sanction

The selective incapacitation approach focuses on those few individuals who commit the greatest number of crimes, whether property crimes or violent crimes. Most attention to date has been placed on individuals classed as chronic, career, or repeat offenders.

According to the criminal sanction approach, the crime rate is a function of the total number of offenders minus those imprisoned (i.e., incapacitated), multiplied by an average number of crimes per offender. Therefore, by incarcerating chronic criminals for long periods of time, the crime rate is lowered.

Research has shown that relatively few offenders are responsible for the vast majority of violent offences. An example of that research is a work by Wolfgang, Figlio, and Sellin titled *Delinquency in a Birth Cohort* (1972), called "the single most important piece of criminal justice research in the last 25 years" (Walker 1993:55). Focusing on 10 000 juvenile males born in Philadelphia in 1945 and living in that city between the ages of 10 and 18, the researchers measured crime as the number of times the police took a juvenile into custody. They discovered that nearly 35 percent of all males had a record of an offence. At least 627 of these males had committed at least five offences. Even more important was the discovery that only 6 percent of the males in the study accounted for over half of all offences committed by the entire group and that that 6 percent accounted for well over half of all violent crimes. Other studies (Hamparian et al. 1978; Shannon 1988; Tracy et al. 1990) resulted in similar findings for both juveniles and adults. These studies identified small groups of high-rate offenders who were responsible for most criminal offences as well as most violent crimes.

The selective incapacitation model does not apply to all offenders; it focuses only on those who are deemed the most dangerous to society. A key feature of this approach is that individuals are considered dangerous not only because of their deeds in the past but because of the crimes they are likely to commit in the future. Future crimes are determined either by the number of prior convictions or by the number of crimes that similar offenders committed once they were released from prison.

In 1990, federal Solicitor General Cadieux recommended the elimination of parole for those convicted of dealing drugs. This policy was to be instituted if members of the National Parole Board suspected convicted drug dealers "will commit further drug offences after release from prison." Such individuals were to be denied parole—were to be punished, in essence, for crimes they had not yet committed. An example of this type of philosophy is found in the State of Washington's "sexual predator" law, which allows the state to "indefinitely lock up anyone who has committed at least one violent sex crime—after he has served his time."

While there is no doubt support for such a policy, there are potential pitfalls in such legislation, as well as problems associated with implementing such policies. Indeed, the most serious criticism of the selective incapacitation of violent offenders is that the criminal justice system lacks the capacity to accurately predict future violent behaviour. This criticism directly challenges the legitimacy of selective incapacitation as a legal sanction. The legal maxim "It is better that ten guilty persons escape, than that one innocent suffer" embodies the value that our society places on individual liberty. Judges would be given the power "to prevent violent offenders … and drug offenders from obtaining parole until they have served half of their sentences." Those identified as dangerous are to be incarcerated longer than those who are not. For Price and Stitt (1986:28), this means that "two offenders could commit the same act but receive different sentences because one is thought to be more likely to commit that or a related act in the future."

The Operation of a Selective Incapacitation-Based Criminal Justice System

According to Price and Stitt, a criminal justice system based on the selective incapacitative approach is based on the idea that the best predictor of future behaviour is previous behaviour. The criminal justice system would operate on the basis of the deterrence doctrine for the vast majority of offenders. However, once an individual enters the system who is considered to be "dangerous," the system assigns special resources and individuals to process the case as quickly as possible. Therefore, only some of the resources of the criminal justice system are dedicated to the selective incapacitation approach. Further, because it contains such a narrow interest, this approach is easily attached to any of the other three models. Such is the case with the State of Washington, which employs the justice model for the majority of its offenders but also exercises a sexual predator law to ensure that certain sex offenders are not released for a long time. In reality, then, this is the most specific of all the models in the sense that it looks only at a select few criminals.

The role of the police would be to arrest suspected offenders, conduct a careful background check, and then place offenders in a pre-trial detention centre if they are considered to be chronic offenders. Plea bargaining would be eliminated, so prosecutors would process all such cases as quickly as possible in order to ensure that offenders aren't released back into the general population. Judges would have little discretion in these cases. Once an offender is determined to be a chronic offender, he would be sentenced to a lengthy determinate prison term. Parole would be abolished and the correctional system would become little more than a holding facility for such offenders. Policies such as "three strikes and you're out" are consistent with the selective incapacitation approach.

The Rehabilitation Approach

History

Supporters of this model assume that the source of crime is determined by factors outside the control of the individual. They argue that since criminals don't freely choose their behaviour, punishment is the wrong policy. Instead, they recommend the individualized treatment of offenders in the hope that the causes of their criminal behaviour are discovered and eliminated. As Allen (1981:2) points out, "the notion is that a primary purpose of penal treatment is to effect in the characters, attitudes, and behavior of convicted offenders, so as to strengthen the social defense against unwanted behavior, but also to contribute to the welfare and satisfaction of the offenders."

EXHIBIT 3.2

The Selective Incapacitation of Sexual Predators

Five months after finishing his sentence for rape, Vance Cunningham looked like a prison success story. He had his high-school equivalency diploma, a promising job as a mechanic on a fishing boat, and, most important, a clean bill of health from a prison psychologist. But the State of Washington's End-of-Sentence Review Committee thought otherwise. Scanning the records of sex offenders, the 10-member panel took note of Cunningham's history: convictions for three rapes and an arrest as a juvenile for demanding oral sex from an adult woman at knifepoint.

Cunningham's past, the committee concluded, made him too great a risk for the state to take a chance on his future. It invoked Washington's "sexual predator" law, in 1992 the only statute of its kind in the United States. The law, enacted in the wake of a sensational 1989 child mutilation case, permits the state to indefinitely lock up anyone who has committed at least one violent sex crime—after he has served his time. Since it was passed, Washington has confined 15 "predators," including Cunningham. None has been charged or even suspected of committing a new crime. Instead, the state contends the men's criminal histories demonstrate that they have a "mental abnormality" requiring confinement until they can be successfully treated.

Supporters of the predator law say this statute reverses trends and puts victims' rights ahead of the rights of criminals. Correctly administered, they say, the law is a legal rifle shot aimed at getting proven sex offenders off the street. Nonpredators are protected by a process that includes the state board, a prosecutor, and a jury. However, the American Civil Liberties Union has filed a brief supporting the challenge and legal experts say the predator law is likely to end up before the U.S. Supreme Court.

No one disputes the horror of the crime that led to the predator statute. Earl Shriner, a former convict with a 24-year history of violent sex crimes against women and children, sexually assaulted a 7-year-old Tacoma, Wash., boy and cut off his penis. While serving a previous prison term, Shriner had boasted that he intended to commit more assaults against youngsters. Prison officials admitted they knew of Shriner's plans but were legally powerless to keep him locked up after he completed his sentence. "There was enormous public concern and demands for action after that little boy was attacked," says Mr. Boerner, a former state and federal prosecutor. One victims' rights group, calling itself the Tennis Shoe Brigade, dumped 8000 sneakers on the steps of the state capital at Olympia, saying they symbolized the demand of victims to be able to walk without fear. "A lot of people said, 'Why do we need these guys anyway? Why not just kill them?'" says Helen Harlow, an organizer of the protest.

Boerner says the Shriner case highlighted a gap in the legal system: "Was society powerless to deal with someone like Earl Shriner, a man known to be dangerous?" The answer, he says, is yes.

In recent years, most mental health experts have moved from regarding sex offences as stemming from mental illness to treating them as antisocial acts—deserving prison, not a psychiatric ward. "Sexual predation in and of itself does not define a mental illness. It defines criminal conduct," says the Washington State Psychiatric Association, which has supported the challenge to the predator law.

Boerner says the state couldn't lock Shriner up as a criminal unless he committed another assault, nor could it cite previous crimes as a reason to confine him as mentally ill. "Apparently," says Boerner, "the law was powerless to protect." While some legislators called for new laws to do everything from mandating by sentence to castrating sex criminals, Boerner says he tried to write a law that matched the contours of the constitution but also gave the state the power to close the legal gap. His solution: the "mental abnormality" classification for suspected predators with a history of at least one violent sex crime. That technically made former offenders treatable, he says, and put them within the state's grasp. Washington's Legislature passed the law unanimously.

"It wouldn't have been fair if we were punishing them," Boerner says. "We're confining people for purposes of public safety and treatment, and the constitution allows that." Critics argue the law is flawed in its belief that future violent behaviour can be predicted from criminals' past sex crimes.

Others say these criticisms miss the point of Washington's predator statute. Alexander D. Brooks, emeritus law professor at Rutgers University and an expert on the rights of the mentally ill, says that by narrowing the pool of sex criminals to those with clear histories of multiple acts of violence, officials ought to be able to pinpoint a likely group of repeaters. More important, he says, the law reflects a shift in concern toward victims' rights. "During the last 25 years we've seen much justifiable attention paid to the rights of prisoners," he says. "But now there is growing concern for the rights of society, especially women and children who are the victims of violent sex crimes." That shift, he says, "in essence is what is being played out in Washington's sexual predator law."

In the rehabilitation approach, more attention is placed on the offender than on the criminal act itself. Criminal sanctions are to be specific to the needs of the offender rather than "based on considerations of social harm and deterrence" (Cullen and Gilbert 1982:34). To facilitate this approach, the indeterminate sentence becomes an essential policy, namely that offenders are to remain in prison for as long as it takes to find the appropriate "cure."

To facilitate an individual-based justice system, probation and parole were introduced along with indeterminate sentences during the late-19th and early-20th centuries. The idea guiding these policies was that the type of punishment (probation or incarceration) would be decided by an offender's need for treatment. If it was decided that the individual needed treatment, the duration of that person's punishment "would be determined by his or her behavior after sentencing as much as by the crime itself" (Clear 1995:460). Inmates who showed improvement would be released earlier than those who resisted treatment or who failed to respond to the proscribed treatment. Treatment at the turn of the century involved "programs of work, moral instruction, discipline, and order," all designed "to develop those personal habits that were prerequisites to a useful law-abiding life" (Carrigan 1991:356).

Probably the test most often used to evaluate the success of rehabilitation programs is whether the offender recidivates, i.e., is convicted of another offence after his sentence is completed. Indicative of the results is a Correctional Services of Canada report that indicated that, five years after they had successfully completed parole, 35.6 percent of former inmates were returned to a federal institution for reoffending. In addition, 39.4 percent of those who served two-thirds of their sentences and were then released on mandatory supervision were reconvicted of another offence (Correctional Service of Canada 1990a). The debate about the worthiness and effectiveness of rehabilitation continues to this day between the advocates of rehabilitation and the other three models.

The Criminal Sanction

Supporters of the rehabilitation model believe it is necessary to look at the criminal and discover the reasons why he committed crime. Once it is discovered what led to the criminal behaviour, an appropriate criminal sanction would be applied. Therefore, punishment would be flexible, based as it is on the needs of the individual. This means that two individuals could commit the identical crime but end up with completely different punishments—perhaps because one individual needs a lengthy treatment program while the other needs another type of treatment. A rehabilitation system is best described as discretionary, with all court and correctional agencies having the power to determine the type and length of sentence to individualize the punishment.

It is important to note that after being subject to a lengthy period of criticism, rehabilitation appears to be gaining support. In a recent national survey in the United States, researchers discovered that prison wardens—though they felt the maintenance of custody and institutional order was their top priority—indicated that the rehabilitation of offenders was a more significant goal than punishment and retribution (Cullen et al. 1993).

The Operation of a Rehabilitation-Based Criminal Justice System

Whereas the other models considered discretion unnecessary and counter-productive, rehabilitation wishes to enhance the discretionary powers of the main agencies of the criminal justice system. Since the focus of this model is on the needs and welfare of the offender, each agency has to make decisions to enhance the chances of the individual's return to society as a better person.

As Price and Stitt point out, this aim to rehabilitate means the criminal justice system would have to focus on the criminal more than on the act committed. Agencies would intervene in the offender's life in order to change the offender, with the hope that the pressures that forced the individual to commit crime are reduced and finally eliminated. Much of the emphasis of the rehabilitation model of criminal justice is thus located at the sentencing and correctional stages of the criminal justice system.

The police role would not change dramatically. Police would continue to arrest criminals and lay charges. Prosecutors would be allowed to plea bargain as much as they wish and there would be few if any restrictions placed on this role. A case would easily be terminated or the total number of charges reduced if the prosecutor felt it would be in the best interests of the offender. Prosecutors would rely on the pre-sentence report and make recommendations about the type of treatment needed. Both the prosecutor and judge would make use of this report during the sentencing of the offender.

Judicial discretion is an essential component of the rehabilitation approach. Prior to handing out any sentence, the judge would receive a pre-sentence report from a probation officer. Any recommendations made in this report could be carefully considered by the judge in the sentencing decision, as would the statements made by the defence lawyer and the Crown prosecutor. The final sentence would reflect the "best interests" of the offender and would involve an indeterminate sentence that fit the "needs" of the offender. As such, offenders would have to serve only the minimum length of their sentence. Under a rehabilitation approach, the correctional system and its related services would probably become the most important agencies of the criminal justice system. Parole services would be expanded, since it would individualize the treatment program for each offender. This individualization would add discretion to the system, since offenders could be released at any time by the parole board after serving the minimum sentence.

Correctional services within the prison would also become more treatment oriented. As Exhibit 3.3 reveals, the correctional system would focus on discov-

EXHIBIT 3.3

Can Rehabilitation Be Effective?

Extensive empirical data now prove that rehabilitation programs work—if they are well designed and effectively implemented. Paul Gendreau, a professor of psychology at the University of New Brunswick, said his research shows that "appropriate" treatment programs reduce recidivism rates by 53 percent. Gendreau told an audience of 350 corrections officials, mental-health practitioners, criminologists, and sociologists that "a reduction in recidivism of 53 percent in six months to two years [follow-up] is not trivial in the least. It is a very powerful effect . . . [we] found that the ability to reduce recidivism through appropriate treatment programs works not only for juveniles but also for adults."

Gendreau said a review of 80 published studies of North American rehabilitation programs that he carried out with Donald Andrews, a professor of psychology at Carleton University, indicated there is reason for hope. The programs most successful in reducing recidivism, he said, are those that employ behavioural-modification techniques that reward pro-social behaviour and "target those anti-social attitudes and values that fuel criminal behaviour." Gendreau said these techniques vary. In some corrections settings, prisoners are given more privileges or money for pro-social behaviour. In many cases, he said, efforts are made to influence an offender's thinking by using role playing to change his or her values.

Effective rehabilitation programs also tend to allow clients some say in establishing the rules, according to Gendreau. They teach offenders skills they can use to keep from committing crimes again. Family therapy can also be helpful, he said. According to Gendreau, several types of treatment have been "shown to be failures," including psychodynamic and nondirective individual therapies, pharmacological approaches, and legal sanctions and punishment. He said, "There are no data indicating that financial restitution, shock incarceration—the disciplinary 'boot camps' that are now being established in an increasing number of states—or electronic monitoring to keep tabs on an offender's whereabouts produce any reduction in recidivism whatsoever." In contrast, positive reinforcements outweigh punishing sanctions in successful rehabilitation programs by a 3-to-1 ratio, Gendreau said. Gendreau said his evaluation of rehabilitation programs shows that community-based programs such as halfway houses are somewhat more effective than prison and other institution-based treatment.

Gendreau said rehabilitation programs show little effect on low-risk clients—offenders who are unlikely to violate the law again with or without treatment. "But the data is very strong," he said. "There's study after study that indicates that if you . . . target medium- to high-risk clients for intervention, then you'll see some very dramatic reductions in recidivism by using primary behavioural strategies."

Source: P. Freiberg, "Rehabilitation Is Effective if Done Well, Studies Say," *APA Monitor*, September 1990. Copyright © 1990 by the American Psychological Association. Adapted with permission.

ering the needs of offenders before it proceeded with a course of treatment. Since treatment is personalized, it could take a long time before that treatment is successful for any individual. Thus, not only might the type of treatment services vary for each offender but also the length of that treatment.

Aboriginal Justice Systems

In the past decade there has been much discussion about the creation of formal aboriginal justice systems throughout Canada. The idea of such systems, specifically those that involve an aboriginal court, has become a major area of interest as it would honour traditional methods of resolving conflict. Many officials accept the notion of an aboriginal justice system, but there has been much controversy about the exact form this justice system should take. In December 1991, for example, the Law Reform Commission of Canada published a report that supported the notion of an aboriginal justice system, although it did not give any indication about the exact type of system it supported. However, the commission (1991:5) discussed the reasons why such a justice system was needed in Canada:

From the Aboriginal perspective, the criminal justice system is an alien one, imposed by the dominant white society . . . not surprisingly, they regard the system as deeply insensitive to their traditions and values: many view it as unremittingly racist.

A few months after the Law Reform Commission released its report, federal Justice Minister Kim Campbell rejected the possibility of a separate system of aboriginal justice in Canada, saying that such a system would be a "cop-out." She favoured a system that integrated certain aspects of traditional aboriginal values into the broader Western legal system. In March 1996, the Liberal federal government followed this position. They continued to reject the idea of aboriginals establishing their own justice system. In particular, they dismissed the idea of aboriginals creating their own criminal law, stating unequivocally that the Charter of Rights and Freedoms applies to aboriginal peoples as much as to all Canadians. It recommended instead that aboriginals be given a greater role in sentencing aboriginal offenders and in assisting in the development of alternatives to prison.

Some provincial governments have rejected the idea of separate legal systems also. To date, most aboriginal systems in Canada have worked together with the existing criminal justice system in order to accommodate their own approach to justice. In Manitoba, for example, the province turned down a proposal for an aboriginal court in January 1993 but proposed a three-year pilot project that would "provide the first comprehensive approach to combine aboriginal methods of conflict resolution with rules and procedures of the existing system." This would involve aboriginal judges, magistrates, and para-legals "handling summary convictions—i.e., crimes where the maximum penalty is six months in jail and a $2,000 fine—accepting guilty pleas, impos-ing sentences and dealing with the Young Offenders Act."

In Saskatchewan, however, the provincial government accepted a recom-mendation from their Indian Justice Review Committee that a separate system of justice for aboriginal peoples be established. Among the first steps taken by the Saskatchewan government was the creation of a justice-of-the-peace program on nine northern reserves. This move toward a parallel justice system was seen as a drive toward the development of an aboriginal justice system.

Models of Aboriginal Justice Systems

How would an aboriginal justice system operate? What shape would it take? There are numerous views on what will constitute such a system, but "funda-mental is the belief that the system must be faithful to aboriginal traditions and cultural values, while adapting them to modern society" (Law Reform Commission of Canada 1991:7). Other essential components of an aboriginal justice system include the interests of the collectivity, the reintegration of the offender back into the community, mediation and conciliation within the community, and the importance of the role of community elders and leaders (Law Reform Commission 1991).

According to Manitoba's Aboriginal Justice Inquiry, the meaning of justice in an aboriginal society differs substantially from that of the broader society. Instead of an adversary system that attempts to "prevent or punish harmful or deviant behaviour," the aboriginal system of justice attempts "to restore the peace and equilibrium within the community, and to reconcile the accused with his or her own conscience and with the individual or family who has been wronged." Thus, the underlying notion of aboriginal justice systems when dealing with crime was "the resolution of disputes, the healing of wounds and the restoration of social harmony" (Report of the Aboriginal Justice Inquiry 1991; Dickson-Gilmore 1992). Ross (1994:262) has identified two essential features of aboriginal justice systems:

TABLE 3.1

Zones of Conflict in the Justice Arena

Aboriginal Approach	Euro-Centric Approach
Regular teaching of community values by elders and others who are respected in the community.	Everyone under obligation to obey set laws as determined by superior state authorities.
Warning and counselling of particular offenders by leaders or by councils representing the community as a whole.	Society reserves the right to protect itself from individuals who threaten to harm its members or its property.
Mediation and negotiation, by elders, community members, and clan leaders, aimed at resolving disputes and reconciling offenders with the victims of the misconduct.	Retributive punishment: justice requires that a man should suffer because of and in proportion to his moral wrong-doing. Punishment is set by legislation; judgment is imposed.
Payment of compensation by offenders (or their clan) to the victims or victim's kin, even in cases as serious as murder.	The perpetrator is the object of sentencing; retributive incarceration and rehabilitation are means to deter and punish offenders.
In court, the defendant presents a front that appears silent, uncommunicative, unresponsive, and withdrawn, based on the desire to maintain personal dignity. This is often interpreted as insolence and evidence of an uncooperative attitude.	Expected behaviour in court: defendant must give appearance of being willing to confront his/her situation and voice admittance to error and show remorse and willingness to change; must express desired motivation for change.
Defendant shows reluctance to testify for or against others or him/herself, based on a general avoidance of confrontation and imposition of opinion or testimony.	Defendant is obligated to testify and defend oneself in order to get at the facts based on an adversarial mode of dealing with legal challenges.
Defendant often pleads guilty on the basis of honesty or nonconfrontational acquiescence.	Expected to plead not guilty on basis that one is innocent until proven guilty.

Source: C. Crow, "Patterns of Discrimination: Aboriginal Justice in Canada," in N. Larson, ed., *The Canadian Criminal Justice System: An Issues Approach to the Administration of Justice* (Toronto: Canadian Scholars' Press, 1994), p. 438. Copyright © 1994 Canadian Scholars' Press. Used with permission.

1. a dispersal of decision-making among many people, as suggested by a regular emphasis on consensus decision-making, and a regular denunciation of such hierarchical decision-making structures as those created by the Indian Act; and
2. a belief that people can neither be understood nor assisted so long as they are seen as isolated individuals . . . people must be seen as participants in a large web of relationships.

Elders play an important role in aboriginal justice systems. They can be both "teachers" and "healers." Healing is an important aspect of the aboriginal justice system, for it allows the spiritual needs of the individual to be addressed. Also underlying the notion of justice for aboriginal peoples are different cultural imperatives. According to Dr. Clare Brant, a Mohawk psychiatrist, these cultural imperatives consist of four major rules in the area of

EXHIBIT 3.4

The Navajo Justice System

Currently in Canada there is much debate surrounding the creation of aboriginal criminal justice systems. However, in the United States, a number of aboriginal systems of justice exist, and one of the most studied is the Courts of the Navajo Nation. Separate aboriginal courts were first formed in 1883, when the Commissioner of Indian Affairs formed the first Indian Court, the Courts of Indian Offenses. However, these courts were established not to promote aboriginal concerns in justice but to eradicate aboriginal cultural practices and to try aboriginals under the dictates of the American justice system.

In 1892 the United States agent to the Navajos formed the Navajo Court of Indian Offenses. This system combined components of the American legal system—particularly the adjudication system with its emphasis on win–lose cases and a powerful central figure (the judge)—with the traditional Navajo system of justice. The Navajo system featured justice based on clan relations, equality, harmony, mediation, leadership by respect, and a focus on making the victims of crime whole.

In 1958 the Navajo Tribal Court was formed in a move by the Navajo Tribal Council to withstand an attempt by the

Arizona legislature to impose Western criminal law on the tribe. But this court was criticized by many because, they felt, it paralleled Western legal concepts too closely. In 1981 an effort was made to integrate the Navajo customary law into the courts. This effort led to the creation of the Navajo Peacemaker Court, a modern system of mediation and arbitration that involves community leaders and traditional methods of resolving conflicts. In 1990 the Navajo Nation Council implemented a task force to examine the operations of the Courts of the Navajo Nation.

The task force made several recommendations in its study, and these dealt with court improvements, continued utilization of Navajo common-law methods, principles, and rules. The next year saw the drafting of a code of judicial ethics and conduct that led to the Navajo Nation Code of Judicial Conduct. This code comprises 11 canons of conduct, and it applies to the justices and judges of the courts and support-staff members who are closely identified with them in the public eye. The code follows traditional legal Navajo values, and it was approved by the Navajo Nation Judicial Conference on November 1, 1991.

The Eleven Codes of Judicial Conduct

Canon One A Navajo Nation judge shall promote Navajo justice.

Principle: A Navajo judge should decide and rule between the Four Sacred Mountains. That means that judges, as Navajos, should apply Navajo concepts and procedures of justice, including the principles of maintaining harmony, establishing order, respecting freedom, and talking things out in free discussion.

Canon Two A Navajo Nation judge shall promote and protect the independence of the courts.
Principle: The Navajo people expect that those who make decisions about their lives and futures will be wise and completely independent, and that the courts will decide without regard to improper influences. They may arise from family, clan, personal, or business relationships; a personal interest in the case before the court; giving into or fearing political influence; or any consideration other than the equality of the parties and the merits of the case.

Canon Three A Navajo Nation judge shall always exercise the inherent powers and duties of the court with impartiality and diligence, in order to encourage free discussion, achieve a prompt and speedy resolution of disputes, and obtain a just resolution of all matters under consideration.
Principle: One of the inherent powers of a court is to regulate proceedings before it. As it is with all court powers, they must

conflict suppression that maintain harmony within the group. Further, they form the very basis of aboriginal life within their communities. The four rules are these:

1. the ethic of noninterference, i.e., the promotion of "positive interpersonal relationships by discouraging coercion of any kind, be it physical, verbal, or psychological"

2. the rule of noncompetitiveness, which acts to eliminate internal group conflict by "averting intragroup rivalry"

3. emotional restraint, which controls those emotional responses that may disrupt the group

be used wisely and well, with impartiality and diligence, so that the end is a prompt and fair disposition of disputes.

Canon Four A Navajo Nation judge shall assume administrative responsibility to oversee the administrative functions of the court. A judge should supervise the activities of the court staff, to assure that the duties and responsibilities of each member are performed.

Canon Five A Navajo Nation judge shall seek continuing education to achieve knowledge of the law, and promote the overall competency of the Navajo Nation judiciary.
Principle: Navajos believe knowledge is power. Knowledge is highly valued and continuously sought. When the Navajo Nation courts were created, a primary goal of the Navajo Tribal Council was the education of the Navajo Nation judges chosen for their wisdom, so each judge must undertake a personal quest for knowledge of the law, in order to meet the expectations of the public.

Canon Six A Navajo Nation judge shall avoid and refrain from engaging in improper political activity.
Principle: Navajo Nation politics and political relationships are different from those in other jurisdictions, because of group, family, and clan participation in the political process. A Navajo judge, as

a leader, should vote and encourage others to vote, participate in chapter meetings, and participate in local affairs.

Canon Seven A Navajo Nation judge shall avoid impropriety and the appearance of impropriety in all activities.
Principle: An "impropriety" is any act that violates any law; and any act or inaction contrary to the duties of judicial office or these canons; or one that undermines public confidence in a judge or the courts.

Canon Eight A Navajo Nation judge shall not use the judicial position to promote financial or business dealings, and shall not engage in business dealings that compromise judicial independence.
Principle: A judge shall not use his or her judicial office for personal gain. Such includes using the status of judge in commercial activities, or obtaining loans and benefits from governmental entities.

Canon Nine A Navajo Nation judge shall not lobby or advocate any position before a legislature or administrative agency, unless done in conjunction with a judicial activity or to improve this Navajo Nation judicial system.
Principle: Given the special public trust of judicial office, the need to avoid even an appearance of impropriety, and the need to avoid political activity, it is inap-

propriate for a judge to lobby, participate in lobbying, provide his or her name for lobbying, or advocate any position before a legislature or administrative body.

Canon Ten A Navajo Nation judge shall not initiate, permit, or condone ex parte communications with parties, counsel, or interested persons, except when provided by law
Principle: Public confidence in the independence and integrity of the judge is undermined, and the judge's decisions are suspect, when there are informal out-of-court communications regarding the merits of a case.

Canon Eleven A Navajo Nation judge shall refuse and disqualify himself or herself where the judge's impartiality might reasonably be questioned.
Principle: The rules of the Navajo Nation courts do not provide for automatic disqualification, and parties are generally required to show bias or prejudice to cause a judicial disqualification.

Source: T. Tso, "Moral Principles, Traditions, and Fairness in the Navajo Nation Code of Judicial Conduct." Adapted from the Navajo Nation Code of Judicial Conduct (1991), in *Judicature* 76, no. 1 (1992).

4. sharing, which means that those who were rich gave away much of their wealth to ensure the survival of the group (Report of the Aboriginal Justice Inquiry 1991).

Beyond these general characteristics there is much diversity. In illustrating these differences, Ross (1994) has described and compared the operation of two different aboriginal justice systems. The Hollow Water Reserve, in northern Manitoba, developed its justice system by requesting that some of the practices of the Western legal system be "modified to accommodate . . . what they wanted to continue doing on their own" (Ross 1994:248). In comparison, the approach taken at Sandy Bay and Attawapiskat (both in Manitoba) requested that they be "granted roles within the Western legal system" in order to cooperate with selected functionaries of the Western legal system.

The Hollow Water Reserve operates a program dealing with sexual abuse. It's called the Community Holistic Healing Program and it combines a healing approach with the Western legal system. It grew from the need to find a concrete solution to a particular community problem. According to the protocol of this justice system, disclosure about sexual abuse is first made to a community team rather than to the police. This community team consists of volunteers, mostly women, including a child protection worker, a community health representative, the nurse-in-charge, representatives from both the local school division and community churches, as well as the local detachment of the RCMP. Criminal charges are laid as quickly as possible after disclosure of the act. The alleged offender is then given a choice: he can decide to proceed through the outside criminal justice system or proceed with the healing support of the team. Either way, he is ultimately sentenced in a court of law. Sentencing is delayed, however, if the individual decides to take part in the healing process.

To be accepted into the healing program, the alleged abuser must accept full responsibility for his actions and enter a guilty plea as soon as possible. The abuser then enters a program that involves 13 different steps "from the initial disclosure to the creation of a healing contract," and if the individual successfully passes them, he proceeds to the cleansing ceremony (Ross 1994:244). This process entails a painful stripping away of all the defences of the abuser over a long period of time: then the rebuilding of the individual begins.

When the accused appears in court for sentencing, the team presents an honest report to the judge about the abuser's sincerity of effort and how much work, if any, still needs to be done. While the Western court would sentence the offender, the healing circle "fiercely" rejects any recommendation of incarceration.

In comparison, both the Sandy Bay and Attawapiskat justice systems focus on integrating traditional aboriginal values into the Western legal system by placing aboriginal peoples into selected advisory roles. At Sandy Bay, the emphasis was placed not on becoming involved in the trial process but rather at the time of sentencing. An elders panel acts together with a provincial court judge or justice of the peace to deliver the sentence. Recommended sentences usually involve some interaction with the community, such as restitution and community service work. If an offender does not fulfil his obligation, he is "banished" to the Western legal system, where he may be subjected to incarceration.

At Attawapiskat, Ross (1994:249) states, the elders have a different role in the sentencing of an offender; they hear the majority of the cases by themselves within a community court, complete with its own summonses and subpoenas. Charges, however, are laid in provincial court but are stayed and can be reactivated at once within a year if the offender fails to follow the sentence of the elders court. Indeed, the cases the elders court tries would not normally involve a period of incarceration. As at Sandy Bay, most of the sentences involve some form of community work.

Models of Criminal Justice and Criminological Theory

Each of the models of criminal justice discussed above are attached to various approaches concerned with explaining the causes of criminal behaviour. As shown in Table 3.2, the most fundamental difference between the **classical** and **positivist** approaches is the emphasis on either the act or the actor. The positivist approach focuses on the criminal offender (the actor), while the classical perspective emphasizes the crime committed by the offender (the act). The basic components of the two criminological approaches are also in conflict with each other.

The deterrence, selective incapacitation, and justice models fit under the classical perspective, which emphasizes the maintenance of social order and, as a result, the protection of society. Individuals are rational actors responsible for their own actions, so each individual, before committing a crime, "evaluates the risk of apprehension, the seriousness of expected punishment, the potential value of the criminal enterprise, and his or her immedi-ate need for criminal gain" (Senna and Siegel 1995:111). If the individual decides the risk of apprehension is too great, he is deterred from committing the crime. The more certain, severe, and swift the punishment, the less likely the crime. In order to attain a society with little crime, the operation of a system of criminal justice is of paramount importance. If the system is effective in its operation, potential criminals make the obvious rational choice: Don't commit a crime.

TABLE 3.2

Early Schools of Criminology		
	Classical	Positivist
(1) Central concern of model's founders	reform of criminal justice system	scientific study of criminal
(2) View of humans	free-will, utilitarian	deterministic: biological, psychological, sociological
(3) Responsibility for actions	yes	no
(4) Way to stop crime	ensure that the costs of crime outweigh the benefits	eliminate factor causing crime
(5) Focus of social control	(a) the law: make penalties severe enough to outweigh benefits of crime	(a) the criminal and his/her condition: criminals are fundamentally different from the rest of us
	(b) no judicial discretion; to ensure that costs outweigh the benefits, punishment must be certain for everyone: punishment fits the crime	(b) judicial discretion; since each criminal and his/her condition may be different, the judge needs the leeway to fit the penalty to the needs of the criminal
	(c) punishments fixed by law (implies the use of determinate sentences)	(c) indeterminate sentences
(6) Purpose of social control	deterrence—if criminal is shown that the costs of crime outweigh the benefits (that "crime doesn't pay"), the person will not commit any more offences; punishment of offender can also deter public from crime	rehabilitate the criminal

Source: F.T. Cullen and K. Gilbert, *Reaffirming Rehabilitation* (Cincinnati: Anderson, 1982), p. 35.

In contrast, the positivist approach assumes that crime "is determined by factors largely outside the control of the individual" (Cullen and Gilbert 1982). These factors may be sociological, psychological, or biological, but all emphasize the differences between criminals and law-abiding citizens. Since the positivist approach does not view criminals as rational actors, positivists would not punish criminals purely on the basis of their criminal acts. Rather, treatment of most offenders is the preferred approach, so the unique causes of individual behaviour need to be discovered before the individual can be treated. The rehabilitation approach was dominant during the first seven decades of criminological theorizing in the United States. Examples of positivist theories include social psychological theories, such as differential association and social learning. Other positivistic theories, notably functionalism and anomie, emphasize the social structural strains, while differential opportunity and subcultural theory stress the strains experienced by members of delinquent subcultures.

Summary

The different approaches and models of justice discussed in this chapter are concerned with the goal of reducing crime in our society. While one model may appear superior to the others in its ability to achieve that goal, such is not the case. One model alone probably couldn't accomplish the goal, given the realities of contemporary society.

It is probably wiser to think of a combined-model approach to attack the problem of crime. The treatment of offenders and the protection of the legal rights of alleged perpetrators are important, but so are the rights of victims and the desire of citizens to live in a crime-free society. How, then, are these issues to be reconciled? Still, it is important to remember that not all offenders—e.g., some dangerous offenders—can be treated. So some offenders can and should be incapacitated for long terms of imprisonment, if not for life.

Overall, however, it appears that although most people want punishment for offenders, they also want justice done as well as the protection of due-process rights granted them by the Charter of Rights and Freedoms. Thus, Canadians should expect to see combinations of the various crime control strategies described above, with the resulting tensions, conflicts, and problems that such approaches bring.

The purpose of our criminal justice system can be interpreted in different ways. The different models that form the basis of our criminal justice system can be categorized according to whether they focus on the act or the actor. Three of the models emphasize the criminal act, and include demands that discretion within the system be removed. These models argue that the discretion of both the prosecutor and the sentencing judge be controlled by guidelines, and that any deviations from these standards must be written down and forwarded to a review agency that assesses their validity. In addition, because prosecutors and judges have the power to shorten sentence lengths, advocates of the justice model support the elimination of parole. The justice model, which forms much of the basis of our criminal justice system today, believes that the accused should be punished only after being found guilty in a court of law, regardless of the factual guilt of the accused. The model's advocates also believe in the control of discretion and the elimination of parole, and so differ from advocates of the deterrence and selective incapacitation models, since they believe that most prison terms should be short in length. In addition, advocates of this position believe in alternatives to imprisonment, especially for first-time offenders. The deterrence model too supports the limitation of discretion throughout the criminal justice process, but it favours much longer periods of incarceration. Violent offenders are the focus of the selective incapacitation approach, which argues that the incarceration of these offenders reduces the rate of violent crime.

The only model of punishment to focus on the actor is the rehabilitation model. Since offenders differ from each other, this approach favours discretion within the criminal justice system so that the "punishment fits the criminal." The goal of this model is the reintegration of offenders back into society, so a wide variety of programs are available for offenders, both inside and outside correctional facilities.

Aboriginal justice systems are now operating in various locations across Canada. To date, they are working to integrate their concerns with those of the Western legal system in order to assist in the social control of as many aboriginal offenders as possible. These systems comprise a large number of groups and individuals, including elders, community members, the offender, the victim, and police officers.

Discussion Questions

1. Which model of criminal justice do you think is most effective in controlling crime in our society?

2. What improvements would you make to our criminal justice system to reduce crime?

3. Why do you think that the majority of the models of criminal justice want to control or eliminate the discretionary powers of criminal justice agents? How would such control reduce the crime rate?

4. Do you think that increasing the number of police on the street, as advocated by the deterrence model, would effectively control crime?

5. How do the views of classical criminologists differ from those of positivist criminologists?

6. Discuss the reasons why aboriginal justice systems are now in operation across Canada.

7. Compare and contrast aboriginal principles of justice with those held by Western legal systems.

8. Why do you think aboriginal justice systems are so successful, when compared to the Western legal system, in processing and treating aboriginal offenders?

Suggested Readings

Canadian Journal of Criminology. "Aboriginal Justice," Volume 34, Nos. 3–4, 1992.

Cullen, F.T., and K. Gilbert. *Reaffirming Rehabilitation.* Cincinnati: Anderson Publishing, 1982.

Duff, A., and D. Garland. *A Reader on Punishment.* New York: Oxford University Press, 1994.

Gordon, D.R. *The Justice Juggernaut: Fighting Street Crime, Controlling Citizens.* New Brunswick, N.J.: Rutgers University Press, 1990.

Hudson, B. *Justice through Punishment: A Critique of the "Justice" Model of Corrections.* London: Macmillan, 1987.

Klein, A. *Alternative Sentencing.* Cincinnati: Anderson Publishing, 1989.

CHAPTER 4

Crime Trends and Patterns in Canada

If the criminal justice system is to effectively control and reduce crime, we need current and accurate information on the nature and extent of crimes in particular locations as well as across Canada. In order to understand the dimensions of any type of crime, we need to be able to measure crime in an accurate fashion. A number of different measures have been developed to assist officials and policy-makers in the collection and interpretation of crime statistics. Official crime statistics are collected by the police or other justice officials from crimes reported to them or by interviewing individual citizens about the times they have been victimized. And while many individuals look at crime or victimization rates for a single year, others are concerned about trends—whether the numbers of crimes are increasing or decreasing over a period of years. As a result, many analysts study crime trends and how particular types of crime change over time.

CHAPTER OBJECTIVES

- understand the Uniform Crime Reporting system in Canada

- understand how violent and property crimes are differentiated

- follow the general trends of criminal victimization in Canada

- know the shortcomings of using crime statistics collected by official agencies

In a recent study, York University psychologist Debra Pepler spent 52 hours observing elementary schoolyards. During this time, she observed some 400 episodes of bullying. In a couple of incidents, knives were drawn and a group of self-appointed playground vigilante groups attacked children who they felt needed to be taught a lesson.

For some people, one of the most disturbing crime trends in Canada today is schoolyard violence. Information about the trends of this violence is limited, but the 1994 Revised Uniform Crime Report indicates that the percentage of violent incidents occurring on school property is small. These data indicate 11 percent of violent incidents directed against children and youths occurred on school property. The majority (81 percent) of the schoolyard incidents were nonsexual assaults, 10 percent were sexual assaults, 4 percent were robberies, and the remainder were other types of violent offences (Johnson 1995:11). The trend of school violence appears to be growing significantly as more attention is placed on it. A federal report on the issue of school violence, based on information collected from 125 school boards across Canada, reported that 819 assaults were reported to the police in 1993, up from 529 in 1990. In addition, reports of weapon possession, largely knives, rose to 141 from 65, and weapons assaults causing bodily harm rose to 221 from 165 (Galt 1996).

In his review of the literature on schoolyard bullies, Farrington (1993) reports that the frequency of bullying by and of students is high in Western nations. Some studies have discovered that approximately 50 percent of all children engage in schoolyard bullying, while over 50 percent are victims of bullies. Boys bully more frequently than girls, but boys' victims are as often girls as boys. Generally, bullies have been found to display the traits of aggressiveness, toughness, strength, confidence, and impulsiveness. Victims tend to be unpopular, lonely, rejected, anxious, depressed, unwilling to retaliate, and lacking in self-esteem. Walker (1994), in his study of school violence, discovered that one or two violent incidents at school have a negative impact on victims' feelings of personal safety and the school as a safe place.

Each year in Canada, the publication of crime statistics on a variety of issues occurs throughout the year. The national crime statistics from any year are usually published in the early summer of the next year, while reports on specialized issues—such as violence in schools, homicide, and robbery—are published at different times. Criminologists are interested in how much crime occurs, whether the overall crime rates increase or decrease, the rate of violent crime, which crimes are the most frequently committed, how many crimes are solved (or cleared) by the police, and which city can lay claim to the title of "murder capital of Canada." But what is meant by these national crime statistics? What are the problems and limitations associated with these figures? Can the figures be manipulated? This chapter discusses the official crime reporting system in Canada. Official crime measures include police-generated crime data and data collected from victimization surveys. In addition, unofficial methods of collecting crime data are also discussed.

Police Data: The Uniform Crime Reporting System

The **Uniform Crime Reporting** (UCR) **system** was instituted in Canada in 1961 and continues, with some changes and modifications, to this day. The UCR is designed to generate reliable crime statistics for use in all aspects of law enforcement, but these statistics are used also by criminologists to study the operation of the criminal justice system and by other people (e.g., politicians) who have an interest in the crime problem. In addition, members of the public are interested in these statistics, since they provide information about crime throughout Canada and in the provinces and cities.

In order to ensure uniformity in the reporting of crime data, standard definitions have been adopted for all offences. This approach is required to eliminate variations in the definitions of offences in different parts of the country. All police agencies are required to submit their crime statistics in accordance with the UCR definitions. Since some offences are "hybrid" offences the UCR does not make a distinction between indictable and summary conviction offences.

The police follow a guidebook, *The Uniform Crime Reporting Manual*, which contains definitions of crime as determined by the Canadian Association of Chiefs of Police and Statistics Canada (Silverman et al. 1991). Between 1961 and 1988, all police departments in Canada summarized their crime data on standardized forms on a monthly basis and forwarded the forms to Statistics Canada. Since 1982 the role of collecting and reporting these data has been the responsibility of an affiliated agency, the Canadian Centre for Justice Statistics. This organization produces the annual crime statistics as well as a "service bulletin" known as **Juristat**. This latter publication is published periodically throughout the year, and features reports that provide insights into specialized areas of Canadian crime statistics as well as the operation of various aspects of the criminal justice system (e.g., corrections).

For the first 27 years of UCR operation, crime was reported on the basis of aggregated statistics. This survey, known as the Aggregate UCR Survey, is still used today alongside the revised system. It records the number of incidents reported to the police and includes the number of reported offences, the number of actual offences (excluding those that are unfounded), the number of offences cleared by charge, the number of adults charged, the number of youths charged, and the gender of those individuals charged. It doesn't include victim characteristics. This approach to collecting statistics has been criticized because it is "less useful for analytic purposes than information based on characteristics of individual crimes" (Silverman et al. 1991:62).

A new system of collecting and reporting crime statistics was introduced in 1988, but it wasn't fully operational until 1992. The new system—referred to as the **Revised UCR Survey** or UCR II—incorporated a key change, as it collected incident-based data rather than summary data and thus allowed for better analyses of crime trends. Other changes included:

1. information on victims: age, sex, victim–accused relationship, level of injury, type of weapon causing injury, drug and/or alcohol use

2. information on the accused: age, sex, type of charges laid or recommended, drug and/or alcohol use

3. information on the circumstances of the incident: type of violation (or crime), target of violation, types of property stolen, dollar value of property affected, dollar value of drugs confiscated, type of weapon present, date, time, and type of location of the incident (Silverman et al. 1991:62–63)

Another difference between the aggregate and revised UCR forms lies in the number of police departments included in the study. The Aggregate UCR Survey includes every police force, while the Revised UCR Survey consists of a sample of 111 police departments across Canada. The police departments included in the Revised UCR Survey are nationally nonrepresentative, however, since about 50 percent are located in Quebec and more than 33 percent are in Ontario.

Since the term "crime rate" is used so often, it is important to know exactly what it means. Crime rates are usually based on 100 000 population. This allows researchers to standardize and compare crime rates across Canada in any given year as well as across a number of years. For example, in 1994, when there were 596 homicides in Canada, the homicide rate dropped to a 25-year low of 2.04 per 100 000 population—a 6-percent reduction over the previous year, when the rate was 2.16 per 100 000 population.

One of the most commonly debated issues about the UCR is how well it measures the crime rate in Canada. Numerous criticisms have been made against police-generated crime statistics. The most common of these criticisms are as follows:

1. There is an unknown (and no doubt large) amount of crime that is not reported to the police and, as a result, does not get recorded in the UCR. This problem can be alleviated with the use of victimization surveys.

2. In a single series of criminal actions reported to the police, only the most serious crime in it is included in the UCR. The most serious offence is usually the one that carries the longest maximum sentence under the Criminal Code of Canada. If, for example, a male breaks and enters a house, sexually assaults a woman level 1, and then kills her (homicide), only the murder is recorded. Although break and enter and homicide both have a maximum penalty of life imprisonment, violent offences always take precedence over nonviolent offences. One exception to this approach is criminal harassment (stalking); all instances of this offence are recorded, not just those in which it is the most serious violation of a series (Hendrick 1995).

3. The overall crime totals misrepresent the crime rate in any given year. When we talk of an increase or a decrease in any given year, we are comparing the totals of all crimes included in the crime statistics with those totals of the previous years. But what if an increase in break and entering corresponds with a decrease in sexual assault level 1? Since one offence is classified as a violent crime and the other a property crime, it is argued these two offences shouldn't have the same weight.

4. There are problems with the way the UCR records criminal incidents for some crimes. For nonviolent crimes, one incident is counted for every distinct or separate incident. But the UCR records violent incidents differently from other incidents. For violent crime, a separate incident is recorded for each victim, so if one person attacks and assaults five individuals, five incidents are recorded. But if five people attack and assault one person, only one incident is recorded. Robbery is an exception to the way violent crimes are recorded. One robbery equals one incident, regardless of the number of victims. This is because a single robbery can involve many victims, so to record the robbery by the number of persons it victimized would overstate the occurrence of robbery (Martin and Ogrodnik 1996).

The next section discusses the patterns and trends of violent crimes reported to the police. As shown in Figure 4.1, violent crimes declined slightly in 1993, the first decline since 1962, the first year that crime statistics were gathered by the UCR survey. However, official crime statistics produced by the police are not a good reflection of the true rate of crime. Other measures, such as victimization surveys, have been developed in an attempt to arrive at a more accurate figure.

Violent Crime

The crimes included in the category of "violent crime" are homicide, attempted murder, assault, sexual assault, other sexual offences, abduction, and robbery. In 1994 overall violent crime declined by 3 percent, the largest

FIGURE 4.1

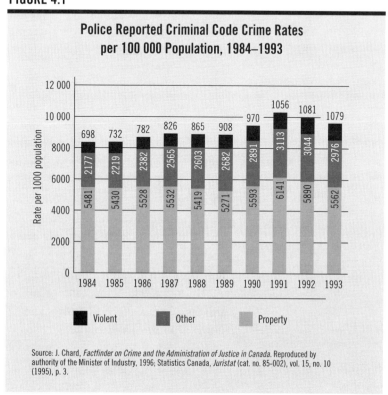

Source: J. Chard, *Factfinder on Crime and the Administration of Justice in Canada*. Reproduced by authority of the Minister of Industry, 1996; Statistics Canada, *Juristat* (cat. no. 85-002), vol. 15, no. 10 (1995), p. 3.

FIGURE 4.2

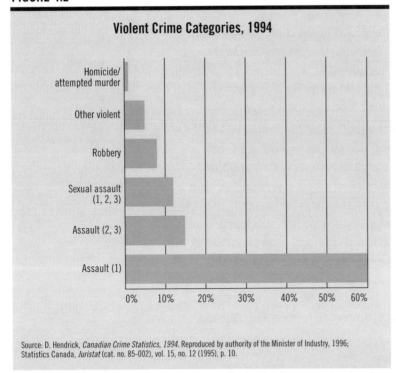

Source: D. Hendrick, *Canadian Crime Statistics, 1994*. Reproduced by authority of the Minister of Industry, 1996; Statistics Canada, *Juristat* (cat. no. 85-002), vol. 15, no. 12 (1995), p. 10.

annual decline since the UCR survey was introduced in 1962. About 303 000 violent crime incidents were reported to the police in 1994, down from just over 310 000 in the previous year. Every type of violent crime decreased in 1994, although by varying degrees. Sexual assaults and other sexual offences declined by 10 percent, attempted murders by 8 percent, abductions by 7 percent, homicides by 6 percent, robberies by 5 percent, and assaults by 2 percent.

As Figure 4.2 indicates, the most common violent crime was assault level 1, which accounted for approximately 60 percent of all violent crime incidents in 1994. The offences of assault level 2 and assault level 3, combined, were the next-highest category, accountable for about 14 percent of all violent offences in 1994. The category of "other violent crime," which includes abductions, other sexual offences, and other assaults, was responsible for 5 percent of all violent crimes recorded in 1994. Homicide was the violent crime least often reported to the police; it accounted for 0.2 percent of violent crime incidents (Hendrick 1995:1).

In 1994, 75 percent of all violent crimes were cleared (51 percent by charge and 24 percent otherwise). To the category of "other sexual offences" belonged the highest total clearance rate (83 percent) for any violent crime. This category was followed by assaults (81 percent), homicide (80 percent), and attempted murder (76 percent). The lowest clearance rates were for the offences of abduction (55 percent) and robbery (33 percent). Different pictures emerge, however, when one considers whether a crime was cleared by charge (i.e., a charge laid against the accused) or "otherwise" (i.e., sufficient evidence to lay a charge exists but none is laid). Homicide and attempted murder were the two crimes most commonly cleared by charge, at 72 percent each. Assault was the offence most commonly "cleared otherwise," at 27 percent.

During 1994, 55 percent of all violent crimes involved physical force. Although 71 percent of all victims knew their accused, women who were victims of a violent crime were more likely to know their attackers than male victims, who were more likely to be victimized by strangers. Fifty percent of violent crime victims were injured during the incident, with 12 percent of these requiring professional medical treatment. Women and men were equally as likely to be victims of a violent crime. However, women were more likely to be victims of sexual assault and assault level 1 and males were more likely to be the victims of robbery and assault level 2 and assault level 3.

Murder

According to the definition used in the Uniform Crime Reports, a murder occurs when an individual either causes the death of another human being or means to cause bodily harm the person knows is likely to cause death. There are four different types of murder in Canada: first-degree murder, second-degree murder, manslaughter, and infanticide (see Exhibit 4.1).

EXHIBIT 4.1

Murder

First-degree murder occurs when

(a) it is planned and deliberate or

(b) the victim is a person employed and acting in the course of his/her work for the preservation and maintenance of the public peace (e.g., police worker, correctional worker) or

(c) the death is caused by a person committing or attempting to commit certain serious offences (e.g., sexual assault, kidnapping, hijacking)

Second-degree murder is all murder that is not first-degree.

Manslaughter is generally considered to be a homicide committed in the heat of passion by sudden provocation. It also includes other culpable homicides that are not murder or homicides.

Infanticide occurs when a female causes the death of her newborn child, and her state of mind is disordered as a result of her having given birth.

Source: O. Fedorowycz, "Homicide in Canada—1994." Reproduced by authority of the Minister of Industry, 1996; Statistics Canada, *Juristat* (cat. no. 85-002), vol. 15, no. 11 (1995), p. 18.

During 1994, 49 percent of all murders were classified as first-degree murders, 41 percent as second-degree murders, 9 percent as manslaughter, and 1 percent as infanticide. The determination of the classification is made by the police during their initial investigation, although the original charge may be changed later by the Crown prosecutor. In addition, a charge of first-degree murder may be reduced to manslaughter by a judge or jury. Not all violent deaths are considered to be homicides, e.g., suicides, death due to an accident, and justifiable homicides.

During 1994, 557 separate homicide incidents involving 596 victims were reported to the police. Ninety-five percent of all homicide incidents involved a single victim. The 30 multiple-victim incidents reported to the police in 1994 involved 23 incidents of 2 victims, 5 incidents of 3 victims, and 2 incidents of 4 victims. Of the 7 incidents involving more than 2 victims, 4 were domestic homicides and 3 involved acquaintances (Federowycz 1995).

Murder has consistently had one of the highest clearance rates of all Criminal Code offences. This high rate surprises many citizens, who read or hear about numerous unsolved murders in the media. Yet since 1984 the percentage of murders cleared by charge in Canada has varied between 77 and 85; in 1994 the percentage was 80. In 1994, of those homicide incidents cleared by charge, 90 percent were cleared when a charge was laid, 9 percent when the accused committed suicide immediately following the offence, and the remaining 1 percent when the accused died from some cause (other than suicide) (Federowycz 1995). However, it must be remembered that because the investigation of a homicide can be very intricate and the process of identifying the alleged offender extremely time-consuming, a homicide incident may not be solved until years after it was originally reported to the police. As a result, these rates usually under-reflect the final clearance rates.

FIGURE 4.3

Homicides by Accused–Victim Relationship, 1984–1994

Source: O. Federowycz, *Homicide in Canada—1994*. Reproduced by authority of the Minister of Industry, 1996; Statistics Canada, *Juristat* (cat. no. 85-002), vol. 15, no. 11 (1995), p. 11.

It is assumed by many members of the public that most murders are committed by persons who are strangers to their victims, but this is not the case. Between 1984 and 1994, the proportion of homicides in which the victim was killed by a stranger has remained relatively stable, averaging 14 percent per year. During this same 10-year period, 40 percent of the victims were slain by a family member and 46 percent were killed by an acquaintance (see Figure 4.3).

In 1994, the age of greatest risk of becoming a homicide victim was less than one year of age. Of the 27 homicide victims under the age of one in 1994, 20 were killed by a parent (11 by the father, nine by the mother), two by a grandfather, one by a sibling, and one by an acquaintance, while the relationship of three of the accused to the victim was unknown. Between 1984 and 1994, there has been an annual average of 20 homicide victims under one year of age, accounting for 2.5 percent to 5 percent of all victims (Federowycz 1995; Johnson 1995).

Murders committed by intimates continue to account for the greatest number of murders in Canada. Figure 4.4 reveals that, between 1974 and 1992, close to 40 percent of all women who were homicide victims were killed by their husbands. A married woman was nine times more likely to be killed by her spouse than by a stranger (Wilson and Daly 1994). Sixty-eight percent of wives killed by their husband were related to them by way of registered marriage (whether co-residing or estranged), and the remaining 32 percent were killed by their common-law husband. Forty-seven percent of the husbands who were homicide victims were slain by their registered-marriage partner while 53 percent were killed by their common-law spouse. During this same period, the 1886 women and men killed by their spouse represent 15 percent of all

Canadian homicide victims—38 percent of all adult women victims and 6 percent of all adult male victims.

Sexual Assault

Sexual assault occurs when an individual is sexually assaulted or molested or when an attempt is being made to sexually assault or molest an individual. A total of 34 764 sexual assault incidents accounted for 11 percent of all violent crimes recorded by the police in 1993. Between 1984 and 1993, the rate of reported sexual assaults more than doubled from 58 to 121 per 100 000 population, an average increase of 9 percent. In 1994, approximately 33 percent of all sexual assault victims were under 12 years of age, and another 33 percent were between the ages of 12 and 17. Thirty-five percent of victims were assaulted by a casual acquaintance, 22 percent by a stranger, 13 percent by another family member, 11 percent by a parent, 8 percent by a close friend, and 6 percent by a business acquaintance (Hendrick 1995).

FIGURE 4.4

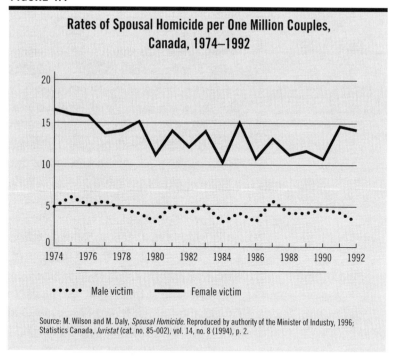

Rates of Spousal Homicide per One Million Couples, Canada, 1974–1992

••••• Male victim   ——— Female victim

Source: M. Wilson and M. Daly, *Spousal Homicide.* Reproduced by authority of the Minister of Industry, 1996; Statistics Canada, *Juristat* (cat. no. 85-002), vol. 14, no. 8 (1994), p. 2.

Sexual assault is divided into three different levels, based on the seriousness of the offence. The least serious type of sexual assault, sexual assault level 1 (Section 271,) occurs when an individual intentionally threatens, attempts, or commits a sexual assault. Sexual assault level 2 (Section 272), involves a weapon, threats to a third party, or bodily harm; and sexual assault level 3 (Section 273), also known as aggravated sexual assault, occurs when an assailant wounds, maims, disfigures, or endangers the life of the victim. Over 90 percent of all sexual assaults are classified as sexual assault level 1. The number of reported incidents of sexual assault level 1 totalled 30 950 in 1994, followed by 768 incidents of sexual assault level 2 and 362 incidents of sexual assault level 3. The maximum penalties for these are 10 years' imprisonment, 14 years' imprisonment, and life imprisonment, respectively. However, sexual assault level 1 is a hybrid offence, and thereby allows Crown prosecutors the discretion to proceed by way of summary conviction.

Assault

An assault level 1 occurs when one individual, without the consent of another, intentionally applies force, or attempts or threatens to apply force to that other person. Assault may occur without violence, but it must include a threatening act or gesture, because words by themselves do not constitute an assault. Assault level 1 is a hybrid offence. Assault level 2, also known as assault causing bodily harm, requires the use or threatened use of a weapon, or the presence of injuries such as broken bones, cuts, and bruises. Aggravated assault is assault level 3, and the victim must be wounded, maimed, disfigured, or have his or her life endangered. The maximum penalties for assault offences are 5, 10, and 14 years' imprisonment respectively.

The category of assault is the most frequently occurring crime in the violent crime category. For example, during the five-year period 1990 to 1994, the total number of violent crimes averaged 297 500 offences per year. During this same period, assault offences averaged 228 000 incidents per year, or about 77 percent of all violent offences. Of all assaults reported to the police between 1990 and 1994, the most common category was common assault (assault level 1), which accounted for 75 percent of all assault offences. The next most frequent category was assault causing bodily harm, or assault level 2, which accounted for 16 percent of all assault offences, followed by aggravated assault, or assault level 3 (9 percent of all assault offences). Common assaults increased by 6 percent from 1993 to 1994, while assault causing bodily harm increased by 2 percent and aggravated assaults decreased by 7 percent. This slight decrease in aggravated assaults is not surprising, since many such assaults stop just short of homicide because the perpetrator's bullet or knife misses its intended target or misses a vital body organ. As a result, these crimes are commonly defined as attempted murder.

In 1994, 78 percent of victims knew the accused. Casual acquaintances were accused in 25 percent of common assaults, while strangers were accused in 22 percent of such offences. These were followed by close friends (8.2 percent), business relations (7.2 percent), parents (3.9 percent), children (1.8 percent), other immediate-family members (2.9 percent), and extended-family members (1.3 percent). As Figure 4.5 reveals, most women victims were assaulted by a spouse or someone they knew very well, such as parents, a child, other family members, or a close friend. Men, on the other hand, were more commonly assaulted by business associates, acquaintances, or strangers.

The rate of clearing assaults by charge has changed considerably since 1975. While reported common-assault offences increased by 102 percent between 1975 and 1992, the rate at which adults were charged with that offence increased by 194 percent—or approximately twice as fast as reported common-assault offences (Kingsley 1993).

Prior to 1983, the rate at which common-assault offences were cleared by charge was 25 percent, compared to 55 percent of these cases cleared "otherwise." After 1983 this pattern changed, with 54 percent of all common assaults cleared by charge in 1994. This increase is attributed to the passage of Bill C-127 (1983), which redefined the sexual- and physical-assault sections of the Criminal Code. Bill C-127 allowed the police to arrest an individual on the basis of "reasonable and probable grounds" if they believed an assault had been committed. The intent of legislators was to enable police officers to arrest individuals suspected of committing acts of domestic violence. However, as Hendrick (1995) points out, this new law also made it easier for the police to lay charges in all types of assault. It has been argued that as much as 46 percent of the increase in the rate of adults charged with common assault can be traced to the changes in charging patterns brought about by the 1983 legislation (Kingsley 1993).

Robbery

Robbery is defined as theft with violence or theft with the threat of violence against persons. The maximum penalty for robbery is life imprisonment. Robbery is sometimes confused with the offence of break and enter (see

FIGURE 4.5

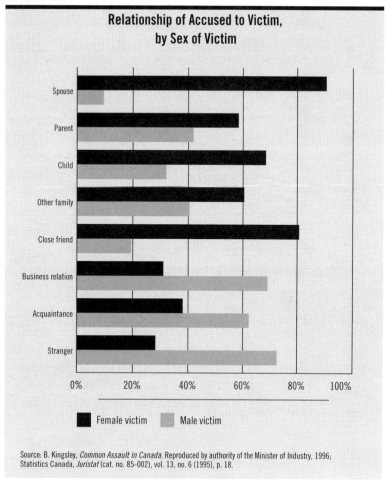

Source: B. Kingsley, *Common Assault in Canada.* Reproduced by authority of the Minister of Industry, 1996; Statistics Canada, *Juristat* (cat. no. 85-002), vol. 13, no. 6 (1995), p. 18.

Chapter 2), but a break and enter involves no violence directed against an individual. Robbery involves the face-to-face confrontation between perpetrator and victim and, as a result, the potential for violence and physical injury. Because robbery involves confrontation, it is greatly feared by the members of the public. One reason for public concern is that robbery is usually committed by a stranger. In 1990, 84 percent of robberies were committed by individuals who were strangers to the victim, while 77 percent of assaults were committed by individuals known to the victim (DuWors 1992). While robbery is classified as a violent crime, it may not involve real violence or even the threat of violence. In 1990, over 74 percent of robbery victims received no physical injury, implying they were threatened. Of the remaining victims, 22 percent received minor physical injuries and 4 percent suffered major physical injuries (i.e., an injury that required professional medical attention at the scene or transportation to a medical facility). According to DuWors (1992:3), most victims in 1990 were harmed by physical force, 20 percent by handguns, 20 percent by knives, 6 percent by sawed-off rifles or shotguns, and the remaining by "diverse weapons."

FIGURE 4.6

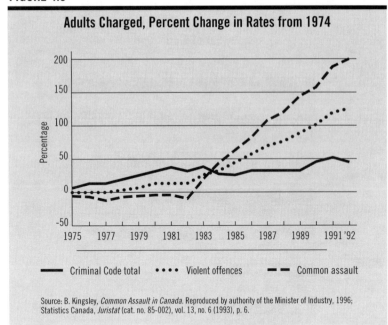

Adults Charged, Percent Change in Rates from 1974

—— Criminal Code total   •••• Violent offences   ▬ ▬ Common assault

Source: B. Kingsley, *Common Assault in Canada*. Reproduced by authority of the Minister of Industry, 1996;
Statistics Canada, *Juristat* (cat. no. 85-002), vol. 13, no. 6 (1993), p. 6.

Figure 4.6 shows the various types of property taken in a sample of 4104 robberies that occurred between 1988 and 1991. Money is the most common type of property stolen (in about 62 percent of cases), followed by "other property" such as stereos (20 percent), personal accessories—for example, jewellery—(20 percent), and consumable goods such as alcohol (6 percent). Identification was the least common type of property stolen (5 percent).

In 1990, 42 percent of robbery victims were women and 58 percent were men. The majority of robbery victims were between 18 and 49 (74 percent of women victims and 65 percent of male victims were in this age bracket). However, a significant number of victims were between the ages of 12 and 17: 17 percent of all male robbery victims and 9 percent of all women robbery victims. Sixteen percent of women victims and 18 percent of male victims were over the age of 49.

The public's fear of robbery is enhanced by the fact that robbery does not have a high clearance rate. In 1990, for example, 49 percent of all violent crimes were cleared by charge, while the corresponding figure for robbery was only 29 percent. Reasons for this low clearance rate are threats made against the victims and the fact that victims may not get a good description of the perpetrator because the crime happens so quickly. Descriptions supplied to the police are usually not good, because the perpetrators have usually left the scene of the crime by the time the police arrive and victims and witnesses give poor information (Brannigan 1984).

Abduction

Abductions remained stable in Canada between 1984 and 1994, accounting for less than 1 percent of all violent crimes annually. In 1990, 1046 abductions were reported to the police. This number increased to 1220 in 1992, and was followed by a decrease to 1130 in 1994. Sixty percent of abductions in 1994 were committed by parents, two-thirds of whom violated a court custody order. Over the past decade, just over half (56 percent) of all abductions were cleared by the police. Abductions by parents or legal guardians were more likely to be cleared (69 percent) than those committed by other individuals.

Criminal Harassment (Stalking)

On August 1, 1993, amendments to the Criminal Code—S. 264 (1)—were introduced to protect persons from harassment. "Criminal harassment" occurs when an individual repeatedly follows or communicates with another person, repeatedly watches someone's house or workplace, or directly threatens another person or any member of that person's family, causing a person to fear for his or her safety or the safety of someone known to that person (see Chapter 2).

In 1994, 3200 incidents of criminal harassment were reported to the police in Canada, with over two-thirds of these reported in Toronto and Montreal. Seventy-five percent of stalking victims were women, while 88 percent of the accused were men. Those arrested for criminal harassment were, in relation to the victim, casual acquaintances (28 percent), ex-spouses (27 percent), close friends (18 percent), strangers (10 percent), spouses (8 percent), other family members (5 percent), and business acquaintances (4 percent). Male victims were harassed by a different profile of offenders: 44 percent of the accused were casual acquaintances, 20 percent were strangers, 12 percent were business acquaintances, 10 percent were other family members, 8 percent were ex-spouses, 5 percent were close friends, and 2 percent were spouses (Hendrick 1995).

Crimes against Property

Property incidents involve unlawful actions with the intent to gain property, but they do not involve the use or threat of violence. Six different types of crime comprise the category of property crime: theft $5000 or under, theft over $5000, possession of stolen goods, fraud, breaking and entering, and possession of stolen goods. In 1994, 1.5 million property crime incidents were reported to the police. These accounted for 58 percent of all Criminal Code incidents. Since 1984 there has been a general decline in property crimes: in 1984, property crimes accounts for 66 percent of Criminal Code incidents, while in 1993 and 1994 this percentage decreased to 58. Rates for all types of property crime decreased in 1993, with the exceptions of motor-vehicle theft and possession of stolen goods.

Breaking and Entering

Breaking and entering occurs when a dwelling or other premise is illegally entered by a person who intends to commit an indictable offence. Break and enter is considered to be the most serious of all property crimes. This is illustrated by the severity of the sentencing provisions in the Criminal Code, where the maximum penalty for an offender convicted of breaking and entering into a dwelling is life imprisonment. In comparison, the maximum punishment for breaking and entering into a business or any other premise is 14 years. In the

FIGURE 4.7

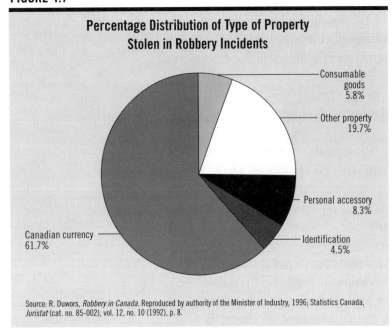

Percentage Distribution of Type of Property Stolen in Robbery Incidents

- Consumable goods 5.8%
- Other property 19.7%
- Personal accessory 8.3%
- Identification 4.5%
- Canadian currency 61.7%

Source: R. Duwors, *Robbery in Canada*. Reproduced by authority of the Minister of Industry, 1996; Statistics Canada, *Juristat* (cat. no. 85-002), vol. 12, no. 10 (1992), p. 8.

FIGURE 4.8

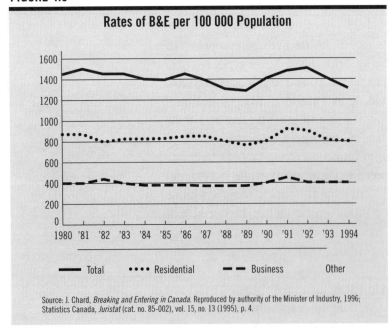

Rates of B&E per 100 000 Population

—— Total   •••• Residential   – – Business   Other

Source: J. Chard, *Breaking and Entering in Canada*. Reproduced by authority of the Minister of Industry, 1996; Statistics Canada, *Juristat* (cat. no. 85-002), vol. 15, no. 13 (1995), p. 4.

Uniform Crime Reports, breaking and entering is divided into three classifications: business, residential, and other (see Figure 4.8).

Two important aspects of breaking and entering offences are the frequency and economic cost. This offence is the most frequently occurring of all property crimes, accounting for 25 percent of all property incidents and 15 percent of all reported Criminal Code offences in 1994. Just over half (58.5 percent) of all break and enters occurred in residences during 1994, followed by business (28 percent) and "other" premises (13.5 percent). The financial cost of break and enters to Canadians is enormous. According to the Insurance Bureau of Canada, losses due to thefts in break and entering incidents totalled more than $373 million in residential insurance claims and $118 million in commercial insurance claims in 1993 (Chard 1995b). Property of some type was stolen in 81 percent of break and enters reported to the police in 1994. In residential break and enters, 28.4 percent of the dollar value of property stolen was between $1000 and $5000 (see Figure 4.9). The largest category for business break and enters was "nothing stolen," while in "other" break and enters the amount of property stolen was valued between $1000 and $5000. The most common type of property items taken from residence were televisions, stereos, and VCRs. In comparison, the most valuable type of property stolen in business break and enters was Canadian currency, money orders, and/or traveller's cheques. Machinery and tools were the most valuable property stolen from other businesses.

Sixty-seven percent of break and enters in 1993 were reported to the police, making it one of the most frequently reported crimes in Canada. Victims who did not report a break and enter to the police felt the incident was too minor to report (48 percent), dealt with the offence in another way (46 percent), felt the police could do nothing (42 percent), and said nothing was taken so they didn't report the incident (36 percent). In 1994, the police cleared 17 percent of break and enters (11 percent by charge, 6 percent otherwise).

And while the offence of break and enter has a maximum punishment of life imprisonment, it is rarely the sentence chosen by judges. In 1993, less than 1 percent (0.2) of break and enter cases resulted in sentences of 5 years or more. While many offenders were imprisoned, it was usually for less than two years, and the sentence usually involved probation, either as the sole punishment or in combination with a short period of incarceration.

FIGURE 4.9

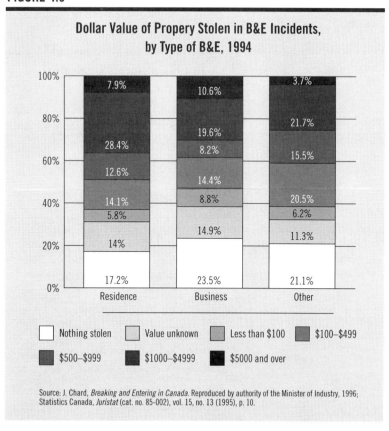

Source: J. Chard, *Breaking and Entering in Canada.* Reproduced by authority of the Minister of Industry, 1996; Statistics Canada, *Juristat* (cat. no. 85-002), vol. 15, no. 13 (1995), p. 10.

Theft

Theft of—or the attempted theft of—personal property involves an incident in which cash or other personal property (e.g., a purse, wallet, credit cards, jewellery, etc.) is taken. Household theft or attempted theft of household property involves, not surprisingly, household property (e.g., bicycle, liquor). Theft comprises two separate offences—"theft over" and "theft under" a certain dollar amount. In 1985, the Canadian Criminal Code was amended to change the cutoff point between them to $1000 from $200. In 1995, the cutoff point was raised to $5000.

Incidents of "theft under $1000" accounted for approximately half (48 percent) of all property crimes in 1994. This percentage represented a 7-percent reduction from 1993, the third consecutive year the number of "theft under" incidents decreased. As Hendrick (1995) notes, due to the large number of "thefts under," the decrease in reported incidents strongly influenced the decrease in both the property crime rate and the overall crime rate. Forty-one percent of these incidents were from motor vehicles in 1994. Next in order was shoplifting (13 percent), then bicycle theft (12 percent). Since many thefts occurred when there were no witnesses, most of the incidents reported to the police were not solved. In 1994, 20 percent of "theft under" incidents were cleared (13 percent were cleared by charge).

In 1994, incidents involving theft over $1000 accounted for 8 percent of all property crimes. This percentage represented a decrease of 2 percent from the previous year, the second consecutive year the rate declined. However, the rate of "theft over" has increased by 53 percent since 1986, the first full year of the $1000 distinction. The most common incident in 1994 involved articles (e.g., stereos) stolen from motor vehicles.

Motor Vehicle Theft

Motor vehicle theft is the stealing of a motor vehicle or the taking of it without permission. Theft *from* a motor vehicle is the theft of automobile accessories as well as personal property found within the vehicle. There were 159 663 incidents of motor vehicle theft in 1994, accounting for 10 percent of all property crimes. The rate of motor vehicle theft in 1994 was 70 percent higher than it was in 1984. Sixty-seven percent of such thefts involved automobiles, followed by trucks, including minivans (26 percent), motorcycles (4 percent), and other motor vehicles (7 percent). Fifteen percent of motor vehicle thefts were cleared in 1994, 10 percent by charge. The rate of recovery of stolen motor vehicles has slowly declined from a high of 81 percent in 1980 to 73 percent in 1990 (Ogrodnik and Paiement 1992; Morrison and Kong 1996).

Motor vehicle thefts usually involve joy-riding, or the theft of a motor vehicle by youths. Individuals between 14 and 19 years of age accounted for 52 percent of all those accused of motor vehicle thefts in 1994. Many of these individuals steal a motor vehicle on a dare or to obtain parts and accessories. Most youths arrested for motor vehicle theft are repeat offenders. A recent study in British Columbia found repeat offenders were responsible for a disproportionate number of auto thefts (Hendrick 1995:19). Another common reason for motor vehicle theft is to use the stolen vehicle in other crimes. Usually a vehicle is stolen as close as possible to the primary crime, thereby reducing the chance that the theft is reported to the police. An increasing number of motor vehicles are stolen and then taken to "chop-shops," which dismantle the vehicle for parts or alter it in some fashion for resale.

Motor vehicle theft is an expensive crime. The 1993 General Social Survey reported that the total value of all property stolen or damaged during motor vehicle crimes totalled $1.6 million, compared to $73 million in losses from credit-card fraud during the 1993–94 fiscal year (Morrison and Kong 1996).

The majority of vehicles are stolen from public streets (38 percent). Next come private residences (20 percent), shopping centres (18 percent), and apartment buildings (14 percent). Almost half (48 percent) of the motor vehicles stolen in 1990 were valued under $5000, while another 25 percent were valued between $5000, and $10 000. Only 1 percent of the vehicles stolen were valued at over $30 000 (Ogrodnik and Paiement 1992).

Other Criminal Code Incidents

Those offences (see Figure 4.10) classified as "other Criminal Code" offences include arson, bail violations, disturbing the peace, mischief, offensive weapons, and prostitution. Some 30 percent of all Criminal Code incidents recorded in 1994 included one of these offences.

In 1994, arson—which is defined as any conduct that causes a fire or explosion, and which is not limited to any specific type of property—was one of the few crimes to increase (by a total of 8 percent) nationally. Offences include arson by negligence, arson with wilful disregard for human life, and possession of incendiary material. In 1990, 57 deaths and 551 injuries were caused by arson and suspected arson incidents. During the same year, the value of property damaged exceeded $244 million, or an average of $24 000 per incident. The number of arson cases cleared by charge is slowly decreasing. In 1974, an accused was identified in 30 percent of arsons, while in 1989 the number of accused had declined to 27 percent and then 21 percent in 1991 (Wolff 1992).

Offensive weapons incidents accounted for 2 percent of all "other Criminal Code" incidents in 1994. Of these offensive weapons, 19 percent involved prohibited weapons; restricted weapons accounted for 12 percent of such incidents. Restricted weapons offences increased by the greatest percentage amount in 1994, up 6 percent from the previous year.

FIGURE 4.10

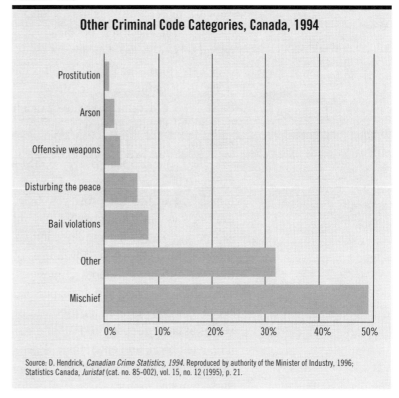

Source: D. Hendrick, *Canadian Crime Statistics, 1994*. Reproduced by authority of the Minister of Industry, 1996; Statistics Canada, *Juristat* (cat. no. 85-002), vol. 15, no. 12 (1995), p. 21.

Victimization Data

The number of unreported crimes represents a large question in the Canadian crime statistics. The exact number and type of these crimes is unknown, and it probably fluctuates from year to year. The official crime rate generated by the UCR is only as accurate as the public contributions of reports make it—as well as the data the police decide to process.

During the past two decades, however, criminologists have started to use victimization surveys in an attempt to gain more information about the volume, type, and rate of crime. Victimization surveys differ from the UCR in that they examine representative samples of a general population in an attempt to discover what crimes occurred in specified time periods. Sometimes researchers collected data from victims concerning a particular type of crime over a specified time period, but this information is of limited value to anyone trying to determine the rate of victimization across Canada for most crimes. Since 1988, a victimization survey of a national sample of personal risk related to criminal victimization was included as part of the General Social Survey program.

The General Social Survey (GSS) is based on a representative sample of about 10 000 Canadians aged 15 years or older, from the noninstitutionalized population in the ten provinces. Selected by computer-assisted telephones utilizing random dialling techniques, interviewers ask respondents about their experiences with crime and the criminal justice system during the previous 12-month period. One of the advantages of the GSS over the UCR is its ability to discover information about crimes not reported by victims to the police. In 1993, the GSS collected data on personal risk and examined the prevalence and social and demographic distribution of eight types of criminal victimization: sexual assault, robbery and attempted robbery, assault, break and enter and attempted break and enter, theft of personal property as well as attempts, theft of household victimization and attempts, vandalism, and motor vehicle theft and attempted motor vehicle theft. Information was collected in other areas of criminal victimization too—including fear and perceptions of crime, police reporting, and perceptions of the criminal justice system.

The GSS surveys are not intended to substitute for the UCR but complement it. Comparisons of the UCR and the GSS are of dubious value, because the ideas behind each system are different. While crime rates in the UCR came from reports of incidents of crime by the public to the police, crime rates in the GSS come from reports of victimizations to survey interviewers. Therefore, GSS data originate from individuals who are actually victimized, and UCR data are based on criminal acts reported to the police. Because their sources of data differ, the GSS and UCR give us different information about crime in Canada.

Criminal Victimization in Canada, 1988–93

General Trends and Patterns

According to Gartner and Doob (1994), 24 percent of Canadians in 1993 were victimized by at least one crime during the previous 12 months, a percentage that was the same as the figure obtained from respondents in 1988. Gartner and Doob report that the chance of victimization for Canadians 15 years and over in 1993 for the crimes of assault, personal property theft, theft of household property, break and enter, and vandalism were the same in 1993 as they were in 1988. However, in 1993 an individual's chance of being victimized of a robbery, sexual assault, assault, or personal theft decreased (see Figure 4.11).

The rate of personal victimization in 1993 was 143 incidents per 1000 Canadians 15 years or older. The rate of assault was the highest of all such offences (67 per 1000 population), followed by theft of personal property (51 per 1000 population), sexual assault (17 per 1000 population), and robbery (9 per 1000 population). The rate of household victimization was higher than personal victimization: 190 incidents per 1000 households. Vandalism had the highest rate (55 per 1000 households), followed by break and enter (50 per 1000 households), theft of household property (48 per 1000 households), and theft of a motor vehicle or motor vehicle parts (37 per 1000 households) (Wright 1995).

There are also regional variations in Canada for both personal and household victims. As Figure 4.12 reveals, the lowest rates of personal victimization were found in Quebec (114 per 1000 population), and individuals in British Columbia had the highest (180 per 1000 population). However, for rates of personal property, the variation among the regions is not great—British Columbia had the lowest rate (45

FIGURE 4.11

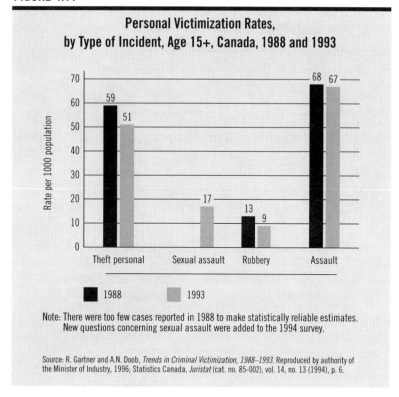

Note: There were too few cases reported in 1988 to make statistically reliable estimates. New questions concerning sexual assault were added to the 1994 survey.

Source: R. Gartner and A.N. Doob, *Trends in Criminal Victimization, 1988–1993*. Reproduced by authority of the Minister of Industry, 1996; Statistics Canada, *Juristat* (cat. no. 85-002), vol. 14, no. 13 (1994), p. 6.

FIGURE 4.12

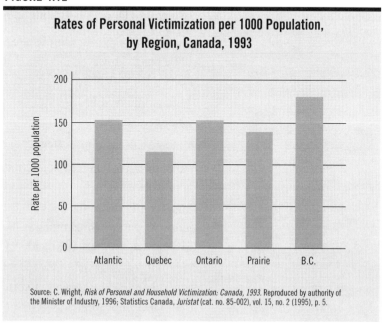

Source: C. Wright, *Risk of Personal and Household Victimization: Canada, 1993*. Reproduced by authority of the Minister of Industry, 1996; Statistics Canada, *Juristat* (cat. no. 85-002), vol. 15, no. 2 (1995), p. 5.

per 1000), and the Prairie region had the highest (59 per 1000).

For violent victimizations, however, not only was the rate higher in each region but there was greater variation between the regions. In 1993, British

FIGURE 4.13

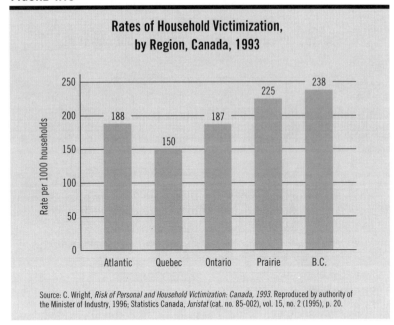

Rates of Household Victimization, by Region, Canada, 1993

Source: C. Wright, *Risk of Personal and Household Victimization: Canada, 1993.* Reproduced by authority of the Minister of Industry, 1996; Statistics Canada, *Juristat* (cat. no. 85-002), vol. 15, no. 2 (1995), p. 20.

Columbia recorded a violent victimization pattern that doubled that of Quebec (134 versus 65 violent victimizations per 1000 population). For household victimizations, British Columbia recorded the highest rate (238 per 1000 households), while Quebec had the lowest (150 per 1000). (See Figure 4.13). The highest rates of individual crimes were those in British Columbia for break and enter and for theft of motor vehicles and motor vehicle parts (65 per 1000 and 45 per 1000 households, respectively). The Prairie region reported the highest rate for theft of household victimization and vandalism (68 per 1000 and 73 per 1000 households, respectively).

Personal Victimization

Certain of the principal findings of the GSS in 1993 are included in the following (Gartner and Doob 1994; Kong 1994; Wright 1995) list:

- Most violent victimizations were committed by strangers and in a public place. However, individuals known by victims were responsible for the violent crimes of sexual assault and assault.

- The majority of robberies and assaults occurred outside of an individual's residence.

- In most victimizations, offenders acted alone and without a weapon.

- Urban dwellers reported higher rates of personal and household victimization.

- Canadians between the ages of 15 and 24 reported a personal victimization rate three times as high as those over the age of 24 (318 incidents versus 106 incidents per 1000).

- The total personal victimization rate for women was 11 percent higher than that for men (151 versus 136 per 1000). For other personal crimes, women reported rates similar to those of men—with the exception of robbery, where the rate for men was double that of women (12 versus 6 per 1000).

- Women's rates of victimization were highest in urban areas, where their rates of victimization exceeded those of males for all types of personal victimization with the exception of robbery.

- Rural women reported a total victimization rate only slightly higher than that of rural men.

- Married men and women had the same total victimization rates (85 per 1000). In contrast, the rate for single women was 24 percent higher than the rate for single men, and the rate for separated and divorced women was double the rate for separated and divorced men.

- For all types of household victimizations, rates for urban households were higher for rural households.

- Household victimization rates rose with household income. Households with incomes of $60 000 or more had victimization rates 65 percent higher than those of households with incomes of less than $15 000.

Victimizations Not Reported to the Police

Of great interest to many who study crime are the reasons why victims do not report crimes to the police. Why do victims not report a crime to the police? Table 4.1 indicates that, in most cases, victims did not report crimes for reasons related to the perceived usefulness of reporting (Gartner

FIGURE 4.14

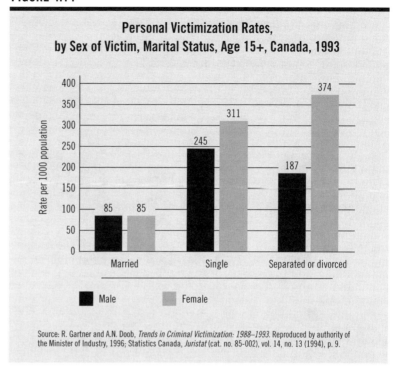

Personal Victimization Rates, by Sex of Victim, Marital Status, Age 15+, Canada, 1993

Source: R. Gartner and A.N. Doob, *Trends in Criminal Victimization: 1988–1993*. Reproduced by authority of the Minister of Industry, 1996; Statistics Canada, *Juristat* (cat. no. 85-002), vol. 14, no. 13 (1994), p. 9.

FIGURE 4.15

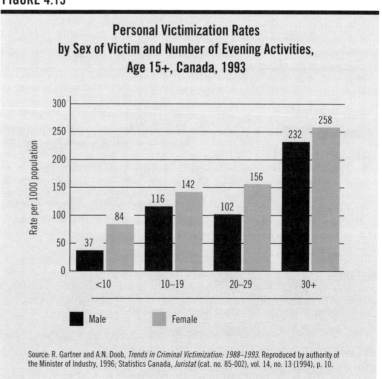

Personal Victimization Rates by Sex of Victim and Number of Evening Activities, Age 15+, Canada, 1993

Source: R. Gartner and A.N. Doob, *Trends in Criminal Victimization: 1988–1993*. Reproduced by authority of the Minister of Industry, 1996; Statistics Canada, *Juristat* (cat. no. 85-002), vol. 14, no. 13 (1994), p. 10.

FIGURE 4.16

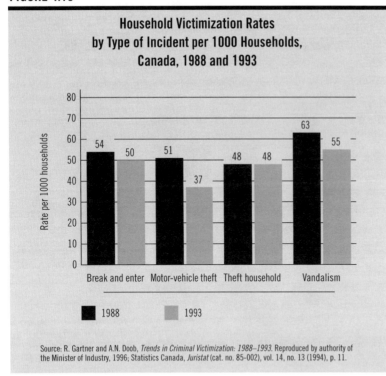

Household Victimization Rates by Type of Incident per 1000 Households, Canada, 1988 and 1993

Source: R. Gartner and A.N. Doob, *Trends in Criminal Victimization: 1988–1993*. Reproduced by authority of the Minister of Industry, 1996; Statistics Canada, *Juristat* (cat. no. 85-002), vol. 14, no. 13 (1994), p. 11.

and Doob 1994). Most victims who didn't report the incident to the police viewed the incident as best dealt with outside of the criminal justice system. That the crime was thought too minor to report or that victims thought the police could do nothing were other important reasons. In about 30 percent of sexual assaults and 20 percent of assaults, a significant reason for not reporting was fear of revenge.

Kong (1994) found that most victims who reported criminal offences to the police resided in an urban area. Forty percent of the total urban incidents were reported to the police as compared to 34 percent of rural incidents. The largest difference was found in

TABLE 4.1

Victimizations Not Reported to the Police by Reason for Not Reporting, by Type of Incident, age 15+, Canada, 1993

	Reason for not reporting to police (%)[1]								
Incident Type	Dealt with another way	Too minor	Fear of revenge	Insurance wouldn't cover	Police couldn't do anything	Police wouldn't help	Didn't want to get involved with police	Nothing taken	Personal matter
Theft personal property – attempt	43	54	—	26	47	21	34	—	32
Sexual assault	65	30	29	—	28	20	50	21	67
Robbery	70	—	—	—	—	—	—	—	—
Assault	64	48	19	7	27	13	47	22	49
Break & enter – attempt	46	48	—	—	42	—	—	36	—
Motor vehicle theft – attempt	33	65	—	—	52	—	—	—	—
Theft household property	36	58	—	—	38	—	27	—	29
Vandalism	45	60	—	—	47	—	37	20	33

[1]Proportions do not add to 100 because these are separate variables.

Source: R. Gartner and A.N. Doob, *Trends in Criminal Victimization: 1988–1993*. Reproduced by authority of the Minister of Industry, 1996; Statistics Canada, *Juristat* (cat. no. 85-002), vol. 14, no. 13 (1994), p. 13.

violent crime victimization: 30 percent of violent crimes against urban residents were reported to the police but only 20 percent of violent incidents against rural residents. According to Kong (1994:11) this difference may be the result of

> greater accessibility and visibility of police in urban areas, the greater rate of stranger violence in urban areas, and the higher percentage of incidents against rural residents that involve perpetrators who are known to the victims.

In contrast, incidents of household victimization were more likely to be reported to the police, and they were reported at similar rates by urban and rural residents.

LaPrairie (1994), in her study of aboriginals in four Canadian inner cities, found that aboriginals expressed similar reasons for not reporting crimes to the police: they didn't think the offence serious enough, they didn't want to "rat," they wanted to "settle [their] own scores," and they feared retribution. One 46-year-old male told researchers, "If you report someone to the police you are called a 'rat' and could end up dead. If I report I'll get it worse. You know what a rat is, eh? I might have ended up in the river" (LaPrairie 1994:35).

Victimization studies have certain limitations, and Sparks (1981) identified two of them:

1. Underreporting to interviewers. While victimization surveys always reveal more crime than the UCR does, they also underreport the crime rate. This is because many crimes are forgotten by victims because those crimes seem insignificant or simply because people can't remember all the crimes committed against them during the previous 12 months.

2. Response bias. Critics of victimization surveys argue that the rate of underreporting is distributed unevenly in society. On the basis of race, whites are more likely than blacks to report having been victimized. In terms of education, college graduates

FIGURE 4.17

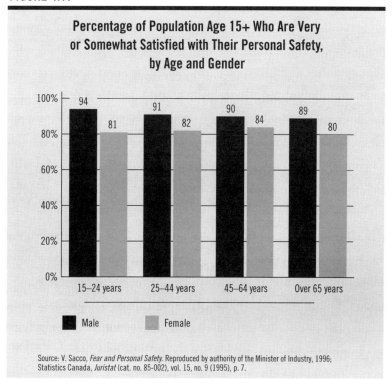

Source: V. Sacco, *Fear and Personal Safety*. Reproduced by authority of the Minister of Industry, 1996; Statistics Canada, *Juristat* (cat. no. 85-002), vol. 15, no. 9 (1995), p. 7.

FIGURE 4.18

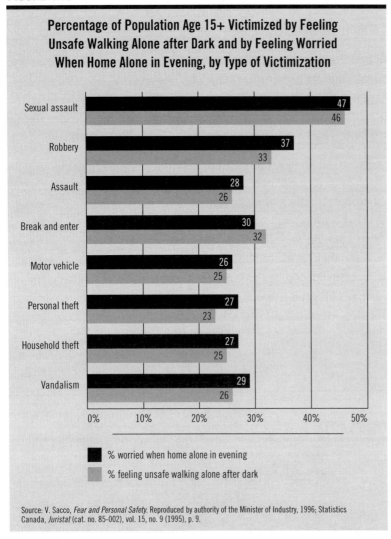

Percentage of Population Age 15+ Victimized by Feeling Unsafe Walking Alone after Dark and by Feeling Worried When Home Alone in Evening, by Type of Victimization

■ % worried when home alone in evening
▨ % feeling unsafe walking alone after dark

Source: V. Sacco, *Fear and Personal Safety*. Reproduced by authority of the Minister of Industry, 1996; Statistics Canada, *Juristat* (cat. no. 85-002), vol. 15, no. 9 (1995), p. 9.

are more likely to report their victimization than those with less education (Beirne and Messerschmidt 1991).

Fear of Crime

According to Sacco (1995:3), fear is defined "as a perception or an attitude rather than as an emotional reaction to imminent danger." Respondents in the 1993 GSS were asked questions about the situations in which they anticipate fear. Researchers found that fear of crime can be a significant factor for many people.

The GSS asked Canadians how safe they felt or would feel if they were walking alone after dark. Twenty-seven percent of Canadians felt "somewhat or very unsafe," while 32 percent reported feeling "very safe" and 12 percent felt "very unsafe." Sacco (1995) found that the fear of crime is a greater problem for women than for men, in all age groups.

As Figure 4.17 indicates, little variation exists between men and women in any of the age categories, although women are less likely than men to say they are very or somewhat satisfied with their personal safety. In addition, individuals who have been recently victimized—especially those who were victims of sexual assault, robbery, or, to a lesser extent, break and enter—are more likely to feel somewhat unsafe when walking alone after dark and worried when they are home alone in the evening (see Figure 4.18).

Summary

Since the 1960s, the traditional mechanism for collecting information about crime in Canada has been the Uniform Crime Reports. This information is based on crimes reported to the police forces across Canada and then tabulated and summarized by the federal government. During the late 1980s, this reporting system was revised to include incident-based data, such as information on the victims, the accused, as well as the circumstances of the incident.

Critics have pointed out a number of limitations in the Uniform Crime Reports. Among them are the fact that many victims don't report crimes to the police and the fact that the police include only the most serious offence in a criminal incident involving numerous criminal actions. Questions have also been raised about the accuracy of police recording practices and how police "clear," or solve, many crimes. As a result of these criticisms, the federal government started to collect crime data from victims. During the past 15 years, the federal government has discovered that many violent crimes are committed that victims don't report to the police. Despite these findings, the police are much more likely to solve violent crimes than they are to solve property crimes. The police are much more likely to solve a murder or sexual assault than they are to solve a motor vehicle theft.

In addition, crimes are placed into one of three categories: violent, property, and "other." In 1994, violent crimes declined by 3 percent, the largest annual decrease in over 30 years. Every type of violent crime decreased in 1994, from 10 percent (sexual assaults and other sexual offences) to assaults (2 percent). Crimes against property are also declining. The 1993 data indicate that all types of property crime are decreasing, with the exception of motor vehicle theft and possession of stolen goods.

Discussion Questions

1. Why did government officials revise the Uniform Crime Reports?
2. What are the three categories into which all crimes in Canada are placed? Do you think the government should develop new categories, such as a sexual offence category or a white-collar crime category? Why or why not?
3. Why is the clearance rate for aggravated assault lower than the clearance rate for first-degree murder?
4. Why is sexual assault one of the most underreported violent crimes?
5. What are the four categories of murder?
6. Why would a police force try to manipulate the number of crimes reported to the various categories?
7. Discuss the differences between the Uniform Crime Reports and victimization surveys.
8. What are the traditional criticisms of the Uniform Crime Reports system?

9. Why is it important to study the fear of crime? Should statistics on the fear of crime be incorporated into official year-end measures of crime as are statistics in the Uniform Crime Reports?

Suggested Readings

Gartner R., and A.N. Doob. *Trends in Criminal Victimization: 1988–1993.* Ottawa: Juristat, 1994.

Hendrick, D. *Canadian Crime Statistics, 1994.* Ottawa: Juristat, 1995.

Sacco, V.F. *Fear and Personal Safety.* Ottawa: Juristat, 1995.

Silverman, R.A., J.J. Teevan, and V.F. Sacco, eds. *Crime in Canadian Society*, 4th ed. Markham, Ont.: Butterworths, 1991.

Solicitor General of Canada. *Victims of Crime*, Canadian Urban Victimization Survey, Bulletin 1. Ottawa: Solicitor General of Canada, 1983.

CHAPTER 5

Police Operations

This chapter starts with a description of the types of police agencies in Canada as they currently exist: municipal, provincial, and federal. This is followed by an overview of the professional model of policing, which was the dominant model of policing from the 1930s to the 1970s.

The basic types of police operations—patrols and criminal investigation—are then reviewed, with particular attention to the various forms of police patrols. Much effort has gone into determining the most effective approach to police patrol over the past 25 years. While criminal investigations have not received as much attention as patrols, the work of detectives is nonetheless important, because detectives are often involved with the most serious crimes. The findings of influential research projects are described as they relate to police patrol and criminal investigations. Later in

CHAPTER OBJECTIVES

- describe the three types of police agencies

- understand the two measures used to estimate the appropriate size of police forces

- understand the traditional organizational structure of the police force

- describe the preventive model of police patrol and new types of police patrols

- identify the similarities and differences between problem-oriented and community-based policing

The Metropolitan Toronto Police Association, which represents the city's 5100 officers, posted this ad in 1995 in response to news that staffing levels had fallen to their lowest levels since the early 1970s. (Photo: Fred Lum/*The Globe and Mail*)

this chapter emerging trends in policing are discussed—problem-oriented policing, community policing, and aboriginal police forces in particular.

One of the most significant components of community policing is the foot patrol officer. A foot patrol officer is a police officer who walks a beat and, as a result, meets the people who live and work in the area. Though public attitudes and perceptions of foot patrol officers are almost always positive, people are sometimes not clear about what foot patrols do and how these officers feel about their work.

In Edmonton, an extensive study of the Edmonton Neighbourhood Foot Patrol included in-depth discussions with the foot patrol officers. The officers reported that foot patrol was much like housekeeping. They have daily routines, including meeting people on the street, checking businesses, and talking to new residents. This enables them to keep tabs on what is happening in their neighbourhood, as the officers can find out who has left the area, who has gone to the hospital, whose house was recently broken into and who just installed a burglar alarm, and which renters have numerous loud parties that lead to noise complaints. Besides obtaining all this information, the foot patrol officers are constantly following up on what happened when they were off duty.

Another housekeeping activity of foot patrol officers is to fill SIRs or Street Information Reports. These reports are filed when an officer stops a person he or she doesn't know and is suspicious about. The person is then questioned and the officer then radios this information to the police communication centre to find out if there is an outstanding warrant for arrest. This "kind of situation, however good-naturedly it is carried out, is a warning to a stranger in the area that a beat cop is on the lookout" (Koller 1990:9).

What sort of experiences do police officers gain as a result of foot patrol? Some officers learn the language spoken by the residents in their beat area, while others participate in fund-raisers, cultural ceremonies, and delivering neighbourhood flyers to some of the local inhabitants. The result of these and other activities leads foot patrol officers to develop attachments to their beats—so much so that many develop a feeling of being "at home." This feeling usually comes from a feeling of trust that develops over time, the result of community members and the police seeing each other as friends. As one foot patrol officer commented, the relationship is one that is based on "person to person, not public to police officer" (Koller 1990:14). This is a marked difference between officers who patrol in vehicles, many of whom "don't like dealing with mistakes."

What are the benefits of this relationship? Changes in the attitudes of the people toward police parallel changes in police attitudes toward citizens. One police officer commented that, after six years on the job, he had a negative attitude toward aboriginals, but when he became a foot patrol officer in an area where there were many aboriginal residents, his attitude changed. Now he has many close friends in the community and his recent experience has led him to an awareness of cultural issues. Other officers, too, found themselves changing in the way they approached the job. Another officer says he used to be aggressive on the job but is now willing to listen more. Thus, foot patrol officers become familiar with, as well as tolerant and understanding of, the residents in their area. This understanding becomes an advantage, not only in day-to-day policing but also in potentially violent situations. For example, foot patrol officers don't feel as threatened in domestic-violence incidents because they usually know both of the individuals involved. As a result, a strong bond is created between the community and the police officer.

The Distribution of the Police in Canada

In 1994, there was a total of 74 902 police personnel in Canada. Of these, 55 855 (or 75 percent) were sworn police officers and the remaining 25 percent were civilian employees. This total represents a reduction of 1036 police officers (or 2 percent) from 1993, the largest annual decrease in police personnel in over 30 years. Since 1962, there have been only four other years when the strength of police departments across Canada declined. In 1978, the number of police officers declined by a total of 59 (a reduction of 0.1 percent), while during the three-year period between 1981 and 1984 the number of police declined by 553, or 1.1 percent. The number of civilian employees working for police agencies is also declining in Canada. That number has declined by 2.9 percent over the past two years, from 19 614 in 1992 to 19 037 in 1994 (Juristat 1996).

In Canada there are three different jurisdictional levels of policing—municipal, provincial, and federal. In 1994, 34 884 (or 62.4 percent) of all police officers in Canada were involved with municipal police agencies. There were 364 "independent" municipal police forces, employing 31 227 police officers, or 90 percent of all municipal police officers in Canada. There were also 201 RCMP municipal contract forces and 13 Ontario Provincial Police municipal contract police forces, which together employed 3430 and 227 police officers, respectively.

Provincial police agencies employed 14 368 police officers, or 25.6 percent of all police personnel in Canada. Provincial police forces enforce the Criminal Code and provincial statutes within areas of a province not serviced by a municipal police force. The three provincial police forces are located in Ontario (the Ontario Provincial Police), Quebec (the Sûreté du Québec), and Newfoundland (where the Royal Newfoundland Constabulatory provides policing services to the three largest municipalities). For the other seven provinces and both territories, provincial policing is provided by the RCMP under contract. The provinces are billed 70 percent of the total contract costs by the RCMP.

The RCMP has complete responsibility in all provinces and territories for enforcing federal statutes, executive orders, security for dignitaries, and airport security. A total of 5180 RCMP officers (or 9.3 percent of all police officers in Canada) were involved in federal policing in 1994. Other responsibilities of the RCMP include forensic laboratory services, the operation of CPIC (an automated national computer system available to all police forces), and telecommunications services for data and radio transmissions to ensure all detachments receive current information. There were 1474 RCMP administrative and law enforcement officers in 1994, accounting for 2.6 percent of all police officers (Juristat 1996).

The largest municipal police agency in 1994 was the Metropolitan Toronto Police Force, with 5311 police officers, or 9.5 percent of all police officers in Canada. The Montreal Urban Community Police Force was the next largest municipal police force, with 4337 (or 7.7 percent) of all police officers. The only other municipal police forces with over 1000 police personnel in 1994 were those in Calgary (1150 officers), Vancouver and Edmonton (both with 1089 officers), the Peel Region in Ontario (1084 officers), and Winnipeg (1078). The largest detachment of the RCMP that provided municipal police services was located in Surrey, B.C., with 309 officers.

There is no single model for determining the appropriate size of a police force or its workload. One key issue is the problem of determining the appropriate population base. Census figures are generally used, but every large city in Canada experiences a substantial influx of persons on most days as people who live outside the city limits drive in for work or pleasure. The actual size of police agencies across Canada can vary significantly, regardless of the size of the community or region it serves. For example, Calgary employs over 1000 police officers to serve a population of 744 000 residents (a population–police ratio of 648:1), while the Surrey, B.C., RCMP has 309 officers to police a city with a population of 278 100 (a population–police ratio of 900:1).

Two measures are generally used to establish the appropriate size of a police force, but they are used mainly to analyze and identify trends in the population. The most common measure used is the population-to-police-officer ratio, which is used to compare the changes in the number of police officers to the changes in the Canadian population (Young 1995). Between 1962 and 1994, the number of sworn police officers increased by 114 percent, while the Canadian population increased by approximately 83 percent. In 1994, the ratio of population to police officer was 523.5:1. From 1962, when the ratio was 711:1, to 1975 the ratio changed until it reached 486:1. The ratio then gradually reversed its trend and reached 515:1 in 1985, only to reverse again, to reach 495:1 in 1991. Since then the ratio has demonstrated yet another reversal to reach its current state, a state similar to the one of 1972 (see Figure 5.1).

By province/territory, the ratios that reflected the lowest

FIGURE 5.1

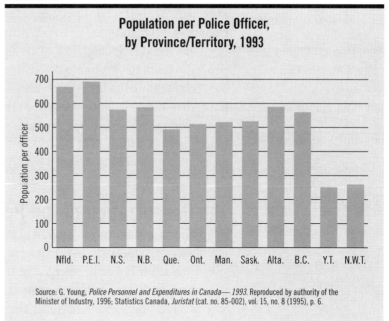

Source: G. Young, *Police Personnel and Expenditures in Canada— 1993*. Reproduced by authority of the Minister of Industry, 1996; Statistics Canada, *Juristat* (cat. no. 85-002), vol. 15, no. 8 (1995), p. 6.

FIGURE 5.2

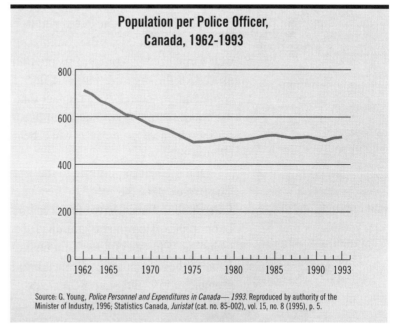

Source: G. Young, *Police Personnel and Expenditures in Canada— 1993*. Reproduced by authority of the Minister of Industry, 1996; Statistics Canada, *Juristat* (cat. no. 85-002), vol. 15, no. 8 (1995), p. 5.

number of police officers per population in 1994 were those in the Yukon, with 266 population to one police officer, and the Northwest Territories, with a ratio of 275:1. At the opposite end of the spectrum were Prince Edward Island (697:1) and Newfoundland (662:1). The cities and regions with a population over 100 000 in 1994 with the greatest population per police officer (see Figure 5.2) were Richmond, B.C. (937:1), Surrey, B.C. (900:1), Halton Regional

Police Force, Ontario (895:1), Nepean, Ontario (855:1), and York Regional Police Force (814:1). The five cities at the other extreme were Montreal (410:1), Halifax (431:1), Toronto (434:1), Vancouver (463:1), and Windsor (487:1).

The second technique used to evaluate the appropriateness of police-force size is to compare the number of Criminal Code incidents (excluding traffic incidents) reported to the police with the number of police officers in the police force that handles those incidents. This ratio is used as an indicator of police workload (Young 1995). The number of Criminal Code incidents per police officer increased from 20 in 1962 to 51.1 in 1991, but since 1991 the number of incidents per officer has declined by 7.5 percent, to 47.1 in 1994.

The Organization of the Police

Police forces are typically organized in bureaucracies. In order to provide polic-ing services as efficiently as possible, an "ideal" model, known as the profes-sional model of policing, emerged in the 1930s and remained the dominant style of policing for the next four decades. This model was characterized by four organizational characteristics. The first was a hierarchical differentiation of the rank structure, with the police chief holding the highest rank and proba-tionary constables the lowest. The second characteristic was functional differ-entiation, where job specializations, such as patrol, homicide investigation, traffic, and robbery, were developed to better deal with the crime problem. The third characteristic was the routinization of procedures and practices, which were formalized in written form and found in policy manuals that dealt with all aspects of the organization. The final characteristic was the centralization of command, which refers to the fact that "ultimate authority rests at the top of the police hierarchy, and decision making within the hierarchy is accountable up the chain of command, while being protected from outside influences" (Reiss 1992:68–72).

Of particular importance to the professional model are specialist job roles. These roles allow the police to operate in a more efficient and effective manner. Large police forces have, in recent decades, developed job specializations. Large police departments are divided into many different operational areas, including field operations, administration, and crime and support services. Each of these components is then broken down into different specialities. For example, crime and support services can be divided into dozens of different units, including homicide, robbery, and stolen-automobile units.

In recent years, however, there have been increasing complaints that this bureaucratic form of organization is unsuited to today's social needs. One complaint is that citizens have a problem determining exactly who is respon-sible for a specific policy or operation. In addition, the number and complexity of police divisions and the lack of a clear relationship among them can lead to internal problems. For example, one division may inadvertently implement a program that overlaps with the activities of another. This overlap illustrates the problem with a traditional "top-down" approach to organization, in which administrators tell supervisors what to do, then supervisors tell divisional commanders what to do, and they in turn tell police officers what to do, then officers tell citizens what to do. The problem with this approach is that there isn't enough information flowing from the bottom to the top, especially when it comes to the sentiments of the public (Kelling and Moore 1988).

The Patrol Function

Police patrol is considered to be the "backbone" of policing, since all new police personnel are expected to spend the first years of their careers on patrol. Police patrols were introduced by Sir Robert Peel in London, England, in 1829. Peel believed the presence of the police would prevent crime, and this idea became a basic assumption concerning the role and function of patrol officers.

The importance of police patrol cannot be underestimated. It continues to be the essential component of police agencies, since patrol officers are the police who are visible to the public. The police patrol is designed to achieve a number of purposes, notably the maintenance of a police presence in the community, a quick response to emergencies, and the detection of crime (Langworthy and Travis 1994). Patrol officers fill an important public role, since they are so visible in the community. And because patrol officers are mobile and therefore located throughout a community, they are usually able to respond quickly to emergencies. Finally, officers on patrol are expected to observe what is going on in the community and prevent potential crime.

Patrol also provides a socializing function for all police officers. Jerome Skolnick, a noted American criminologist and specialist in the area of police studies, noted the importance of this socializing function 30 years ago. According to Skolnick (1966:43–44), a police officer's "working personality is most highly developed in his constabulatory role," and it is this role that forms "the common background" of all future police experiences.

Patrol officers are the most visible component of the police, and perhaps of the whole criminal justice system. When criminal incidents occur, patrol officers are usually first to arrive and deal with the incident. They are typically seen in marked patrol vehicles, but they also patrol on foot, on bicycles, and on horses. They perform their duties within a designated area, or beat, and rarely leave unless in pursuit of a suspect or to back up other patrol officers. Police beats are patrolled 24 hours a day, by different shifts of officers.

Activities of Patrol Officers

The specific activities of patrol officers are hard to identify because this position is, in many ways, a generalist role—i.e., a patrol officer performs a multitude of roles while on the job. Cordner and Hale (1992) identified the major roles of a patrol officer:

Field Practice 5.1
Patrols

Example 1. Mall Security

Over 100 youths met in a mall parking lot to watch a fight between two teenage males. Due to the extreme cold, a decision was made to have the fight in the mall. Once the group entered the mall, store owners rushed to close their shops, although none of the teenagers entered any shop. Fearful of a swarming incident, the store owners called the police. Police were informed that "hundreds" of youths were swarming and looting stores. All available patrol units were pulled from the city and sent to the mall. Twelve patrol vehicles showed up, but the police found no thefts, no damages, no fight—just a large group of youths in the centre court. In addition to the 12 patrol units, two K-9 units were sent, as well as four detectives and two supervisors. While this incident was going on, only three patrol units were left to police the remaining areas of the city for almost two hours.

Example 2. Random Patrol

Two police patrol officers developed their own procedure to check certain locations on their beat where a large number of criminal incidents had taken place during the previous six months. The essence of their procedure was to visit these designated locations randomly, i.e., at unpredictable times. They visited each location at least 15 times during the eight-hour shift, sometimes as often as 25 times. When not responding to calls for assistance, the patrol officers varied their location checks, sometimes doubling back to a location they had checked just minutes before. The result of their efforts: a reduction in the number of crimes and the apprehension of seven individuals, all charged with break and enters.

Example 3. Citizen Patrol

Due to the ever-decreasing number of police patrolling the streets, some citizens decided to create their own patrol to assist police. Over 40 volunteers, mostly retirees, move about in pairs on a four-hour shift at least twice a month. The volunteers organized a number of fund-raisers to buy radios to allow them to contact police if they saw anything suspicious. Patrol hours are from 10 P.M. and 6 A.M., seven nights a week. After the first year of the citizens' operation, the police reported a 47-percent reduction in break and enters and twice the number of volunteers who contacted the police about assaults.

- to deter criminals through a visible police presence
- to maintain order
- to respond to citizens' calls for service as quickly as possible
- to assist those in need
- to take part in crowd control
- to obtain statements from crime victims and witnesses
- to arrest individuals and transport them to a police facility for interrogation

Field Practice 5.2

Proactive Policing

Example 1. A 'John' Sting

In an attempt to crack down on prostitution, female vice-division police officers dressed like hookers and situated themselves in an area frequented by prostitutes. Over two nights they arrested 15 men, ranging in age from 25 to 56, all of whom approached the undercover officers. All 15 men were released on appearance notices and were to be charged with communicating for the purpose of prostitution.

Police officer Lisabet Atkinson in uniform, left, and in her undercover outfit when posing as a prostitute in Toronto's Parkdale neighbourhood, where the sex-and-heroin trade flourishes. (Photos: Randy Velocci/*The Globe and Mail*)

Example 2. Taking the Bite Out of Crime

To combat a 56-percent increase in robberies on city streets, a deputy police chief decided to "take a bite out of crime" by having some of her officers pose as potential victims for street muggers. Four officers wandered around a section of the downtown core, feigning intoxication to attract potential muggers. Each officer carried a case of 24 beer. Once robbed, each officer gave a preassigned signal to backup officers, which led to an immediate arrest in each case. After one month of operation, 15 police officers had been mugged and 19 individuals had been arrested and charged. Although the program was ongoing, the deputy chief decided to publicize it in the hope that it would deter would-be muggers and make the streets safer.

Field Practice 5.3

Aggressive Policing

Example 1

Residents near a park placed numerous complaints about bush parties held in that park. These parties were attended mostly by youths, and involved drinking, drugs, and often serious acts of vandalism of park and private property. Warning signs about this type of behaviour were ignored, and so were signs that announced the park's daily closing time. In order to deal with the increasing number of complaints, police officials decided to order their officers to stop and question all young people they encountered on their numerous patrols through the park. In addition, a mandatory arrest policy was instituted, with every youth arrested who was found in the park after closing.

Example 2

Police officers received hundreds of calls from irate citizens about the new renters in a house on their street. These renters were operating a booze can—an after-hours club where people go after the legitimate bars had closed. In addition to the serving of alcohol without a licence, the club was subject to complaints about noise, prostitution, drugs, vandalism, and hit-and-run traffic accidents. Since these activities were occurring between 2 A.M. and 6 A.M., when police patrols were infrequent, many of the complaints went unheeded by police. In addition, the residents did not know who the landlord was, only that he lived in another part of the city and never appeared at his rented house. One police officer then decided to leave the landlord's phone number lying on her desk, as though inadvertently, for a few residents to see while the officer was called away from her desk. Phone calls to the landlord's office during the day were not returned, but the landlord took action against the tenants after irate neighbours phoned him during the early hours of the morning to let him listen to the noise over the telephone.

Example 3

Youth crime was increasing—especially violent crime. Most of this violent crime was taking place in three areas of the city, so police officials decided to create a tactical unit that comprised 50 police officers. These officers then moved into a specific area and "swept" it. That is, all youths on the street were stopped, questioned, and sometimes searched for weapons and drugs. In addition, the hangouts of youths were targeted and searched, with the result that police usually left behind a ransacked building. It was a highly successful tactic. In the first month of its operation, over 100 knives and guns were confiscated, as well as various drugs, and over 300 items reported stolen were retrieved from the hangouts.

Sometimes patrol officers receive a detailed assignment, such as traffic patrol or security checks at business establishments. Their typical role, however, is that of "routine observation," in which officers drive around a particular beat and respond to citizens' calls for service. Most of the activities of patrol officers are unrelated to crime. It has been estimated that at least 80 percent of all calls for police assistance involve noncrime incidents. This means that officers on patrol commonly deal with issues such as neighbourhood disputes, animal control, noise complaints, and locating lost children.

Incident-Driven Patrol

The police patrol vehicle and two-way communications revolutionized police departments in the 1930s. New communications technology enabled the police patrols to be in constant contact with headquarters, and the motor vehicle allowed them to respond to criminal incidents almost immediately. This led to a type of policing known as incident-driven policing, where the primary role of the police is to respond to citizens' calls for help. Since incident-driven policing was viewed as the most efficient manner in which to organize patrols, police administrators moved all patrol officers into motor vehicles.

Incident-driven policing is also referred to as reactive policing. When the police receive an emergency call a patrol officer is immediately dispatched to the scene of a crime. Patrol officers are also involved with proactive policing. This means that the police initiate their own crime control activities. Requesting information from citizens or stopping and questioning a citizen who looks like a suspect are examples of this approach to policing. When police departments decide to crack down on the street drug trade or street prostitution, or to set up fencing operations, they are engaged in proactive policing.

Most studies in the United States (e.g., Reiss 1967; Sykes and Brent 1983) have reported that at least 80 percent of patrol work is reactive. However, in his study of a regional police force in southern Ontario, Ericson (1982) discovered that patrol officers he was observing were involved much more in proactive policing than the other studies suggested. In fact, his observations revealed a different perspective on the nature of work experienced by patrol officers' work. In the 1323 contacts between patrol officers and citizens, 52.6 percent were the result of reactive mobilization, while the remaining 47.4 percent were proactive in nature.

Ericson did find differences between proactive and reactive policing, particularly as they related to the location of occurrence. Two-thirds of the proactive activities of patrol officers took place in public areas. Proactive activities usually involved either routine stops of citizens who may have violated the Highway Traffic Act or stops of citizens suspected of driving-related criminal violation (e.g., impaired driving). The remainder of the proactive activities of the police involved patrolling parks, fast-food establishments, and shopping malls in the hope of discovering youths violating liquor and drug laws.

In contrast, Ericson found reactive-style policing involved police responding to a different type of location—specifically, private residences. Ninety-five percent of reactive policing resulted from citizen calls to the police dispatch centre, while the other 5 percent resulted from citizens gaining the attention of police while they were patrolling. Property and interpersonal disputes, calls about possible criminal activity, and automobile-related matters accounted for the vast majority of reactive calls in Ericson's study.

Proactive and reactive policing styles are thought to be separate functions of the police, but they may be used in conjunction with each other. For example, a city may be experiencing an increasing number of break and enters. When a citizen calls the police after realizing that his or her residence has been broken into, the police respond by investigating the incident. At the same time, the police could respond proactively by analyzing all such recent incidents in the hope that a pattern emerges. If a pattern is detected, the police may decide to identify potential burglary sites and stake them out.

Changing Patrol Strategy

Until the late 1960s police patrol in most major North American communities involved two officers patrolling a beat in a marked cruiser. They would randomly patrol their beat and they responded with service to citizen calls relayed to them by a dispatcher. This approach is known as preventive patrol and is based on two assumptions: first, that highly visible patrol vehicles deterred crime and, second, that the presence of patrol vehicles makes citizens feel safer. In the late 1960s, however, a number of police agencies in the United States began to raise questions about the effectiveness of this style of patrol. Some of the findings of major research efforts concerning the success of different types of police patrol—as well as different types of nontraditional patrol that have emerged over the past few decades—are presented below.

Kansas City Preventive Patrol Experiment

The Kansas City Preventive Patrol Experiment is considered by many to be the most influential study on motor vehicle patrols (Kelling et al. 1974). The results of this study led to a substantial revision of traditional police patrol practices. At the time, Kansas City was using preventive patrols throughout the city. The idea behind this experiment was developed by police officers themselves. The police chief had issued a directive that all officers in the five patrol divisions discuss the major crime issues confronting them as well as the public, and develop a study that might lead to an improvement in police services and a reduction in crime. The officers in one patrol division raised questions about the effectiveness of preventive patrols, so the police conducted an experiment to determine the effect of different types of patrol on crime rates and citizens' fear of crime and feelings of safety.

The Study Design

One police division was restructured and divided into 15 patrol beats, which were then divided into three different categories of five beats each. The boundaries of each of the 15 beats were drawn up in order to be as similar as possible to all other beats on the basis of crime rates, selected population characteristics such as the racial composition and length of residence of the citizens, and calls for service. Three different types of patrol were instituted: reactive, proactive, and control (i.e., preventive patrol). The reactive beats involved no preventive patrol activity whatsoever. Patrol officers who worked reactive patrol beats entered their beat only to respond to calls for assistance. When not responding to calls, the patrol officers patrolled neighbouring proactive police beats. Proactive beats were assigned two to three times the number of police patrol units through the addition of patrol vehicles from the reactive beats. Proactive patrols were highly visible and the officers patrolled in an aggressive style, meaning that they stopped vehicles and citizens if they felt there was sufficient reason to do so. The control beats maintained the normal level of patrols that were operational at that time—one car per beat.

Results of the Study

Before the study started, most observers felt proactive patrols would be the most successful in reducing crime and improving citizens' feelings of safety, because of the greater number of patrol vehicles and the more aggressive patrol approach. But the results, after one year of this experiment, did not support this idea. In fact, the results revealed that the different types of patrol did not affect (1) crime rates (as measured by the number of burglaries, motor vehicle thefts, thefts including motor vehicle accessories, robberies, and vandalism, all considered to be highly deterrable crimes), (2) citizens' attitudes toward police services, (3) citizens' fear of crime, or (4) rates of reported crimes. These findings were both revealing and controversial.

They were revealing because police departments had always considered routine preventive patrol to be the most effective approach to patrolling. Yet the results of this study concluded that preventive patrol was no more effective than reactive patrol, and adding more patrol units (as in the case of proactive units) does not automatically lead to a reduction of crime rates or citizens' fear of crime. As Klockars and Mastrofski (1991:131) stated, this experiment led to the conclusion that it "makes about as much sense to have police patrol routinely in cars to fight crime as it does to have firemen patrol routinely in firetrucks to fight fire."

Policy Recommendations

This study had a tremendous impact on the traditional assumptions held about preventive patrol. While it is necessary to have police patrols, the presence of more patrol officers didn't lower the crime rates. This led to the *mayonnaise theory of police patrol*, which states that the quantity of police patrols is similar to the amount of mayonnaise required to make a sandwich. Just as a small amount of mayonnaise goes a long way to make a good sandwich, though personal tastes may vary, so too does a little police patrol go a long way. If an area has no patrol, starting one there will reduce the crime rate, but adding more patrols to an area that already has some appears to have little, if any, impact on crime.

According to Walker (1994), there are several reasons why increasing police patrols has so limited an impact on crime. First, patrol officers are so spread out across a beat that the visibility of a patrol vehicle may be a chance encounter rather than a daily occurrence. Second, many crimes are not deterrable by police patrols. Crimes that occur in residences, such as murders, sexual assaults, and child abuse, are not going to stop because more police are patrolling the streets. And third, some people are not deterred by increasing numbers of police. Robbers, for example, will change their approach to committing an offence rather than stop their criminal behaviour altogether (Desroches 1995).

Impact of the Study

The findings were controversial because some police executives and observers interpreted the results as proof that preventive patrol has no effect on crime. What the study revealed was that additional police patrols do not lower the crime rate. This study gave police administrators evidence that changing the number of patrols doesn't deter crime or raise the level of satisfaction felt by the public for police services. Yet police patrols, whether in the form of reactive, proactive, or preventive, are needed no matter which style of policing is required. Police leaders used this study to start other types of patrols in the hope that those others have a greater impact than preventive patrol.

Directed Patrol

Directed patrol is the type in which officers spend some of their time in certain locations and watch for specific crimes. This type of patrol is usually a result of crime analysis information. Results of directed patrols indicate that the police can reduce the target crime, although it is not known if directed patrols actually reduce crime or force it into other areas.

One form of directed patrol is referred to as "hot spots" patrol. This requires an analysis of all incoming calls based on their geographical origin. In the Hot Spots Patrol Experiment conducted in Minneapolis, Minn., the police discovered that over 50 percent of all crime calls came from just 3.3 percent of all addresses and intersections (Sherman et al. 1989). The highest number of calls over a one-year period came from a large discount store, from where 810 calls for police service were recorded. Next was a large department store, which produced 686 calls, and an intersection with a bar and a 24-hour convenience store, which produced 607. In an attempt to control crime in selected hot spots, a marked patrol vehicle parked there when not responding to an emergency call elsewhere. As a result, these areas received increased presence of patrols, always of a proactive nature. After a year, there was a 250-percent reduction in total calls for service in the area under study.

In large part the formation of the Neighbourhood Foot Patrol Program (NFPP) in Edmonton in 1987 was based on an analysis of calls for service. Through an analysis of 153 000 calls for service during 1986, the 21 hottest areas of the city were located. Over 80 percent of the calls in these areas came from repeat addresses. Twenty-one foot patrol officers were then permanently assigned to a beat that encompassed a hot spot. The presence of foot patrol officers was supplemented by 80 motor vehicle patrol officers. One year after the creation of the NFPP, the number of calls per address and the addresses which accounted for at least two calls the year before were examined. A slight reduction in the number of calls to repeat addresses (from 4014 to 3918) was noted, as well as a reduction in the total number of calls (from 21 001 to 19 612) (Koller 1990; Hornick et al. 1993).

The benefits of directed patrol are that more information about crimes and criminals is obtained from local citizens and that citizen awareness of the police is raised, both of which increase the likelihood of offender arrest (Cordner 1981).

Management of Demand Patrol

Another type of police patrol is **management of demand,** or managing the demand for services, which requires the police to categorize demands for services and then match these with different types of police responses. For example, emergency calls are responded to immediately, while nonthreatening incidents are placed on a waiting list and left alone until an officer is free to investigate the complaint.

The first study of this type of patrol was conducted in Wilmington, Del., where the police developed a differential police response to citizens' calls for services. An evaluation study of this program found city residents were very supportive of this type of patrol and that crime did not increase. When calls for service were studied, the bulk of these calls were found to be nonlaw-enforcement related. Many calls for service concerning criminal activity didn't require an immediate response because the alleged perpetrator had already left the scene of the crime. This differential-response approach gained favour because it frees patrol officers from responding to minor public concerns and allows them more time to perform other more important activities (Cahn and Tien 1981). This approach is standard policy for police departments across North America. Calls for service are now routinely screened by dispatchers, categorized, and, if the call is high-priority, patrol officers are sent to the location immediately. In their analysis of calls for service, for example, the Edmonton Police Force discovered "consistently, month after month, . . . only about five percent of all incoming phone calls are high priority in nature" (Braiden 1993:219). In Halifax, only 17 percent of incoming calls were found to require an immediate police response, and many of these were false alarms (Clairmont 1990).

Analysis of calls for service allows police administrators to restructure their patrol activities without diminishing public satisfaction with the police and without affecting adversely the crime rate. It also allows some patrol officers to

Toronto police constable Helio Pereira, left, spot-checks a cyclist to ensure that her bike has the required safety equipment. Pereira says bicycle officers' shorts and bikes are conversation pieces and get people talking. (Photo: Peter Moon/*The Globe and Mail*)

become active in other areas of police operations, such as criminal investigations and crime prevention.

Foot Patrol

Foot patrol, once the mainstay of police forces in the late-19th and early-20th centuries, all but disappeared with the introduction of motor vehicle patrol in the 1930s. However, foot patrols began to reappear in the late 1970s as citizens complained about the lack of contact with patrol officers in motor vehicles. A common feature of foot patrols today is their emphasis on greater interaction with the community and the solving of underlying community problems that may lead to crime and disorder. Most municipal police forces in Canada today have foot patrols, although many forces maintain such patrols only in the downtown core or other densely populated areas.

An experiment involving foot patrol officers in Flint, Mich., became the source of renewed interest across North America (Trojanowicz and Bucqueroux 1990). An evaluation revealed that while foot patrol may reduce crime only slightly, it did occasion a significant reduction in citizens' fear of crime and a positive change in police–citizen relationships. For example, the Flint Neighborhood Foot Patrol Program lowered crime rates by about 9 percent in all categories of crimes with the exceptions of burglary and rob-bery, both of which increased by about 10 percent. Calls for service decreased by over 40 percent and public support for the police increased. After four years, 64 percent of the citizens surveyed indicated they were satisfied by the police, while 68 percent felt safer in their neighbourhood.

Police forces in Canada have implemented a variety of foot patrols. In Toronto, Division 31 police commanders instituted foot patrols in the

Jane–Finch area in 1977 to "defuse escalating tensions between the police and, in particular, members of the ethnic community" (Asbury 1989:165). This area was selected for its long history of tension between police and community, its high population density, and its high rate of serious crime. Foot patrol officers designed and became involved in various "community-building" activities in an attempt to help residents increase community cohesion and gain control of their community. Some residents reported "a 1000-percent" improvement in the community after the introduction of foot patrols and felt much safer.

Another major foot patrol initiative came from the Edmonton Police Force and its Neighbourhood Foot Patrol Program (NFPP). Twenty-one foot patrol areas were selected for foot patrol on the basis of calls for service (see Directed Patrol section, above). The results of this program have been mostly positive. An evaluation of the program discovered that it has worked best in stable middle-class neighbourhoods, but not as well in the inner city (Bayley 1993). A survey of users of police services in these 21 beats revealed that foot patrol was favoured over motor vehicle patrol. In addition, foot patrol officers held a higher degree of satisfaction with their job than did motor vehicle patrol officers.

The evidence to date indicates that if foot patrol is to be successful, it must operate in locations where there is a possibility of frequent interaction with large numbers of community members, such as at shopping centres, in high-density neighbourhoods, and in the downtown core. The size of the foot patrol beat should be small, in some instances covering no more than a few blocks, thereby enabling the police to walk their beat area at least once a day (Trojanowicz and Bucqueroux 1990).

Proactive–Reactive Patrol

While the terms reactive and proactive usually refer to different types of patrolling, some police forces have combined both styles. This style of policing is referred to as the "proactive-reactive split" or split-force patrolling. This style is practised by the Halton Regional Police Force, in southwestern Ontario. It involves a "separation of function and also of structure in the major role played by patrol officers in the community" and was introduced to make better use of existing resources as well as to increase service to the community. This style of policing was designed to give its officers greater responsibility and account-ability. In each patrol area some officers were given the responsibility of performing a proactive and preventive role, which allowed them to work closely on specific projects with community members. Many of these projects were developed by patrol officers themselves, who were given considerable latitude by police administrators. The remainder of the police officers conducted their activities in the traditional, reactive style of policing.

At the core of this style of policing is the concept of "constable-generalist." This concept counters the idea that police forces need to become increasingly specialized. Instead, it supports the idea that a police officer better meets "the needs and the community as a generalist; one who can respond to a wide variety of situations and who has the ability to work proactively." This does not mean police departments are no longer specialized, but that the number of specialists is substantially reduced and placed in a more centralized support function for all patrol areas (Loree 1993).

Criminal Investigations

If patrol officers are unable to apprehend a suspect, they submit their report to a criminal investigator, or detective. Detectives can follow up on information given to them directly by citizens or informants also. Detectives are usually organized under a different division of a police agency than patrol officers. They are organized into various sections that specialize in a particular type of criminal activity, such as vice operations (gambling, homicide, robbery, and prostitution) or support services, such as a polygraph operator. While most detective work is reactive, detectives are involved also with proactive activities, such as vice squads and sting squads. A vice squad may pose a police officer as a prostitute in order to arrest customers, or, in a sting operation, detectives may set up an operation that buys stolen goods and videotape everyone who brings in stolen goods.

As was the case with the effectiveness of preventive patrol, no questions were raised about the effectiveness of detective work until the late 1960s. In 1975, the Rand Corporation, a San Francisco-based research organization, studied criminal investigators across the United States. The results led many to question the traditional assumptions of detective work.

The Study Design

The investigators studied criminal investigators in all U.S. police departments employing more than 150 police officers or serving jurisdictions of more than 100 000 people. They conducted in-depth interviews with detectives in 25 of the locations and observed detectives in another 156 police agencies. The goal of their study was to describe and assess the investigation process, in the hope of identifying the most effective investigation techniques as well as to evaluate the contribution of various technological advances to successful investigation outcomes (Greenwood and Petersilia 1975). Their data were collected from interviews, annual crime reports, criminal investigation files, and internal information collected from police departments. Of prime concern to the researchers was the relationship between the organization of detectives and their clearance rate.

Policy Recommendations

Much like the Kansas City Preventive Patrol Experiment, the researchers found themselves questioning traditional assumptions about the importance and significance of detective work as it was then practised. Significantly, the researchers discovered that the single most important factor in the clearing of

Police investigators were still a long way from making an arrest when the body of student Kristen French was found beside a country road in Burlington, Ont., two weeks after her kidnapping. (Photo: Tibor Kolley/*The Globe and Mail*)

a case (as measured by the identification of the accused) was the information obtained by the patrol officer who originally responded to the complaint. If the patrol officer was unable to identify a suspect, detectives rarely cleared the case. The researchers did find that some detective work did lead to cleared cases, particularly when special task forces were created to deal with a particular type of criminal activity. Detectives spent most of their efforts on cases going to trial, such as interviewing witnesses and ensuring files were in order. As a result, the researchers recommended that patrol officers be given an expanded role for the preliminary investigation of crimes and end the duplication of this work by detectives.

Their second recommendation was that post-arrest investigations be coordinated with prosecutors so more cases would be prosecuted. Another recommendation was that police agencies create guidelines so that cases requiring only routine processing be given to clerks and those that require investigation be handed over to detectives. The final recommendation was that police forces improve their systems for organizing and searching fingerprint files.

EXHIBIT 5.1

Criminal Investigations

Detective work is structured in accordance with different organizational policies. The three studies discussed briefly below highlight different approaches taken by criminal investigators.

Ericson (1981), in his study of detectives in the Greater Toronto Area, found detectives were usually given information about a particular crime from the files forwarded to them by patrol officers. Detectives spent most of their time interviewing victims, complainants, and informants for information in a specific case. It was rare for a detective to arrest a suspect, and many of the suspects they charged were in fact arrested by patrol officers. Ericson also found 50 percent of detectives' time was spent in the office, not including time spent interviewing citizens or suspects at the police station. The most common activity of detectives was sitting at their desk in the office "to type reports, review files, call citizens connected with case investi-

gation, and to hold both formal and informal meetings about a variety of matters relating to investigation priorities and procedures, and office routine." These observations support findings by Greenwood and Petersilia (1975), who concluded that it is "not appropriate to view the investigator's role as that of solving crimes. Investigators do not spend much time on activities that lead to clearances, and most of their work in this connection could be performed by clerical personnel." Detectives do not produce high rates of solved crimes. According to Ericson (1981), collective cooperation and quality—rather than quantity of arrests, charges, and clearance rates—are emphasized by detectives.

Eck (1983; 1992), in his work on detectives investigating robberies in the United States, argued that while detectives solved a significant number of crimes, they did so only after a reasonable amount of investigation in cases they classified as "solvable." Seventy-five percent of robbery cases were dropped after the first day of investiga-

tion, and the average case was investigated no longer than four hours over three days. An essential feature of a cleared case was that the initial investigation was conducted by patrol officers. In those robberies where the suspects' identity was not known immediately after the crime was committed, detectives were able to clear the incident by arrest in less than 10 percent of all cases.

In his study of bank robbers in Canada, Desroches found detectives' expertise lay in their ability to obtain confessions, review cases prior to a court trial, make suspects plead guilty, and gain long sentences. All are important aspects of their job. And detectives accomplished all these things with basic police procedure and hard work; rarely did they try to clear a case by enticing suspects with deals of leniency. Indeed, much effort went toward the arrest and charging of repeat offenders and career criminals, since once they arrest a suspect they "automatically assume that he or she has committed multiple robberies—a valid assumption in most cases" (Desroches 1995:240).

Impact of the Study

The impact of this study did not lead to significant changes in the operations of detectives. Some police agencies developed investigation guideline policies that separated cases most likely to be solved by investigation from those that likely couldn't be solved. This led to the development of a "solvability index" based on the presence or absence of factors related to high clearance rates. Perhaps the most significant result of this study was that more police agencies allowed patrol officers to investigate crimes, in particular robberies and break and enters (Eck 1983). These crimes were usually cleared with four hours of investigation, allowing detectives to handle the more sophisticated cases.

Recent Changes in Policing

Due to concerns about the proper role of the police in contemporary society, police administrators and analysts began to study what was wrong with traditional styles of policing and start to develop and experiment with new types of policing. By the mid-1980s, two decades of research revealed the limits of traditional styles of policing. Police patrols didn't reduce the crime rate, and detectives didn't solve a lot of crimes, and arrests don't necessarily deter criminals.

Field Practice 5.4
Problem-Oriented Policing

Example 1

A lot of crime occurs in places where it is difficult for police officers to conduct surveillance; narrow pathways and dead-ends, for example, are areas that are virtually impossible for police vehicles to patrol. A new patrol technique allows the police to overcome these problems—bicycle patrol, which has turned into a highly effective tool of police patrol. By operating on the principles of speed and silence, bike patrol officers are able to penetrate these areas and surprise criminals. In Toronto, two bike patrol officers negotiated a sharp turn between two buildings and startled two men passing something between them. The officers rode up to the two men and dismounted their bicycles. The two men started running. A constable chased one of them on foot but couldn't catch him. The other constable chased the other man on his bicycle and caught him. The individual arrested had a criminal record and was charged with the possession of hashish. Without their bicycles, the officers would not have been able to get close enough to the drug deal to make an arrest.

Source: P. Moon, "Bike Officers Pedal New Type of Policing," *The Globe and Mail,* August 8, 1994, pp. A1–A2.

Example 2

Problem-oriented policing is effective on the streets of a community, but it can also be effective with focal groups on a preventive basis. In Edmonton, foot patrol officers become involved with students, especially junior-high students, as some turn to crime during the summer months. Some officers have been successful at setting up a summer youth program by receiving a grant, while others inform the students about possible jobs or volunteer positions in a variety of places. One police officer proposed and formed a native arts program at a local school, funded by the provincial government. His object is to teach junior-high students the value of education in a work-experience setting as they plan, make, advertise, and market their crafts after school and on Saturdays. The hope is that all these students will continue their high-school studies, since a requirement of the program is that all participants must be enrolled in school. Teachers noticed an improvement in the students' punctuality and attendance, because students who are late or miss classes are not allowed to become involved in the after-school program.

Source: K. Koller, "The Edmonton Neighbourhood Foot Patrol," Edmonton Police Service, 1990.

The majority of police work remained reactive, but that didn't seem to work too well. Victim surveys discovered citizens didn't report crimes to the police and that victims had lost faith in the police to respond quickly and effectively. If the police did respond, many citizens were never informed about the progress of the case until they were notified to appear at a preliminary hearing or court trial. Further, officers became removed from the concerns of the neighbourhood, and as a result seemed unreliable, with the result that citizens didn't call the police to report crimes and lived with significant fear of crime (Sherman 1986).

At the same time, some communities began to hire private security companies to protect them from criminals because of their lack of faith in the ability of the police do so (Shearing 1992). As a result, some police administrators felt there was a need for fundamental change. What emerged is called community policing, which attempts to close the gap between the police and their communities. There are many types of community policing; but no matter the degree to which a police force practises this new type of policing, almost all police forces in North America are involved with some aspect of it. In fact, it is seen by many as the future style of policing. How did this new type of policing develop in such a short time?

Problem-Oriented Policing

In 1979 Herman Goldstein published an article in which he laid out a new style of policing that he called **problem-oriented policing.** This style of policing, according to Goldstein, represented a fundamental change in the way the

---

EXHIBIT 5.2

The Ten Principles of Community Policing

1. Community policing is both a philosophy and an organizational strategy that allows the police and community residents to work closely together in new ways to solve the problems of crime and fear of crime.

2. Community policing's organizational strategy first demands that everyone in the department, including both civilian and sworn personnel, must investigate ways to translate the philosophy into practice.

3. To implement true community policing, police departments must create and develop a new breed of line officer, the Community Policing Officer (CPO), who acts as the direct link between the police and people in the community.

4. The CPOs' broad role demands continuous, sustained contact with the law-abiding people in the community, so that together they can explore creative new solutions to local concerns involving crime, fear of crime, disorder, and decay, with private citizens serving as unpaid volunteers.

5. Community policing implies a new contract between the police and the citizens it serves, one that offers the hope of overcoming widespread apathy, and at the same time it restrains any impulse to vigilantism.

6. Community policing adds a vital proactive element to the traditional reactive role of the police, resulting in full-spectrum police service.

7. Community policing stresses exploring new ways to protect and enhance the lives of those who are most vulnerable—juveniles, the elderly, minorities, the poor, the disabled, the homeless.

8. Community policing promotes the judicious use of technology, but it also rests on the belief that nothing surpasses what dedicated human beings, talking and working together, can achieve.

9. Community policing must be a fully integrated approach that involves everyone in the department, with the CPOs as specialists in bridging the gap between the police and the people they serve.

10. Community policing provides decentralized, personalized police service to the community. It recognizes that the police cannot impose order on the community from outside, but that people must be encouraged to think of the police as a resource they can use in helping to solve contemporary community concerns.

Source: R.C. Trojanowicz and B. Bucqueroux, *Community Policing: A Contemporary Perspective* (Cincinnati: Anderson, 1990).

police operate: rather than spend most of their time responding to citizens' calls involving criminal incidents, the police would direct their energy to the causes of crimes and complaints in an attempt to eliminate these sources. This involved a fundamental change in the way the police operated, in particular in their developing strategies to eliminate the sources of crime. And unless the underlying causes of crime are eliminated, the problem will persist, leading to more criminal incidents and citizens' greater fear of crime.

As problem-oriented policing began to come into practice, four stages of the problem-solving process were developed. The first is referred to as "scanning," where a police officer identifies an issue and then assesses whether it really is a problem. In the second stage, "analysis," the officer collects as much information as possible about the problem. In the next stage, "response," all relevant information is collected to start to develop and then implement solutions. In the final stage, "assessment," police officers collect information about the effectiveness of their approach, changing any particular tactics if doing so is considered necessary, or even developing an entirely new approach.

The essence of the problem-oriented approach is in the analysis stage, where a problem is broken into three components—(1) actions, specifically victims, offenders, and others involved in the events, (2) incidents, which deals with the social context, physical setting, and actions taken before, during, and after the event(s), and (3) responses, where the perceptions and receptions of citizens and private and public institutions are applied to the problem (Eck and Spelman 1987).

Community Policing

One flaw of the problem-oriented approach was that the police didn't always include the community when studying a crime problem. As Moore and Trojanowicz (1988) point out, **community policing** involves community groups, such as businesspeople, residents, and school teachers, as "key partners . . . in the creation of safe, secure communities. The success of the police depends not only on the development of their own skills and capabilities, but also on the creation of competent communities."

The goal of this style of policing was not to fight crime but to encourage public safety and confidence, reduce citizens' fear of crime, and encourage citizen involvement. The development of community support would be facilitated by decentralized, neighbourhood-based policing operating out of mini-stations or storefronts.

While each police department needs to create its own community policing style in a manner that reflects the diversity and needs of the local citizens, certain characteristics are nevertheless identified as essential to the success of any community policing effort:

1. the mission of police officers as peace officers
2. community consultation

3. a proactive approach to policing

4. a problem-oriented strategy

5. crime prevention activities

6. interagency cooperation

7. interactive policing

8. a reduction of the fear of victimization

9. development of police officers as generalists

10. decentralized police management

11. development of flatter organizational structures and accountability to the community (Normandeau and Leighton 1990)

A crucial goal of a community policing strategy is the reduction of fear of crime in the community. Fear of crime has been divided into three types. First is the intense fear suffered by the victims of crime as well as their family, friends, and neighbours. This fear includes physical injury, property loss, economic costs (such as hospital bills and loss of wages at work), and psychological trauma such as depression and anxiety. Victims can also suffer from what has been called "double-victimization"—that is, when they report the crime they are treated as second-class citizens by the agencies in the criminal justice system. The second type of fear is known as the concrete fear of crime, which refers to fear of specific crimes, especially violent crimes. Studies have identified high-risk groups—people who live in large urban areas, the young, women, and racial minorities—who are most susceptible to concrete fear. They fear being sexually assaulted, physically assaulted, robbed, and murdered. Formless fear of crime, the third type, is the feeling that one is unsafe. Research has found the groups displaying the highest levels of formless fear include the elderly, the marginally employed, and those with low incomes. Studies focusing on the fear of crime note that while people are afraid of serious crime, they are just as concerned, if not more concerned, about petty crimes and social disorder. In the past, the police failed to understand that when people say they are afraid of crime, they are talking about all types of crime and disorder, not just serious, violent crimes (Trojanowicz and Bucqueroux 1990).

To community police officers, the reduction of the fear of crime is an essential component of their job, and it's also a way to increase citizen–police cooperation. A variety of techniques can be employed to reduce the fear of crime in a community, including a police–community newsletter, a police–community contact centre staffed by patrol officers and civilians, and a variety of programs in which police officers contact victims of crime to inform them of police action on the case. Whatever programs are developed, the most successful allow officers the time to identify key issues with local residents and to use both personal initiative and community input to solve problems. And while not all programs are successful, evidence shows that foot patrol officers are actually able to reduce the level of fear in the community.

Aboriginal Police Forces

One outgrowth of the community policing model has been the creation of aboriginal policing on reserves, or First Nations police forces. These have been the result of federal and provincial commissions of inquiry into aboriginal issues in Canada, most of which understood there were problems with the way aboriginal communities were policed by their RCMP or provincial police force counterparts in Ontario and Quebec. One of the key recommendations of these inquiries was for aboriginal peoples to be involved in their own criminal justice systems. As a result, many provinces and the federal government began to explore the possibility of aboriginal police forces, and by the spring of 1994 there were 793 police officers and band constables funded by federal and provincial governments. In Ontario there were 243 aboriginal police officers in 70 communities, while in Quebec there were 175 in 54 settlements (Moon 1994).

One of the earliest undertakings of aboriginal police forces occurred in Quebec, where in 1978 25 aboriginal reserves in Quebec were policed by a semi-autonomous police force known as the Amerindian Police. These forces were created because of the dependency of native communities on outside police forces, a dependency that "increases the likelihood of police interventions and 'criminalizes' behaviors that would not necessarily be considered criminal if other agencies were involved" (Hyde 1992:370). Aboriginal police forces were founded to give a greater understanding of, and sensitivity to, the issues that confront the peoples living in aboriginal communities.

Amerindian police force members were most commonly requested to perform a service function within the community. Approximately 6000 out of the total 17 000 requests for police assistance recorded between 1978 and 1983 were for noncriminal incidents. Most were requests for services. Almost 45 percent of all service calls ended up with police making referrals to other agencies, such as social and health services, probation officers, and psychiatric specialists. Hyde (1992:370) believes that "peace keeping, crime prevention, and crisis-intervention functions of the police are, in part, the raison d'être for the establishment of the force."

Most of the crimes committed by aboriginals in communities policed by the Amerindian police forces involve the least serious Criminal Code and provincial offences. These include public order offences, interpersonal disputes, liquor and drug offences, and break and enters. The most typical police response to an incident is "no charge," meaning the police take no action, while the next most common response is "suspect detained," meaning an individual is detained by the police overnight (Depew 1992). As a result, the Amerindian police play an important role in the area of crisis intervention as well as in the provision of social services. LaPrairie and Diamond (1992) found many criminal cases were dealt with without the invoking of formal criminal justice measures. They discovered that only about 33 percent of reported criminal or potential criminal offences were officially recorded, and only 12 percent of those officially recorded made it to court.

Recognizing the importance of aboriginal police officers on reserves, the federal government created the First Nations Policing Policy in June 1991. Aboriginal communities now have more control over the operations and management of policing on reserves. This can be established in one of two ways: (1) they may decide to develop and administer their own police force or (2) they may elect to hire an existing police force that employs aboriginal police officers (Royal Canadian Mounted Police n.d.). Regardless of the type of policing a community adopts, the purpose of the First Nations Policing Policy is to improve the administration of justice and the maintenance of social order, public security, and personal safety in aboriginal communities on reserves. The objectives of the policy are

1. to provide First Nations communities with on-reserve policing services equal in quality to those provided in non-First Nations communities

2. to provide First Nations communities with police services that suit their needs and respect their culture and beliefs

3. to accommodate local and regional variations in policing services

4. to ensure that First Nations policing services are responsible for enforcing all laws normally assigned to police officers

5. to ensure that implementation of new policing arrangements is undertaken in a planned and coordinated manner to guarantee a high probability of success

6. to ensure Firsts Nations policing services are consistent with generally accepted practice and due process related to public complaints, grievances, and redress

7. to support and encourage evolving self-government in First Nations communities

8. to ensure on-reserve police services are independent of the First Nations or band governance authority, yet accountable to the communities they serve (First Nations Policing Policy 1992:2)

According to Depew (1992:475) a community-policing approach on the part of aboriginal communities involves an approach to community planning that takes into consideration "community-level political and economic development to ensure stability and coherence in local social organization and an appropriate legislative framework to sustain inter-governmental cooperation, coordination, and support for new native policing arrangements."

Summary

Police forces have traditionally operated in a militaristic style of organization. Many questions have been raised about the effectiveness of policing, especially patrol work. Police officials have spent the past two decades experimenting with different patrol styles, some of which appear to be effective in catching criminals and deterring further criminal actions.

In order to improve their effectiveness, many police forces have introduced community-based policing. Although the exact nature of this type of policing varies from location to location, most include the elements of community involvement and problem-solving. These new approaches have led many police forces into a new era of policing, using their resources differently in an attempt to achieve better results for their efforts. While these new models have established themselves as the future of policing in our society, many issues have yet to be resolved. Police forces are reluctant to change their organizational structure, particularly in any way that would decentralize their decision-making authority and share that authority with the community. There is also the issue of changes occurring among the police; much more research is needed to understand the nature and extent of these changes in all aspects of policing.

Aboriginal police forces have emerged in recent decades in an attempt to deal more effectively with the issues facing individuals who live in aboriginal communities. In many ways, the members of those forces are peacekeepers, because they combine the role of police officer, social worker, and community activist. The origins of aboriginal policing are found in the community policing model.

Discussion Questions

1. What should be the primary function of the police in our society?
2. Should the police become more proactive? If so, how could this be accomplished, and what would the impact be?
3. What are the problems and benefits associated with a highly structured model of police organization?
4. Would there be benefits to a decentralized model of police organization?
5. Why do you think many officers resist attempts to move police departments toward a community policing model?
6. Can the efficiency of detectives be increased? How?
7. Discuss the positive aspects of community policing for the police and the public. Can the police and community ever form a unified front to fight crime?

8. Discuss the impact of aboriginal police forces. What are the benefits of aboriginal police forces?

Suggested Readings

Canadian Journal of Criminology. "Police and Society in Canada." Volume 33, Nos. 3–4, 1991.

Chacko, J., and S.E. Nancoo, eds. *Community Policing in Canada.* Toronto: Criminal Justice Press, 1993.

Forcese, P. *Policing Canadian Society.* Scarborough, Ont.: Prentice-Hall, 1992.

Martin, M.A. *Urban Policing in Canada: Anatomy of an Aging Craft.* Montreal: McGill–Queen's University Press, 1995.

Normandeau, A., and B. Leighton. *A Vision of the Future of Policing in Canada: Police Challenge 2000.* Ottawa: Solicitor General of Canada, 1990.

Stansfield, R.T. *Issues in Policing: A Canadian Perspective.* Toronto: Thompson Educational Publishing, 1996.

Trojanowicz, R.C., and B. Bucqueroux. *Community Policing: A Contemporary Perspective.* Cincinnati: Anderson, 1990.

CHAPTER 6

Issues in Canadian Policing

T his chapter focuses on a number of topics that relate to policing in the 1990s: discretion, the recruitment of women and racial minorities, use of deadly force, and police misconduct.

The long-standing issue of police discretion is concerned with questions of fairness in police decisions to arrest and charge. In this discussion, we review the three areas thought to influence the use of discretion.

The discussion of women and racial minority police officers addresses some of the problems related to recruitment. The current status of women and racial minority police officers in Canadian police agencies is reviewed. Concern about the performance of women police officers is also considered, as well as gender conflicts at work.

CHAPTER OBJECTIVES

- discuss the practice of police discretion

- examine the changing social composition of the police, including women and minorities

- discuss the various issues surrounding the hiring of more women and minority police officers

- discuss the use of deadly force by and against police officers in Canada

- examine the amount and types of police misconduct and attempts to control these actions by outside agencies

The examination of police use of deadly force and police misconduct reviews various studies on these issues in Canada. In addition, the attempt to control police misconduct by external agencies is also discussed.

In the early morning hours of December 14, 1993, a black Montreal taxi driver Richard Barnabe, depressed over the fact that he was not granted visiting rights to his son over Christmas, went to his church to talk to a priest. While banging on the building to wake the priest, he accidentally broke a church window. When police arrived after receiving a report from a citizen, Barnabe fled the scene and led police on a 10-kilometre pursuit through city streets at speeds exceeding 100 kilometres an hour. When Barnabe finally stopped, in front of his brother's house, he was arrested, taken to the local police station, and strip-searched with six police officers present.

When they began their strip-search at 4:21 a.m., Barnabe was "conscious and coherent" enough to refuse medical assistance, but when handcuffs were placed back on Barnabe 29 minutes later, he was bloodied, bruised, and in full cardiac arrest. At hospital, he was diagnosed as having three broken ribs, a broken nose, bruises, and suffering from irreversible brain damage.

All the police officers involved were suspended without pay, but received the equivalent of their take-home pay from their union, the Montreal Police Brotherhood. After a police investigation, the six officers involved were charged with assault causing bodily harm, a charge that carries a maximum 10-year sentence. A jury found four of the officers guilty as charged. Three were sentenced to jail terms of 60 to 90 days, to be served on weekends, and one year of probation. The weekend sentences allowed the officers to maintain their jobs. The fourth officer convicted was ordered to perform 10 hours of community work in a palliative care hospital and given two years' probation. His sentence was lighter because he arrived only after the strip-search had started and was implicated only in tying Barnabe's legs. The fifth officer was acquitted, and the judge imposed a publication ban on the remaining officer's testimony and forbade any mention of his name or his role in the events.

A youth who has just injected a speed ball that will have him writhing in a police cell is arrested by police constables. (Photo: Christopher Grabowski/*The Globe and Mail*)

According to the Quebec Superior Court judge, the sentences "had to reflect society's revulsion and the suffering of the officers from public scorn." Despite Barnabe's injury, the judge ruled that "no gratuitous blows were delivered" and the actions of the police were "neither premeditated nor malevolent." In addition, he cited their lack of prior criminal records, the likelihood they would be fired, and the poor training given to the officers. The judge also considered the fact that the officers were "not criminals in the normal sense of the word" and posed no danger to society and had already been punished and stigmatized by the media. However, the judge added that the jail terms were necessary to reflect "public revulsion" and that the "role of the court is not to please public opinion, but to dispense justice."

While the lawyers for the four officers felt the sentences were "reasonable and fair," they immediately filed appeals. Barnabe's sister considered the sentences to be "candy-coated" and demanded the officers be fired. Just one week before, her family received about $215 000 from the Montreal Urban Community Police Force in a civil lawsuit (Picard 1995).

Police Discretion

What if Richard Barnabe had been white and had been driving an expensive car? Would the police have reacted differently? Would they have just warned him and then let him drive home? In theory, the police have no legal authority to arrest certain individuals and ignore others committing the same crime.

While it wasn't developed to deal specifically with police use of discretion, Section 15 (1) of the Charter stipulates that numerous "extra-legal" factors are not to be considered within the law or the application of the law. According to Section 15 (1):

> Every individual is equal before and under the law and has the right to
> the equal protection and equal benefit of the law without discrimination
> and, in particular, without discrimination based on race, national or
> ethnic origin, colour, religion, sex, age or mental or physical orientation.

Discretion is the choice or decision on the part of the police to arrest and charge only a select group of individuals. In reality, it is difficult for the police to arrest and charge everyone they catch breaking the law because they lack the resources to do so. In addition, many citizens fully expect to be let off with a warning. As Stansfield (1996:142) states, the question is not whether the police decide to arrest someone or charge them, but "which criteria police use when enforcing the law."

Police discretion usually becomes a factor when officers must use their powers of arrest or investigate an alleged criminal offence although the available evidence indicates they should not. According to Roberg and Kuykendall (1993), police discretion involves three elements: (1) deciding whether or not to get involved in an incident in the first place, although this may not be a choice if the officer is responding to a citizen complaint; (2) determining how to behave in any particular incident, or how to interact with the victim, witnesses, or the public; and (3) selecting from various alternatives to deal with the problem. In any given situation, a police officer may decide not to do anything even though she or he observed the commission of a criminal offence or let one person off with a warning while arresting another for the same offence. Both of these are discretionary acts.

Goldstein (1960) categorized police discretion in terms of enforcing the criminal law into two classes: invocation discretion and noninvocation discretion. Invocation discretion refers to situations in which a police officer decides to arrest an individual. Noninvocation discretion involves those circumstances in which police officers could arrest someone but choose not to. Goldstein was most concerned about noninvocation discretion because such decisions have "low visibility" and are not reviewed by superiors. The low visibility of police discretion means that, unlike the other criminal justice agencies, the police can "hide" or "obscure" their discretionary decisions. Thus, discretion "may sometimes deteriorate into discrimination, violence, and other abusive practices" (Senna and Siegel 1995:233).

Police decisions to arrest and charge may result in discriminatory practices against members of a particular group. As a result, members this group may be overrepresented in arrest and charge statistics.

Situational Variables

Most studies on police use of discretion focus on the specific factors that led to an officer's decision to make an arrest. The most common factors were the citizen's social class, age, sex, and race. Other variables included the relationship between the victim and the complainant, the amount of respect or deference they give to the police officer, the nature of the offence, or problem, and the amount and quality of the evidence. These are called *situational variables*. The dynamics of any situation may vary, thereby allowing police officers to vary in their responses to the incident.

Another important factor in police discretion involves the location of the incident. Police usually arrest suspects more frequently in public settings than in private ones. Still, a number of different agents can influence police use of discretion in these situations, such as the seriousness of the crime and the need to be in control of the situation, especially if members of the public are watching. The presence of other police officers is also another influence on police discretion—if a police officer thinks other police officers expect him to respond in a punitive manner, he will probably do so. Indeed, police officers working alone behave much differently than if they are working with a partner—they usually make more arrests since they are concerned with gaining control of a situation as quickly as possible. However, Sherman (1985) and Brooks (1989), in their studies of police use of discretion in the United States, found that while two officers patrolling together will not make as many arrests as a single patrol officer, they treat suspects more harshly because each officer is concerned about performing properly in front of his or her partner.

Situational variables can have a significant influence on police work. Table 6.1 illustrates those variables relating to the suspect and the complainant that appear to have an influential impact on police discretion in the United States. Any one of these variables, or a combination of them, could influence the investigating officer's decision to do nothing, to give warnings, or to arrest someone.

Community Variables

An important factor in police decision-making involves the

TABLE 6.1

Critical Variables Influencing Police Behaviour

Variables	Role of Citizen	
	Suspect	Victim
Race	X	0
Demeanour	X	X
Relation to victim	X	0
Social class	X	0
Age	X	0
Sex	X	0
Preference of public/private setting	X	X
Number of citizens	X	X
Proactive/reactive	X	0
Number of officers	X	0

X = Consistent relationship found
0 = No consistent relationship found

Source: L.W. Sherman, "Causes of Police Behavior," in A.S. Blumberg and E. Niederhoffer, eds., *The Ambivalent Force*, 3rd ed. (New York: Holt, Rinehart and Winston, 1985), pp. 183–85.

racial and social class composition of a community. Research conducted in Canada and the United States has found police officers make more arrests in minority and working-class communities. The police view these communities as locations where more violent crimes are likely to occur and where more residents challenge their authority. Police, as a result, are more suspicious and concerned about their safety when they are in these areas. These feelings revolve around the idea of a symbolic assailant, an individual who, the police believe, tends to be potentially dangerous or troublesome (Skolnick 1966).

Some communities have higher rates of reported crime, and higher rates of crime can influence a police officer's perception of danger. The greater danger a police officer perceives, the more likely he or she will respond with an arrest. But, at the same time, police officers tend to ignore certain types of criminal activity in these areas, perhaps because of the greater amount of police work they become involved in or the fact they are more tolerant of minor violations. In addition, the attitudes of citizens in a particular community can influence police behaviour, since most police–citizen encounters result from a citizen calling the police. In his study of the Royal Newfoundland Constabulatory in St. John's, McGahan (1984) found police perceived the city to be a "mosaic of 'trouble areas.'" Specific communities were known to the police for their high rate of calls for service, and as the location of known and suspected criminals and repeat offenders. McGahan (1984:53) found these "trouble areas" were defined by the police as "concentrations of low-rent and subsidized housing—

defined as rowhousing or townhousing," which some police officers referred to as a "ghetto." In the mind of police officers, there is "a direct and clear correlation between rowhousing/public housing and crime." Overall, McGahan found that police would form a "model" of troubled areas which they used to predict the type of calls and the most appropriate response, allowing them "to cope with a threatening and troublesome segment of their environment."

Extra-Legal Factors

Perhaps the most controversial issue surrounding police use of discretion is whether the police take into account the race, class, and gender of the suspect when deciding to make an arrest—that is, whether police discretion favours the members of a certain social class or racial groups. Bienvenue and Latif (1974) studied 1969 arrest data for the city of Winnipeg to see if there were any differences in the arrest and charge rates between aboriginals and whites. They concluded that aboriginal women and men were overrepresented for all offences except drug and traffic violations. However, when the distribution of offences within each group was compared, aboriginals were found to be arrested more for minor offences while whites were arrested more frequently for the most serious, indictable offences. While Bienvenue and Latif point out these differential arrest patterns may reflect variations in socioeconomic status, they also suggest this may be the result of discrimination in the police use of discretion. When they looked at police decisions to charge, they found that aboriginals were also overrepresented for every type of charge at the time of sentencing.

In another Winnipeg study, Gunn and Minch (1988) found extensive use of police discretion in sexual assault cases. Of 211 charges laid against offenders, 122 (or 58 percent) were terminated, either because the police officer decided no sexual assault had occurred or because he or she foresaw difficulties for the complainant. Another 18 percent of the cases were terminated because of issues related to the victim, including her refusal to give a formal complaint to the police or because she decided to drop the charges. Finally, 11 percent of charges were dropped because the suspect could not be located.

Since police were using discretionary powers not to arrest or charge alleged offenders, mandatory arrest and charge policies in sexual assault cases became policy for most Canadian police forces in 1983. For example, in 1992, the Metropolitan Toronto Police Force required all its officers to lay charges when the evidence supported such an action; if the officer did not lay a charge, she or he had to file a report indicating the reason(s) for inaction.

Fleming (1981) provide further evidence of police discretion in his study of police decisions not to proceed with an investigation after it is learned that the victim of a violent crime is gay. As Abell and Sheehy (1993:225) note, when these reports are investigated by police, the "violence and homophobia and lesbophobia underlying it are often downplayed or excused." They argue that assailants receive more lenient treatment simply because "their crimes are crimes against gay men or lesbians." Petersen (1993:246) states that official responses to such crimes "typically range from indifference to brutality."

Other studies have found that the race of the victim rather than the criminal is the basis for the police decision to use discretion. Smith et al. (1984), for example, in their study of discretion in an American police force, found that officers are more likely to arrest the suspect when the victim of the crime is white rather than when the victim is a member of a minority group.

The Changing Composition of the Police

During the past 15 years Canadian police forces have started to hire more women and visible-minority police officers in order to better represent and serve the communities they serve. For many people, a police force that represents the sexual, ethnic, and racial composition of their community is "an essential feature in effective policing" and "provides a psychologically positive attitude on the part of visible minorities who have felt left out and alienated from the mainstream of society" (Jayewardene and Talbot 1990; Normandeau 1990). A police force that reflects the demographics of its community can be an essential approach "in gaining the public's confidence by helping to dispel the view that police departments are generally bigoted or biased organizations" (Senna and Siegel 1995:239).

In Canada, pressure to increase the numbers of women and visible minorities in police forces did not emerge until the 1970s, over 10 years after similar issues were raised in the United States. According to Forcese (1992), this change was the result of increasing numbers of visible-minority immigrants to Canada. Questions about the appropriate composition of the police were raised, including whether or not the police are isolated from the community, how important it is to have visible-minority and female representation in police departments, and what type of individuals should be recruited as police officers. While the responses to these questions varied, some police officials actively began to increase the number of visible minorities and women in their departments. It was not until the mid- to late 1980s that significant steps were achieved, although these increases still remained small in the overall context of Canadian policing.

Women and Policing

The number of women police officers in Canada has always been small. Throughout the 1960s, for example, the percentage of female police officers remained at less than 1 percent, rising to 2 percent only by 1980. This figure increased to 3.6 percent in 1985, 6.4 percent in 1990, and 8 percent in 1993 (see Figure 6.1). In 1994, the number of women police officers increased 10.9 percent over the previous year to a total of 5056. While the number of sworn police officers has declined since 1992 (see Chapter 5), the number of women police officers increased by 770. In 1994, 93 percent of all women police

FIGURE 6.1

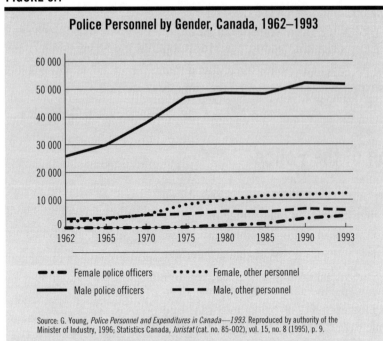

Police Personnel by Gender, Canada, 1962–1993

- **– · –** Female police officers
- **●●●●●** Female, other personnel
- **——** Male police officers
- **– – –** Male, other personnel

Source: G. Young, *Police Personnel and Expenditures in Canada—1993*. Reproduced by authority of the Minister of Industry, 1996; Statistics Canada, *Juristat* (cat. no. 85-002), vol. 15, no. 8 (1995), p. 9.

officers occupied the rank of constable, while 6 percent were noncommissioned officers. Less than 1 percent had reached officer status (Juristat 1996). In fact, the first women chief of police was appointed in Guelph, Ontario, in the fall of 1994. The first woman chief of police appointed in a city over 100 000 population was in Calgary, Alberta, in the summer of 1995. In comparison, 67.9 percent of male police officers were constables, 27.3 percent were non-commissioned officers, and 4.8 percent were officers.

Unequal Treatment

Before the increase in the number of women police officers in Canada in the mid-1980s, the role of women in policing was generally restricted to assignments involving social service issues, including juvenile issues, and family matters. Women were seen as adding some value to specialized police activities and units, as opposed to contributing to overall law enforcement activities. It should be noted that it was commonly believed men were more effective administrators and "were less likely to become irritable and overcritical under emotional stress" (Wilson and McLaren 1977).

Although these stereotypes of women and men in police work would ultimately be challenged, the initial breakthrough for equal treatment for women was the elimination of exclusionary physical requirements. For example, until 1979 the Ontario Provincial Police and the Ottawa Police Force turned down women applicants unless they were 5'1" tall and at least 160 pounds. Complaints to the Ontario government resulted in changes to these standards to accommodate the recruitment of more women (Forcese 1992). Police agencies started to advertise for more women interested in policing as a career. In 1987, the Metropolitan Toronto Police Force, which employed more than 5000 officers, had only 226 female sworn officers, approximately 4 percent of the total. The percentage of women in the RCMP, which didn't hire its first women officers until 1975, was only 7 percent in 1988.

Probably the most significant breakthrough for women police officers was the policy of **employment equity**. According to the Report of the Royal Commission on Equality in Employment (1984), employment equity is a policy of purposefully identifying any significant differences between participation and availability of four targeted minority groups—visible minorities, women, people with disabilities, and aboriginals—as well as any employment policies and/or practices that disadvantage these groups. The legal foundation of employment equity policies is the Canadian Human Rights Act (1977). Section 16 (1) of this act states that it is not discriminatory to start a special program designed to prevent, eliminate, or reduce disadvantages experienced by individuals due to their race, national or ethnic origin, religion, age, sex, family status, marital status, or disability.

Some observers have noted that the major problem facing police departments is not the recruitment of women, but rather their retention. This is because "many police departments are locked in a 'time-warp' that perpetuates the myth that only men can do patrol" (Hale and Wyland 1993:4). The presence of women in a traditionally male domain is threatening to many male officers regardless of rank and they are treated as outsiders, effectively eliminating them from learning tasks that would help them to be promoted at a later date (Padavic and Reskin 1990; Hunt 1990). Crawford and Stark-Adamec (1994) studied why women and men left four major Canadian police forces. The primary reason women gave for leaving their job as a police officer was raising a family (56 percent), moving to another city (17 percent), joining a new police force (11 percent), burnout/negative views on life (6 percent), feelings of inadequacy as a police officer (6 percent), and dissatisfaction with shift work (6 percent). Male officers, in contrast, left primarily due to a change in occupation (41 percent), disillusionment with policing or the criminal justice system (32 percent), burnout/negative views on life (23 percent), dissatisfaction with shift work (18 percent), family-related issues (9 percent), and danger inherent in the job (5 percent).

The Performance of Women Police Officers

In 1979, Canadian police administrators, apparently concerned about the possibility of an increase in the number of women police officers, were "anxious to receive some feedback on the effectiveness of women officers on general patrol in order to establish policies and practices" (Linden and Fillmore 1993:93). Linden and Minch (1982) studied the issue of women in policing in various RCMP detachments located in the lower mainland of B.C. as well as in the Vancouver City Police Department. They discovered that the supervisory performance ratings of male and female police officers were very similar. In addition, supervisors indicated positive opinions about the quality of female officers' work. However, many male officers expressed dissatisfaction with women patrol officers when questions concerning possible injuries were discussed. The general finding of the researchers was that "a substantial number of male officers in both forces felt that people would continue fighting and that both the male and female officer would be more likely to be injured than if both partners were male" (Linden and Fillmore 1993:105). Generally, male officers were concerned most about the need for using either strength or physical force. However, 80 percent of male patrol officers who had been part-ners of women officers were in favour of them working a regular patrol shift.

When questioned about their experience on the job, approximately 60 percent of the women police officers felt they had to work harder than men to receive credit for their work. Most said that their competence was repeatedly questioned, they were judged by different standards, and that any mistakes they made were attributed to their gender.

A number of U.S. studies have also investigated this issue. Researchers there also found that the major concern surrounding women as police officers was that they couldn't handle the "physically demanding" aspects of their job. Bloch and Anderson (1974) conducted a study of women police officers on patrol in Washington, D.C., during 1973. A matched group of 86 newly trained women and men police officers were evaluated for one year on the basis of their performance on patrol. They performed the same jobs and handled similar situations, and, at the conclusion of the study, women and men officers were found to be equally effective in their jobs. While women made fewer arrests, they were found to be more effective than their male counterparts in defusing potentially violent situations. In addition, they were found to use a less aggres-sive style of policing and less likely to engage in and be charged for improper conduct.

Sherman (1975), comparing male and female recruits, found that women were as effective as men in patrol work, that citizens found them to be more sensitive and responsive to their needs, and that they handled service calls, especially domestic disturbances, better than men. Similar results were found by Sichel et al. (1978) in their study of New York City police officers. Basing their conclusions on 3625 hours of observation on patrols and on approxi-mately 2400 police–citizen encounters, they reported that both female and male police officers performed the same on patrol, but that citizens found women officers more respectful, pleasant, and competent.

These findings have led to the conclusion that women police officers, because they are more compassionate, less aggressive, and less competitive, see their job from a different perspective and therefore develop different policing styles than do men. As suggested by these studies, these differences are a source of concern for some male officers and administrators, but also a source of optimism among observers who are sceptical about the social value of tradi-tional police styles. However, Worden (1993), analyzing 24 police departments in three metropolitan areas in the United States, found there is little proof that women police officers define their role or view the public differently than male police officers.

Women Police Officers: Gender Conflicts at Work

Despite the evidence that female and male police officers perform equally, policewomen have sometimes experienced difficulty being fully accepted by their male colleagues. According to Balkin (1988:33) male officers perceive

EXHIBIT 6.1

Women Police Officers

In 1980, the Los Angeles Police Department doubled the number of its women police officers. Commander Ken Hickman, a Ph.D. candidate, used this opportunity to study the records of 68 women police officers with an equal number of male officers hired at the same time. In his analysis of 6000 daily field report activities, he discovered male–female officer teams were just as productive in initiating potentially hazardous calls as were all-male teams. He also found that the leading initiators of potentially hazardous activities were women. Commander Hickman also found that recruit training officers rated men lower than women in the area of tactics, initiative and self-confidence, writing and communication skills, and public contact. Also, the IQs of the women recruits were higher, and academically the women surpassed their male classmates in the LAPD recruit training academy. In terms of physical fitness and height, Hickman found that these traits were correlated with success in the field

for only 4 percent of all police officers. Women received substantially more commendations from the public, and their superior communication skills allowed them to better handle domestic situations. It was also found that both female and male police officers received similar numbers of complaints from the public.

These results in many ways proved the predictors of Lewis Sherman, who wrote that having women patrol officers would lead to the following benefits:

1. a reduction in the incidence of violence between police officers and citizens

2. increased quality of police service because women accentuate the service role of police work more than men

3. improved police–community relations because women are more visible than men, make more contacts, and citizens will assist policewomen upon request

4. policemen can learn from policewomen that an officer can be efficient without using force

5. policewomen are more effective than policemen in settling problems reported by women from low-income neighbourhoods

6. a police department becomes more democratic and responsive to the community by hiring personnel who are more representative of the community's population

7. lawsuits charging sex discrimination could be avoided by police departments that develop and implement job-related selection, recruitment, and promotional standards and tests

Source: M.K. Elias, "The Urban Cop: A Job for a Woman," *MS.* 12 (1984); D.C. Hale and S.M. Wyland, "Dragons and Dinosaurs: The Plight of Patrol Women," *Police Forum* 3, 1993; and L.J. Sherman, "An Evaluation of Policewoman Patrol in a Suburban Police Department," *Journal of Police Science and Administration* 3, 1975. Reprinted from *Journal of Police Science* 3, pp. 383, 384 (1975). Copyright held by the International Chiefs of Police, 515 North Washington Street, Alexandria, Va. 22714, USA. Further reproduction without express written permission from IACP is strictly prohibited.

policewomen to lack both the physical and emotional strength to perform well in violent confrontations. Overall, male police officers hold "almost uniformly negative . . . attitudes toward policewomen." Baunach and Rafter (1982), Peterson (1982), and Martin (1991) have pointed out that since male police officers associate masculinity with the use of physical force, and view the use of physical force as the defining feature of police work, they are concerned and threatened by women being successfully integrated into police work. However, Hunt (1990) reports that male and female police officers develop similar attitudes toward their occupational duties and job satisfaction (see Table 6.2).

However, this is not to say that women officers do not continue to experience gender conflicts at work. Martin (1990), in her national assessment of women police officers in the United States in the 1980s, found that a high percentage of female officers experienced some form of bias, and that 75 percent of both new and experienced police officers reported being the victims of sexual harassment. In fact, a higher proportion (35 percent) of rookie

TABLE 6.2

| Police Cultural Oppositions | |
Female	Male
Formal	Informal
Academy	Street
Inside	Outside
Management	Streep cop
Administration	Crimefighting
Social service	Rescue activity
Paperwork	Crimefighting
Formal rules	Informal rules
Legal money	Clean and dirty money
Legal force	Normal and brutal force
Marital sex	Illicit sex
Domestic women	Whore/dyke
Emotional	Instrumental
Intellectual	Physical
Clean	Dirty

Source: J.C. Hunt, "The Logic of Sexism among Police," *Women and Criminal Justice* 1, no. 2 (1990), p. 118.

women officers as opposed to rookie men officers (8 percent) reported their primary problem as new patrol officers was harassment by other police officers (see Table 6.2). This harassment included displays of pornography, jokes or comments based on sexual stereotypes of women, and remarks on women's sexuality. Crawford and Stark-Adamec (1994) reached similar conclusions in their study of 50 female and 68 male police officers and ex–police officers in four major Canadian police departments. Eighteen percent of the women in the study referred to sexually related problems on the job, including sexual harassment and sexual discrimination.

Questions have been asked about the potential effectiveness of women in the top ranks of police agencies. Male officers may find it difficult to take orders from women supervisors, and some women members of police agencies may decide not to seek promotion as they fear rejection from male officers (Wexler and Quinn 1985).

Visible Minorities and Policing

Very little has been written about visible-minority police officers in Canada, no doubt because very few visible minorities have become police officers. For example, in 1986, a total of 645 sworn police officers in Canada were members of visible minority groups, or 1.1 percent of the total of all sworn officers in this country (see Table 6.3). The largest group of visible minorities was located in Ontario, where 395 officers—1.9 percent of all sworn police officers—were members of visible minorities; there were no visible-minority police officers in either Newfoundland or Prince Edward Island.

In 1989, 242 (or 4.2 percent) visible-minority police officers worked for the Metropolitan Toronto Police Force, in a city that had in excess of one million people belonging to visible-minority groups. The largest number of visible minorities were found in the rank of constable (195, or 4.7 percent of all constables), followed by sergeant (18, or 2.0 percent), staff sergeant (8, or

2.7 percent), inspector (2, or 4.4 percent), and staff inspector (1, or 3.0 percent) (Suriya 1993).

The limited number of visible minorities in Canadian police forces is a result of their limited access to the law enforcement profession. To date, studies have found that unrelated job requirements have deterred large numbers of visible minorities from applying to police forces across Canada (Jayewardene and Talbot 1990). For example, the debates surrounding Sikh RCMP officers wearing turbans as part of their uniform focused on the issue of RCMP tradition rather than the legal issue of whether the wearing of turbans interferes with the performance of duty. Hiring policies that create such obstacles for police officers have been termed a form of "systematic discrimination," since these policies place an arbitrary barrier between an individual's ability and his employment opportunities in his chosen area of work (Abella 1984). According to the Canadian Employment Act, the

TABLE 6.3

Government Police Officers and Detectives by Ethnicity, 1988

	Total	Caucasian		Visible Minority	
Canada	**57380**	Total **55475**	% **96.7%**	Total **645**	% **1.1**
Nfld.	1085	1085	100.0	0	0
P.E.I.	285	285	100.0	0	0
N.S.	1605	1570	97.8	10	0.6
N.B.	1400	1355	96.8	10	0.7
Que.	16290	15925	97.8	55	0.3
Ont.	20510	19760	96.3	396	1.9
Man.	2145	2035	94.9	10	0.5
Sask.	2320	2225	95.9	15	0.6
Alta.	4895	4690	95.8	55	1.1
B.C.	6450	6240	96.7	55	1.3
Halifax	620	610	98.4	10	1.6
Montreal	7935	7785	98.1	40	0.5
Toronto	7550	7160	94.8	315	4.2
Winnipeg	1215	1200	98.8	0	0
Regina	630	615	97.6	0	0
Calgary	1540	1500	97.4	15	1.0
Edmonton	1735	1665	96.0	30	1.7
Vancouver	3315	3206	96.7	55	1.7

Source: S.K. Suriya, "The Representation of Visible Minorities in Canadian Police: Employment Equity beyond Rhetoric," *Police Studies* 16, no. 2 (1993), p. 48.

goal of selecting the appropriate individual "has to be so structured as to increase the reliability of its objectivity" (Suriya 1993:47).

In his investigation of the recruitment process by Canadian police forces, Jain (1994) recommends the need for proactive recruitment methods, such as community outreach programs. These programs involve strategies such as providing visible-minority role models, trained recruiters, giving high-school presentations with visible-minority role models, and requesting high-school teachers and others to identify potential visible-minority candidates. Other related issues include the reassessment of mental ability tasks, which may be biased against those not raised in Canada or North America as well as against female applicants. Interviews may be a questionable component of the hiring process, since they have relatively low reliability (e.g., different interviewers reach different conclusions) as well as low validity (e.g., interview ratings and job performance scores are not closely related), and, as a result, involve subjective assessments and are therefore "susceptible to the covert prejudices of individual interviewers" (Jain 1994:105). Interviews have also been criticized because they are "not conducive to objective results" (Jayewardene and Talbot 1990:6). In addition, the Advisory Committee on Multicultural Police Recruitment and Selection of the Ottawa Police Force (1989) found that psychological tests, unless carefully reviewed, could readily lead to "many areas where sexual, religious, and cultural assumptions could lead to misinterpretations of the responses." Furthermore, they stress the importance of including an individual "with multicultural experience or training at the final interview as well as throughout entire selection process."

The Ontario Task Force on Race Relations and Policing (1989) reports that members of visible minorities consider policing a dead-end job with few promotional opportunities. The Task Force found that the "effective ceiling" for visible-minority promotions is the rank of staff sergeant. They also concluded that many visible-minority police officers have served for many years to obtain promotions "which have not been forthcoming" (Wood 1989).

Another significant reason for the low numbers of visible minorities in policing is the unequal treatment they receive in such areas as work assignments, evaluations, and promotions. Research conducted in the United States has shown that black police officers performed their duties only in black communities and were able to arrest only black citizens. If a white person committed a crime in a black community, a white police officer would be contacted to make the arrest. Rudwick (1962) found that, of 130 cities and counties in various southern states in 1959, 69 required white officers to arrest

Court sheriffs in Abbotsford, B.C., escort the car carrying Terry Driver in May 1996 as it leaves the courthouse. Driver was charged with the first-degree murder of Tanya Smith. (Photo: Chuck Stoody/Canadian Press)

white suspects, and 107 cities had a policy that only black officers could patrol in black areas. The few studies that have focused on this issue have reached different conclusions. In their research on the aftermath of the Miami riots of the early 1980s, Berg et al. (1984) discovered that black officers were closer to the community than either white or Hispanic officers. In contrast, Felknes (1991) found black officers had trouble relating to the black community since they tended to identify with their white colleagues, who had a limited understanding of cultural differences. This has led to the further marginalization of minority police officers, who find opposition in the police department and apathy from minority citizens.

Deadly Force

Deadly force is defined as force that is used with the intent to cause bodily injury or death. Police use of deadly force refers to those situations in which the police use firearms in encounters with citizens. Citizens may also be injured or killed as the result of other types of force used by the police: for example, choke holds, which can cause death, should be included in any definition of deadly force (Fyfe 1988). High-speed chases ending in death can also be seen as a type of deadly force; however, such cases are not included here because the deaths that occur are unintentional and often accidental.

Section 25 of the Criminal Code allows Canadian police to use lethal force:

> 25. (1) Every one who is required or authorized by law to do anything in the administration or enforcement of the law
>   (a) as a private person,
>   (b) as a peace officer or public officer,
>   (c) in aid of a peace officer or public officer, or
>   (d) by virtue of his office,
>   is, if he acts on reasonable grounds, justified in doing what he is required or authorized to do and in using as much force as is necessary for that purpose . . .
>
> (3) Subject to subsection (4), a person is not justified for the purposes of subsection (1) in using force that is intended or is likely to cause death or grievous bodily harm unless he believes on reasonable grounds that it is necessary for the purpose of preserving himself or any one under his protection from death or grievous bodily harm.
>
> (4) A peace office who is proceeding lawfully to arrest, with or without warrant, any person for an offence for which that person may be arrested without warrant, and everyone lawfully assisting the police officer, is justified, if the person to be arrested takes flight to avoid arrest, in using as much force as

is necessary to prevent the escape by flight, unless the escape can be prevented by reasonable means in a less violent manner.

Subsection (1) of Section 25 of the Criminal Code states that any individual, including a peace (police) officer, can use "as much force as necessary" in the "administration of the law" if they "act on reasonable grounds." Furthermore, if a police officer is to be justified in using deadly force, he or she must believe on "reasonable grounds" that it is necessary to use force in order to protect themselves or an individual in their care from "death or grievous bodily harm."

As Stansfield (1996:111) points out, this approach to deadly force raises a number of problems. First, the phrase "as much force as necessary" makes it appear that police can use as much force as they feel is necessary to resolve any particular incident. Second, it does not state exactly how much force should be used.

A number of mechanisms have been implemented in an attempt to control the police use of deadly force. In Canada, the Criminal Code clearly states that a police officer does not have to be physically attacked before using potentially deadly force. These laws and regulations possess a *reasonableness standard* for the use of force, namely that force will be considered excessive when, after the officer has evaluated all the circumstances at the time of the incident, the force was determined to be unreasonable. However, even if police investigators and Crown prosecutors determine excessive force was used, it is still difficult to gain a conviction. Police witnesses have traditionally been reluctant to assist Crown prosecutors, which has led to a revision of the Ontario Police Act, which stipulates that officers must cooperate with any investigation. When cases have proceeded to court, jurors have acquitted the officers in almost every case.

Information on the police use of deadly force in Canada is limited to estimates about the number of people killed by the police as a result of their use of deadly force. But the definition of deadly force used here has three categories that need to be examined if the full extent of this issue is to be fully determined:

1. *Death:* police use a deadly weapon, and as a result the individual dies.
2. *Injury:* the police use a deadly weapon, but the individual is wounded and does not die.
3. *Noninjury:* the police use a deadly weapon, but the individual against whom it is directed is not injured.

As Roberg and Kuykendall (1993) point out, a fourth category would cover the total number of times a police officer fires his or her weapon. An individual who is shot at and killed or wounded may be shot at many times, not just once. Geller and Scott (1991) found police officers miss their target 60 to 85 percent of time. An officer could shoot six bullets at a suspect and miss him altogether, or hit him once, injuring or killing him.

Systematic data for the first category of deadly force is hard to find in Canada since such records are not kept for public consumption. Case studies taken from newspapers cannot be analyzed with the purpose of studying anything beyond the dynamics of the situation, such as police regulations and the final results of any investigation (Forcese 1992). In the United States, however, the "cause of homicide" category published annually by the National Center for Health Statistics has included the subcategory of "police or legal" intervention since 1949. Between 1949 and 1990, police in the United States killed approximately 13 000 people. However, Sherman and Consworthy (1979) point out that these statistics underestimate such incidents by 25 to 50 percent, stating that the real number is closer to 30 000 or 40 000.

The following discussion of police use of deadly force in Canada, therefore, is limited to the few studies that have attempted to empirically analyze this issue. While Abraham et al. (1981) focused on the Metropolitan Toronto Police Force, Chappell and Graham (1985) looked at national and British Columbia data.

Variations among Provinces and Cities

The frequency with which police use Category 1 deadly force varies according to the province or territory. Between 1970 and 1981, 119 deaths in Canada were the result of police use of deadly force. Quebec experienced the greatest number of deadly force incidents during this time period (37 percent), followed by Ontario (27.7 percent) and British Columbia (11.8 percent). However, when the number of deaths caused by police use of deadly force is measured by 100 000 population, the Northwest Territories had the highest rate (2.43 per 100 000 population), followed by Manitoba (1.18) and Quebec (0.70 per 100 000 population).

The size of a police force is thought to influence the police use of deadly force, which is said to increase as the size of the police force grows larger. This idea is based on the argument that larger centres harbour more criminals and have more crime and more weapons, and that the police are more likely to intervene in situations in which they think deadly force is the appropriate response. As Chappell and Graham (1985) found, between 1970 and 1981 there was no discernible evidence that such a relationship existed in Canada. Although Chappell and Graham did not analyze their data in this matter, American researchers (Fyfe 1988; Kania and Mackey 1977; Sherman and Langworthy 1979) have all found a relationship between lack of social cohesion in a community (e.g., poverty and high divorce rates) and police involvement in potentially dangerous situations.

Another important factor is the police organization itself: the organizational values, policies, and practices of police administrators. For example, restrictive shooting policies will no doubt lead to a significant decrease in the number of times deadly force is used. Also, police training and their response to dangerous incidents may have an impact on their use of deadly force. For example, some police departments may tell their officers how to deal with certain incidents, such as waiting for "backup support" or acting in an aggressive manner (Fyfe 1988).

Race

According to historical data collected in the United States, blacks have been killed by the police at a rate disproportionate with their numbers in the broader population (Takagi 1974; Blumberg 1980). Since 1970, fewer blacks have been killed by the police, largely due to the fact that more restrictive policies were formalized and implemented in most police departments (Sherman and Cohen 1986). Fyfe (1982) attempted to assess whether or not the New York police discriminated against blacks when they used deadly force. Studying police shootings over a five-year period, Fyfe found that police officers shot armed suspects and became involved in violent confrontations. Once these factors were included in the analysis, Fyfe found that racial differences decreased. He also discovered that black police officers were almost twice as likely as white officers to use deadly force. This was attributed to the fact that black police officers patrolled in higher crime areas where the use of weapons is more common and that they were on patrols more often than white officers.

Abraham et al. (1981), in their study of the use of deadly force by Metropolitan Toronto police officers, described seven incidents as "confrontation situations." All victims were armed at the time of the shootings: one had a shotgun, another had an inoperative shotgun; there were also two toy weapons, two kitchen knives, a gardening tool, and a police officer's night stick. According to Abraham et al. (1981:234), the key problem in all seven incidents was that the police involved themselves in a way that led to a confrontation, reflecting "fundamental training defects in the Metro police."

In their study of police use of deadly force in British Columbia between 1970 and 1982, Chappell and Graham (1985:110–11) reported that all 13 victims were males aged 17 to 52. One of the victims was black, another was of Asian descent, and all others were white. Seven of the victims were armed at the time of the shooting incident, and two victims were not in possession of a weapon when they were confronted by the police (these two individuals were in the possession of a weapon at the time of their criminal offence but were unarmed when they were shot by police). In addition, three individuals were not armed, and in the remaining case no weapon was discovered on the victim's body in the field, though an unloaded weapon was discovered tucked into his belt at the autopsy.

Deadly Force against Police Officers

Police officers can be the recipients of deadly force. The danger of their daily activity was underscored in the summer of 1995 when a police chief in Quebec was shot and killed while responding to a domestic violence incident. The death of a police officer on duty is a rare event in Canada; on average, two or three officers are killed each year. In comparison, approximately 70 police officers a year are shot and killed in the United States.

A study by the Canadian Centre for Justice Statistics (1982) investigated the shooting deaths of 77 Canadian police officers over the years 1961 to 1980. During this period, 73 Canadian police officers were murdered in 65 incidents. Seventy-one of the 73 homicides were committed by firearms—32 by handguns, 27 by rifles, and 12 by shotguns and sawed-off rifles. Between 1961 and 1970, 19 (53 percent) of the police homicides were committed by rifles, while during the 1970s handguns accounted for 21 (57 percent) of the police deaths.

A total of 87 individuals (three men and four women) were arrested for the killing of the police officers, and 68 were subsequently charged with murder. Nineteen of the suspects died before charges could be laid—six were killed in a violent confrontation with the police, while the other 13 took their own lives after the commission of the crime. Twenty-eight of the suspects were found guilty of first-degree murder, 14 of second-degree murder, and 13 were acquitted by reason of insanity.

Police Misconduct

Police deviance has been defined as "a generic description of police officer activities which are inconsistent with the officer's legal authority, organizational authority, and standards of ethical conduct" (Barker and Carter 1986:1–7). Barker and Carter divide police deviance into two categories: occupational deviancy and abuse of authority. Occupational deviancy is defined as "criminal and noncriminal [behaviour] committed during the cause of normal work activities or committed under the guise of the police officer's authority" (Barker and Carter 1986:4). Examples of police occupational deviancy include misconduct such as sleeping on duty, insubordination, and misuse of firearms. Police abuse of authority involves the use of various types of coercion when the police are interacting with citizens. According to Roberg and Kuykendall (1993:200), there are four types of coercion that are used by the police:

1. verbal coercion: the use of deceit, promises, threats, and derogatory language

2. physical coercion: the use of the officers physical strength and body

3. nonlethal coercion: the use of a weapon instead of or in addition to the officer's body

4. lethal coercion: the use of a deadly weapon in such a manner that a person is likely to be seriously injured or killed

How common is police brutality? Claims have been made throughout the 20th century that Canadian police forces have used brutality. Jamieson (1973) and Brown and Brown (1978) have found that various police forces across Canada have harassed and intimidated striking workers. More recently, it was reported that some Regina police force officers patrolled with unleashed police dogs and that during 1981–82, 85 people were bitten, 52 of them native people (Forcese 1992).

Incidents of police brutality are reported almost weekly by the media across Canada. But what form does police brutality take? Reiss (1974), in an American study, used college students to observe police–citizen interactions in high-crime areas in Washington, D.C., Chicago, and Boston. The students reported verbal abuse was common but that the excessive use of force was relatively rare, occurring in 44 cases out of the 5360 observations. There was little difference in the way police treated blacks and whites, and when force was used, it was typically directed toward selective groups—those who were disrespectful of the police or who disregarded police authority after they were arrested. Sherman (1980) reported that police use of any form of violence was rare, while Bayley and Garofolo (1989) found that when police use force, it usually involves grabbing and restraining, but rarely if ever are weapons used.

However, despite these research findings, widely publicized incidents of police brutality have continued to haunt police departments in both the United States and Canada (Forcese 1992:172–76). In Canada, it has been charged police frequently rely on excessive physical force to obtain confessions from suspects (Hagan 1977), a situation that leads Brannigan (1984:57) to conclude that "the police appear to routinely trample over the rights of accused people." For example, in 1976, as a result of allegations of police brutality in the Metropolitan Toronto Police Force, a Royal Commission was created to investigate the charges. The chairman of the Royal Commission, Mr. Justice Donald Morand, concluded that of the 17 incidents he studied, six involved the use of excessive force.

Controlling Police Misconduct

As incidents of police brutality drive a wedge between police–community relations, a number of efforts have been devised to deal with such issues with the hope that they will not occur in the future. Community policing is one such development, and so are new policies detailing how police officers are supposed to use force in various situations with the public. However, Senna and Siegel (1995:248) point out that such regulations are often "haphazard" and "usually a reaction to a crisis situation . . . rather than part of a systematic effort to improve police–citizen interactions."

It is thought that one of the best ways to control police brutality is to create a separate civilian commission or review agency to investigate allegations of such behaviour. The goal of establishing an external review board is to make the police accountable. The first such organization was created in 1981 in Toronto to investigate allegations of police brutality of Metropolitan Toronto police officers. This commission was later expanded to a province-wide jurisdiction in 1992. In 1981, the Office of the Public Complaints Commissioner was established as a three-year pilot project. The duties of the office were to:

- review and, if necessary, re-investigate complaints made by persons dissatisfied with decisions made by the police

- monitor initial police complaints investigations and decisions made by police chiefs, the Ontario police commissioner, and decisions reached in internal disciplinary hearings
- receive and record complaints from the public
- refer cases to a civilian board of inquiry, if necessary, after reviews
- conduct initial investigations into "two-force" complaints—allegations against officers from more than one force
- make recommendations to the police to improve police practices in order to avoid re-occurrence of certain types of complaints

In order to carry out an investigation, the Public Complaints Commissioner was granted considerable powers of search and seizure, to subpoena witnesses, and to order a hearing before a Board of Inquiry that held direct disciplinary powers. One-third of the Board of Inquiry were to be lawyers, one-third individuals jointly recommended by the Board of Police Commissioners and the Metropolitan Toronto Police Association, and one-third appointed by the Toronto City Council (MacMahon 1988). Misconduct needed to be established beyond a reasonable doubt, a standard usually applied to criminal matters. Between 1988 and 1990, almost 98 percent of the cases in which civilians filed a complaint against police stemmed from an incident in which they were charged (Ellis and DeKeseredy 1996).

The Public Complaints Commissioner further categorized allegations of police brutality as follows:

1. failure to act according to police procedure
2. nonphysical: verbal threats
3. physical: assault or excessive force
4. misuse of authority

The annual reports of the Public Complaints Commissioner for the period 1988 to 1991 are summarized by Ellis and DeKeseredy (1996). They found that nonphysical and physical assaults by police account for approximately one-half of all complaints. The largest category was "failure to act according to police procedure," such as neglect of duty, which accounted for 43 percent of all complaints. Landau's (1994) study of the nature of allegations revealed that "improper police behavior" accounted for 49 percent of complaints, followed by physical abuse (34 percent), verbal abuse (32 percent), unprofessional conduct (29 percent), and neglect of duty (25 percent).

According to Ellis and DeKeseredy, the rate of complaints increased each year. In 1988, the rate was 6 percent, increasing to 9.8 percent in 1989 and 12.7 percent in 1990. Between 1988 and 1990, 1915 complaints were heard by the police disciplinary board or by the complaints board (Ellis and DeKeseredy 1996:117–18). Discipline occurred in 82 of these cases—21 complaints led to informal disciplinary measures and 61 complaints led to formal disciplinary action. In his study of complainants, Landau (1994) found that the largest percentage of decisions by both the police chief and the Public Complaints Commissioner for a 15-month period in 1992 and early 1993 resulted in "no action taken" because of insufficient evidence, which accounted for 52 percent of all "resolved" complaints. Two other categories—"no further action— evidence supports officer" and "no further action—complainant lodged in bad faith"—accounted for 16 and 23 percent of all complaints respectively. Thus, no further action was taken in 70 (or 91 percent) of 77 decisions.

Of the 1915 incidents that led to an investigation, Ellis and DeKeseredy found most complaints to result from police–citizen contact on the street (48 percent). The next-largest categories were "residence," "police building," and "public place," which accounted for another 46 percent of the remaining incident locations. Similar results were obtained by Landau. Just over 78 percent of all complaints in her study came from incidents "on the street or in public" (54 percent) and the complainant's residence (24 percent).

In his study, Landau found 30 percent of complainants were black, 8 percent were Asian, and 4 percent were Hispanic. These rates are considered to be an "unreliable indicator of the current state of relations between police and visible minority, particularly black members of the community" (Annual Report of the Public Complaints Commissioner 1989:15). Ellis and DeKeseredy (1996:119) agree with this view, pointing out these rates "greatly underestimate the actual number of occasions in which blacks and other visible minority community members experienced racially or ethnically biased police conduct."

Summary

In our society today police forces and their officers face many critical issues as they develop policies, enforce the law, and interact with the public. One central issue concerns the best way to measure the overall effectiveness of the police. Some people assert that the police should always arrest an individual whenever there is enough evidence, regardless of the infraction. This move toward "zero tolerance" policies has led to a debate about the practice of police discretion. Studies of the arrest practices of the police in Canada indicate that the police do not "over" arrest the members of any particular group, but that situational and community factors play a crucial role in the decisions made by the police.

Social issues also affect police operations. Women and minority group members are now entering police ranks in increasing numbers, with research indicating that their performance is as good as or even better than other police officers. However, the percentage of women and minority group members on police forces still does not reflect their representation in the population. As their numbers increase, an important issue involves the number of women and minorities in the higher echelons of the police department.

Other critical issues involve police use of deadly force and police deviance. While the studies of deadly force are rare, it can be concluded that it is an uncommon occurrence for the police to kill a citizen in Canada. More information, however, is available on police deviance. Recent initiatives by the province of Ontario reveal that many citizens have concerns about the police overextending their powers in their contacts with citizens.

Discussion Questions

1. What are some possible negative and positive consequences of the police use of discretion?

2. What are some factors that influence the use of police discretion?

3. Why have women and minority group members been excluded from joining police forces throughout the 20th century?

4. What are the advantages and/or disadvantages for police departments of hiring women and members of minority groups?

5. Are women as effective as men in all types of police work? Why or why not?

6. Discuss why the police in Canada use less deadly force than their counterparts in the United States.

7. Do you think police deviance is as serious a problem as it was 10 or more years ago?

8. What do you think is the best way to control police deviance?

Suggested Readings

Chappell, Duncan, and L.P. Graham. *Police Use of Deadly Force: Canadian Perspectives*. Centre of Criminology, University of Toronto, 1985.

Ellis, Desmond, and W. DeKeseredy. *The Wrong Stuff*, 2nd ed. Scarborough, Ont.: Allyn and Bacon, 1996.

Forcese, Dennis P. *Policing Canadian Society*. Scarborough: Prentice-Hall, 1992.

Landau, Tammy. *Public Complaints against the Police: A View from Complainants*. Centre of Criminology, University of Toronto, 1994.

Linden, R., and C. Minch. *Women in Policing: A Review*. Ottawa: Solicitor General of Canada, 1982.

Shearing, C.D., ed. *Organizational Police Deviance*. Toronto: Butterworths, 1981.

CHAPTER 7

Pre-Trial Procedures

Between an arrest and a trial lies a series of events that are essential components in the processing of defendants in the criminal justice system. Pre-trial procedures are important because most criminal cases are never formally heard in the courts but are resolved informally. Although most Canadians have seen television courtroom dramas with juries, defence lawyers, and prosecutors arguing over details in front of a judge, such formal trials occur infrequently. As a result, it is important to study pre-trial procedures in order to understand the reality of most individuals who enter into the criminal justice system.

In July 1984, the body of Lorraine Briggs was found wrapped in green garbage bags under the stairwell of her home in Edmonton, Alberta. She had been strangled, perhaps a week earlier.

CHAPTER OBJECTIVES

- **explain the key components of pre-trial procedures**
- **consider the importance of the defendant's right to legal counsel**
- **discuss the rules governing search and seizure in Canada**
- **consider the different types of warrants used by the police in Canada, including warrantless searches**
- **consider the laws governing police use of electronic surveillance**
- **examine the laws controlling the police interrogation while the suspect is in custody**

During the police investigation the palm print of her 16-year-old grandson, Emerson Broyles, was found on one of the garbage bags. In addition, he had been seen driving her van in the days before the body was found. By the time the body was found, he was in custody, charged with forging his grandmother's name to cheques.

However, all of the evidence against Broyles was circumstantial. The police decided to recruit a friend to visit him in detention while wearing a tape recorder that would record their conversation. During this visit Broyles denied murdering his grandmother, but admitted to his friend that he was aware that she was dead and knew the location of the body before police discovered it. On the basis of this conversation, Broyles was convicted of second-degree murder and sentenced to life in prison with no parole for 10 years.

On appeal, the Supreme Court of Canada ruled that the police cannot recruit informers to get a confession from an accused person. The justices unanimously agreed to order a new trial for Broyles because a key piece of evidence was obtained in violation of his right to remain silent. The Court said the police action violated the defendant's constitutional right of silence when in the custody of authorities. The Supreme Court further ruled that informers are acting as police agents. Once it is established that the incriminating statement has been made to a police agent, the only other legal issue is whether the agent elicited the statement.

Arrest

The power to arrest means that the police can restrain the liberty of an individual. During the course of their duties, a police officer may stop and question a large number of people for a number of reasons. They may want to obtain information about a crime or question someone about what he or she is doing in a particular location.

To legally arrest someone, the police officer has to verbally inform the individual in question that he or she is under arrest. Section 10(a) of the Charter of Rights and Freedoms stipulates that "everyone has the right on arrest or detention to be informed promptly of the reasons thereof."

Police may arrest someone without a warrant (see Chapter 1). For this to happen, a police officer may arrest

- anyone he finds committing any criminal offence (indictable, summary conviction, and federal statute)
- anyone about to commit on indictable offence
- anyone who the police officer believes has an outstanding warrant within the territorial jurisdiction in which the person is located

A police officer's power to arrest without a warrant is restricted by Section 495(2) of the Criminal Code, which states that no arrest shall occur where the public interest is satisfied and no reasonable grounds exist to believe the accused will fail to appear in court (see below). Also, in the case of a summary conviction offence, an arrest cannot be made when the offence has been committed or is about to be committed.

Arrests can be made with or without an arrest warrant (see Chapter 1). A police officer has a duty not to arrest an individual for certain types of offences, as outlined by the Criminal Code:

> 495. (2) A peace officer shall not arrest a person without warrant for
>> (a) an indictable offence mentioned in Section 553,
>> (b) an offence for which the person may be prosecuted by indictment or for which he is punishable on summary conviction, or
>> (c) an offence punishable on summary conviction, in any case where
>> (d) he believes on reasonable grounds that the public interest, having regard to all the circumstances including the need to
>>> (i) establish the identity of the person,
>>> (ii) secure or preserve the identity of the person,
>>> (iii) prevent the continuation or repetition of the offence or the commission of another offence,
>> may be satisfied without so arresting the person, and
>> (e) he has no reasonable grounds to believe that, if he does not so arrest the person, the person will fail to attend court in order to be dealt with according to law. (Source: Justice Canada)

If the police are going to arrest someone with a warrant, they must suspect that the individual committed a crime and that his or her appearance cannot be compelled by a summons (see Chapter 1). To obtain a warrant, the police must ordinarily go before a justice of the peace and lay an information alleging that a criminal offence has been committed. However, an arrest can be made without a warrant if the police observe a crime involving an any type of offence being committed. But if the police decide they are going to detain the individual for a period of time, he or she must be brought before a justice of the peace as soon as possible. Section 503 (1) of the Criminal Code states that when a justice is available within 24 hours of an arrest, the accused must be taken before him within this period of time, or within a reasonable period if a justice is not available. If the accused does not appear before a justice within a certain amount of time, the case may be terminated on the grounds of "unreasonable delay." The Supreme Court of Canada dealt with the meaning of "unreasonable delay" in *R. v. Storey* (1990), in which it ruled that the police were allowed an 18-hour delay so that a line-up could be put together. However, when an accused was detained for 36 hours in *R. v. Charles* (1987), it was considered to be a violation of Section 9 of the Charter.

Custodial Interrogation

The police can place an accused in custody at the time of arrest, whether it be on the street, in a house, in a police station, or in a police vehicle. The individual must be informed of his or her right to silence and counsel before the police start questioning. According to Section 7 of the Charter, everyone has the right to life, liberty, and security of the person and the right not to be deprived thereof except in accordance with the principles of fundamental justice. Thus, the police must inform the individual they have taken into custody that he or she has certain rights. Currently, the police must read the following to any person they arrest:

1. *Notice upon arrest:* I am arresting you for ... (briefly describe reasons for arrest).
2. *Right to counsel:* It is my duty to inform you that you have the right to retain and instruct counsel without delay. Do you understand?
3. *Caution to charged person:* You (are charged, will be charged) with ... Do you wish to say anything in answer to the charge? You are not obligated to say anything unless you wish to do so, but whatever you say may be given in evidence.
4. *Secondary caution to charged person:* If you have spoken to any police officer or anyone with authority or if any such person has spoken to you in connection with this case, I want it clearly understood that I do not want it to influence you in making any statement. (Source: Justice Canada)

Many suspects choose to remain silent, and since both oral and written statements are admissible in court, police officers sometimes stop their questioning until defence counsel are present. If the accused decides to answer the questions, he or she may decide to stop at any time and refuse to answer more questions until a lawyer arrives. Suspects may waive this right only if they are aware of what they are doing and are able to contact a lawyer at any time if they so wish. In a study published before the enactment of the Charter of Rights and Freedoms, Ericson and Baranek (1982) found that almost 60 percent of defendants gave verbal statements to the police before any contact with a lawyer. The authors also reported that almost 70 percent of those requested by police to provide a written statement did so prior to contacting a lawyer. Perhaps many Canadians arrested behave like Guy Paul Morin, who thought it better to answer police questions because "by refusing to talk or asserting his rights would imply guilt" (Makin 1992:200).

Traditionally, Canadian courts have stated that an out-of-court statement by an accused person constitutes appropriate evidence, if it is voluntary. In *R. v. Rickett* (1975), it was determined that when an issue arises over the voluntariness of a statement, it must be proved beyond a reasonable doubt that the statement was voluntary. In essence, Section 7 of the Charter seeks to impose limits on the powers the state and its agents (such as the police) have over the detained individual. This protects the accused against the superior resources of the police. However, the police have the power to deprive an individual of his or her life, liberty, or security as long as they respect the fundamental principles of justice.

Right to Counsel

According to Section 9 of the Charter of Rights and Freedoms, everyone has the right not to be arbitrarily detained or imprisoned. But even if detention is justified, the right to legal counsel found in Section 10 of the Charter "emerges in the face of any detention" (Abell and Sheehy 1993:269).

> 10. Everyone has the right on arrest or detention
>   (a) to be informed promptly of the reasons therefore
>   (b) to retain and instruct counsel without delay and to be informed of that right
>   (c) to have the validity of that detention determined by way of **habeas corpus** and to be released if detention is not lawful (Source: Justice Canada)

According to the interpretation of Section 10(b) of the Charter, the right to contact a lawyer without delay is a central Charter right. This means that when an accused requests counsel, that request must be allowed. A number of issues have been raised over this issue, including what the right to counsel encompasses, when and how the police must inform the accused of the right to counsel, what the accused must do to assert the right to counsel, and when it is reasonable to limit the right to counsel under Section 1 of the Charter (Abell and Sheehy 1993:269).

The accused must be given a reasonable opportunity to consult a lawyer; they also have the right to talk to legal counsel privately. However, the accused cannot delay the investigation by deciding to contact counsel after several hours. The burden is on the accused to prove that it was impossible to contact his lawyer when the police offer him the opportunity (*R. v. Smith* 1989).

The right to counsel in Canada is not absolute, and is available only to someone under arrest or being detained. In *R. v. Bazinet* (1986) the suspect voluntarily agreed to accompany the police to the police station. While answering questions about a murder, the suspect confessed to committing the crime. At this point, the police informed him of his right to counsel. On appeal, it was ruled that the police followed proper procedure since there was no evidence to indicate that the accused felt he was deprived of his liberty and had to accompany the police.

But what happens if a suspect requests to "see" a lawyer—can the police continue to interrogate him while he is waiting for the lawyer to appear? The answer depends on the type of question the police are asking. If the questions are "innocuous" (e.g., asking questions such as the accused's name and address) then they are allowed. However, questions concerning the facts of the case are not allowed until legal counsel has talked with his or her client. In *R. v. Manninen* (1983), the accused had requested to see his lawyer. However, a police officer continued to question him, asking the accused the location of a knife that was allegedly used to rob a store. The accused then proceeded to tell the officers that he only had a gun while committing the robbery. The Ontario Court of Appeal ruled that this question was in violation of Manninen's rights because it was "based on a presumption of guilt and the answer was devastating to the defence" and was asked "as if the appellant had expressed no desire to remain silent." As a result, the accused's admission of guilt was excluded.

In *R. v. Black* (1989), the accused was originally charged for the attempted murder of another woman. She contacted her lawyer by telephone, but a few hours later, the victim died. The police advised her that she was now being charged with first-degree murder. The accused requested to speak to her lawyer again, but the lawyer could not be reached. The officers then suggested she speak to another lawyer, a suggestion she refused. Shortly after, the police questioned the accused again, and she confessed to the crime. The Supreme Court ruled that since the accused had not waived her right to a lawyer, it was a violation of her right to legal counsel, and consequently, her statement was excluded from the evidence.

An individual can give up the right to counsel, but he must appreciate the consequences of giving up that right. If he is not so instructed by the police, anything he tells the police will be excluded. In *R. v. Clarkson* (1986), a woman confessed to the police that she murdered her husband, even though her aunt, who was present during the questioning, told her to contact a lawyer. Since the accused was intoxicated at the time, the Supreme Court later ruled the confession to be inadmissible because the police should have waited to question her when she was sober since everyone must be fully aware of the consequences of waiving their right to counsel.

How long does an accused have to make a call? It depends on the seriousness of the charge. In the case of *R. v. Joey Smith* (1989), the accused was arrested for robbery and requested to contact a lawyer after 9 p.m. Finding only a business telephone number, the accused decided to try again in the morning, despite police recommendations that he call that evening. The accused refused. When the police questioned him later, he ultimately made a statement "off the record" that was later used as evidence to convict him. On appeal, the Supreme Court of Canada ruled the statement to be admissible because the crime was

Field Practice 7.1

Release on Recognizance

Poor and Out of Work

An 18-year-old male was arrested for stealing two loaves of bread and some canned meat. He requested to be released on recognizance, claiming that he was well known in the area and too poor to leave. An investigation discovered that he lived with his unemployed girl-friend, had never held a long-term job, had dropped out of school in Grade 10, and was indeed poor. His prior record consisted of only a shoplifting infraction, for which he had paid restitution to the shop owner on time. The investigator recommended pre-trial release, but the justice of the peace remanded him to the local remand centre to await his trial.

White-Collar Offender

A 40-year-old male was arrested for defrauding 22 senior citizens of their life savings, which totalled over $250 000. He had set up an elaborate series of financial institutions and fake financial statements to prove to his victims that they would be investing in a "can't lose" company, and promised (in writing) a return of a minimum of 10 percent on their investment. Once they had invested in the company, the victims received glowing financial statements and at least two cheques representing some of the profits allegedly made by the company. After his arrest, the police discovered he had a previous conviction for the same offence in another city. The accused requested to be released on recognizance, a request readily agreed to by the judge.

Strong-Arm Robber

A strong 22-year-old male was arrested after a series of purse-snatchings committed against elderly women. Employed as a labourer at a nearby factory, he lived at home, and had a good work history, no prior record, and a clean driving record. The accused requested release on recognizance, but the judge refused, citing the impact of his violent action. Instead, the judge set bail at $10 000, a sum the accused could not afford. The accused was sent to remand to await his trial date.

not considered a serious offence. If it had been a serious offence, he would have been granted an additional opportunity to contact legal counsel.

Compelling Appearance, Interim Release, and Pre-Trial Detention

After an individual is arrested, he or she may be taken to the police station, where the police record the criminal charges and obtain other information relevant to the case. This process is commonly referred to as "lodging a complaint," and it usually includes a description of the suspect and, if necessary, circumstances relating to the offence. If the suspect was caught in the act of committing a crime (as opposed to being arrested by a warrant or summons), the arresting officer proceeds to swear an information and present it to a justice of the peace as soon as possible.

What actually happens to the accused depends on the charge. If the charge is a summary conviction offence, in all likelihood the accused will be released immediately on his own recognizance and after a promise to appear in court on the trial date. This is standard operating procedure in Canada, and it expedites the processing of such cases and saves the police from searching for the accused to serve him with an arrest warrant or summons.

When an indictable or hybrid offence is involved, the police need reasonable and probable grounds that a crime was committed. In all provinces except New Brunswick, Quebec, and British Columbia, Crown prosecutors do not review any charges before they are laid. This means that anyone (usually a police officer) who has reasonable and probable grounds that an individual has committed an indictable offence can swear an information before a justice of the peace (Section 504 of the Criminal Code). The justice of the peace must accept the information and decide whether to proceed by way of a summons or arrest warrant (Section 507 of the Criminal Code).

The procedure of initiating charges has been criticized by the Law Reform Commission of Canada (1990:70) as "a mere formality." As a result, the protections offered individuals through the Charter "are largely lost," and "the resources of the court can be wasted by the initiation of prosecutions that have little chance of success." However, the theory behind this process is to require the justice of the peace to evaluate the worthiness of the charge(s).

Unlike summary conviction offences, individuals charged with indictable offences are usually processed at a police station. This can involve fingerprinting and photographing the accused. Afterward, depending on the charge, the accused may be released on his own recognizance; however, if there is a belief that the individual may not appear at the court trial, the police may keep the individual locked up in a jail cell and/or send him to a remand centre to await a hearing on the charges and bail. If the accused enters a guilty plea when the charges are read into court, he is admitting to all the elements of the crime, and the court will usually schedule a sentencing date. A plea of not guilty sets the stage for a trial, and such a case may ultimately involve a plea bargain.

If the accused is charged with what is referred to as a Section 469 crime— e.g., murder—a superior court justice decides whether or not to order the accused into a detention facility. In these cases, a reverse onus applies—that is, it is up to the accused to show why he should be released.

1. the accused is charged with an indictable offence while already on judicial interim release or is in the process of appealing another indictable offence

2. the accused commits an indictable offence but is not a resident of Canada

3. the accused allegedly has broken a previous interim release order

4. the accused has committed or conspired to commit an offence under Sections 4 and 5 of the Narcotics Control Act (i.e., trafficking, exporting, or importing)

In almost every case, the prosecutor has to *show cause*—to demonstrate that detaining the accused is justified. Otherwise, the accused has to be released. The judge cannot impose any more control over the accused unless the prosecutor shows that it is necessary. Certain conditions—e.g., reporting to a police officer—may be imposed when he is released. The prosecutor may want the accused to enter into a recognizance to forfeit some money (but without asking for any cash) if he fails to appear in court, that one or more sureties agree to forfeit money if there is a failure to appear. Alternatively, the accused may be requested to deposit an amount of money with the court. Both a surety and a cash deposit may be required if the accused is not a resident of the province or lives beyond 200 kilometres of where he is being held. Of course, the accused may be detained if the justice of the peace feels it is necessary, but the reasons must be recorded.

Bail Reform

In 1971, Parliament passed the Bail Reform Act (1972), creating the system of judicial interim release described above. Amended four years later, the act is the basis for bail in Canada today. It was largely the result of the Ouimet Committee, which recommended that suspects should not be placed in detention unless it was believed that this was the only means to ensure that the accused would appear in court. This recommendation was based on a Canadian study on pre-trial detention and a U.S. study on how bail discriminates against the poor. In the Canadian study, Milton Friedland (1965) concluded that "the overwhelming majority of persons in Toronto charged with offences against the Criminal Code were arrested rather than summoned." In the 6000 cases he studied, Friedland found that the accused was arrested in 92 percent of the cases, and that 84 percent of those arrested remained in custody until their first court appearance.

The U.S. study, referred to as the Manhattan Bail Project, took place in New York City in the early 1960s. The Vera Institute, a private, nonprofit research organization dedicated to improving the criminal justice system, designed an experimental pre-trial program that investigated arrested individuals who could not afford bail in order to see who would appear in court for their trials if they were released back into the community following their initial court appearance. The researchers found that the appearance rate of those released on their own recognizance was consistently the same as or better than the rate of those released on monetary bail. As a result, release-on-recognizance programs were influential in changing the nature of the bail process across North America.

The Manhattan Bail Project also led to the introduction of different types of pre-trial release. One such innovation became known as stationhouse release, a process in which a suspect is issued a citation to appear in court at a later date, thereby bypassing the costly exercise of pre-trial detention. This experiment was also successful, as most suspects released back into the community appeared in court on the duly appointed date. As a result of these studies, "the prevailing view became that release should be available, regardless of financial circumstances, unless overwhelming factors preclude it" (Anderson and Newman 1993:216).

The Bail Reform Act therefore emphasized the need to release most offenders into the community pending their trial. The new legislation instructed police officers to issue an appearance notice to the accused rather than arrest her unless the public was in jeopardy or she had committed a serious indictable offence. In addition, the officer in charge of the lockup must release a person charged with most offences and compel the accused to appear in court by a summons, promise to appear, or on her own recognizance.

In addition, the legislation provided that a justice or magistrate has to release the accused unless the prosecutor shows cause why the release should not occur. There also exists what is known as the "ladder effect" when determining the release of the accused. This means that a prosecutor must persuade the justice why, for most offences, a less severe release mechanism is not appropriate in any given case. The "ladder" is mentioned in Section 515(2) of the Criminal Code, which establishes that almost every individual can be released on recognizance if she promises to appear for trial on a designated date. Unsecured bail does not require the defendant to pay money to the court, but she remains liable for the full amount if she fails to appear at her trial. Fully secured bail requires the defendant to post the full amount of bail with the court. The amount of bail cannot be fixed so high that it becomes, in effect, a detention order.

The number of individuals held in preventive detention varies significantly across Canada. Jails and remand centres are a controversial issue because conditions tend to be poor, with very little, if any, rehabilitation services. During the early 1980s, evidence showed that aboriginal peoples were placed in preventive detention at a higher rate than any other racial group in Ontario (Birkenmayer and Jolly 1981). Statistics released by the Canadian Centre for Justice Statistics for 1988–89 revealed some provincial variation in the use of pre-trial detention. Two provinces (Manitoba and Quebec) were found to have more individuals in custody awaiting a court appearance, trial, or sentence than those sentenced to a term of imprisonment.

One major concern of the judiciary is that preventive detention is based on the prediction that the accused will do something wrong in the future. In this sense, it is very much like the concerns raised about selective incapacitation (see Chapter 3). Such factors as previous criminal record and seriousness of the current offence may lead a Crown prosecutor to request for preventive detention.

Search and Seizure

Do the police have the right to conduct frisk searches whenever they want after an individual has been lawfully arrested? Should the police be able to use excessive physical force or psychological intimidation beyond what is "reasonable" in order to accomplish the search? The answers to these questions are found in the laws governing search and seizure in Canada. Because the issue of search and seizure encompasses a variety of situations throughout the criminal justice process, many debates exist over appropriate behaviour by the police or other government agents. As a result, the laws governing this area are constantly challenged in court.

One of the most fundamental rights of Canadian citizens is the protection against unreasonable search and seizure. This right gives a citizen the right to be left alone by the government or its agents unless there are grounds that allow them to intrude. A search involves the intrusion of a government representative into an individual's reasonable and justifiable expectation of privacy. A seizure is defined as the exercise of control by a government representative over an individual and/or item. Generally, a search warrant is required before a search of an individual or a place may be legally conducted. There are three different legal areas that govern searches and seizures in Canada: common law, the Criminal Code, and the Charter of Rights and Freedoms.

The common law is concerned with the search of persons as well as places. In most cases, the police must have a search warrant granted by a member of the judiciary in order to search an individual. However, the common law gives police the right to conduct general body searches when arresting a suspect. This includes combing out hair samples for forensic evidence, but it does not include the taking of blood samples, which are considered to be an invasive search. For an invasive search, special statutory authorization is required, and this is usually found in the Criminal Code.

Most of what the police do in this area of law is regulated by Section 487 of the Criminal Code. All police officers must obtain a search warrant by swearing an information on oath in front of a justice of the peace. The search warrant provides police officers with the power to search places but not individuals (which is covered by common law). Currently, a warrant can be obtained for:

(a) any items on or in respect of which an offence under any federal act has been committed

(b) anything that will provide evidence of any evidence under federal legislation

(c) anything intended to be used to commit an offence against the person for which an arrest without a warrant may be made (Source: Justice Canada)

The police officer must specify the offence, describe the items as well as the place(s) that will be searched, and explain how the search will turn up the items mentioned in the warrant application (Sections 488, 488.1, and 489 of the Criminal Code).

Police officers have the legal right to seize items not mentioned in the warrant if there are reasonable grounds to believe they were obtained by or used in the commission of an offence. The Law Reform Commission of Canada (1991) maintains that the Criminal Code contains only minimal regulations covering search and seizure and therefore there is a lack of certainty within the law itself.

Two sections of the Charter of Rights and Freedoms specifically relate to search and seizure. Section 8 of the Charter states that "everyone has the right to be secure against unreasonable search and seizure," while Section 24(2) points out that if evidence

> was obtained in a manner that infringed or denied any rights or freedoms guaranteed by the Charter, the evidence shall be excluded if it is established that . . . the admission of it in the proceedings would bring the administration of justice into disrepute. (Source: Justice Canada)

Requirements for Search Warrants

The 'Reasonableness' Test

This test, as it applies to searches and seizures, generally refers to the question of whether or not a police officer has overstepped his or her authority. Most searches are judged to be unreasonable if a police officer does not have sufficient information to justify the search. The appropriate standard of proof is one of "reasonable and probable grounds" rather than proof beyond a reasonable doubt; in other words, a search warrant can be granted only if the request for it is accompanied by facts that indicate to the court that a crime has been committed or is being committed.

Particularity

This refers to the search warrant itself. A search warrant must specify the place to be searched and the reasons for searching it. When the police request a search warrant, the warrant must identify the premises and the personal property to be seized, and it must be signed by a police officer. The facts and information justifying the need for a search warrant are also set out in an affidavit requesting the warrant.

Searches Needing a Warrant

The issue of whether the police are required to obtain a **warrant** as a prerequisite to a search or seizure has been a key component of the Supreme Court of Canada's interpretation of Section 8 of the Charter of Rights and Freedoms. During the early years of the Charter, the courts took two different positions on the necessity of warrants. First, some judges and justices of the peace focused on the issue of the reasonableness of police conduct, meaning that a critical evaluation of the "reasonableness" of the search can be determined after the search or seizure takes place if the issue arises. The presence or absence of a warrant, or the information found in the warrant, is not always considered as the most important criterion in determining whether the search or seizure was reasonable. The Law Reform Commission (1983:83), in its study of **search warrants** in seven Canadian cities (Edmonton, Fredericton, Montreal, St. John's, Toronto, Winnipeg, and Vancouver), concluded that "there is a clear gap between legal rules for issuing and obtaining search warrants and the daily realities of practice." In some locations, police gave only minimal information to support their request for a warrant and, as a result, provided the "adjudication no objective basis for making a judicial determination as to whether or not to issue a warrant." This does not mean that the police are involved in illegal searches, but, rather, that proper procedures have not been followed, thereby raising concerns about the "reasonableness" of a search. The Law Reform Commission (1983:86) concluded, after an analysis of all the documents, that

> no decisive relationship [exists] between the legality of the search and the eventual seizure of the specified item. This argues against the possibility that the widespread illegality of warrants is attributable to police decisions to search in inappropriate cases. Rather the indication is that the problem resides with adherence to procedures. In other words, the necessary factual basis for a search may well exist, but the warrant is nonetheless being issued improperly.

The second position was taken by judges and justices of the peace who interpreted Section 8 of the Charter differently. They emphasized that failure to obtain a warrant without all pertinent information is "unreasonable" except in the most extraordinary situations. In other words, the Charter exists to prevent unreasonable searches and seizures from taking place at all, not to determine if they were reasonable or unreasonable after the fact.

Invoking strict standards for warrants involving searches and seizures promotes adherence to the law in three ways. First, it requires police officers to make an objective assessment of the "reasonableness" of their evidence before they act. Second, it provides judges with the exact information a police officer has obtained to date, giving them the grounds to make a more informed decision about the legality of the warrant. Third, it provides a neutral and objective assessment of the evidence by a "detached" individual rather than relying on a decision made by a police officer "in the heat of the chase." According to the advocates of the third position, a proper system for issuing search warrants "can only be accomplished by a system of prior authorization not one of subsequent validation" (Martin's Annual Criminal Code 1994).

This issue has not yet been resolved in Canada. In their decision in *Hunter v. Southam Inc.* (1984), the Supreme Court of Canada took the position that "for any type of search of premises, the person or a vehicle, the question is whether a warrant is feasible." Therefore, according to the Supreme Court, there can be exceptions to the requirement of a warrant in every case, since it may not be "feasible" to obtain one. In essence, the test is whether a warrant is feasible for any type of search of a place, person, or motor vehicle. What this ruling did was to protect citizens from unreasonable searches and seizures through a minimum-standards approach.

Warrantless Searches in Exigent Circumstances

A case involving a **warrantless search** is liable to be deemed illegal and therefore "thrown" out of court. However, in Canada, a warrantless search can be considered reasonable depending upon the exigent (i.e., immediate) circumstances of the case. But what are considered to be acceptable exigent circumstances in Canada? And just when can a police officer conduct a search without a warrant? After all, the Canadian courts have ruled that the police cannot go on "fishing expeditions" for evidence. What is important are the circumstances of the case and how the police conduct their activities.

Illegal searches are not always ruled to be unreasonable. In *R. v. Heisler* (1984), for example, the Alberta Court of Appeal ruled that searching an individual's purse when entering a rock concert was not illegal although there had not been any prior reasonable grounds. And in *R. v. Harris* (1987), Mr. Justice Martin of the Ontario Court of Appeal stated that minor or technical defects in a warrant would not automatically make unconstitutional a search or seizure under Section 8 of the Charter.

Drug convictions are sometimes appealed on the issue of warrantless cases. This is because police officers observe possession of the drug but don't have the time to obtain a search warrant prior to the use or selling of the drug. In *R. v. Collins* (1987), police officers in British Columbia, conducting a heroin investigation, observed two suspects in a village pub. When one individual left to go to his car, the police approached him, searched the car, and found a quantity of heroin. Back in the pub, an officer approached the other suspect and proceeded to grab her by the throat to prevent her from swallowing any evidence. The suspect dropped a balloon containing heroin. The trial judge ruled the search unreasonable since the police had used unnecessary force. The

Supreme Court of Canada, however, overturned this decision, stating that there was nothing to suggest the collection of evidence in this manner made the trial unfair.

In determining the reasonableness of a search, the courts examine the following issues:

1. whether the information predicting the commission of a criminal offence was compelling

2. whether the information was based on an informant's tip, and whether the source was credible

3. whether the information was corroborated by a police investigation before the decision to conduct the search was made

The police are also able to take into account the accused's past record and reputation, provided that such information is relevant to the circumstances of the search.

Searches Incident to an Arrest

Another exception to the search warrant requirement involves searches incident to an arrest. This power is granted to the police by the common law and allows the police to search the suspect for weapons and evidence of a crime without first obtaining a search warrant. The courts have allowed this exception on a number of grounds, including

1. the need to protect the arresting officers

2. the need to prevent the arrestee from destroying any evidence in their possession

3. the intrusiveness of the lawful arrest being already so great that the incidental search is of only minor consequence

4. the fact that the individual could in any event be subjected to an inventory search at the police station

In *Cloutier v. Langlois* (1990), the police stopped a motorist for making an illegal right-hand turn. Contact with the dispatcher revealed that the motorist had several unpaid traffic fines. Subsequently, the driver became agitated and abusive toward the police, who then proceeded to place him by the car, spread his legs, and frisk him. The motorist later sued the police officers for assaulting him. The Supreme Court ruled that reasonable grounds are not necessary for a frisk search incident to an arrest, and that such searches are necessary for "the effective and safe enforcement of the law . . . [and] ensuring the freedom and dignity of individuals." In this case, the police were justified in believing that the search was necessary for their safety.

However, the courts have also stated that before conducting a frisk search the police must inform the suspect of his or her right to counsel. But the police do not have to wait until the suspect contacts a lawyer before a search is made. The Supreme Court has established the following limits on the common law and the right to search an individual incident to arrest:

1. The police have discretion whether a search is necessary for the effective and safe application of the law.
2. The search must be for a valid criminal objective (e.g., to check for weapons or to prevent an escape).
3. The search cannot be used to intimidate, ridicule, or pressure the accused to gain admissions.
4. The search must not be conducted in an abusive way.

There are exceptions to these rights. In *R. v. Tomaso* (1989), the accused appealed his conviction of dangerous driving, arguing that the police collected blood from his bleeding ear while he was unconscious in hospital. The blood sample revealed the accused was impaired at the time of the accident. However, the Ontario Court of Appeal determined the seizure was unreasonable—but only because the accused was not charged until two weeks later.

Warrantless Searches in Motor Vehicles

The Supreme Court of Canada has established that a warrantless search of a vehicle may be reasonable if there are grounds for believing that the vehicle contains drugs or other contraband. However, the power to search a vehicle without a warrant must be found in statute or at common law (e.g., a search incident to a valid arrest).

The legality of searching motor vehicles has proved to be a difficult issue for the police. Can a police officer search the interior of a vehicle? Or a locked suitcase or closed briefcase? In *R. v. Mellenthin* (1992), the Supreme Court of Canada ruled the accused's rights were violated when, at a police check stop, the accused was questioned about the contents of a bag. The suspect handed over the bag, which was found to contain narcotics. However, the officer had no idea or suspicion that the accused was in possession of these illegal drugs when he asked to search the bag. According to the Supreme Court, the purpose of a police check stop is to detect impaired drivers or dangerous vehicles but not to conduct unreasonable searches. In this case, there was no informed consent.

Other Types of Warrantless Searches

The Doctrine of Plain View

The police can search for and seize evidence without a warrant if the illegal object is in plain view. For example, if a police officer arrives at a home responding to a domestic violence incident and notices marijuana on the coffee table, the officer could seize the evidence and arrest the suspect. However, if the officer is suspicious that more drugs may be in the house, he or she would have to apply for and receive an authorized search warrant before investigating any further.

Reasonable Grounds

If a police officer stops a motor vehicle concerning a defective tail-light, and the driver leans over, the officer may become suspicious that an illegal item is being hidden. There is nothing in the act of leaning over itself that can make a police officer suspicious, but when the officer talks to the motorist, and the motorist appears nervous and says nothing, an experienced officer can come to the reasonable conclusion that the motorist is hiding something. This might give the officer reasonable cause to search the vehicle (Salhany 1986).

The rationale for "reasonable grounds" is found in Section 101(1) of the Criminal Code. It allows a police officer to search without a warrant when that officer believes he or she has reasonable grounds to believe that an offence is being committed or has been committed. The section also deals with prohibited weapons, restricted weapons, firearms or ammunition, and evidence that an offence is likely to be found on a person, in a vehicle, or in any place or premises other than a dwelling place. In *R. v. Singh* (1983) the accused fit the description of a suspect wanted for interrogation about a multiple shooting. The incident had occurred just a few minutes before, when the suspect was seen in the same vicinity. When stopped by police, the suspect had a noticeable bulge in his pocket and refused to make eye contact with the police. The police then searched the suspect and found the weapon used in the crime. In this case, the Ontario Court of Appeal ruled there was no unreasonable search and seizure as specified by Section 8 of the Charter of Rights. In *R. v. Ducharme* (1990), police officers saw a man running into a lane with a full garbage bag at 3 a.m. When they stopped the individual, they noticed the man's hands were cut and bleeding. An officer then searched the bag, without consent, and found 32 cartons of cigarettes. It was later reported that a glass door of a store had been broken and cigarettes stolen from the store. The accused was convicted, but the defence lawyer appealed the case arguing that the officer had performed an improper search. However, the British Columbia Court of Appeal ruled that since the search occurred peacefully in a public place, no invasion of the body occurred; under incriminating conditions, it was "reasonable" for the officer to search the garbage bag. It was not necessary to arrest the accused before looking into the bag. In both cases, the courts ruled police officers can search if they have reasonable grounds for suspicion.

Section 489 of the Criminal Code also permits police officers to seize items not mentioned on a warrant. The key issue here is that the officer has to believe on reasonable grounds that the item in question has been obtained by, or has been used in the commission of, an offence.

Consent Searches

Police officers may also make a warrantless search when an individual voluntarily consents to the search. Those individuals who choose to consent to a search are waiving their constitutional rights. Thus, the police may have to prove in court that the consent was voluntarily given to them.

The major legal issue in most consent searches is whether the police can prove that consent was given to them voluntarily. In *R. v. Willis* (1992), the Supreme Court of Canada provided guidelines for judging whether or not a voluntary consent was given.

1. The giver of the consent had the authority to give the consent in question.
2. The consent was voluntary in the sense it was free from coercion and not the result of police oppression, coercion, or other external conduct which negated the freedom to choose whether or not the police should continue.
3. The giver of the consent was aware of his right to refuse the police to engage in the conduct requested.
4. The giver of the consent was aware of the potential consequences of giving the consent.

Electronic Surveillance

The use of wiretaps to intercept conversations between individuals has had a significant impact on police work. These electronic devices allow people to listen to and record the private discussions between people over telephones, as well as through the walls and windows of houses. Using a variety of techniques, police are able to listen to private discussions and obtain information concerning criminal activity.

The earliest and most commonly used type of electronic surveillance is wiretapping. With an approved search warrant from the courts, police officers can listen to and record conversations over telephone lines. This evidence is considered admissible and is often the key evidence that leads to the conviction of the accused.

The Law of Electronic Surveillance

In Canada, the judiciary can authorize the interception of private communications and the use of the information obtained as evidence. It appears that most applications for authorizations for electronic eavesdropping are accepted. Between 1985 and 1989, for example, only three applications out of a possible 2222 were rejected. According to the Solicitor General of Canada (1991), who collects and publishes these figures, this extremely low number of rejections reflects the fact that (1) strict procedures are being followed and (2) judges return an unknown number of applications to the police to provide more information about the case before any authorization will be granted. The Solicitor General points out that almost every one of the 408 authorizations granted in 1989 involved conspiracies to commit serious drug offences. This has led to the comment that electronic surveillance is a necessary feature in the fight against organized drug rings.

Charter defences have been used by drug offenders in an attempt to argue that the police use of electronic surveillance brings the administration of justice into disrepute. However, the Supreme Court has ruled that if the police acted in good faith—that is, they acted in accordance with what they understood the law to be—then the evidence should be admitted. In *R. v. Duarte* (1990), the Supreme Court of Canada ruled on the issue of the police acting in good faith. In this case, members of the Ontario Provincial Police and the Metropolitan Toronto police force were involved in a joint drug investigation concerning large quantities of cocaine. This investigation also involved a police informant and an undercover police officer. Both of them consented to having electronic surveillance equipment in the walls of the apartment occupied by the informant and paid for by the police. In this situation, a court authorization was not required by law since both the informant and undercover operator agreed to the use of such equipment. The lower court judge agreed with the defendant that the practice of conducting electronic surveillance by the police without judicial authorization, even when one of the individuals consents to the surveillance, violates Section 8 of the Charter.

Stay of Proceedings

What happens when an individual commits a crime a number of years before the laying of charges? Judges in Canada have the discretion to stay the proceedings when they believe such a situation abuses the rights of the accused. Delay in the charging and prosecution of an accused for sexual offences cannot justify a staying of proceedings. Sometimes the information concerning a sexual offence will come to the attention of the police years after the reported incident occurred. The police may take months or years to decide that they have the reasonable and probable grounds to lay charges.

In *R. v. L. (W.K.)*, the accused was charged in 1987 with 17 counts of sexual assault, gross indecency, and assault involving his two daughters and step-daughter. The victims complained to the police in 1986, although the first incident had reportedly occurred in 1957 and the last in 1985. The trial judge stayed the proceedings, since to do otherwise would violate the accused's right to fundamental justice. Both the British Columbia Court of Appeal and the Supreme Court of Canada ruled that the trial should not have been stayed. According to the Supreme Court's ruling, the fairness of a trial is not automatically jeopardized by a lengthy pre-charge delay. In fact, this delay may favour the accused, since the police may not be able to find witnesses or any corroborating evidence, if needed.

In some cases, the complainant may make charges of illegal sexual activity on the part of the accused but may not wish the case to proceed to court and give evidence. In *R. v. D.(E.)*, this is exactly what happened, and the police decided not to proceed with the charges if the accused agreed to have no more contact with the family. Four years later, the victims decided to press charges against the accused, and charges were laid by the police. The accused argued his rights had been violated, and the judge agreed that this case would consti-tute an abuse of process and ordered a stay of proceedings. The Crown appealed and won. The Court of Appeal rested its decision on the fact that the accused gave no formal statement to the police in 1984, talking to them on a "non-caution, no-charge basis." The Appeal Court stated that an abuse of process would have occurred only if the prosecution had unfairly reneged on the expectations it gave to the accused.

Legal Aid

Since the earliest days of our criminal justice system, defence lawyers have played an important role in the protection of the accused. However, when defendants could not afford their own lawyers, they were susceptible to local provisions concerning free legal representation. Such a system was clearly problematic, and many critics argued that this system discriminated against people on the basis of wealth and income. An important legal decision in the United States illustrated the problems of not having access to free legal coun-sel, and this case led to the development of formal legal aid systems in Canada. The case in question was *Gideon v. Wainright* (1963), which led to a U.S. Supreme Court decision that is considered to have had the greatest impact on the criminal court process than any other Supreme Court case. Gideon was charged in a Florida state court with breaking and entering into a poolroom. When he gave his plea, Gideon requested the court to appoint a lawyer to represent him. However, the court refused, since free legal representation was only available if the accused was charged with an offence that was punishable by death. Gideon argued that it was his constitutional right to be represented by a lawyer, citing the Sixth Amendment to the U.S. Constitution, which states, in part, that "in all criminal prosecutions, the accused shall enjoy the right . . . to have the Assistance of Counsel for his defense."

The state court judge refused Gideon's request, with the result that he conducted his own defence. Defending himself as best he could with his lim-ited legal knowledge, Gideon made an opening statement to the jury, cross-examined the prosecution's witnesses, called his own witnesses, and gave a concluding statement arguing that he was innocent of the charge. The jury found him guilty, and the judge sentenced him to five years in prison. Gideon appealed his case to the Florida Supreme Court, arguing that the state's refusal to appoint him legal counsel denied him his constitutional rights. The Florida Supreme Court upheld the conviction. Gideon then wrote a letter to the U.S. Supreme Court, which agreed to hear his case. They appointed him free legal counsel and ultimately agreed with his argument.

In Canada, the first province to provide a **legal aid** system was Ontario, in 1967. In 1973, the federal government started to provide funds to provincial legal aid programs; to receive these funds, all such programs had to offer criminal law services when an accused was charged with an indictable offence, or when the accused faced the loss of liberty or livelihood in a summary conviction offence.

The cost of providing legal aid services has increased dramatically in the past decade. In 1987–88, the total cost of legal aid programs in Canada totalled approximately $260 million, increasing to $412 million in 1990–91 and over $600 million in 1992–93. The federal government has reduced its contributions significantly during the past few years, making provincial governments pay more of the costs. As a result, some provinces have stopped funding legal aid programs, forcing provincial bar associations to pay for continued existence of the program.

The cost of legal aid is growing faster than all other justice services. Between 1988–89 and 1992–93, civil and criminal legal aid costs more than doubled. Adjusting for inflation, this represents an increase of over 70 percent. During this five-year period, approved legal aid applications in both civil and criminal cases increased 43 percent from 541 314 to 772 338. Of total legal aid funding, 88 percent goes into expenditures directly related to the provision of legal services, such as legal advice, legal representation, private lawyer fees, and the cost of running legal aid offices. Central administrative costs account for 10 percent of the budget, while legal research and public legal education make up 2 percent (Young 1994).

Legal aid is provided only to those individuals who receive social assistance or whose family incomes are below social assistance levels (Canadian Centre for Justice Statistics 1992). In Manitoba during 1992, for example, approximately 97 percent of all legal aid clients had a gross family income under $11 000, while 82 percent reported a gross family income of less than $5000. Legal aid programs provide a variety of services, from representation in criminal and civil law cases to family court cases, as well as general information about legal rights in Canada. Despite these restrictions, approved applications for legal aid increased from approximately 860 000 in 1990–91 to 1 000 000 in 1992–93. In the same period, the number of requests for legal aid approved in both British Columbia and Ontario more than doubled, an increase largely attributed to the recession. What does this mean for legal aid lawyers? One legal aid lawyer in Saskatchewan who once worked on 250 to 300 cases about ten years ago now handles 350 to 400 cases. For a major criminal case, it is not unusual to work 15-hour days seven days a week (Fine 1994a).

Three models for providing legal aid for those who qualify are in practice in Canada. These are the **judicare** model, the **public defender** program, and a combination of these two approaches, called the combined approach. The judicare model operates in the provinces of New Brunswick, Ontario, and Alberta, and in Yukon and the Northwest Territories. In this program, qualified legal aid recipients receive a certificate and are allowed to select their own lawyer. The major benefits of this system involve costs, the availability of services, and the fact that one lawyer handles the case from beginning to end. Usually, lawyers are paid a set fee for their services, but this amount is typically too low to cover their costs. Rural areas are better served by this system since the population base is too small to justify the maintenance of a permanent legal aid office funded by the government. It is far less costly to allow clients to select legal counsel from those already in the area. Other benefits of this system are: (1) legal aid recipients are able to select their own lawyer; (2) normal lawyer–client relationships can be maintained for poor defendants; and (3) clients can select lawyers they feel will best serve their interests (Burns and Reid 1981).

The public defender system operates in Nova Scotia and Prince Edward Island. In this system, lawyers are, in effect, employers of the provincial government. One of the benefits of this system is that the lawyers involved are salaried lawyers—thereby assuring that the client receives competent legal counsel—and do not take any money for their services from their clients or their clients' families. Another advantage is that the public defenders representing a legal aid case are able to contact other public defenders, allowing them to benefit from group resources and expertise.

According to Burns and Reid (1981:414–16), the benefits of this approach include:

- better representation, because lawyers are specialists, with some becoming spokespersons for the poor
- lower costs
- greater efficiency, because it is centralized
- better service of the interests of clients, because lawyers are salaried and therefore do not need to use legal tactics that benefit them

The combined approach (also referred to as the "mixed" approach) is found in British Columbia, Saskatchewan, Manitoba, Quebec, and Newfoundland.

Does a person receiving legal aid have a greater chance of being convicted? In her study comparing judicare legal counsel and public defenders in British Columbia, Brantingham (1985) found no differences between them in terms of conviction rates (guilty outcome rates) and similar patterns of sentence severity (the amount and length of jail term). However, she did discover that these two types of legal aid varied substantially on sentencing outcome. Specifically,

EXHIBIT 7.1

Issues in the Criminal Justice System: Cut-Rate Justice

Due to large increases in the number of people being approved for legal aid despite decreasing federal government funding, provincial governments have had to reconsider the way legal aid programs operate. In 1995, the Ontario Conservative government felt that a viable approach was to take complete control of the province's legal aid system and, without paying lawyers for work already completed, create a new system of legal assistance that would only support cases involving those accused of the most serious criminal offences, such as murder.

Two alternative legal aid plans have been introduced in Manitoba during the 1990s. Legal Aid Manitoba took the unusual step of putting its cases up for auction. Manitoba legal firms were offered 11 files, each of which contained 50 future cases involving minor youth offences, such as vandalism and break and enters. To "win" these files, legal firms had to submit sealed bids, with the companies charging the lowest rates receiving the file. According to the executive director of Legal Aid Manitoba, this move made perfect sense at the time, but defence lawyers felt otherwise. The president of the Manitoba Association of Rights and Liberties argued that this program was "a denial of due process" since legal aid recipients get only the

lawyer who has submitted the lowest bid. And if the legal firm that wins a file decides to take all the cases contained within it to trial, it could easily end up losing money. This could lead to pressures on the clients to accept plea bargains that are not in their favour. The president of the Manitoba Defence Lawyers Association in 1992 called the auctions "a new evil in the legal system" since there is incentive for a firm to complete the cases as quickly as possible by entering guilty pleas and plea bargaining the charges or sentence. Although he felt that "most lawyers are honorable" and would not practise this way, the "appearance of justice is lacking." He may be right as it appears that legal firms are viewing the auction as a chance to ultimately gain new clients through repeat business—not just in criminal cases, but also by representing them in the future in divorce cases as well as conducting the legal work on mortgages. The competition for new clients is so intense that some firms are now offering to take young-offender cases free of charge rather than have another legal firm represent them through legal aid. This policy is based on the notion "that once you snag a young offender, you've got a client for life."

In another, more recent change, legal aid lawyers must submit Crown prosecutor position sheets to Crown attorneys when they are handling a legal aid case involving a criminal charge. On these sheets the Crown specifies what type of disposition it will be asking for, such as

a jail sentence or fine. If the Crown prosecutor decides to request a jail sentence, a legal aid certificate will be awarded to the lawyer, meaning that the client's legal costs will be covered. But if the Crown prosecutor decides to request another disposition, clients will have to cover legal costs themselves. In a number of instances, the accused has pleaded guilty to a change in order to avoid legal bills.

Both these programs are viewed positively by the head of Legal Aid Manitoba. Legal aid clients receive good legal representation and there are less claims for the money help by the organization. As a result, expenditures of Legal Aid Manitoba since the beginning of the decade have been among the lowest in Canada. But what happens if the economy approves? It is predicted that as more Manitobans and Canadians go back to work, demand for legal aid will decrease. In addition, revenues will increase, allowing the old system to re-emerge.

Source: "Lawyers Have a Big Stake in Legal-Aid System," *The Globe and Mail*, September 29, 1994, p. A6; Tony Davis, "For Sale: Justice for All?" *Winnipeg Free Press*, February 7, 1995, p. B3; Sean Fine, "Lawyers Object to Changes in Legal Aid," *The Globe and Mail*, September 24, 1994, p. A1; Margot Gibb-Clark, "Ontario Lawyers Postpone Legal Aid Work," *The Globe and Mail*, September 12, 1995, p. B1; Martin Mittelstaedt and D. Downey, "Tories Withdraw Legal-Aid Threats," *The Globe and Mail*, September 14, 1995, p. A3.

judicare clients received more jail sentences or absolute discharges, while the clients of public defenders were given more sentences involving probation orders, restitution, community work orders, and fines. Brantingham (1985:77) attributed these differences to the fact that clients of public defenders were sentenced after guilty pleas, "particularly guilty pleas following discussions between the public defenders and the Crown counsel."

Morse and Lock (1988:36), interviewing aboriginal offenders concerning their perceptions of the criminal justice system, found considerable criticism of legal aid lawyers. In particular, they pointed to the fact that legal aid "is overworked so lawyers tell 75 percent–90 percent of accused to plead guilty" and that there "is no real choice in who gets to act as your lawyer." Furthermore, the native offenders complained that legal aid lawyers do not invest much time with them and their cases and "often don't see them in custody until five minutes before appearing in court." Only 41 percent of the offenders indicated they were "satisfied" with their legal representation, while 48 percent said they were "dissatisfied."

Summary

Police officers have the power to use many different techniques to investigate and apprehend suspects. These include searches, electronic surveillance, interrogation, the use of informants, and the disclosure of evidence to the defence. Since the introduction of the Charter of Rights and Freedoms, the Supreme Court of Canada has placed numerous constitutional limits on the police. For example, the police are required to obtain properly authorized warrants to conduct searches except in clearly defined contexts. The police must follow these legal procedures exactly or risk the chance of losing the case due to "technical" reasons.

The interrogation procedures of the police are carefully controlled. However, a number of issues continue to surround police conduct during interrogations, such as when they can legitimately start to question a suspect, especially after a vague or ambiguous request to have a lawyer present.

A significant issue for the accused is whether or not he or she receives interim release or is detained for part or all of the time preceding the trial. During the past 25 years, bail provisions have been loosened, allowing most individuals charged with a crime to be free while awaiting their trial. However, recent crimes involving individuals released on bail have led to a tougher scrutiny of the rules regarding bail, with the result that offenders charged with certain types of crimes are now refused any type of pre-trial release.

Discussion Questions

1. Should guilty individuals go free because the police did not follow established legal procedures when they arrested the suspect(s)? Explain your answer.
2. Should evidence that is obtained illegally be excluded from trial? Explain.
3. Do you think that the police should be held personally accountable if they violate a citizen's constitutional rights? Why or why not?

4. Should suspects have fewer constitutional rights? Should the courts be more concerned with the rights of victims? Explain your answers.

5. When can the police legally search a dwelling or person without a search warrant?

6. What would happen if police officers were required without exception to obtain a search warrant before they search any person or dwelling?

7. Should all defendants accused of a criminal offence be allowed to plea bargain for a reduced sentence in exchange for a guilty plea? Why or why not?

8. Can the Bail Reform Act be revised to protect the public more from those charged with violent offences? Explain.

9. Should legal aid be available to all individuals accused of a crime? Give reasons for your answer.

10. How can an individual be denied interim release?

11. What inequities exist in the bail system in Canada? In the legal aid system?

Suggested Readings

Atreis, J., P.T. Burns, and J. Taylor, eds. *Criminal Procedure: Canadian Law and Practice*. Vancouver: Butterworths, 1991.

Brannigan, A. *Crimes, Courts, and Corrections: An Introduction to Crime and Social Control in Canada*. Toronto: Holt, Rinehart, and Winston, 1984.

Doob, A.N., P.M. Baranek, and S.M. Addario. *Understanding Justices: A Study of Canadian Justices of the Peace*. Toronto: Centre of Criminology, University of Toronto, 1991.

Grosman, B. *The Prosecutor*. Toronto: University of Toronto Press, 1969.

Hann, R. *Decision-Making in a Canadian Criminal Court System: A Systems Approach*. Toronto: Centre of Criminology, University of Toronto, 1973.

Klein, J.F. *Let's Make a Deal: Negotiating Justice*. Lexington, Mass.: Lexington Books, 1979.

Pink, J.E., and D. Perrier. *From Crime to Punishment: An Introduction to the Criminal Law System*. Toronto: Carswell, 1988.

Wilkins, J.L. *Legal Aid in the Criminal Courts*. Toronto: University of Toronto Press, 1975.

Wilkins, J.L. *The Prosecution and the Courts*. Toronto: Centre of Criminology, University of Toronto, 1979.

CHAPTER 8

The Courts and Trial Procedure

On October 24, 1993, the RCMP arrived at the farm of Robert Latimer in Wilkie, Saskatchewan, responding to a call concerning the death of his 12-year-old daughter, Tracy. During their subsequent questioning, Latimer confessed to the police that he had killed his daughter because she was suffering from the most extreme form of cerebral palsy and he wanted to relieve her from her constant pain. He confessed to police that he had poisoned Tracy in the front seat of the truck with carbon monoxide from the truck's exhaust pipe while he sat in the back of the truck watching her die and timing her death. He then proceeded to draw a diagram for the police officers of the elaborate apparatus to pipe the exhaust fumes into the cab of the truck.

Because of the evidence supplied by Latimer through his confession and diagram, he was charged with first-degree murder. During the trial, held in Battleford, Saskatchewan, Latimer's lawyer argued the defence of necessity

CHAPTER OBJECTIVES

- discuss the operation of the different levels of our court system

- understand the roles of the defence lawyer, Crown prosecutor, and judge

- understand that the court is designed to provide an impartial forum for the facts of the case

- discuss the role of plea bargaining in the Canadian criminal justice system

for his client, which is generally used in situations of imminent danger, but applied it in this case by arguing that his client was trying to prevent a greater tragedy. The trial judge, however, rejected this line of argument. Latimer was found guilty of second-degree murder after a jury deliberation of less than four hours. He was sentenced to the minimum jail term of life in prison, with no chance of parole for 10 years. His lawyer immediately filed for an appeal, and Latimer was allowed to be released while on bail.

Latimer's appeal to the Saskatchewan Court of Appeal was rejected on July 18, 1995. However, the appeal court was split in their decision concerning whether or not the 10-year minimum sentence was appropriate. The dissenting judge wrote that Mr. Latimer's sentence "exposes a stark inequality in the administration of justice in Canada in this sphere of wrongdoing." The majority argued that while Latimer acted in order to relieve his daughter's suffering, he acted "as a self-appointed surrogate decision-maker, he was not entitled to take the criminal law into his own hands and terminate her life."

Over the next few months, however, a number of disconcerting facts about this case emerged. One was that the RCMP were instructed by the Crown prosecutor to ask prospective jurors about their ethical beliefs on mercy killing without informing either the judge or defence lawyer. Another issue concerned the RCMP's questioning of Latimer; in particular, the issue was whether the police in Canada have the right to question and detain a suspect without first arresting and then charging him or her with a crime. The Supreme Court of Canada agreed to hear the case on the second issue, preferring not to deal with the former. However, the Crown prosecutor was charged with a criminal offence in June 1996 for his actions.

Many of the actions of prosecutors and defence lawyers are governed by trial procedure within the court system. The court is the location of many of the most important actions and decisions of the criminal justice system, including plea bargaining, the determination of guilt and innocence, and sentencing. In this chapter, the operation of Canada's criminal courts is examined as well as the role of the defence lawyer, Crown prosecutor, and judge.

The Courts

The word "court" refers to a complex part of the criminal justice system. Only a court or a court-appointed official can decide to detain an accused prior to trial, and only the courts can decide on her or his guilt or innocence. In addition, the court must decide on the appropriate type and length of sanction. The word "court" can also be used to refer to a number of different places or individuals. It can refer to a room where a case is being heard, to a group of judges (e.g., the Supreme Court of Canada), or to a single judge.

A judge is an officer of the government who is in charge of a court of law. The duties of a judge include deciding which evidence can be admitted in trial, the appropriate questions to be asked, and any procedural issues that may arise. In a jury trial, the judge has to "charge" (i.e., instruct) the members of the jury about the evidence and charges prior to their departure to the jury room to decide on the guilt or innocence of the accused. If the trial is to be decided by judge alone, he or she determines the guilt or innocence of the accused.

It is common practice to refer to the "lower" and "higher" courts in Canada. The former refers to provincial courts, which try all provincial and summary conviction offences; superior, or "higher," courts hear only indictable offences. The "higher" courts also refer to the provincial appeal courts, such as the Ontario Court of Appeal, as well as the Supreme Court of Canada. Appeal courts are also known as the "courts of last resort," meaning that they are the final authorities in cases under their jurisdiction. All individuals, however, have the right to petition the Supreme Court of Canada to appeal their case, even if the provincial appeal court has denied their application for an appeal.

Field Practice 8.1

Compensation, Diversion, Overcharging

Compensation

A provincial legislature approved a $100 000 settlement to reimburse the family of an individual wrongfully convicted for murder in order to cover their legal expenses. The original agreement made by a special committee was for $200 000, but the premier reduced it by half, saying the original settlement was too generous when the crime was taken into account. The family agreed to take the reduced amount and to drop their lawsuit against the government. The individual had been accused of stalking his victim (criminal harassment), breaking into her apartment, stabbing her twice, and attempting to rape her. His lawyer revealed that the prosecutor had but did not reveal evidence of another suspect in the case.

Diversion

A 17-year-old male was charged with intrafamilial sexual abuse. Since this was his first offence, the prosecutor recommended that he be placed in a diversion program for such offenders. He wanted to spare the victim from testifying in court, save the family from financial expenses and the stigma of a trial, and allow the offender to participate in a treatment program that had successfully treated others like him.

Overcharging

A prosecutor was worried about the ability of a sexual assault victim to testify against her assailant in court. As a result, he decided to proceed against the accused with all 12 charges laid against him by the police. As a result, the accused pleaded guilty to the lesser offences of breaking and entering and robbery, thereby eliminating the need for the victim to testify.

The Court System in Canada

Decorum is required from all participants and observers in all the different levels of the court. If an individual upsets the court proceedings, he or she can be forcefully removed from the court and held in contempt of court, leading to a fine or a period of incarceration. Whenever a judge (or judges, in the case of the appeal courts) enters the court, everyone in the court must rise. The defence lawyer and Crown prosecutor sit at separate tables with their associates and/or clients, while the judge sits on an elevated bench at the front of the courtroom. The public is separated from the actual proceedings by a railing. If the trial involves a jury, they are set to one side of the courtroom in a jury box.

Court procedures are rigidly followed and controlled by law, tradition, and judicial authority, for example, who may speak, when they may speak, and in what order they may speak. In addition, what can be said and not said in court is dictated by the rules of evidence and any determination about the admissibility of the evidence as determined by the judge.

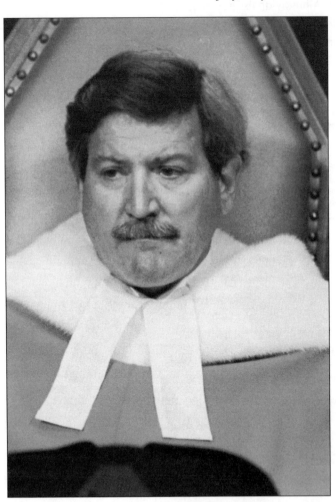

Chief Justice Antonio Lamer wrote a precedent-setting judgment on intoxication as a defence. (Photo: Canadian Press)

The Daily Business of the Courts

Studies of the provincial courts across Canada have consistently shown the majority of cases involve the accused pleading guilty to the charge as laid when making his or her first appearance in court. For example, Ericson and Baranek (1982) found 91 of 131 accused (70 percent) individuals pleaded guilty to at least one charge when they appeared in court. Only 21 individuals pleaded not guilty, with 15 (11.5 percent) being found guilty on at least one criminal charge and 6 (4.6 percent) being acquitted of all charges. Furthermore, only 17 (13 percent) had their charges withdrawn or dismissed, and the remaining two cases did not appear in court to face the charges laid against them.

While the majority of the accused pleaded guilty, the next most common method in which prosecutors deal with a case is to terminate cases by withdrawing charges or dismissing them altogether. Prosecutors may use their discretion to screen out weak cases and negotiate plea actions.

Other studies of the lower courts have reported similar results. A study in British Columbia found that almost 25 percent of all cases were dealt with through a stay of proceedings or a withdrawal of charges (Griffiths et al. 1980). Hann (1973) found that all counts were dropped or withdrawn in one-third of the cases in his study, while Friedland (1965), in his study of 5539 cases heard in Toronto's magistrate's courts during 1961–62, reported 682 (12 percent) were concluded by a withdrawal of charges. One reason for these case withdrawals and dismissals are the scheduling delays that lead to the charges being dismissed without the court's ever hearing the merits of the case (Wheeler 1987).

At the lower court level, the police may also play an important role in prosecutorial discretion. Crown prosecutors often have limited time to prepare for a case, and, for the sake of expediency, must rely on the information of the police. In some instances, prosecutors will follow the suggestions of the police officer(s) involved in the investigation of the case. In Ericson's (1980) study of detectives, he found that they worked hard at arriving at a satisfactory plea settlement with both Crown prosecutors and defence counsel. He cites a case in which the Crown prosecutor, the defence counsel, and the investigating detective had lunch together. They quickly negotiated a plea, with the result that the charge was reduced to attempted theft from attempted robbery. After lunch, the plea was entered in court in accordance with the negotiated settlement.

According to Ericson, detectives have considerable control in the lower courts because of several factors related to the organization of the courts. One factor is that the Crown attorney depends on detectives for the production and construction of evidence. Another factor is the heavy workload of Crown prosecutors, who usually handle 20 or more cases daily, and rarely have detailed knowledge of any of them. In some instances, they do not read the case file until moments before court is about to begin. Under these conditions, Crown prosecutors are very likely to follow much of the information provided to them by detectives (Ericson 1981; Wheeler 1987). Some researchers argue that detectives themselves strike most of the deals with defence counsel, subject to the approval of the Crown prosecutor. In his study of robbers, Desroches (1995:244) found that police work closely with Crown prosecutors "to avoid lengthy trials that tie up courts, judges, police officers, prosecuting attorney, and witnesses." If they are successful in obtaining a statement of guilt from the accused, they can bargain with the defence counsel from a position of strength. In the majority of these cases (about 60 percent), offenders were given no concessions for their guilty pleas. And those who were able to successfully reduce the number of charges against them in return for a guilty plea were given no guarantee of a shorter sentence.

These studies point to the fact that the police and defence counsel have a significant impact on the prosecution of cases, particularly in the lower courts. As Osborne (1983) concluded in her study of prosecutors in Ontario, they played a "limited role . . . in the pre-trial period which ultimately circum-scribes . . . control over the construction and outcome of cases." This role of the police has emerged because they maintain control of the case as it proceeds toward the court system, while different prosecutors handle the case, usually for brief periods of time.

Prosecutors, of course, can decide to use their own discretion to stay proceedings, withdraw charges, or dismiss the charges altogether. They may decide, given the circumstances of the case, to use their discretion to expedite matters for the victims. For example, in their study of the prosecution of child sexual abuse cases in the Hamilton-Wentworth (Ontario) region, Campbell Research Associates (1992) found that prosecutors used their discretionary powers to settle cases before the actual trial to speed up the decision-making in the criminal justice system as well as to protect child victims from the trauma of appearing and testifying in court. Numerous case-related factors have been found to influence prosecutorial discretion, including the attitude of the victim, the cost of prosecuting a case, the potential of using alternative approaches to deal with the case, and the willingness of the suspect to cooperate with the authorities (Miller 1970).

Other reasons for prosecutors deciding not to prosecute a case include insufficient evidence, witness problems, due process problems, a plea on another charge, and referral to another jurisdiction for prosecution. For example, Vinglis et al. (1990) found that Crown prosecutors in Ontario with-drew charges in drinking-driving cases because witnesses were not available (8.4 percent of the cases), errors were found by prosecutors in the technical requirements of the Criminal Code (5.6 percent), the police failed to collect available evidence (4.3 percent), the evidence did not substantiate the charge (6.5 percent), and the information was improperly worded (3.2 percent). Cases were also dismissed because the accused was charged in a number of different cases, the prosecutor decided to dismiss charges in exchange for a guilty plea, the accused agreed to attend a diversion program, or the accused is wanted for a more serious crime in another jurisdiction.

The Defence Lawyer

After arrest and interrogation, the defence lawyer reviews the relevant informa-tion and evidence the police have collected, and perhaps interviews the arrest-ing police officers as well as the Crown's witnesses to the crime. The primary responsibility of the defence lawyer is to represent his or her client, who has the legal right to legal counsel. The defence lawyer is also responsible for the preparation of the case and selecting a strategy with which to attack and ques-tion the prosecutor. Since most defendants are not trained in the operation of the law, they are unsure of how to proceed. Defence lawyers ideally help their clients to understand what is happening in court and the consequences of the charges if they are found guilty. In some cases, the defence lawyer may hire individuals to investigate certain aspects of the case or contact other experts in the field to get a second opinion.

Some of the most significant work of the defence lawyer is conversation with the police and the prosecutor. The defence has probably worked with the investigating officers and the prosecutors on previous occasions. Usually, they discuss the strength of their client's case and assess the chance of gaining a satisfactory plea bargain (see below).

The defence lawyer represents the accused at all stages of the criminal justice process, including bail hearings, plea negotiations, and preliminary inquiries. If a trial is held, defence lawyers question prospective jurors, cross-examine Crown witnesses, and call defence witnesses. If their client is convicted, defence lawyers attempt to get them the best possible sentence. They may also file an appeal with the hope that a court of appeal will agree to other arguments and reverse the lower court's decision or reduce the sentence.

Throughout the trial process, the formal function of the defence lawyer is to "exercise his professional skill and judgment in the conduct of the case . . . (and) fearlessly uphold the interest of his client without regard to any unpleasant consequence to himself or any other person" (Martin 1970:376). If the accused admits to the defence lawyer that she or he committed the crime in question, the lawyer, if convinced that the statements are true, can contest the case by objecting to such legal issues as the form of the indictment and the admissibility or sufficiency of the evidence. However, they cannot suggest that another individual committed the crime in question or introduce any evidence they believe is false or that has the purpose of establishing an alibi for the accused.

One of the most common questions asked of criminal defence lawyers is how they can defend someone they know is guilty. According to the Canadian Bar Association's Code of Professional Conduct (1987), defence lawyers are required, even in those cases where they know their client is guilty as charged, to protect their client as much as possible. Our legal system demands that accused have the legal right to use every legitimate resource to defend themselves. This means that defence lawyers have to question the evidence given by witnesses called by the prosecution and attempt to point out that the evidence taken as a whole "is insufficient to amount to proof that the accused is guilty of the offence charged," but "the lawyer should go no further than that" (Martin 1970). Some view the role of defence lawyers as necessary to protect the integrity of our legal system; if they refuse to protect the guilty, "the right of a defendant to be represented by counsel is eliminated and with it the entire traditional trial" (Swartz 1973:62).

The Crown Prosecutor

Crown prosecutors play a pivotal role in the courts, as they are responsible for presenting the state's case against the defendant. According to the Canadian

Bar Association's Code of Professional Conduct (1987) for Crown prosecutors, their prime duty is not to gain a conviction, but rather to enforce the law and maintain justice by presenting all the evidence relevant to the crime being tried in criminal court. For example, the prosecutor must disclose "to the accused or defence counsel . . . all relevant facts and known witnesses" that could influence "the guilt or innocence, or that would affect the punishment of the accused."

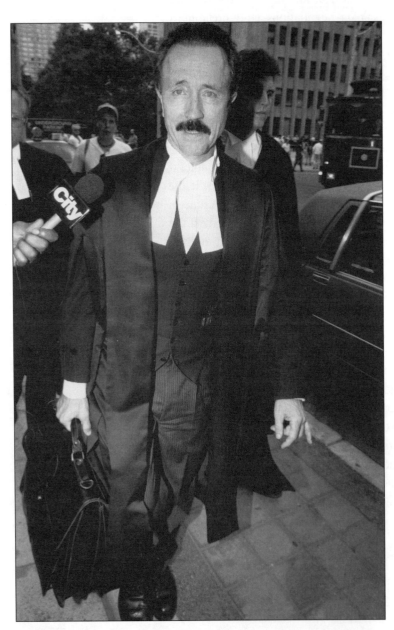

Crown attorney Ray Houlahan was in the driver's seat as the Niagara and Scarborough regional offices disagreed over which charges against Paul Bernardo should be tried first. (Photo: Fred Lum/*The Globe and Mail*)

However, many prosecutors are faced with the dilemma of maintaining an impartial role in the court and attempting to find the defendant guilty as charged. According to Grosman (1969:63), there is strong pressure on prosecutors to gain as many convictions as possible once a decision has been made to prosecute the case. This pressure to succeed at trial stems from two considerations. The first is that in order to "maintain his administrative credibility and to encourage guilty pleas the prosecutor must demonstrate that he is able . . . to . . . succeed consistently at trial." If not, more cases would be taken to court, because the defence counsel would feel that it had a good chance to gain a favourable result for its client. The second consideration is that "confidence in present administrative practices is maintained only if the acquittal rate is not substantial." Therefore, to maintain their credibility, prosecutors must attempt to gain as many guilty verdicts as possible.

Some argue that this role makes prosecutors more powerful simply by enabling them to virtually define the parameters of a court case. For example, the prosecutor presents the Crown's side of the case in an opening address to the judge and jury before the jury has heard anything else. While the opening address may be criticized in court, it makes a significant first impression. Karp and Rosner (1991:74) argue that in the David Milgaard case, the Crown prosecutor gave a "damning and convincing argument" to the jury, taking "full advantage" of the tradition that allows the Crown to speak first, and providing "a lengthy exposition of what he expected the forty-two witnesses to say when called to the stand."

The Responsibilities of the Crown Prosecutor

The Crown prosecutor can be viewed as the chief law enforcement officer within the provincial and federal court systems. They represent provincial or federal attorneys general and ministers of justice in all phases of their work, from discussing a case with the police to making sentencing recommendations to the judge and perhaps filing an appeal. The most obvious responsibility of the Crown prosecutor is to try indictable and summary conviction offences in a court of law. They have a large number of responsibilities associated with trying a case, such as examining court documents sent by a variety of individuals, including coroners and the police, in order to determine if further evidence is required. In addition, Crown prosecutors interview victims and subpoena witnesses to give testimony during the court trial. They also may decide not to try a case, even if the police have laid charges, by requesting an adjournment of the case until a future date, withdrawing the charges, or deciding to offer no evidence so that the court will dismiss the charges and the case (Osborne 1984; Law Reform Commission 1990b).

Crown prosecutors are responsible for trying a wide spectrum of cases involving a variety of charges, including child sexual assault, domestic violence, and white-collar and property crimes. Because a Crown prosecutor may be assigned to one particular courtroom as opposed to a specific case, one case can be worked on by different Crown prosecutors as it progresses through the court system. In recent years, however, there has been a trend toward specialization, in which special prosecution units try only cases involving specific charges, such as financial or economic crimes and domestic violence. In Manitoba, for example, when the Department of Justice implemented the Family Violence Court (see Chapter 1) six prosecutors were trained to prosecute family violence cases. Two of the objectives for appointing specialized prosecutors are (1) to process cases expeditiously, aiming for a three-month average processing time from first appearance to disposition, and (2) to increase victim/witness information and cooperation and to reduce case attrition, particularly at the prosecutorial level through a stay of proceedings (Ursel 1994:2).

For a variety of reasons, a prosecutor may decide not to proceed with a case although the police feel charges should be laid or have already laid charges against the suspect. In three provinces (British Columbia, Quebec, and New Brunswick), the police are required to allow prosecutors to review and approve evidence before changes are laid. In all other jurisdictions in Canada, charges can be laid without prosecutorial approval, although they may decide not to prosecute the case at a later date. For indictable offences, defence counsel may decide to contest the evidence at a preliminary inquiry in order to question whether there is sufficient evidence to proceed to criminal trial. In such cases, the prosecutor attempts to show a judge that sufficient evidence does exist by reviewing the physical evidence and questioning and cross-examining witnesses.

Criminal Trial Procedure

The criminal trial is the start of the **adjudication** stage of the criminal justice system. If the accused pleads guilty, a date will be set for the sentencing (see Chapter 9). However, if the accused elects trial by judge and jury, the next step is jury selection. Jury trials are relatively rare in Canada, as only about 5 percent of all cases are heard at the superior court level. Because these cases involve serious crimes, juries and courtroom dramas have become, for many Canadians, typical of what happens in the Canadian justice system (see Chapter 1).

The Plea

In most cases, a defendant appearing in criminal court for an indictable offence will enter a plea of guilty or not guilty. It is estimated that 90 percent of defendants plead guilty prior to trial or when they appear in the lower courts for the first time. If the defendant pleads not guilty to an indictable offence, a trial date is set. For certain charges, the accused can indicate whether he or she wishes to be tried by a judge alone or by judge and jury. There may be a trial even if the accused pleads guilty. If the accused pleads guilty to a lesser offence, the judge may decide to proceed with the more serious charge. If the accused is acquitted on the latter, the judge can sentence him or her on the prior plea of guilty (*R. v. St. Jean* 1970). In addition, judges hold the discretion to accept a guilty plea, if the facts of the case support a trial for the more serious charge. Thus, a plea bargain made between the defence and prosecution may not be accepted by the trial court judge.

When an individual pleads guilty, it must be a free and voluntary act. The accused also gives up his or her constitutional rights, including the right to cross-examine witnesses and to have a trial by jury (if applicable). However, a judge may decide to review the evidence, and if it appears that the accused wishes to change his or her plea, the judge has the discretion to allow the change in plea. As a result, a judge must take caution when accepting the accused's plea of guilty. The judge must believe that the facts of the case warrant such a plea and that the plea is made voluntarily by the accused. The accused, if not represented by defence counsel, must be informed of that right, and the judge may insist on the presence of a defence lawyer before the plea is accepted by the court. In addition, the judge has the right to allow the accused

EXHIBIT 8.1

Malicious Prosecution

What happens when a Crown prosecutor prosecutes a case when he or she has insufficient evidence? The decision to prosecute may lead to claims of "malicious prosecution" if the accused is found not guilty. What recourse is open to those who feel they have been wrongfully prosecuted in Canada?

Malicious prosecution cases invariably end up in failure for the plaintiff. They are either thrown out by judges before trial, end when the plaintiff runs out of resources or patience, or finish because of a compensation award received from the government.

Some of the more notable malicious prosecution lawsuits in recent years have been the following:

- Susan Nelles. The nurse was charged with the murder of four babies at Toronto's Hospital for Sick Children and was discharged after a preliminary inquiry.

- John Popowich. The Saskatoon police officer was acquitted of child sexual abuse charges in connection with the Martensville affair.

- Alain Chapleau. He was acquitted of arson in a major fire involving PCB-laden waste at St-Basil-Le-Grand, Quebec.

- John Munro. The former federal cabinet minister endured an 11-month trial for breach of trust, corruption, and several other charges only to have all charges dismissed or withdrawn.

- Patti Starr. Starr was the figure at the centre of an Ontario political fund-raising scandal in the late 1980s. She was convicted of fraud and breach of trust and served two months of a six-month sentence.

- Michael (Subway Elvis) McTaggot. He spent 20 months in jail before being cleared in seven bank and trust company robberies. It later turned out two key eyewitnesses had identified someone else as the robber.

The following people resolved malicious prosecution suits through other means:

- Donald Marshall. An order-in-council from the Nova Scotia government compensated him and his parents for the 11 years he spent in prison for a murder he did not commit.

- Wilson Nepoose. After spending five years in an Alberta prison for a crime he did not commit, Nepoose was compensated by the Alberta government under federal–provincial compensation guidelines.

- Richard Norris. The Ontario government was exonerated after Norris had spent about two years in jail for sexual assault. He was compensated under federal–provincial guidelines.

Source: K. Makin, "A Lawsuit Nearly Impossible to Win," *The Globe and Mail*, November 16, 1995, p. A8.

to withdraw a plea of guilty if he or she was "in a disturbed state of mind at the time" of the guilty plea (*R. v. Hansen* 1977).

Preliminary Hearing

Before there can be a trial for certain indictable offences at the superior court level, a justice of the peace or provincial court judge can be requested to conduct a **preliminary inquiry** to see if there is enough evidence to proceed to a criminal trial. The purpose of the preliminary inquiry is to protect the accused from being put on trial unnecessarily. During the preliminary inquiry, a judge examines the evidence and hears witnesses.

The preliminary inquiry is much like a regular trial. It is conducted before a provincial court judge and, in most cases, is open to the public. The defendant is also present, as is defence counsel (if one has been retained) and the Crown prosecutor. The purpose of the preliminary inquiry is to establish whether there exists sufficient evidence to proceed to a trial, not for the accused to plead his or her guilt or innocence. The accused can also request for a prohibition of the publication of the proceedings of the preliminary inquiry until charges are either discharged or, if a trial is held, until the trial has finished. The publication ban order is mandatory when requested by the accused at the opening of the inquiry, but discretionary when applied for by the prosecutor.

The prosecution presents its evidence and witnesses, and the accused has the right to cross-examine any or all witnesses and to challenge the prosecutor's evidence. After all the evidence is presented to the court, the judge decides whether or not sufficient evidence has been presented by the Crown to prosecute the accused. If the judge believes there is enough evidence, then a trial will be scheduled, but if there is not, the charges are dropped and the defendant is freed. The judge weighs the evidence on the same basis he or she assesses the evidence at a criminal trial.

In Canada, the accused in most cases has the right to waive the preliminary inquiry. A defendant is most likely to waive a preliminary inquiry for one of three reasons:

1. the accused has decided to enter a plea of guilty
2. the accused wants to speed up the criminal justice process and have a trial date set as early as possible
3. the accused hopes to avoid the negative publicity that might result from the inquiry

However, a prosecutor may not want to see a preliminary inquiry waived, since it can provide a record of witness testimony. Thus, evidence given at the preliminary inquiry can be of assistance during the trial.

The Right to a Jury Trial

In Canada, the right to a jury trial is set out in Section 11(f) of the Charter of Rights and Freedoms, which states that any person charged with an offence has the right to trial by jury where the maximum punishment for the offence is imprisonment for five years or more.

This distinction was challenged in *R. v. D. (S)* (1992) in which the defendant wanted the right to a jury trial, though the offence he was charged with carried a maximum punishment of less than five years. The court held that no principle of fundamental justice was violated as no right exists that entitles the accused to a jury trial in every criminal case. Once an accused is convicted and there are further proceedings based on this conviction, there cannot be another jury trial. For example, when convicted murderer Paul Bernardo was declared a dangerous offender, his defence lawyer made no attempt to have the case heard by both a judge and jury since Bernardo had already been found guilty and, as such, was not an individual "charged with an offence" as specified by Section 11(f) of the Charter. This ruling was based on a previous case heard by the Supreme Court of Canada, which ruled that it would be wrong to allow an individual already convicted to have the right to request a jury trial after he had already been convicted (*R. v. Lyons* 1987).

Jury Selection

If the accused decides to be tried by a judge and jury, jury selection follows a four-step procedure. Three of these occur outside the court and are a provincial responsibility; the fourth takes place in the court and is governed by federal legislation (the Criminal Code). The three out-of-court selection stages are:

1. the assembly of a source list of persons who may be qualified, under provincial law, to serve as jurors (most provincial jury acts specify some or all of the sources to be consulted to prepare the list but some do not)

2. a determination of the identity of those on the source list who are qualified to serve, according to the relevant provincial jury act, and the disqualification or exemption from service of those on the service list who, for various reasons, are usually also specified in the appropriate jury act

3. the selection from the names remaining on the source list of a jury panel, who are, as appropriate, summoned to appear in court accordance with the procedures set out in each provincial jury act

A list of initial candidates is compiled in various ways in the different provinces. This initial list, referred to as *venire* (or jury array), provides the government with a group of citizens who are all potential jurors. Each province has a jury act specifying who may be selected for the jury array. Section 626 of the Criminal Code allows each province to determine the qualification for potential selection, but Section 626(2) specifically precludes discrimination on the basis of sex. Approximately 100 individuals for the juror list appear in court, where there is an in-court selection process. The framework for this in-court procedure is found in Section 631 of the Criminal Code. Generally, names are randomly selected from the list of jurors present, and each individual is interviewed and challenged by the defence lawyer and prosecutor.

A "challenge" occurs when either the prosecutor or the accused (or, in most cases, his or her lawyer) objects to a potential juror. There are two types of challenges in Canada: the "challenge for cause" and the "peremptory" challenge. The purpose of both challenges is to eliminate those jurors considered by either side to be unqualified or not impartial. In this process, all potential jurors are challenged by the prosecution and defence lawyer to assess their appropriateness to sit on the jury. Each potential juror is questioned under oath about such things as their personal background, occupation, residence, interest in the case, and attitudes about certain relevant issues. Any citizen who is thought to have a bias for or against the accused—e.g., if they are a friend of the accused or if they have already formed an opinion—will be eliminated.

If there is a "challenge for cause," a reason must be provided and the judge must determine if the reason given for the challenge is appropriate. The usual approach is for either side to challenge for cause first, as the number of peremptory challenges is limited. A potential juror may be challenged if, for example, they were convicted of an offence and incarcerated for over 12 months, they are physically unable to serve on the jury, they cannot speak either official language of Canada, or they are non-Canadian or a landed immigrant (Mewett 1996).

If a potential juror is challenged peremptorily, no reason has to be given. Before 1992, the Crown was allowed only four peremptory challenges for any type of offence, but they also had the power to "stand by" up to 48 prospective jurors. In contrast, the defence lawyer had up to 20 peremptory challenges if the minimum punishment was life imprisonment or 12 such challenges for all other offences. However, the Supreme Court of Canada, in *R. v. Barnes* (1991), ruled this process gave unfair advantage to the Crown and violated Section 11(d) of the Charter. Section 634(1) of the Criminal Code was changed to allow both the prosecutor and defence to have 20 peremptory challenges when the accused is charged with high treason or first-degree murder, 12 challenges when the accused is charged with all other offences punishable by imprisonment of five years or more, or four peremptory challenges for all other offences.

Only the trial judge has the right to "stand aside" a prospective juror, and then only in limited circumstances. A juror may ask a judge to be stood aside

A TV cameraman films only the feet of prospective jurors in the Bernardo murder trial in a Toronto hotel. Photographers were complying with a ban on identifying prospective jurors. (Photo: Moe Doiron/Canadian Press)

for reasons of personal hardship or any other reasonable cause (Section 633 of the Criminal Code). This allows the judge, in those situations in which a full jury has not been sworn, to call back jurors in the hope that both sides agree on their role as a juror. In these cases, however, the jurors are subject to the same challenges as all other jurors (Section 641 of the Criminal Code). If a full jury still has not been formed, further individuals will be selected from another jury list until the process is complete.

In Canada, a jury always consists of 12 individuals. Until 1992, the Yukon and Northwest Territories were allowed to select only six individuals. However, the Court of Appeal of the Northwest Territories held that such a jury was in violation of Section 15 of the Charter. The Latimer case discussed at the beginning of this chapter was tried by a jury consisting of 11 people. This is because a judge has the power to discharge a juror due to illness or any other "reasonable" cause. A trial can continue as long as there are 10 jurors, but if there is less than 10, the jury must be discharged and the whole process started over, as specified by Section 634 of the Criminal Code.

At one time, it was a regular occurrence for jurors to be sequestered in a hotel for the length of a trial until they reached a verdict. Today, however, juries are sequestered only during their deliberations concerning the guilt or innocence of the accused.

Legal Rights and Criminal Trials

Every trial involves certain legal principles concerning the rights of the accused as specified by the Charter and rules of evidence. These rights have been introduced to ensure the accused will be given a fair trial and are found within Section 7 of the Charter (see Chapter 2). According to Section 11(a) of the Charter, everyone has the right "to be presumed innocent until proven guilty according to law in a fair and public hearing." What follows is a discussion of the most fundamental rights that accused persons possess within the Canadian legal system.

The Right of the Accused to Confront the Accuser

The right of the accused to confront the accuser is essential to a fair trial since it controls the type of evidence used in court. Hearsay evidence—that is, second-hand information—is only accepted as evidence in rare circumstances, for example, information revealed by a dying person. This is precisely what happened in a famous U.S. case involving the Ford Motor Company and one of its vehicles, the Ford Pinto (Cullen et al. 1987). In this case, a death-bed statement to a nurse by a victim of a traffic accident involving a Pinto led to that statement's being entered into the court record, though it could not be corroborated. As a result, crucial evidence was entered into the case, and this was a major factor in the outcome of the case.

Furthermore, the accused (usually through his lawyer) has the right to cross-examine all witnesses and victims testifying against him. This allows the defence to challenge any statement or testimony given by a prosecution witness or a victim, with the hope of discrediting such information.

Child sexual assault legislation allows a child to testify outside the courtroom when the accused is charged with certain sexual offences (see Chapter 1). Judges are permitted to allow a child to testify from behind a screen or via closed-circuit television from another room in the courthouse. However, the provisions found in this legislation protecting children from seeing the alleged abuser have not always been accepted outright by members of the judiciary. In *R. v. Ross* (1989), the Nova Scotia Court of Appeal upheld the constitutionality of the provision, ruling that "the right to face one's accusers is not, in this day and age, to be taken in a literal sense … It is simply the right of the accused person to be present in court."

The use of videotapes as the sole evidence of the victim's testimony, however, has proved to be a more problematic issue. In *R. v. Meddoui* (1990), heard in the Court of Queen's Bench of Alberta, the trial judge accepted the videotape of the victim as evidence. However, in another case that same year *(R. v. Thompson),* also heard before the Court of Queen's Bench of Alberta, the use of videotapes was ruled as violating sections 7 and 11(d) of the Charter. In future, therefore, the use of videotapes as prima facie evidence will likely be rare in Canadian courts.

The Right to a Speedy Trial

One of the most serious problems facing the courts today are delays in hearing a criminal case. These delays may result from a variety of legal options, such as plea bargaining, procedural and evidentiary issues, as well as court cancellations. These delays, however, may contravene Section 11(b) of the Charter, which guarantees that any person charged with an offence has the right "to be tried within a reasonable time."

The right to a speedy trial is also considered to be a part of fundamental justice protected by Section 7 of the Charter. This right was clarified in *R. v. Askov* (1990). In this case, three men charged with numerous weapons offences were denied bail in November 1983. They were released on bail in May 1984, but their court trial was put over until September 1985, due to a backlog of cases. The lawyers for the accused argued their clients' right to a fair trial was unfairly violated by courtroom delays. The presiding judge agreed, but the Ontario Court of Appeal overturned his decision. However, the Supreme Court of Canada agreed with the trial judge. In addition, when the Supreme Court made their decision, they identified four factors to be considered whenever a judge had to rule on whether there had been an unreasonable delay. The four factors they identified were:

1. *The length of the delay.* While there is no absolute time limit identified by the Supreme Court of Canada, they ruled that "it is clear that the longer the delay, the more difficult it should be for a court to excuse it." This factor is to be balanced along with all the other factors, including "the standard maintained by the next comparable jurisdiction in the country."

2. *The explanation for the delay.* Two key factors were identified: (a) the conduct of the Crown and (b) systematic or institutional delays. In addition, the accused cannot unduly cause a delay in the proceedings, although if the accused were to make a deliberate attempt to delay the trial, the courts would not rule in their favour and the burden of proof would be in the hands of the accused.

3. *Waiver.* In this situation, the accused indicates that he has understood that he has a Section 11(b) guarantee, and has waived the right provided by that guarantee.

4. *Prejudice to the accused.* This allows the Crown to proceed in those cases in which, despite a long delay, no resulting damage has been suffered by the accused.

The Right to a Public Trial

Do members of the media have a right to attend trials? While this issue is not specifically covered by the Charter, Section 2(b) guarantees freedom of the press and other forms of the mass media. However, freedom of the press is limited by Section 1 of the Charter, where it has been held that freedom of the press is not an absolute right since it can be circumscribed by the rights of others, a fact inherent in the concept of democratic freedom.

While most criminal trials are open to reporting by the media, a public trial is for the benefit of the accused. Section 11(b) of the Charter states that any person charged with an offence has the right "to be presumed innocent until proven guilty according to law in a fair and public hearing." This means that justice cannot be served by secret court trials.

But, as noted previously, the accused can request the judge to order a ban on the publication of certain evidence emerging in a preliminary inquiry. In such a case, the name of the accused can be published, but specific evidence presented in court cannot be published as "this might jeopardize the ability of the accused to receive a fair trial" (Boyd 1995:141). The rationale is that the media could give out information that might possibly bias potential jurors or judges. As a result, great care is taken to protect the accused.

The issue of publication bans is controversial. When Karla Homolka and Paul Bernardo were tried separately, a publication ban was ordered on the Homolka trial to protect Bernardo's right to a fair trial. A judge even ordered certain information contained in the book *Karla's Web* to be blacked out because defence counsel argued it might bias Bernardo's trial.

EXHIBIT 8.2

R. v. Askov

The case of *R. v. Askov* (1990) illustrates how the Supreme Court of Canada interpreted the right to speedy justice for the accused. This decision relates to Section 11(b) of the Canadian Charter of Rights and Freedoms, which states that any person charged with an offence has the right "to be tried within a reasonable time."

Facts of the Case

In November 1983, Askov (along with a few associates) was charged with the possession of a prohibited weapon, possession of a weapon for a purpose dangerous to the public, pointing a firearm, and assault with a weapon. He was denied bail in November 1983, but he was released on bail in May 1994 on a recognizance of $50 000. A preliminary inquiry, originally started in July 1984, took until September 1984 to complete. There was enough evidence to proceed to trial, but the trial was booked to start 13 months later due to scheduling problems. Almost two years had passed since the original charges were laid. The case was then rescheduled to be heard in September 1986; when the trial started, defence counsel argued it should be stayed because of the length it had taken to come to trial (now almost three years). The trial judge denied the request, stating that "insufficient institutional resources" were the source of the delay. This ruling was confirmed by the Ontario Court of Appeal.

Decision

Askov appealed this decision to the Supreme Court, which heard the case in October 1990. The court ruled in favour of Askov, setting out a number of factors to be used by the courts when determining if the delay for a case to come to trial is excessive. These included the length of the delay, the explanation for the delay, the accused's waiver of rights, and prejudice to the accused. In addition, the court stated that a waiting period of five to eight months for a case to come to trial was acceptable.

Significance of the Case

The impact of *Askov* was described by a judge on the Ontario Court of Appeal as "staggering." In the six months following the court's decision, over 34 000 charges were stayed, dismissed, or withdrawn. This included 8600 impaired driving charges, 6000 cases involving theft under $1000, a substantial number of charges involving assaults and frauds, 500 sexual assaults, in excess of 1000 drug offences, and thousands of violations of provincial statutes.

Update

Seventeen months later, the Supreme Court of Canada, in *R. v. Morin* (1992), changed the acceptable waiting period to eight to ten months. In addition, it introduced a number of other tests, making it no longer necessary for the prosecutor to prove that the delay was caused by the accused, that institutional delay was justified, or that the accused had waived his or her rights under Section 11(b) of the Charter.

Another important issue revolves around whether or not trials should be televised as a matter of right. The situation in Canada is different from that in the United States, where, in 1981, the U.S. Supreme Court removed all constitutional obstacles to the use of television over the complaints of the accused. As a result, during the summer of 1995, many Canadians watched the live coverage of the O.J. Simpson trial on their televisions, while they could only view artists' sketches of the Paul Bernardo trial.

According to Section 486(1) of the Criminal Code, a judge has the right to exclude the public for all or part of the trial if he or she feels it is in the "interest of public morals, the maintenance of order, or the proper order of administration." This is most commonly done when a child or mentally challenged person is going to testify and the judge feels it will assist them if the court is cleared.

Perhaps the most controversial decision a judge can make is to exclude the media. Rarely are members of the media banned from the courtroom. Instead, it is more common for a superior court judge to issue a nonpublication order to protect "the integrity of the court." In addition, Section 486(3) expressly allows a trial judge to ban the publication of anything that would identify the

EXHIBIT 8.3

TV in the Courtroom

The judiciary in Canada has traditionally been reluctant to allow television in courtrooms. In the United States, however, over 30 states currently allow cameras in their courts. Almost one-half of these states give the accused an unconditional right to object to television coverage of their trials and six restrict the presence of television cameras in civil trials and the appeal courts. In the early 1990s, COURT TV, a cable television channel specializing in covering major U.S. court trials, went on the air. The network covered such cases as the William Kennedy Smith rape trial in Florida, the Jeffrey Dahmer trial in Milwaukee, Wisconsin, and the Mike Tyson trial in Indianapolis, Indiana.

The controversy surrounding television in Canadian courtrooms revolves around the issue of whether television is qualitatively different from the reports provided by other media. While everyone has the right to a fair trial, the argument goes, each member of the public also has the right to be informed. Thus, to keep television out of the courtroom "offends some other deep-seated principle operating within the legal process" (Hutchinson 1984:7)

The main argument against television in the courts of Canada is that the presence of cameras will so adversely affect the behaviour of the judge, jury, lawyers, and witnesses that it would diminish the accused's right to a fair trial. Another argument is that the objectivity and fairness of jurors would be threatened, the quality and reliability of witnesses' testimony would be reduced, and additional judicial pressures would be added. Concerns for the accused include the fact that they may have a difficult time handling and presenting themselves in a favourable manner, and that the public may recognize defendants in their community and react to them in a negative manner, even if they are not convicted.

Advocates of television coverage of trials point out that these problems are not specific to television. They recommend that adequate safeguards accompany the introduction of televised trials. For example, the accused would have to consent to the coverage, to detailed editing of the courtroom activities and instructions. Reasonable limits would be introduced, such as a case that excludes television cameras to safeguard victims of child sexual assault. In addition, the proponents of television in the courtroom point out that it educates the public about the law. Observing lawyers, prosecutors, judges, and experts in various fields such as forensics can give the public significant insights into the law and legal procedure.

Hutchinson (1984:7) points out that the opposition to televised proceedings by lawyers and the judiciary may stem from the fact that, through television, their revered status may become myths and the "introduction of TV cameras, able to render the courtroom commonplace and reveal the mundane and prosaic nature of the justice system, would help that illusion."

Source: Allan C. Hutchinson, "A Case for TV in the Courtroom," *The Globe and Mail*, March 9, 1984, p. 7; J. Lazerson, "Court TV: Can It Increase Understanding of Law and the Legal Process?" *Judicature* 76, no. 2 (August 1992).

The Paul Bernardo murder trial attracted more publicity than any other criminal trial in Canada's history. (Photo: Roger Hallett/*The Globe and Mail*)

Despite public petitions and organized protests, a judicial enquiry concluded the plea bargain Karla Homolka negotiated with prosecutors cannot be retracted, nor can additional charges be laid. (Photo: Roger Hallett/*The Globe and Mail*)

names of the complainant and/or witnesses in trials involving sexual offences.

Prosecutor Discretion

Once the police arrest and lay charges against a suspect, it is not an automatic fact that the prosecutor will try the case. For numerous reasons, a large number of defendants are never brought to trial. Crown prosecutors "have virtually unfettered discretion as to when to charge, what to charge, when the charge should be reduced or dropped" (Delisle and Stuart 1994:525). Therefore, the prosecutor has the power to decide whether a case should be tried in court according to the charges laid by the police, to plea bargain, to stay proceedings, or to dismiss the charges outright. In addition, the prosecutor has the discretion to proceed by way of indictment or summary conviction in hybrid offences. Their discretionary powers exist at all levels of criminal trials.

Plea Bargaining

Section 10(b) of the Charter of Rights and Freedoms states that an essential aspect of prosecutor discretion is negotiating a bargain with defendants and their lawyers concerning a criminal case. In plea bargaining, the defendant agrees to plead guilty to a criminal charge and receives some benefit in return (Law Reform Commission of Canada 1989:2–3). Although an agreement is reached by all the key actors involved in a trial, the judge may not accept the deal, since he or she is not legally bound to approve it. Plea bargaining exists because it serves a variety of purposes:

1. It improves the administrative efficiency of the courts.
2. It lowers the cost of prosecution.
3. It permits the prosecution to devote additional time to more important cases. (Wheatley 1974)

Since prosecutors prefer to devote their time to serious crimes or cases that have a good chance for conviction, they may agree to accept a guilty plea to a lesser charge because it saves the court's time and money, and reduces the risk of losing the case should it proceed to trial. In addition, the prosecutor may gain certain information about other criminals that will help solve other crimes.

A variety of options are open to the prosecutor when offering or considering a plea bargain. One common option is to offer the defendant a lesser charge in return for a plea of guilty. Another common form of plea bargaining involves sentence bargaining, in which the prosecutor agrees to recommend a shorter sentence to the judge or proceed in the court trial by way of summary conviction in a hybrid offence. For example, a Crown prosecutor may agree to proceed against an individual charged with sexual assault (level 1) on the basis of a summary conviction charge instead of as an indictable offence. Defendants may also plea bargain for dropped charges. An example of this type of plea bargain involves the dropping of extraneous illegal actions that are contained in the complaint. For example, the prosecutor may agree to drop an auto theft charge accompanying a drug offence.

The three main types of plea bargaining practised in Canada are charge bargaining, sentencing bargaining, and fact bargaining.

Charge bargaining involves three primary activities:

- the reduction of the charge to a lesser or included offence
- the withdrawal or stay of other charges or the promise not to proceed on other possible charges
- the promise not to charge friends or family of the defendant

Another common form of plea bargaining is known as sentence bargaining. Prosecutors and defence lawyers recommend to the presiding judge an appropriate sentence for the accused. While judges do not have to accept this recommendation, they usually do. Sentence bargaining usually includes the following:

- a promise to proceed summarily rather than by way of indictment
- a promise that the Crown will make a particular recommendation in relation to sentence
- a promise not to oppose defence counsel's sentence recommendation
- a promise not to appeal against sentence imposed at trial
- a promise not to apply for a more severe penalty
- a promise not to apply for a period of preventive detention
- a promise to make a representation as to the place of imprisonment, type of treatment, etc.
- a promise to arrange sentencing before a particular judge

In fact bargaining the prosecutor and defence lawyer agree not to submit certain facts about the case or the background of the offender into court. In this manner, it is hoped that the accused will receive a lighter sentence. Such a practice usually involves:

EXHIBIT 8.4

Negotiating a Reduction in Charges: *R. v. Kienapple* (1974)

In this case, the Supreme Court of Canada ruled on the issue of multiple convictions and punishments stemming from the same act. This case had a significant impact on plea bargaining in Canada, as it shaped policy on the reduction of charges in criminal cases.

Facts of the Case

Kienapple was charged and convicted of rape and unlawful sexual intercourse with a 13-year-old female. The jury convicted him on both counts and the judge sentenced the accused to two concurrent terms of imprisonment of 10 years each. The Ontario Court of Appeal dismissed the accused's appeal, but the Supreme Court of Canada agreed to hear the case.

At issue was the principle of *res judicata*, which means that the second charge—in this case, the crime of having unlawful carnal knowledge of a female under 14 years of age, contrary to Section 146(1) of the Criminal Code—was not an independent offence, but rather an "essential" part of the first offence. This means that a conviction on the first charge effectively eliminates a finding of guilt for all the remaining charges.

Decision

The Supreme Court of Canada, in a five-to-four decision, decided that the second charge was indeed an essential part of the first offence. They ruled that the second charge shared certain aspects of the first charge, because the girl involved was under 14 years of age, thereby lacking consent, and this overlapped with the charge of rape, since lack of consent was a necessary component of the offence of rape.

Significance of the Case

This decision is significant for the issue of charge reduction in Canada. When an individual is charged with more than two offences, the question arises as to whether one charge overlaps with the other. If it does, an individual may plead guilty to one of the offences, although, legally, that individual could be convicted of only one of the offences. This means that individuals may think they are receiving a lesser sentence, but in reality they could not be sentenced for both offences if they negotiate a guilty plea for only one offence in return for the Crown's dropping the other charges.

- a promise not to "volunteer" information about the accused (for example, not to submit evidence as to the defendant's previous convictions)

- a promise not to mention a circumstance of the offence that may be interpreted by the judge as an aggravating factor (and, therefore, deserving a greater degree of severity of punishment)

The practice of plea bargaining has been criticized and defended by a wide variety of individuals and professional bodies involved with the criminal justice system. In 1975, the Law Reform Commission (1975:14) referred to plea bargaining as "something for which a decent criminal justice system has no place." Nine years later, however, the Commission (1984) changed its view, calling plea bargaining a normal practice in the criminal justice system; in 1989 it commented that plea bargaining is not a "shameful practice" (Law Reform Commission 1989:8).

The Criminal Trial

A criminal trial is a formal process that strictly follows rules of evidence, procedure, and criminal law. This definition is in sharp contrast to the trials shown on most television shows and movies, which can present the courtroom as a "no-holds-barred" forum with defence lawyers and prosecutors asking leading questions, acting in a prejudicial manner, and winning a case by courtroom trickery. Each criminal trial follows a particular procedure that must be observed by all parties involved. As a result, trials are extremely complicated, with the judge having to make decisions about technical questions of procedure and what evidence can be allowed to enter the court.

The key actors are the prosecutor and defence lawyer, who try to present their case the best they can and in such a manner that will lead to a successful adjudication. Prosecutors will use police reports, testimony from witnesses and victims, as well as physical evidence in an attempt to persuade the court the defendant is guilty. The defence lawyer will try to point out the limits and problems in the prosecutor's case, while at the same time presenting evidence beneficial to the accused. The defence lawyer will try to ensure that his or her client's constitutional rights are protected. Since only one side can win, both the prosecutor and defence lawyer will assess the trial in order to see if an appeal is necessary.

The Opening Statement

Once the jury has been selected and the trial begins, the criminal charge(s) are read to the jurors by a court employee. Then, both the prosecutor and defence lawyer have the right to make opening statements to the jury. In Canada, the prosecutor always presents the first opening statement. This usually involves a summation of the criminal charges, the facts of the case, and how the Crown will proceed. However, the prosecutor cannot be biased or impartial in her opening comments, since the prosecutor's role is to assist the jury in arriving at the truth. As a result, Crown prosecutors have a duty to be impartial, and this excludes any notion of winning or losing. They must guard against stating information likely to excite and inflame the jury against the accused. Nor may they "express a personal opinion as to the guilt of the accused or state that the Crown ... [is] ... satisfied as to the accused's guilt" (Salhany 1986:274).

The defence does not have to make a opening statement if he does not wish to. The defence lawyer also outlines the case, but informs the jury how he intends to show that the defendant is, in fact, innocent of all charges. This involves describing how he will prove the prosecution's case to be inadequate.

Prosecutors must be extremely careful when outlining their case. For example, they cannot promise evidence that they will not bring into court. If they mention the name of a particular witness, and their expected testimony, and this individual does not appear, the judge may rule the statement was prejudicial toward the accused and subsequently set aside any verdict of guilt. In addition, the prosecutor cannot mention any evidence that she knows will be inadmissible or the prior record of the accused, if it exists.

If the trial does not involve a jury, the opening statements can be brief, as the judge is probably knowledgeable about the case, the appropriate rule of law, as well as some of the evidence that may already have been discussed in a preliminary inquiry.

All evidence submitted in the court in an attempt to prove the defendant innocent or guilty must meet the highest standard of proof. The standard is "guilty beyond a reasonable doubt" and is viewed as the basis for reducing the risk of conviction if there are questions about certain facts that were presented during the trial. This has led to the belief that it is better to release one hundred guilty persons than to convict someone who is innocent.

Trial Evidence

Once the opening statements have concluded, the prosecution starts its case by presenting evidence. Usually the first evidence to be presented comes from sworn witnesses (e.g., police officers, medical examiners, victims, etc.) providing testimony. This type of testimony consists of anything that the witnesses saw, heard, or touched. Sometimes it involves the opinions of witnesses; for example, an eyewitness may give an opinion as to whether the defendant appeared confused. Expert witnesses are specialists in certain areas that apply to the case. For example, a medical examiner can give expert testimony about the time of death or how injuries occurred. No more than five expert witnesses may be used by the prosecution or defence without the approval of the judge. When the prosecution has finished her questioning, the defence has the right to cross-examine the witness. Cross-examination can focus on the oral and written statements of the witness. Testimony is but one form of evidence that may be used during a trial. Other types of evidence are:

- *Real evidence.* This type of evidence consists of exhibits such as weapons, clothing, fingerprints, etc. Real evidence must be the original evidence. However, photographs and duplicates may be introduced as evidence.
- *Direct evidence.* This type of evidence consists of the observations of eyewitnesses.
- *Circumstantial evidence.* This type of evidence proves a subsidiary fact from which the guilt or innocence of the accused may be inferred.

All evidence presented in court is governed by the rules of evidence. The judge acts as an impartial arbitrator and rules on whether certain types of evidence can be allowed into the trial. Judges may decide to exclude certain evidence from the trial. One such type of evidence that is excluded is known as *hearsay evidence*. This is information that a witness hears about from someone else. The courts have ruled that such information represents a denial of the defendant's right to cross-examination since witnesses do not have the ability to establish the truth of the information.

The Defence Lawyer's Presentation of Evidence

The defence lawyer has the right to introduce any number of witnesses at a trial or none at all. If he does introduce a witness, the prosecution has the right to cross-examine that individual. One of the most critical decisions a defence lawyer has to make is whether or not the client should give testimony under oath. During a criminal trial, the defendant has the right to be free from self-incrimination (i.e., the right to remain silent), which refers to the fact the accused has the right not to testify.

Closing Arguments

Section 651 of the Criminal Code determines whether the prosecution or defence presents their arguments first. If the defence presents evidence or the defendant testifies, the defence must address the jury before the prosecution. If no defence evidence is called, the prosecutor presents his or her evidence first. During their closing arguments, both prosecution and defence are allowed to offer reasonable inferences about the evidence and show how the facts of the case prove or disprove the defendant's guilt. However, they are not allowed to comment on evidence not used during the trial.

The Charge to the Jury

After the defence lawyer and prosecutor make their final presentations to the court, the judge instructs, or **charges,** the jury on the relevant principles of law that they have to take into account when deciding the guilt or innocence of the defendant. The judge will include information such as the elements of the alleged offence, the evidence required to prove each charge, as well as the degree of proof required to obtain a guilty verdict. It is essential for the judge to clearly explain the relevant laws and evidence requirements as well as the meaning of reasonable doubt. In addition, judges also have to instruct the jury on the procedures they should use when making their decision. These instructions are very important since they may prove to be the grounds of an appeal.

On paper, these instructions seem simple and reasonable. However, in reality, they may confuse jurors and lead them to make incorrect evaluations of the evidence or select the wrong verdict. The final instructions given to the jury apply to issues of evidence and testimony and usually include mention of (1) the definition of the crime with which the defendant is charged; (2) the presumption of the defendant's innocence; (3) the burden of proof that lies with the prosecution; and (4) the fact that if, after extensive discussion, there remains reasonable doubt among the jurors as to the guilt or innocence of the defendant, he or she must be acquitted.

The judge also instructs jurors about the possible verdicts they might consider. While the jury may decide to reach a verdict on the guilt or innocence of the defendant on the original charge, they usually have the option to decide on the degree of the offence in many cases (e.g., second-degree murder or manslaughter).

The Verdict

After the judge has reviewed the case and the charges, the jury move to a separate room to consider the verdict. The jury verdict in a criminal case usually must be unanimous. Juries may take a few hours, a number of days, or many weeks to review all aspects of the case before they reach a decision.

If a jury remains deadlocked after a lengthy deliberation, it may return to the courtroom and inform the judge of their situation. The judge may then request the jurors to return to the jury room for a final attempt to arrive at a verdict; in most cases the judge specifies a designated time period. If all reasonable attempts have been made to reach a verdict but none is forthcoming, a "hung jury" results. In such cases, the judge proceeds to dismiss the jury and declare a mistrial. It is then up to the prosecution to decide to retry the case, a decision that must be made within a specified time period. If a new trial is ordered, a new jury has to be appointed.

If the jury reaches a verdict of guilty, the judge sets a sentencing date. In the duration, the judge can request a presentence report from a probation officer before the sentence is imposed. In such cases, the defence lawyer can start the process of appeal. Defendants may be released while awaiting sentencing or held in custody.

The jury has no role in sentencing, with the exception of second-degree murder. In such cases, the jury can make a recommendation to the judge that the length of time before parole be increased from 10 years to a longer period, which cannot exceed 25 years. However, this is only a recommendation and the trial judge is not bound by it.

One of the important roles of a jury is referred to as *jury nullification*. This happens when a jury does not follow the court's interpretation of the law in every situation, thereby "nullifying" (i.e., suspending) the requirements of strict legal procedure. In these cases, jurors may decide to disregard what the judge told them about specific aspects of the law or evidence because they consider the application of the law to the defendant to be unjust. Jury nullification can occur in two ways. The first occurs when a verdict of guilty is reached and the judge decides this to be an erroneous decision. In such a case, the judge may refuse to abide by the verdict and may instruct the jury to acquit the defendant. The second happens when the judge requests a jury to "arrest" its verdict of guilty and acquit the accused.

Appeals

Canada's criminal justice system allows all those convicted of a crime a direct criminal appeal. This means that the defendant or the prosecution has the right to appeal the decision in a case. The convicted individual has the right to appeal his conviction, or the sentence, or not being found mentally unfit or criminally responsible to stand trial due to a mental disorder, or not being found to be unfit to stand trial.

For the prosecution, the terms of an appeal vary according to whether the trial involves an indictable or summary conviction offence. In a summary conviction case, the prosecutor can appeal against a dismissal or the sentence. If the case involves an indictable offence, the prosecution can appeal the sentence, if the accused was acquitted, if it was found that the accused was not criminally responsible on the basis of a mental disorder, or if the accused was found to be unfit to stand trial.

There are limits on the amount of time allowed to file an appeal, but extensions can be made for a variety of legitimate reasons. During an appeal it is not uncommon for the convicted individual to apply for bail or another form of pre-trial release.

The appeal court can order a new trial or acquit the convicted individual if it finds that the trial judge made an error concerning the law, that the verdict was unreasonable and not supported by the evidence, or that there was a miscarriage of justice. If it appears that the position of the prosecutor is no longer valid, the appeal court usually grants an acquittal. But if it decides there is still enough evidence for the prosecutor to argue the case, it will order a new trial.

If the appeal court decides the appeal registered by the prosecution is valid, it normally grants a new trial. However, it can convict and sentence the accused if the trial was by judge and jury and there was enough evidence presented to the court.

The Supreme Court hears some appeals, but only if the cases involve important questions of law. The Court also considers appeals from the prosecution against acquittals.

For summary conviction offences, the convicted individual usually appeals a conviction or sentence to a federally appointed judge in a superior court. Once again, the accused may be released pending the outcome of the appeal. It is rare for a summary conviction offence to be heard by the Supreme Court of Canada, and then only if it involves an important legal issue.

Summary

Our court systems are organized at the federal and provincial levels. Because the accused is presumed to be innocent until proved guilty, it is up to the prosecutor to prove guilt beyond a reasonable doubt. The major actors in the courts are the judge, the prosecutor, and the defence lawyers. The prosecutor represents the interests of the state, while defence lawyers provide essential services to their clients. The prosecutor uses evidence collected by the police to convince the court that the defendant is guilty, while the defence lawyer attacks the prosecution's case.

An important part of the trial is the selection of members of the public to serve as jurors. These individuals are chosen by a procedure called "voir dire," a system that allows both lawyers to question prospective jurors. The law allows each side to challenge any prospective juror on the basis of cause or for peremptory reasons.

Trials are controlled by rules of evidence and criminal procedure. These rules are enforced by judges who, during a trial, act as an arbitrator over issues that may arise. Evidence must be reliable and relevant, otherwise it is inadmissible.

The issue of discretion is probably the key issue at this stage of the criminal justice system. Since the number of individuals charged with crimes far exceeds the number of courts, plea bargaining becomes an essential component in the day-to-day functioning of our criminal justice system. Many cases are never heard formally in a courtroom because they are plea bargained.

Discussion Questions

1. Should the Crown prosecutor have absolute discretion over which cases are heard in court? Why or why not?

2. What qualities should a prosecutor have?

3. Do you think the right to a jury trial should be expanded to all defendants? Explain your answer.

4. Discuss the role of the jury during a trial. Should jurors be passive listeners, or should they be allowed to ask questions directly to the prosecutor, defence lawyer, and witnesses?

5. Briefly describe the selection process for jurors.

6. What do prosecutors and defence lawyers attempt to accomplish in their opening statements?

7. Why should a "speedy" trial be a legal right for defendants?

8. Should all defendants accused of a criminal offence be allowed to plea bargain for a reduced sentence in exchange for a guilty plea? Explain.

9. What is the role and function of a preliminary inquiry?

10. Should judges be formally required to participate in all plea bargains? Give your reasons.

11. What are the disadvantages for a defendant who does not receive interim release? What are the advantages for those who do receive it?

12. Should the Bail Reform Act be revised to give the public more protection from those charged with violent offences? Explain.

13. Should plea bargaining be abolished? Give reasons.

Suggested Readings

Karp, C., and C. Rosner. *When Justice Fails: The David Milgaard Story*. Toronto: McClelland and Stewart, 1991.

Russell, P.H. *The Judiciary in Canada: The Third Branch of Government*. Toronto: McGraw-Hill Ryerson, 1987.

CHAPTER 9

Sentencing

After the accused is convicted at the end of a criminal trial, the court must adjudicate an appropriate sentence. Our criminal justice system operates on the belief that justice at sentencing must prevail; that is, guilty people must be punished for the crime. This stage is one of the most controversial since the public is very concerned about the type and length of punishment. Some people argue that sentences are too short while others believe they are too long.

Sentencing is the process by which judges impose a punishment on an convicted criminal. The punishments available to the sentencing judge vary according to the type of offence, but there is a wide variation of punishments to select from. Sentences can include incarceration, fines, community service orders, or probation.

An important issue in the area of sentencing is the discretion held by judges. Judges hold substantial

CHAPTER OBJECTIVES

- explain the four major goals of criminal sentencing

- outline the various sentences available to a judge

- be familiar with some of the recent innovations at the sentencing stage

- discuss disparity in sentencing

- discuss changes to sentencing practices and review the literature to see if they are successful

Name: Paul Kenneth Bernardo

Born: August 27, 1964, in Toronto, the youngest of three children. Family moved to suburban Scarborough in 1965.

Education: Attended Elizabeth Simcoe Junior Public School, Jack Miner Senior Public School, Sir Wilfrid Laurier Collegiate Institute, graduating in 1982; University of Toronto, Scarborough campus, B.A. (Business), 1987.

Career: Enrolled in CA courses of the Institute of Chartered Accountants of Ontario but failed exam. Worked for brief periods at Price Waterhouse and Goldfarb Schulman Patel & Co. Declared personal bankruptcy May 24, 1990. After moving to St. Catharines, Ont., in 1991, listed his occupation as self-employed bookkeeper. (Photo: Roger Hallett/*The Globe and Mail*)

discretion and are largely unaccountable for their actions. In addition, disparity and discrimination in sentences have led to the demand that judicial discretion be controlled.

After the court has reached the decision that the accused has done something wrong, a punishment must be handed out. In the example that follows, it is clear that both men violated the law. But the question then becomes what should the courts do to indicate their disapproval?

On the same day in June 1985, Robert Rowbotham, 35, of Toronto, and Michael Waite, 22, of Drayton, Ontario, were sentenced in different Ontario courtrooms for the crimes of drug trafficking and criminal negligence causing death, respectively. Both charges carried a maximum sentence of life imprisonment. Rowbotham got 20 years; Waite got two years less a day. When observers compared the sentences with the immediate harm inflicted on the victims, something deeply troubled them. Lawyer Harold Levy, an adviser to the Law Reform Commission of Canada, was quoted as saying that "something was clearly out of kilter. There was a sense of the system not working" (Gibb-Clark 1985:A4).

Rowbotham was sentenced to 20 years in a federal prison for his part in a large marijuana importing drug operation. At the time, it was the longest sentence ever handed out for a soft-drug offence in Canada. Waite received a sentence of two years less a day in a provincial jail after killing four teenagers on a hayride. He was driving down the wrong side of a road with only his foglights on in the dark, after drinking seven bottles of beer. In both cases, the defendants were found guilty by a jury.

The Rowbotham case had already dragged on for 13 months after a preliminary hearing that had lasted three months. The jury found Rowbotham and 10 others guilty of a number of drug importing and trafficking offences. These individuals were responsible for importing an estimated 6000 kg of marijuana and hashish worth an estimated $5 million on the street. At the sentencing, the judge called the defendants "social bloodsuckers." He also criticized the defendants for their "somewhat jocular air" during the trial, saying that some had treated the legal process as a big joke. Rowbotham, who was considered to be the mastermind of the drug operation, was out of prison on parole from a 1976 sentence for which he had received a sentence of 14 years (later reduced to nine years on appeal) on similar drug offences.

Waite was originally charged with criminal negligence causing death, which carries a life sentence. One cannot blame the judge for the light sentence because, for whatever reason, the members of the jury decided to convict him of the lesser sentence of dangerous driving, an offence punishable by imprisonment for a period not to exceed five years. Indeed, the judge was quoted as saying that he could not remember "in my 22 years as a judge and lawyer . . . a

Robert Rowbotham, left, with the B.A. diploma he earned as an inmate, got 20 years for drug-related offences. Michael Waite, right, got two years less a day after being found guilty of five counts of dangerous driving that resulted in the death of four teenagers. (Rowbotham photo: Ian MacAlpine, Canada Wide Photo Services; Waite photo: Canadian Press)

more flagrant case of dangerous driving." The jury decided on the lighter charge and sentence despite that, three hours after the accident, Waite had taken a breathalyzer test that indicated his blood alcohol percentage was still over the legal limit (Gibb-Clark 1985).

While the sentences obviously differed in these two cases, it is unrealistic to criticize the judge for the seemingly light sentence imposed on Michael Waite. Although the jury found him guilty, they convicted him of an offence that in effect eliminated the possibility of the judge's imposing a more severe disposition. Comparisons of dispositions such as these will always be controversial and lead to much criticism of sentencing practices.

Goals of Sentencing

Sentencing is considered by many to be the most important stage in the criminal justice system, since it is at this point that the offender is punished. But punishment covers a wide spectrum of sentences in Canada, including a fine, probation, community service, imprisonment, an intermittent sentence, or a recognizance to keep the peace. It is also possible for a judge to combine certain of these punishments into what is referred to as a *split sentence*—for example, a fine and a probation order.

Determining the appropriate sentence length for a convicted offender is perhaps the most difficult decision a judge has to make. This is because, when it comes to determining the actual length of the sentence, judges usually have considerable discretion about its type and length. In some instances, such as first- and second-degree murder and manslaughter, there are fixed minimum sentences that a judge cannot change. But judges still hold discretion in the sense that they can recommend a parole application date that varies among convicted offenders.

What is the source of this judicial discretion? Is it the result of the personal preferences of a particular judge, the legal seriousness of the crime, the defendant's race, the quality of the arguments given by the defence attorney and Crown prosecutor during the trial, or perhaps the impact of the crime on the victims? All of these factors may in some way contribute to the judge's final decision.

If you were a judge, with the responsibility of deciding which offenders go to a correctional facility and who stays in the community, how would you decide who is to receive a prison sentence? Furthermore, what criteria would you use to determine your sentence? Criminal sentences in Canada vary widely, from a discharge to long-term imprisonment, although the type of crime the offender is convicted for will guide your final decision. This is because, in most cases, the Criminal Code determines the maximum length of punishment for the offence. When you make your final decision, it is not only of concern to the offender, but also the community, the police, and the victims. And, of course, your decision may be a mistake. What happens, for example, if you decide that a convicted offender should receive a probation order but while on probation he or she commits a series of violent crimes? Would you change your overall sentencing approach in the future or would you view this as simply an aberration because it has not happened before?

Underlying all such decisions are a number of goals—deterrence, selective incapacitation, justice, or rehabilitation—that are important to the sentencing of offenders because our system of justice is supposed "to accomplish something, to achieve some social utility beyond merely solving crimes and catching criminals" (Anderson and Newman 1993:288). Two factors are important here: sentencing and dispositions.

Sentencing has been defined as a

> process in which the court or officials, having inquired into an alleged offence, give a reasoned statement making clear what values are at stake and what is involved in the offence. As the sentence is carried out, it may be necessary from time to time, as in probation, to change or amend conditions relating to the sentence. (Law Reform Commission of Canada 1974:4)

Sentencing therefore includes a number of issues and should be distinguished from the actual sentence imposed on the offender.

A disposition refers to "the actual sanction imposed in sentencing" (Law Reform Commission of Canada 1974:4) or "the judicial determination of legal sanction to be imposed on a person found guilty of an offence" (Canadian Sentencing Commission 1987:153).

Of course, before someone receives a disposition, he must plead guilty or be found guilty in a court of law. If someone commits an offence and admits that he did, in fact, commit the crime, one assumes they will be found guilty. What then becomes an issue is the type and length of the disposition. If the crime involves a serious, violent act, is it not reasonable to expect a lengthy period of imprisonment as the disposition? While one expects this to be true, what happens during the court trial and the factors surrounding the commission of the act may have significant weight in determining the final disposition.

When Jane Stafford (see Chapter 1) was acquitted by a jury of the charge of first-degree murder for the killing of her abusive husband (a crime for which she admitted responsibility when questioned by the RCMP), it was obvious to practitioners within the criminal justice system that Jane would receive life imprisonment. However, the jury decided much differently. During their discussions on the appropriate disposition, they looked at the facts surrounding the case and the reasons for Stafford's actions, and acquitted her of the charge. This led to a great deal of commentary, not only among the public but also in the legal community. According to the latter, the fact that Stafford had committed the offence (and admitted to it) was reason enough to give her the only disposition possible: 25 years before parole. As one law professor commented on the final decision of the jury, "few people would suggest that Jane Stafford deserved a severe criminal penalty. She was clearly a victim of her tragic circumstances and did not have many realistic options. However, those factors would normally relate to the severity of her sentence, not to whether she committed the crime" (Vallee 1986:184–85).

Because of this type of reasoning, the Crown successfully appealed the verdict, but this time Stafford pleaded guilty to the lesser charge of manslaughter. The punishment for manslaughter ranges from a minimum punishment of probation to a maximum punishment of life imprisonment. Since there is no minimum punishment for the charge of manslaughter, a judge has considerable discretion when deciding the final disposition. What sort of factors became important to the judge when he started the process of determining his sentence? The different views on the appropriate sentence can be summed up by comparing the final arguments of Stafford's lawyer and the Crown prosecutor at the sentencing hearing. The Crown prosecutor argued for a jail term so as "to discourage others from taking the law into their own hands," while her lawyer requested a suspended sentence, based upon the circumstances of her actions and a recent Ontario case with similar facts in which the judge gave the defendant a suspended sentence (Vallee 1986:198).

However, the judge disagreed with Stafford's lawyer, noting that she was "judge, jury, and executioner." He also recognized that Stafford was taking a certified nursing course but that, at the same time, "there must be deterrence" (Vallee 1986:199). Stafford was sentenced to six months, to be served at a provincial correctional facility, and two years' probation. In addition, the judge recommended that she be allowed to commute to her nursing course while at the facility. While all parties involved believed that Stafford would never commit a crime like this again, the factors that went into their professional reasoning became important features during both trials. Should the sentence reflect society's disapproval of her actions? Is Stafford a good candidate for rehabilitation? The answers to these questions are important, because they reflect different views of the nature of sentencing an offender.

All sentences, from probation to life imprisonment, have a number of goals. The foundation of these goals is found within the theories guiding our criminal justice system. Any sentence can reflect one or a combination of these goals. The specific goal of any sentence imposed on an offender is to reduce "the crime rate by stopping the criminal activities of apprehended offenders and deterring others from committing crimes" (Anderson and Newman 1993:288). How best to achieve this is, of course, open to opinion and debate. What follows below is an outline of the four major goals that are used at the sentencing stage within our criminal justice system: deterrence, selective incapacitation, rehabilitation, and the justice model. While these major sentencing goals are presented as separate and distinct from one another, some observers (e.g., Havemann 1986; Doob 1992) have noted that sentences in Canada reflect a combination of these goals at any one time.

Deterrence

By punishing an offender, the state indicates its intent to control crime and deter potential offenders. **Deterrence**, the oldest of the four main sentencing goals, refers to the protection of society through the prevention of criminal acts. This is accomplished by punishing offenders according to the nature of their offence—too lenient a sentence might encourage more people to engage in criminal activity because they may not fear the punishment for their offence; too severe a sentence might reduce the ability of the criminal justice system to impose punishment that is thought to be both fair and impartial, and might actually encourage more criminal activity. For example, if all convicted robbers were to receive a minimum of 10 years for their crimes, they may kill their victims if they are the only witnesses who could identify them. For the deterrence approach to work, it must strike a balance between fear and justice among both offenders and law-abiding citizens.

There are two types of deterrence: specific deterrence and general deterrence. **Specific deterrence** attempts to deter, through punishment, an individual offender from committing another crime (or recidivating) in the future. **General deterrence** refers to a sentence that is severe enough to stop people from committing crimes. To date, there is some evidence that specific deterrence does work, although only in certain instances, such as domestic violence (Sherman and Berk 1984). However, many more studies have found that specific deterrence does not stop people from committing a crime again once they have served their punishment (Wheeler and Hissong 1988; Fagan 1989).

It is hoped that general deterrence, by punishing an offender, will make an impact on the members of society. More specifically, punishing an offender sends the message that if someone commits the same offence, he or she will receive the same punishment—i.e., crime doesn't pay (Wilson and Abrahamse 1992). Therefore, the purpose of the law and the criminal justice system is to create a "threat system" (Van Den Haag 1982). However, an increasing amount of research has revealed that people may not be deterred from committing crimes even though they know there is certainty of punishment if they are caught (Tunnell 1990; Williams and Rodeheaver 1991). Critics also point out that if fear of formal sanctions translates into high rates of deterrence, the United States would have a much lower crime rate than it has due to the large number of severe punishments imposed on offenders (Walker 1993).

Selective Incapacitation

If an offender is considered to be a significant risk to society, he or she may be sentenced to serve a long prison term. **Selective incapacitation** as a punishment justifies long sentences because the offenders are considered to pose a serious threat to the safety of society. It is believed that incarcerating those individuals (referred to as chronic offenders) who commit the most heinous and/or the greatest number of criminal offences will reduce the crime rate. In essence, the goal of the selective incapacitation approach is to prevent future crimes by imprisoning individuals based on their past criminal offences. While the selective incapacitation and deterrence approaches both focus on punishing criminals for the express purpose of protecting society, selective incapacitation differs from deterrence because it favours extremely long sentences.

At present there is considerable debate surrounding the effectiveness of this sentencing approach (Visher 1987). Research on the use of incapacitation policies to reduce crime originally predicted a 10 to 30 percent reduction in the crime rate, although studies of the long-term effects of such policies have discovered the actual reductions may be only 5 percent at most. In addition, these policies also have the potential to increase prison populations.

A recent selective incapacitation approach that has appeared in the United States is the "three strikes and you're out" sentencing policy, which requires an offender convicted of three felony offences to serve anywhere from a 25-year sentence to a mandatory life sentence. This approach is controversial since an individual can receive a life sentence for committing two minor crimes if they are categorized as felonies (some states, like California, require that the third felony be designated as "violent" or "serious") (*Criminal Justice Newsletter* 1993). Crime rates in those states that have implemented this type of sentencing policy have not declined, either in the overall amount of crime or in specific offence categories such as sexual assault. While these laws may put chronic offenders behind bars for extremely long periods of time, many now question the real impact it will have on the crime rate. For example, Mauer (1994) argues that the "three strikes" approach may have little more than symbolic value. This is because "three time losers" are close to "aging out" of crime, and locking them up for life may have little influence on the crime rate. In fact, it may be more practical to jail young criminals, perhaps those only convicted of one criminal offence, since their rates of future criminality will no doubt be higher. Mauer also points out that current sentences for chronic offenders are already lengthy and that adding a few more years to their sentences will not help bring down the crime rate in any significant fashion.

Rehabilitation

A sentencing approach based on **rehabilitation** believes that many (not all) offenders can be effectively treated so that, in the future, they will live "crime-free" lives in their communities. Supporters of rehabilitative sentences argue it is fairer and more productive to treat certain offenders rather than punish them without treatment. Since it is not known exactly how long it will take to rehabilitate an offender, this approach supports indeterminate sentences. Since every offender is potentially different in the type and length of treatment needed, the sentence has to reflect this.

Rehabilitative sentences, in contrast to the deterrence and selective incapacitation approaches, do not always include imprisonment. In fact, offenders may be sentenced to serve their punishment within the community if more appropriate services are available to them. In *R. v. Preston* (1990), the B.C. Court of Appeal upheld a lower court judge's decision that a drug addict could serve her sentence in the community, provided there was a reasonable chance for her successful rehabilitation. According to the evidence, Leslie Rae Preston had 23 prior convictions, including trafficking in heroin and prostitution. Her current charge was possession of heroin, worth more than $6000 on the street. After she was charged, the accused entered a methadone treatment program, and by the time of her court trial she had stopped using drugs and was doing well in her treatment program. The judge found her guilty as charged, but gave her a suspended sentence so she could continue her rehabilitation program.

This sentence represented a significant change in the sentencing practice of the lower courts, as in the recent past they had "always emphasized deterrent sentences for drug offences, especially for hard drugs and when a repeat offence is involved." But Preston's lawyer argued that there "is no credible basis for expecting that a term of imprisonment will rehabilitate the addict," and that when the sentence was completed, "the addict who emerges from custody poses the same threat as before." As a result, deterrence should be given less weight than the "reasonable chance of rehabilitation" (*Justice Report* 1990:16).

Justice Model

According to the **justice model**, offenders should be punished no more or less than what their actions deserve. In particular, the severity of their sentence should be based on how serious their crime was and the extent of their prior criminal record (von Hirsch 1976; Cullen and Gilbert 1982). This approach specifies that all punishments be equally and fairly given to those with the same number of prior criminal convictions and who have committed the same crime. The focus is on the crime committed, rather than any attributes of the individual. Extra-legal factors such as race, gender, and/or social class are not to be considered. In essence, then, all individuals convicted of the same crime must receive the same sentence.

While the justice model favours a determinate sentencing approach, it differs from the deterrence and selective incapacitation approaches because (1) it focuses on an offender's past behaviour as the rationale for sentencing rather than on his or her future criminality and the protection of society and (2) it believes that sentences, while determinate, should be shorter than longer. This means that for a specific criminal offence, justice model advocates would support a sentence of five years (with no parole), while supporters of the deterrence approach would prefer a much longer sentence (also with no parole). In theory, then, the justice model advocates a sentencing approach that utilizes short periods of incarceration in comparison to the lengthier sentences favoured by the deterrence and selective incapacitation models.

In 1990, the federal government published a report entitled "Sentencing: Directions for Reform," which revealed the direction it would like sentencing to take in the future. The following are excerpts from the government's initiative, which reflects a strong justice model orientation.

(1) The fundamental purpose of sentencing is to contribute to the maintenance of a just, peaceful, and safe society through the imposition of just sanctions . . .

(3) . . . a court that sentences an offender for an offence shall exercise its discretion within the limitations prescribed by this or any act of parliament, and in accordance with the following principles:

  (a) a sentence should be proportionate to the gravity of the offence, the degree of responsibility of the offender for the offence, and any other aggravating or mitigating circumstances;

  (b) a sentence should be the least onerous alternative appropriate in the circumstances;

  (c) a sentence should be similar to sentences imposed on other offenders for similar offences committed in similar circumstances;

  (d) the maximum punishment prescribed should be imposed only in the most serious cases of the commission of the offence;

  (e) the court should consider the total effect of the sentence and the combined effect of that sentence and the other sentences imposed on the offender; and

  (f) a term of imprisonment should be imposed only:

    (i) to protect the public from crimes of violence;

    (ii) where any other sanction would not sufficiently reflect the gravity of an offence or the repetitive nature of the criminal conduct of an offender, or adequately protect the public or the integrity of the administration of justice;

    (iii) to penalize an offender for wilful noncompliance with the term of any other sentence that has been imposed on the offender where no other sanction appears to compel compliance. (Source: Justice Canada)

Issues in Sentencing

In recent years, a number of critical issues have been raised about the role and purpose of sentencing in Canada. A general concern is that there is no coherent rationale for sentencing in Canada. As the members of the Canadian Sentencing Commission (1987:77) noted, "the primary difficulty of sentencing . . . is that there is no consensus on how sentencing should be approached." A coherent and consistent sentencing policy would eliminate this problem as it would make the sentencing process "understandable, accessible, and predictable—to judges, the public, correctional officers, and the offender." This would be achieved by a clear explanation "of legal sanctions while a statement of the goals of sentencing would justify the sanction and explain variations" (Campbell 1990:390).

Beyond this general issue lie specific problems. One of these deals with judicial discretion: in particular, the fact that judges have the opportunity to discriminate against members of certain social groups, that is, "to base their sentences on factors such as race and socioeconomic class, that are objectionable on moral or legal grounds" (Myers 1995:417). Another problem in recent years is the fact that judges do not punish consistently—that is, offenders who have been convicted for similar offences receive different sentences (Blumstein et al., 1983). Another issue concerns alternative sanctioning bodies and the introduction of alternative groups into the final decision on sentences imposed by judges. Examples include aboriginal sentencing circles, which have been introduced in a number of Canadian provinces to deal with aboriginal offenders, and federal legislation that institutionalizes the role of victims in the sentencing process through victim impact statements.

Such practices are an attempt to reduce sentencing discrimination and inconsistent sentencing practices as well as to introduce alternative voices into the sentencing process. In an attempt to correct this situation, the Canadian Sentencing Commission proposed a justice model–based approach to sentencing. In particular, they recommended a structured sentencing rationale similar to that developed and practised in Minnesota. This approach emphasizes the protection of individual rights and liberties, equity, and fairness, as well as crime prevention and the protection of the public (Campbell 1990). Furthermore, the commission argued that sentencing should be fair and equal for all Canadians, regardless of who they are and where they live, and stressed the need for alternatives in the sentencing process.

Public Opinion and Sentencing

Research conducted in a number of Western countries in recent years indicates that members of the public select harsher sentences than judges. Studies have long pointed out that there is a wide gap between the sentencing lengths of judges and those the public would have handed out for exactly the same case. However, research comparing the relative punitiveness of public and judicial attitudes toward the punishment of offenders has come to a different conclusion (Roberts 1988b; Roberts and Doob 1989; Zamble 1990; Zamble and Kalm 1990). In the study conducted by Roberts and Doob (1989), 62 percent of the public and 63 percent of the judiciary agreed on those offenders who should be incarcerated. These same researchers discovered that when they presented the public with sufficient information about different sentencing options available to judges, they actually became less punitive than judges. The public recommended incarcerating a total of 81 863 offenders in the study, while, in reality, judges had incarcerated a total of 92 415 offenders.

However, does the public agree with judges about the type of offences that should lead to incarceration of the offender? When Roberts and Doob compared the rank-orderings of the public with the actual actions of the judiciary on 10 offences, substantial differences were found between the two groups. Of the 10 offences, the public suggested more punitive sentences on five of them (arson, assaulting a police officer, forgery, theft over $1000, and fraud over $1000) and gave virtually the same response for two offences (possession of dangerous weapons and kidnapping). Those offences for which the judiciary gave more punitive responses were robbery, perjury, and break and enter.

While it appears that the public may be more punitive than judges when sentencing offenders, they tend to support a variety of sentencing goals. For example, in a U.S. study, Jamieson and Flanagan (1989) found the greatest support for deterrence (79 percent of the respondents rated it as "very important") with almost as much support (72 percent) for rehabilitation. Overall, at least two-thirds of those interviewed rated all sentencing goals as "very important." Once again, substantial variation is found for each sentencing goal among the public when they are questioned on specific cases. Jacoby and Dunn (1987) discovered, in their U.S. sample, that rehabilitation was supported by 85 percent of the respondents as the appropriate sentencing goal for the violent crime of arson, but only 50 percent of the same group selected rehabilitation for the violent crime of forcible rape. A Canadian study discovered that when a crime was judged relatively "minor," the sentencing goal supported by most of the public was deterrence. However, the public responded differently when they were presented with serious violent crimes. For violent crimes such as robbery and sexual assault, the public showed minimal approval for deterrence, with selective incapacitation receiving the majority of support (Canadian Sentencing Commission 1987).

Sentencing Guidelines

Canada currently has no established sentencing policy (Doob 1992). What this means is that sentences imposed by judges are designed to meet their own personal criteria as to what an appropriate sentence is, as opposed to following specific guidelines or a punishment rationale. As a result, judges are able to sentence offenders on the basis of different criteria that pertain to the offender and/or the circumstances surrounding the offence. Judges are then free to decide what sentence they want to use to achieve these different goals. As Doob (1992:424) has commented, "the policy that judges have created in Canada is better described as the absence of a policy" as a number of purposes are involved such as "rehabilitation of this offender, deterrence of this offender, incapacitation of this offender, deterrence of others, and denunciation of criminal behavior. The only problem is that the policy, such that it is, does not indicate how these different purposes are to be blended, or which is to dominate the decision in particular cases."

One approach developed to counteract this "nonpolicy" is referred to as *structured sentencing*, which follows the justice model of sentencing. This approach uses written standards or guidelines to control a judge's sentencing decision. The goal of sentencing guidelines is to promote sentencing neutrality and eliminate any discrimination and disparities that may exist in the imposition of sentencing. Currently 22 U.S. states have existing or proposed sentencing guidelines.

In 1987, the Canadian Sentencing Commission released its report on sentencing, called *Sentencing Reform: A Canadian Approach*. This report—as well as some of the individual studies commissioned for it—reviewed many of the problems associated with sentencing in Canada at that time. The commission proposed an alternative sentencing system that would represent the "just deserts" philosophy toward sentencing and punishment, particularly as it was constructed and operating in Minnesota (see Chapter 3). While the recommendations within the report failed to be enacted as a total package, much of the spirit of the document pervades the Canadian justice system.

Why were members of the Canadian Sentencing Commission so impressed by the Minnesota sentencing guidelines? To answer that question, it is important to know the underlying philosophy of the sentencing guidelines, why they were introduced, how they are supposed to work, and how successful they are in achieving their goals.

Sentencing guidelines were introduced by advocates of the justice model in an attempt to control judicial discretion in sentencing. They argued that sentencing systems that allowed the discretionary powers of judges to remain unchecked ultimately led to disparity in sentencing decisions. Such disparity was evident when the trial outcomes of different groups were compared, that is, "when 'like cases' with respect to case attributes—regardless of their legitimacy—are sentenced." In order to eliminate disparity, sentencing reformers argued judicial discretion—i.e., the "latitude of decision provided by law by someone in imposing sentence"—needed to be curtailed or, better yet, completely banned (Blumstein et al. 1983). For the criminal justice system to be fair, sentencing decisions had to be based on legal factors, ignoring any extra-legal factors (e.g., race, gender, social class) of the offender and/or victims.

The Minnesota Sentencing Guidelines were introduced in 1980 in an attempt to eliminate sentencing disparity by controlling judicial discretion at the sentencing stage. The guidelines stated that sentencing should be done without regard to the race, gender, or social or economic status of the defendant. In their original form, the guidelines allowed judges to make sentencing decisions based solely on two factors: (1) the severity of the crime for which the offender was convicted, and (2) the prior record of the offender. As a result, the guidelines regulated both the decision to commit an offender to prison as well as the length of their imprisonment. The guidelines were also designed to control the state prison population. To achieve this goal, the guidelines were constructed to imprison those convicted of serious violent crimes as well as

TABLE 9.1

The Sentencing Commission's Guiding Principles

After examining closely our system of sentencing offenders and identifying its strengths and weaknesses, the Canadian Sentencing Commission was guided, in making its recommendations, by the principles found in the first column below. The second column contains a summary of the current situation.

Guiding Principle	Current
Role of Parliament The sentencing of criminal offenders should be governed, in the first instance, by principles laid down by Parliament.	Parliament has thus far never stated what principles should guide sentencing
Purpose The fundamental purpose of sentencing is to preserve the authority of and to promote respect for the law through the imposition of just sanctions.	There are at least five main purposes with no explicit system of priorities. In a given case, these purposes may conflict.
Priority The paramount principle governing the determination of sentence is that the sentence be proportionate to the gravity of the offence and the degree of responsibility of the offender for the offence.	As noted above, there is no paramount principle. Judges choose among these purposes and combine them as they see fit. There are no rules determining the priority of these purposes.
Trial Judges Within the limits set by Parliament, the sanction imposed on an offender in Canada should ultimately be determined by an impartial and independent person with the best knowledge of the case: the trial judge.	This is the current situation. The Commission maintained this as an important principle in its recommendation.
Statutory Maximum Penalties The upper limit of maximum penalties should provide sufficient scope to allow the imposition of appropriate sentences. However, the range available should not be so wide as to provide no guidance.	At the moment, many maximum penalties are so high that they are rarely if ever used. Therefore, at present, the maxima provide little guidance and in many instances give a false impression of what sentences might be expected.
Restraint In line with the recommendations of numerous Canadian commissions that have reported in the past, sentences of imprisonment should be used more sparingly, especially for those convicted of minor property offences. Sentences of imprisonment should normally be reserved for the most serious offences, particularly those involving violence. People should not be imprisoned because of an inability to pay fines.	Canada presently imprisons more people than do most Western democracies. A substantial proportion are imprisoned for minor property offences or for non-payment of fines.
Guidelines Within the statutory limits, judges should be given explicit guidance on the nature and length of the sanction to impose. This guidance should not preclude the judge from selecting the most appropriate sanction from the full range of sanctions prescribed by Parliament.	Parliament, directly or by implication, provides no guidance to the sentencing judge in determining the appropriate sentence to impose. Courts of Appeal give some guidance, but because the Supreme Court of Canada does not hear sentence appeals, there is no opportunity for a uniform approach across Canada.

(Table continues next page.)

TABLE 9.1, continued

Guiding Principle	Current
Comprehensibility The sentence imposed by the court should bear a close and predictable relationship to the administration and execution of that sentence. We should move much closer, then, to "real time" sentencing. "Real time" sentencing reduces the discrepancy between the sentence as pronounced by the judge and as administered by correctional authorities.	The sentence pronounced in court, in many instances, varies substantially with what actually happens to an offender because of the manner in which a sentence is administered and executed. Those sentenced to a term of imprisonment may be granted day release after serving one-sixth of the sentence and full release on parole after serving one-third thereof.
Equity The system to be proposed should, as much as possible, promote equity and enhance clarity and predictability in sentencing.	There is unwarranted disparity in sentences such that the sentence is determined by factors beyond the seriousness of the case, the blameworthiness of the offender, and the circumstances surrounding the commission of the offence. Sentences are, in most instances, not predictable unless one knows not only the facts of the case but also factors such as the identity of the trial judge and agreements that might have transpired between defence and Crown counsel. Given the uncertainty and unnecessary complexity of the system, it is not surprising that most people do not understand sentencing.

Source: Canadian Sentencing Commission, *Report of the Canadian Sentencing Commission* (Ottawa: Supply and Services, 1987), pp. xxv–xxvii. Reprinted by permission of Carswell, a division of Thomson Canada Ltd.

those who had long prior criminal records. Most property offenders would not be imprisoned until they had been convicted of a number of offences.

Minnesota's sentencing guidelines, known formally as *presumptive guidelines*, are the most common type of structured sentencing since they require all sentences to fall within a narrow range established by law. Any deviation from the sentence guideline requires judges to explain the reasoning for their actions. The popularity of such guidelines results in large part from their rationale that as prior record and offence severity increase, so does the recommended sentence. However, if an offender commits a serious crime but has no prior record, he or she will have to serve a sentence involving a specified time of imprisonment. And if an offender continues to commit low-severity crimes, probation no longer becomes an option, and she or he will have to serve time in prison. For example, if someone with no prior record is convicted of aggravated robbery (severity level of conviction offence is "7" and criminal history score is "0") he or she will receive a sentence of 48 months. However, if two people commit a crime involving theft under $2500 (an offence with a severity level of 3) and for one offender it is her first offence and for the other it is her sixth, the former will receive 12 months' probation compared with her accomplice's sentence of 25 months' imprisonment. Another popular aspect of this sentencing rationale is that it ignores all features pertaining to the offender because it only focuses on the act(s) for which the offender is convicted in a court of law. Because the gender, race, or social class of the offender is irrelevant to the sentence, advocates of this approach point out that it is fair and equal to all.

Presumptive sentencing guideline models include four elements:

1. a standard sentencing range established by law
2. a statutory presumption that sentences, as established by sentencing judges, will fall within the legally defined range
3. a legal proviso allowing sentencing judges to move sentences outside the guidelines in light of aggravating or mitigating circumstances unique to each individual case
4. a requirement that sentencing judges make formal written justification in the event a sentence falls outside guidelines (Eskridge 1985)

Presumptive guidelines were recommended by the Canadian Sentencing Commission (1987). In its final report, the commission mentioned many problems of sentencing, which they attributed to the structure in which sentencing decisions are made rather than to judges themselves. Some of the problems identified by the commission were these:

- Maximum penalties are unrealistically high and do not always reflect the relative seriousness of offences.

- Mandatory minimum sentences create injustices by unnecessarily restricting judicial discretion without accomplishing other functions ascribed to them.

- Systematic information about current sentencing practice is lacking. For policy-makers and sentencing judges alike, easily accessible information on sentencing does not exist. (Stuart and Delisle 1995:903)

As a result of these problems, the Canadian Sentencing Commission (1987) recommended a "fundamental overhaul" of the then-current sentencing practices in Canada. The recommended changes were:

1. a new rationale for sentencing
2. elimination of all mandatory minimum penalties (other than for murder and high treason)
3. replacement of the current penalty structure for all offences other than murder and high treason of maximum penalties of 12 years, 9 years, 6 years, 3 years, a year or 6 months. In exceptional cases, for the most serious offences which carry a maximum sentence of either 12 or 9 years, provision is made to exceed these maxima
4. elimination of full parole release (other than for sentences of life imprisonment)
5. provision for a reduction of time served for those inmates who display good behavior while in prison. The portion that can be remitted would be reduced from one-third to one-quarter of the sentence imposed

6. an increase in the use of community sanctions. The Commission recommends greater use of sanctions which do not imply incarceration (e.g., community service orders, compensation to the victim or community and also fines, which do not involve any segregation of the offender from the community)

7. elimination of "automatic" imprisonment for the fine default to reduce the likelihood that a person who cannot pay a fine will go to jail

8. creation of a presumption for each offence respecting whether a person should normally be incarcerated or not. The judge could depart from the presumption by providing reasons for the departure

9. creation of a "presumption range" for each offence normally requiring incarceration (again the Judge could depart by providing reasons)

10. creation of a permanent sentencing commission to complete the development of guideline ranges for all offences, to collect and distribute information about current sentencing practice, and to review, in appropriate cases to modify (with the assent of the House of Commons) the presumptive sentences in light of current practice and appellate decisions

But do sentencing guidelines actually achieve their goals of fairness and equity? Initial analyses of sentences in Minnesota revealed greater uniformity and neutrality in criminal sanctions. Since the guidelines were explicitly developed to make extra-legal variables such as race, gender, and social class irrelevant factors at sentencing, the advocates of this sentencing approach agreed that their approach was, in fact, successful. Miethe and Moore (1985), for example, studied the impact of defendants' social class on sentences during the first year of the operation of the Minnesota sentencing guidelines. They found that judges were following the guidelines by giving greater weight to offence-based characteristics, such as the use of a weapon and the severity of the criminal action. Differential treatment of offenders on the basis of race, employment status, and gender declined, as did variations between judicial jurisdictions. In addition, Miethe and Moore (1985) reported that tighter controls on judicial discretion did not lead to greater discretion "upstream" in the criminal justice system, such as increased prosecutorial discretion. These results were confirmed by other research efforts. Kramer et al. (1989), for example, reported that judges continued to follow the sentencing guidelines four years after the introduction of the guidelines. Stolzenberg and D'Alessio (1994) confirmed these same conclusions in their study, which analyzed judicial sentences during the first 10 years of sentencing guidelines in Minnesota.

However, this type of sentencing reform may be limited in its scope of impact. Stolzenberg and D'Alessio (1994) and D'Alessio and Stolzenberg

(1995) found considerable deviation from sentencing guidelines the longer they were in effect. Specifically, they discovered that judges were not giving first-time violent offenders prison terms although a period of incarceration was stipulated by the guidelines. This was attributed to the Minnesota Sentencing Commission's "imperative to maintain the prison population within acceptable limits" (D'Alessio and Stolzenberg 1995:298). In addition, Frase (1991) reported that sentencing guidelines were increasingly circumvented by prosecutors reducing the charges or by recommending leniency because of offender-based criteria, such as family background. What these researchers have discovered is that the Minnesota Sentencing Guidelines continued to be affected by offender traits such as race and social class, particularly when judges determined sentence lengths (Moore and Miethe 1986; Stolzenberg and D'Alessio 1994).

Sentencing Disparity

The precise nature of sentencing disparity varies according to the individual defining the term. Disparity is most evident when examining trial outcomes, "when 'like cases' with respect to case attributes—regardless of their legitimacy—are sentenced" (Blumstein et al. 1983). Disparity can also be seen in the variations in sentences found within a specific jurisdiction or across jurisdictions. Becker (1968), for example, views disparity as the imposition of the same penalty (e.g., a fine) regardless of the differences among individuals.

In their research of sentencing disparity in Canada, the Canadian Sentencing Commission (1987) identified three types of sentencing disparity:

1. case to case, where the same judge imposes different sentences to similar offenders convicted of the same offence committed in similar circumstances

2. judge to judge, where different judges impose different sentences in similar cases

3. court to court, where different courts in a particular jurisdiction use different standards for what is considered an appropriate sentence for specific types of cases

The commission interviewed 400 judges, who admitted that there was variation among their sentencing practices, largely due to different personal attitudes. In addition, over 80 percent of almost 700 Crown prosecutors and defence lawyers believed there was unwarranted variation in sentences in their jurisdictions, and almost 90 percent stated that they felt there was unwarranted variation across Canada.

Two research studies have attempted to assess how similar court cases may be treated differently by judges. Hogarth (1971) studied the sentencing patterns of 71 magistrates in Ontario and found a great deal of variation in their sentencing decisions. In particular, he discovered that the judges' penal philosophy and attitudes determined what they considered important during a trial and ultimately influenced the type and length of sentences they imposed. Hogarth estimated that the legal facts of a case accounted for only 9 percent of the sentencing variations found in his study.

Palys and Divorski (1986) studied judicial variation in sentencing by presenting 206 Canadian provincial court judges with five hypothetical cases and requesting them to indicate what sentence they would impose on the offender. While judges were found to vary in their sentencing decisions in all five cases, the greatest differences were discovered in a case involving assault causing bodily harm. The judges' sentences varied from a $500 fine and six months' probation to five years in a federal institution.

Race and Sentencing Disparity in Canada

Research into sentencing **disparity** in Canada has usually focused on whether or not white offenders receive different or less harsh sentences than aboriginal offenders. Numerous provincial and federal inquiries into aboriginals and their experience with the dominant justice system have documented the impact of sentencing upon aboriginals. In 1991, for example, the Law Reform Commission published a report, *Aboriginal Peoples and Criminal Justice*, that concluded that the "impact of the justice system on Aboriginal persons is most apparent at the sentencing stage." The commissioner felt that the sentencing of aboriginals reflects a bias in the operation of the criminal justice system due to the overrepresentation of aboriginals in federal correctional facilities. In 1988, for example, nearly one in three inmates in Prairie penitentiaries were of aboriginal ancestry.

Two early studies reached different conclusions on this issue. Dubienski and Skelly (1970), studying arrest data in Winnipeg, found relatively fair treatment of aboriginals and whites for all offences. The exception was for violations of regulatory statutes where aboriginals were incarcerated more mainly because they were unable to pay fines. Hagan (1977), studying the impact of pre-sentence reports on the incarceration of offenders, concluded that race had little effect on sentencing outcome. However, he did find that aboriginals were treated more unfairly in rural areas.

Renner and Warner's (1981) study of cases heard by three magistrate and two county courts in Halifax, Nova Scotia, indicated that first-time white offenders convicted of summary charges were given discharges in 23 percent of the cases they studied. In contrast, first-time black offenders never received a discharge. A 1988 study conducted with the support of the Legal Services Society in British Columbia found some differences in the sentencing of aboriginals and nonaboriginals in summary conviction courts for the single-charge offences of common assault and theft under $1000. In the study, aboriginals were charged in 29.3 percent of the common assault cases and 21 percent of the cases of theft under $1000. After studying the courts for a nine-month period, the researchers concluded that "individuals of Native ancestry with prior criminal convictions were acquitted less frequently and found guilty more often . . . than non-Native individuals in similar circumstances." However, the researchers found that when aboriginals had no prior convictions, they were granted stay of proceedings more frequently and found not guilty more often than nonaboriginals (Lewis 1992).

Boldt et al. (1983), however, found no evidence of disparity among the sentences imposed on aboriginal and nonaboriginal offenders in the Yukon. Studying pre-sentence reports on aboriginal offenders, they found that while aboriginals do "receive proportionately more recommendations for incarceration than non-Natives," the difference was largely explained by the legal factors of offence severity and prior conviction(s).

Moyer et al. (1985), using data on cases of Canadian homicide between 1962 and 1984, compared the processing of male and female aboriginals and nonaboriginals through the Canadian courts. Their data revealed that the outcome of preliminary hearings indicated no differences by race or gender. During the 1960s and 1970s, the conviction rate of aboriginals and nonaboriginals was about the same. But between 1976 and 1980, Moyer et al. discovered that although the conviction rate did not differ by race, there was a notable difference between aboriginals and nonaboriginals in the type of offence they were convicted for. Aboriginals were more likely to be convicted of manslaughter charges than nonaboriginals (76.3 percent and 73.7 percent of aboriginal males and females, respectively, compared with 45.6 percent and 56.4 percent for nonaboriginal males and females). Nonaboriginals were more likely to be charged with first- and second-degree murder. Only 4 percent of aboriginal males were convicted of first-degree murder charges, compared with 13.5 percent of nonaboriginal males. After reviewing the data, Moyer et al. concluded that they could find little discrimination in the sentencing and criminal justice processing of aboriginals. In addition, Moyer and her colleagues examined sentence length by offence type for aboriginal and nonaboriginal admissions to federal, provincial, and territorial correctional institutions. They concluded that the data reveal little differences between the two groups in terms of admissions based on Criminal Code and provincial offences.

According to LaPrairie (1990:434), these studies, taken together, "provide no definitive answers to the questions of racial bias or unwarranted bias in the sentencing of aboriginal people, but highlight some of the contradictions that exist." However, some U.S. researchers now argue that factors of legal relevance can hide prior discriminatory actions in the criminal justice system. As Welch and Spohn (1986) report, indirect discrimination can occur when judges rely more on the offender's prior record of incarceration when setting type and length of sentence rather than on prior arrest or conviction. Thus, judges place most weight on a legally relevant factor that is the culmination of numerous discretionary decisions by various actors within the criminal justice system, including prior sentences. Myers (1995:420) noted in her review of U.S. sentencing practice that "any decision that led to a prior incarceration could incorporate discrimination based on legally irrelevant factors." Some researchers (Welch et al. 1984; Miethe and Moore 1986) also argue that the importance given to legally relevant factors varies according to offender characteristics and jurisdiction, particularly when the defendant is a member of a racial minority group.

Disparity in Sentence Length

In contrast to the numerous studies that have explored disparity in sentencing by type of sentence, only a few have examined differences in terms of sentence length. According to Moyer (1987), aboriginal offenders convicted of homicide offences receive shorter sentences than do nonaboriginals for the same categories of offences. She found almost 50 percent of nonaboriginals convicted of homicide received life sentences, compared with 20 percent of aboriginals, and that almost 50 percent of aboriginals received sentence lengths of less than five years compared with less than 25 percent of nonaboriginals.

Canfield and Drinan (1981) studied admissions to federal correctional facilities between 1976 and 1980 and discovered a disparity in sentence lengths that favoured aboriginal offenders. When they examined sentences for specific offences they found aboriginals consistently received shorter sentences for the same offences. For example, 55 percent of aboriginals received sentences of less than four years for attempted murder, compared with 23 percent of nonaboriginals, while 34 percent of aboriginals received sentences of more than six years, compared with 60 percent of nonaboriginals.

These findings reflect much of the diversity of conclusions found in this area to date. As Griffiths and Verdun-Jones (1994:429) have commented in their review of these studies, "the research is inconclusive as to whether there is a racial bias in Canadian sentencing practices." After a review of the literature, LaPrairie (1990) concluded that the data concerning the role of judicial discretion in causing the alleged statistical overrepresentation of aboriginal people in correctional institutions remains contradictory and unclear. Some of the problems experienced by these studies can be attributed to insufficient data. Also, different research trends have emerged in an attempt to discover whether there is discrimination against certain groups at the sentencing stage. For example, it is possible to look at discrimination in the type of sentences received by offenders as well as for possible differences in sentence lengths. Incomplete data about crimes can also confound studies. In some research projects, such key factors as the race of the victim may not be noted.

Victim Participation in Sentencing

It has been argued that many judges are extremely reluctant to take into consideration the feelings and concerns of victims when it comes to sentencing offenders. The courtroom is their domain, and while outsiders can inform the judiciary of their experiences, there is no guarantee that the victims will have any influence on their decision.

Since 1989, victims in Canada have the right to complete a **victim impact statement,** a document that requests victims to detail the effect of the crime on them. It is then forwarded to the judge for consideration in sentencing. When these forms were introduced, it was hoped they would have a significant influence on the sentencing decision. It was an attempt to bring victims "back into" the criminal justice system by giving them an opportunity, either through a written form or by speaking before a judge in the courtroom, to inform the court about the impact of the crime and, in some cases, what sort of sentence the offender should receive.

The effect of these statements on the sentencing decision is largely unknown since it is rare for a judge to mention a victim impact statement. However, some judges have made it a habit to mention the victim impact statement in certain court cases. This is particularly so when they feel that aggravating circumstances in the offence have severely traumatized the victim, thereby leading them to hand out a tougher sentence.

Most of the detailed research into the impact of victim participation on the sentencing of criminal offenders has taken place in the United States. Erez and Tontodonato (1990) studied 500 felony cases in Ohio and found that victims filled out impact statements more often when a violent crime was committed against them, when they suffered a physical injury, when the victim was "vulnerable" (for example, the victim was elderly, a minor, or pregnant), when the crime occurred in the victim's home, and when the offender was known to the victim. They also found victim impact statements were filled out more often when the defendant was a male and had prior convictions.

Erez and Tontodonato also studied what happened when a victim appeared before a judge in an attempt to influence the sentence. The impact of this activity was limited because the judge's decision on sentencing appeared to be determined primarily by legal factors, not by the victim's appearing in court. The authors also discovered that the inclusion of a victim impact statement in the defendant's file influenced the likelihood that a prison sentence (as opposed to probation) would be given to the defendant, but it did not affect the length of the prison sentence.

In a later study, Erez and Tontodonato (1992) examined the extent of victims' involvement in the criminal justice system and the effect of this experience on their satisfaction with the system. Previous studies (Kelly 1984; Forst and Hernon 1985; Shapland, Willmoew, and Duff 1985) had all reported that victims' complaints were concerned more with criminal justice procedures, particularly the inability of victims to influence the decision-making process, than with the apparent injustice of the outcome of the criminal trial. However, in their study, Erez and Tontodonato found the most significant predictor influencing victims' satisfaction with justice was their perception of the fairness of the sentence. Another factor was the type of offence. Erez and Tontodonato discovered victims of crime against the person were more satisfied with the justice system than victims of property crimes, who usually saw those charged with such offences receiving shorter sentences.

To evaluate the effectiveness of victim impact statements in Canada, the Department of Justice conducted studies in six Canadian cities during 1986 (Giliberti 1990). One part of the study evaluated the effects of victim impact statements on victims. To their surprise, researchers discovered no difference in the degree of victims' satisfaction with justice when their impact statements were used in court and when they were not. According to the victims, the most important feature of the program was the opportunity it gave them to discuss the offence and its effects and to have this information given to the court, to be given useful feedback about the case, and to be able to contact someone should they experience any difficulties. Researchers also discovered that this led to victims being better informed about what was happening in their cases as they progressed through the criminal justice system. However, researchers report that the impact of this program was the same for both participants and nonparticipants in terms of the level of their participation in the criminal justice system, their satisfaction with how the case was handled, and their future reporting of incidents to the police. It was also found that the majority of all victims held negative attitudes toward sentencing both before and after their cases.

The effect of victim impact statements on the criminal justice system varied across the six study sites. For example, in Victoria, very few victim impact statements were used in court when their use was at the discretion of prosecutors. Prosecutors indicated that they did not use them because they felt they contained no new information, that too many were vague or contained largely irrelevant information, that they were of doubtful accuracy, and that they contributed to higher operating costs of the criminal justice system. In Toronto, prosecutors felt that victim impact statements could have a significant role in court. As a result, two-thirds of the victim impact statements in Toronto were entered into court trials as exhibits and one-third were used as Crown submissions. For all Crown prosecutors, victim impact statements had the greatest impact in sexual assault and sexual abuse cases. In addition, these statements were considered helpful in raising prosecutors' awareness of the long-term emotional impact on victims, which had not been captured in other documents available to prosecutors (Roberts 1992:67). Victim statements had some impact on judges. Of the 13 judges who responded to the question "Have victim impact statements actually affected sentences that you have passed?", seven judges responded positively while six answered no. However, in British Columbia, Roberts (1992:77) reported a "minor change" in sentences imposed by judges in cases where a victim impact statement was used, while "occasionally sentences have been dramatically higher."

Raymond Raven plays a drum for his father, Raymond Sr., at the entrance to an Ojibway sweat lodge. (Photo: Peter Moon/*The Globe and Mail*)

Healing Circles

In recent years, much attention has been given to the overrepresentation of aboriginals in the federal and provincial correctional systems. Quigley (1994:270) has summarized the implications of this overrepresentation of aboriginals in the Canadian correctional system:

- Aboriginal accused persons are more likely to be denied bail. This in turn tends to increase the likelihood of incarceration upon conviction.

- Aboriginal offenders are more likely to be committed to jail for nonpayment of fines. In Saskatchewan during the 1992–93 fiscal year, almost 75 percent of admissions to jails for fine default were aboriginals.

- Aboriginal offenders are less likely to receive probation as a sentence than are nonaboriginal offenders.

From this evidence, Quigley (1994:271) recommends an attempt "to decrease the preponderance of Aboriginal people within the prison system." One proposal has been to reintroduce sentencing and healing circles, in which a group of elders participate with a judge in the sentencing process in an attempt to heal the accused, the victim, and the community.

The exact nature of sentencing circles varies across Canada, but there are some common features. Quigley notes that modern sentencing circles are, in reality, a hybrid of the traditional form of aboriginal community justice and the Western legal system. In essence, judges retain the right to give final approval to a sentence imposed by a sentencing circle. What is different, however, is the process by which the sentence is arrived at. The difference, according to Quigley (1994:288), is that "sentencing circles are a variation in procedure, not necessarily a change in the substance of sentencing." The sentencing circle

Field Practice 9.1

A. Sexual Assault

At a party, five men sexually assaulted a woman who had too much to drink and was passed out in a bedroom. It took the woman almost a week to discover what had happened. All the assailants were charged with Sexual Assault Level I, and since it was the first offence for all involved, the prosecutor decided to proceed by way of summary conviction. All the defendants pleaded guilty to the single charge, which carries a maximum sentence of six months or a fine of $2000. The judge fined each of the assailants $1000. When the victim heard about the punishments, she said she was a double-victim, raped once by the men and the other time by the criminal justice system.

B. White-Collar Criminal

A securities officer was convicted of stealing money from his clients over an eight-year period. The police estimate that he stole over $10 million from over 2500 people. The judge fined him $1 million (the maximum allowed) and sentenced him to four years' imprisonment, but agreed to reduce the sentence to one year on probation if he agreed to build 10 shelters for the homeless in the city. In addition, he would have to completely fund these shelters for a total of five years out of his own pocket. The defendant agreed to the sentence with a smile on his face.

C. Child Sexual Assault

A 74-year-old man was convicted of sexually assaulting his daughters for periods up to five years during the 1940s. In addition, the prosecutor and police suspected that he had also sexually assaulted his two granddaughters, although they did not charge him with these offences because they felt the evidence wasn't strong enough. The judge heard testimony from all the victims, who informed her of the trauma they had experienced. The judge, upon pronouncing a sentence of six months' suspended sentence, pointed to the age and failing health of the convicted individual.

operates on a similar basis as the Western legal system in some of its procedures. For example, if there are disputes on factual matters, they are resolved by calling for evidence, examination, and cross-examination of witnesses. What does differ is that, through discussion around a sentencing circle, "respected members of the community, the victim, the police, the accused, the family of the accused, Crown and defence counsel, and the judge try to jointly arrive at a decision that is acceptable to all."

Once a sentence is agreed upon, it is not an automatic fact that the sentence will be accepted by the Western legal system. For example, the Saskatchewan Court of Appeal overturned the sentence handed down by a sentencing circle to Ivan Morin. In 1992, Morin, a 34-year-old Métis, was convicted of robbing a gasoline station of $131 and choking a female attendant. He was sentenced to jail for 18 months instead of the six to eight years requested by the Crown. The Crown's sentence proposal was based on the fact that Morin had 34 prior criminal convictions ranging from drunk driving and small-time break-ins to attempted murder and kidnapping. When the trial judge accepted the recommendation of the sentencing circle, the Crown appealed the case. Their appeal was based largely on their opinion that Morin was using the sentencing circle to receive the lowest sentence possible and did not show real remorse or interest in rehabilitation. In their review of this case, the Saskatchewan Court of Appeal noted that judges should accept the decisions of sentencing circles in cases where (1) the accused agreed to be referred to a sentencing circle; (2) the accused has deep roots in the community in which the circle is held; (3) the elders are willing to support the offender; and (4) the victim voluntarily participates (Abbate 1995). Since Morin appeared to be trying to take advantage of the lighter sentences associated with sentencing circles, the judges on the Saskatchewan Court of Appeal decided to accept the argument presented by the Crown and increased the sentence. Such appeals are rare. In Saskatchewan, over 200 cases have been heard and the Crown has appealed only five of them.

The benefits of sentencing circles are many. According to a court in the Yukon, the benefits of sentencing circles involve numerous modifications to the decision-making process:

1. The monopoly of professionals is reduced.
2. Lay participation is encouraged.
3. Information flow is increased.
4. There is a creative search for new options.
5. The sharing of responsibility for the decision is promoted.
6. The participation of the accused is encouraged.
7. Victims are involved in the process.
8. A more constructive environment is created.
9. There is greater understanding of the limitations of the justice system.
10. It extends the focus of the criminal justice system.
11. There is greater mobilization of community resources.
12. There is an opportunity to merge the values of Aboriginal Nations and the larger society. (*R. v. Moses* 1992)

Summary

The sentencing of a convicted person is one of the most crucial decisions made within our criminal justice system. In Canada judges have considerable discretion determining the length of a sentence, and their decision reflects how they wish the accused to be punished. However, in most cases, the decision of the judge is not final since the members of the parole board may decide to grant full parole before the completion of the sentence.

No matter the reason for a sentence, the object is to reduce crime by incarcerating criminals and deterring others from committing crimes. Deterrence, selective incapacitation, rehabilitation, and the justice model all vary in terms of their emphasis on how best to deal with offenders through sentencing.

In Canada, the federal government has attempted in recent years to shift the focus of sentencing to a justice model perspective. The Canadian Sentencing Commission was formed in 1987 to investigate the problems with the current sentencing approach and to suggest an alternative approach that is both coherent and consistent.

A number of significant problems have been identified with the sentencing practices of judges in Canada. These include sentencing practices that lead to discrimination and disparity. In an attempt to correct these problems, a structured (or determinate) sentencing approach has been proposed. In addition, sentencing circles have been introduced in aboriginal communities in an attempt to eliminate concerns over racial disparity in sentencing.

Discussion Questions

1. Why is sentencing considered by many to be the most critical phase in our system of justice?

2. Why does sentencing disparity exist? How can we reduce these disparities? Should all individuals who commit the same offence receive the same sentence?

3. Compare the different types of sentence affiliated with each of the different models of criminal justice. What are the benefits and disadvantages of each?

4. Are there any crimes for which the Canadian government should pass mandatory sentencing law?

5. Should public opinion affect sentencing decisions made by judges?

6. Should Canada have a well-defined sentencing policy? If so, what would be the impact of such a policy?

7. Should victims have a greater role in the sentencing of offenders? How could this be done?

8. Discuss the reasons why aboriginal sentencing circles are so successful.

9. Should Canada reintroduce the death penalty as a sentence for first-degree murder? Explain your answer.

Suggested Readings

Canadian Sentencing Commission. *Sentencing Reform: A Canadian Approach*. Ottawa: Minister of Supply and Services, 1987.

Rock, P. *A View from the Shadows*. Oxford: Clarendon Press, 1986.

Samuelson, L., and B. Schissel, eds. *Criminal Justice: Sentencing Issues and Reform*. Toronto: Garamond Press, 1991.

CHAPTER 10

Contemporary Corrections in Canada

W hen a defendant is convicted of a criminal offence, he or she may be sentenced to a period of confinement in a federal or provincial correctional institution. To meet the growing number of individuals sentenced to a term of incarceration in one of these institutions, a large and costly correctional system has developed over the last 160 years. The correctional system as we know it today started in the early 1800s in Ontario with the opening of the Kingston Penitentiary. Today, there are over 60 federal institutions and over 100 provincial correctional facilities. Our correctional facilities operate on the basis of security levels—maximum, medium, and minimum—although it is difficult for the authorities to always make the proper distinctions between them.

After a discussion of correctional facilities and a profile of the adult correctional population, this chapter covers some of the most important issues facing Canadian corrections today. This includes coping with prison

CHAPTER OBJECTIVES

- examine the adult correctional population in Canada today

- discuss the facilities for women offenders in the federal correctional system

- discuss the legal rights of inmates

- understand the effects of being sentenced to prison, including prison violence and suicide

life, prison violence, and prison suicide. In addition, the legal rights of inmates are discussed, including the requirement for the Correctional Service of Canada to operate in a fair manner in its treatment of inmates.

Prisons have evolved constantly since their introduction into Canada in the early 19th century. From a single facility, the correctional system has grown into a system differentiated by security levels of the offenders. While prisons have always been controversial in our society, a current issue revolves around the idea of private prisons. Such prisons would be built and operated by private corporations specializing in corrections, and serving the purpose of saving large amounts of money for both federal and provincial governments.

In the spring of 1995, the province of New Brunswick signed a contract with a private corporation specializing in the building and management of correctional facilities—Wackenhut Corrections Corp. of Coral Gables, Florida—to build and operate a young-offender facility. At the same time, it also announced they were exploring the possibility of calling for proposals to build and possibly operate an 80-bed adult facility. The Nova Scotia government then released a press statement stating that they were looking at the feasibility of involving the private sector in operating its nine provincial correctional centres. Both provincial governments cited cost savings as their rationale in exploring the private prison alternative. New Brunswick noted it could save as much as 15 percent of the costs of building and operating a facility, while Nova Scotia stated it was looking for ways to reduce the provincial debt. In the United Sates, cost savings are estimated at approximately $10 (U.S.) for each inmate per day (Cox 1995). While the government of New Brunswick later decided to staff the new facility with provincial employees, it raised issues concerning private prisons in Canada.

The History of Prisons in Canada

It is only in recent decades that Canada, like all other Western nations, has increased its use of confinement as the main approach to punishing offenders. Between 1832, when the first federal prison was built in Kingston, Ontario, and 1950, a total of eight federal prisons were constructed. During the 1950s, three federal institutions were built, followed by eight in the 1960s, five in the 1970s, and six during the 1980s.

The first prisons in North America were built in the United States. Two different types were originally constructed. The **Pennsylvania system** reflected a strong Quaker influence. Inmates were isolated not only from the outside, but also from each other. They were given one hour a day to exercise by themselves in an outside yard; for the rest of the time they were expected to remain in their small cells, read the Bible provided to them, reflect on their illegal actions, and "repent" their crimes (Jackson 1983).

Another style of prison was built in Auburn, New York. Referred to as the **Auburn prison system**, this institution held inmates in what is known as the *congregate system*. This system was based on the belief that the most efficient way for inmates to reform their actions was through hard work. During the day, inmates worked together both inside and outside the walls, although they were not supposed to talk to each other. Prisoners ate together, but also in complete silence. If the inmates were not working or eating, they were locked in their cells. A different prison architectural style characterized the Auburn system. While the Pennsylvania prison was built on one floor, the Auburn system had a number of floors of cells built on top of each other, in tiers, as they were called (Rothman 1971). The Auburn system, originally built between 1819 and 1823, quickly became the most copied style of prison and ultimately became the "international prototype of a maximum-security prison" (Anderson and Newman 1993:349). The Auburn system was to become the basis for the first Canadian federal prison located at Kingston, Ontario (Taylor 1979).

The Pennsylvania system continued to survive in one particular form: solitary confinement. Most correctional institutions today contain within them areas set aside for more severe forms of punishment for inmates who violated prison rules and regulations or who are considered to be "troublemakers."

The Adult Correctional Population in Canada Today

From 1989–90 to 1993–94, the total correctional caseload for both federal and provincial institutions increased from 117 571 to 154 106 inmates, a 31-percent increase. Of these, 27 573 were inmates serving custodial sentences, 14 251 (or 52 percent) were in provincial or territorial facilities, while 13 322 (or 48 percent) were in federal institutions. Of the 5230 inmates in provincial facilities who were not serving a sentence, 5130 (or 98 percent) were remanded in custody and waiting for judicial action on their cases, and the remaining 100 (or 2 percent) were on temporary detention. In addition, 121 403 offenders were serving a sentence or part of their sentence under community supervision. Most of these offenders (102 402, or 84 percent) were on probation supervision, while the remaining 19 001 (or 16 percent) were placed in the community on parole or another type of conditional release, excluding offenders on temporary absences from federal institutions (Reed 1995:3).

In provincial institutions, during 1993–94, men represented 91 percent of the total sentenced population, while women accounted for the remaining 9 percent, a ratio that has remained constant since 1989–90. Aboriginals accounted for 17 percent of the total number of sentenced offenders, a decrease of 1 percent since 1989–90 and 6 percent since 1992–93. The median age (29) of sentenced offenders increased from 1989–90, when it was 27.

In federal correctional institutions, males accounted for the vast majority of admissions during 1993–94 (97 percent). Aboriginals made up 12 percent of all admissions, an increase of 1 percent since 1989–90. The age of the average federal offender was 31 in 1993–94, the same as it was in 1989–90 (Reed 1995:4–5).

FIGURE 10.1

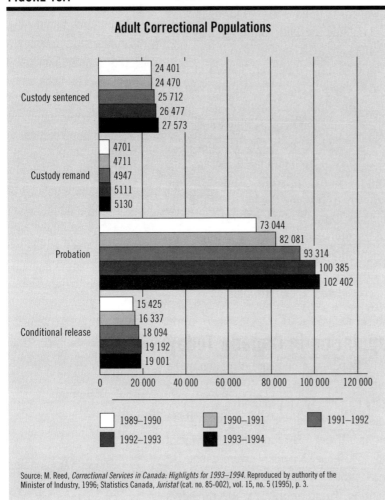

Adult Correctional Populations

Custody sentenced
- 24 401
- 24 470
- 25 712
- 26 477
- 27 573

Custody remand
- 4701
- 4711
- 4947
- 5111
- 5130

Probation
- 73 044
- 82 081
- 93 314
- 100 385
- 102 402

Conditional release
- 15 425
- 16 337
- 18 094
- 19 192
- 19 001

0   20 000   40 000   60 000   80 000   100 000   120 000

☐ 1989–1990   ◻ 1990–1991   ■ 1991–1992
■ 1992–1993   ■ 1993–1994

Source: M. Reed, *Correctional Services in Canada: Highlights for 1993–1994*. Reproduced by authority of the Minister of Industry, 1996; Statistics Canada, *Juristat* (cat. no. 85-002), vol. 15, no. 5 (1995), p. 3.

Federal Correctional Institutions

At present, 41 federal correctional facilities (excluding halfway houses) are operating under the jurisdiction of the Correctional Service of Canada. Four of these facilities are located in the Atlantic region, 11 in Quebec, 10 in Ontario, and the Prairie and Pacific regions each have eight. Eleven institutions are classified as minimum-security facilities, 16 are medium-security facilities, and 14 are maximum-security facilities. The capacity of these facilities varies from 78 to 501 inmates, with an average of 259 inmates. The average capacity of minimum-security facilities is 121 inmates, while medium- and maximum-security institutions have average capacities of 377 and 235, respectively. According to the Correctional Service of Canada, the majority of inmates in the federal correctional system are housed in facilities built between 10 and 50 years ago. Of the 41 federal institutions, 29 were built between 10 and 50 years ago, while six are over 50 years old and six are under 10 years of age (*Forum on Corrections Research* 1991).

Security Levels

Since the major objective of correctional institutions is confinement, the primary factor in determining the classification level of an inmate is security. On a general level, security has three components: (1) the likelihood an inmate will escape or attempt to escape; (2) the likelihood an inmate will place a correctional officer or another inmate in danger; and (3) the likelihood an inmate will attempt to violate institutional rules (Anderson and Newman 1993). Until 1981–82, the Correctional Service of Canada employed a classification system of offenders based on the likelihood an offender would escape from an institution and the potential harm to the community if he did.

According to the Correctional Service of Canada, the three levels of security were defined as follows:

1. *Maximum security.* The inmate is likely to escape and would cause serious harm in the community.
2. *Medium security.* The inmate is likely to escape but would not cause serious harm in the community.
3. *Minimum security.* The inmate is not likely to escape but, if he did, would not cause harm in the community. (Eckstedt and Griffiths 1988:191)

Inmates are given a security classification when they enter a federal correctional institution by parole officers of the Correctional Service of Canada. This is followed in most cases by an interview with a placement officer who assesses the inmate to deter-

FIGURE 10.2

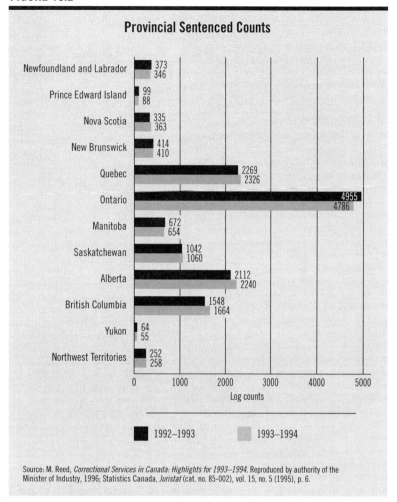

Source: M. Reed, *Correctional Services in Canada: Highlights for 1993–1994*. Reproduced by authority of the Minister of Industry, 1996; Statistics Canada, *Juristat* (cat. no. 85-002), vol. 15, no. 5 (1995), p. 6.

mine his or her security needs. This initial assessment does not necessarily determine the type of security-level facility the inmate will be sent to, however. An inmate classified as maximum-security may be sent to a medium-security institution, depending on their prior record as well as the type of programs offered by the institution.

Maximum-security facilities are usually surrounded by high fences or walls (depending on when they were built), usually around 20 feet tall and surrounded by guard towers at strategic positions. Intrusion detection systems ensure that the perimeter is not being "compromised." Parts of the facility are separated by gates, fences, and walls, and inmates are usually required to have special permission forms when they are moving between sections of the institution outside of normal times of movement. A number of inmates live in solitary confinement, either because of behavioural issues or out of concern that they will be attacked by other inmates, usually because of their crimes (e.g., sex offenders). Maximum-security facilities usually have a number of educational and treatment programs, such as adult basic education, high-school equivalency courses, and various skills-development programs, such as carpentry.

Medium-security institutions are typically enclosed by chain-link fences topped with barbed and razor wire. Compared with maximum-security facilities, medium-security institutions allow more freedom of movement for inmates. Many of these facilities have modern surroundings and training centres. In addition, they also have a variety of educational and treatment facilities available.

Minimum-security prisons usually have no fences or walls around them. In fact, an inmate can walk out of the facility since security around the facility is much more relaxed. There are no armed guards, no towers, no barbed wire, or electronic surveillance equipment to ensure prisoners stay within the institution. Staff and inmates often mingle and are indistinguishable from each other since prison clothes are not issued. Inmates are also housed in better living arrangements, in private or semi-private rooms. In addition, inmates may be on work release programs that allow them to hold jobs during the day.

Since 1981–82, the Correctional Service of Canada has operated on the basis of seven different security levels. Level 1 facilities are community correctional centres, while level 2 institutions have such minimum-security facilities as forestry and work camps. Levels 3, 4, and 5 represent medium-security facilities, while level 6 represents a maximum-security institution. Level 7 is the highest level of security risk, and is reserved for violent offenders who are placed into what are referred to as special handling units, or "super-max" institutions.

Women in Federal Correctional Institutions

Most women remanded or sentenced to a correctional facility in Canada today are placed in provincial institutions. In 1991, approximately 13 500 women were serving a sentence and about 8500 were on remand in provincial or territorial facilities. The majority of provincial sentences for women were for six months or less, and almost 40 percent for 14 days or less. Thirty percent were jailed due to their failure to pay fines, and more than 25 percent of all women serving a sentence in a provincial institution were there for a property offence, mostly shoplifting or fraud charges. Only 9 percent had committed a violent offence, the majority of these being minor assault charges. Approximately 25 percent of the women in provincial correctional institutions were repeat offenders, usually having been sentenced previously for such criminal offences as drinking, prostitution, theft, and fraud.

In comparison to their provincial counterparts, women serving federal sentences had no prior convictions, 50 percent had never been in prison before, and 87 percent were serving their first federal sentence, a much higher percentage than for federally sentenced men (Shaw 1994).

Until recently, the only federal facility for women in Canada was the Prison for Women, located in Kingston, Ontario, with an average population of 115. Beginning in 1978, approximately one-third of all federally sentenced women have been permitted to serve their sentences in provincial facilities in their own province. In the late 1980s, however, the federal government appointed the Task Force on Federally Sentenced Women to study the quality and quantity of programs and facilities for women in the federal correctional system as well as the experiences and needs of women offenders, particularly with regard to physical and sexual abuse. One of the central goals of the inquiry was to evaluate whether or not the correctional model used for the male prison population is appropriate for women. The final report of the task force, entitled *Creating Choices: Report of the Task Force on Federally Sentenced Women* (Correctional Service of Canada 1990b), recommended that the Prison for Women be replaced by five new correctional facilities for women, all of which would feature community-based programs. The federal government agreed and started to build new facilities in the following locations:

1. Truro, Nova Scotia, site for the Atlantic regional facility

2. Joliette, Quebec, the location for the Quebec regional facility

3. Kitchener, Ontario, for the Ontario regional facility

4. Maple Creek–Nekaneet, Saskatchewan, for the Healing Lodge for aboriginal women

5. Edmonton, Alberta, for the Prairies regional facility.

In addition, the Burnaby Correctional Centre, already operating in Burnaby, B.C., would serve as the Pacific regional facility.

The first goal of the task force, however, was to identify the needs of federally sentenced women. The task force reported that the ages of the women serving federal sentences ranged from 19 to 74, that 15 percent were aboriginal women, and that approximately 70 percent were mothers, many of whom were sole supporters of their children. In addition, most women had limited education background and few marketable skills, and were either on social assistance or working at low-paying jobs when they were arrested (LeBlanc 1994). The task force further reported that 75 percent of nonaboriginal women federal offenders and 85 percent of aboriginal women federal offenders were victims of physical and/or sexual abuse in their communities.

To facilitate the reintegration of federally sentenced women into the community, innovative program models were developed for each of the regional centres. For example, at the Truro Federal Women's Facility, with a maximum capacity of 30 offenders, the program goals were "community oriented, holistic, women-centred, culturally sensitive, supportive of autonomy and self-esteem, and oriented toward release" (LeBlanc 1994:12). Programs take place both on and off-site, with an emphasis on off-site programming if the offender does not pose a risk to the community. All programs are aimed at helping women make informed and meaningful decisions about their lives. In addition, the Truro facility contains a multifaceted children's program. Some children are allowed to visit their mothers on a temporary basis, while others actually live with their mothers in the institution (LeBlanc 1994).

Prison Life

Most people believe that prisons can change the lives of inmates. Prisoners are separated from the outside world, experience a life under the constant scrutiny of prison guards and other staff, and are required to follow strict daily regimes or endure strict disciplinary sanctions. Prisons are commonly referred to as **total institutions**. According to Goffman (1961), total institutions have four distinct elements:

1. The inmate lives under the watchful eye of a centralized institutional authority.
2. The inmate shares his or her space with other inmates, who are all treated alike and forced to enact the same routines.
3. All of an inmate's time is tightly scheduled by a body of rules and administrative orders imposed by those in charge.
4. The entire system of enforced activities, and time and space control, is organized around the institutional goals of correction and/or treatment.

According to Goffman, prisons are total institutions that force inmates to live regimented and dehumanizing lives. Extensive control over the lives of

Inmates at the Prison for Women, in Kingston, Ont., stand by their cells. These cells are part of a corridor of cells called the Range. (Photo: Alex Cairns/Canadian Press)

inmates has thus forced them to "fight back" against this authority, leading them to commit more criminal acts. Recently, however, this traditionally accepted view of prisons as total institutions has been challenged. Farrington (1992) argues that prisons can better be described as "not-so-total" institutions, pointing out that Goffman's view is no longer consistent with the one that underlies most modern prisons. He states that prisons are never totally isolated from society, as most require a constant supply of goods and services from the broader society. In addition, prison staff work only in the prison, and by leaving everyday, take the prison into the community. Moreover, they bring back information from outside the prison, telling the inmates stories about the questions they ask. Furthermore, inmates are able to maintain contacts with many aspects of their former lives. In addition, the trend toward relatively shorter sentences and various programs that allow inmates to leave the prison for brief periods of time mean they have consistent contact with their communities. In addition, the correctional system today, through its emphasis on community corrections, emphasizes reintegration of inmates.

Despite Farrington's view, prisons remain in many ways a total institution. Residents must dress according to institutional rules, and many human activities are strictly curtailed, including family relations, friendships, heterosexual activities, and a choice in deciding what daily activities one wants to participate in.

Inmate Society

For decades, experts on prisons and prison life have stated that inmates formed their own world, with a unique set of norms and rules referred to as *inmate subculture* (Irwin 1974). The basis of inmate subculture, they argue, is a unique social code of unwritten rules and guidelines that tell inmates how to behave, think, and interact with prison staff and other inmates. Clemmer (1958) introduced the idea of inmate social codes when he wrote about life in a maximum-security prison. He identified a unique language used by prisoners, known as *argot* (Caron 1982), consisting of such words as "jointman" (a prisoner who behaves like a guard) and "yard" ($100). Clemmer also identified what he termed the *prisonization process*—the manner in which an individual assimilates into the inmate subculture by adhering to norms of behaviour, sexual conduct, and language. According to Clemmer, inmates who become the most "prisonized" are the most difficult to reintegrate into mainstream society.

Sykes (1958) and Sykes and Messinger (1960) used Clemmer's work to identify the most important aspects of inmate subculture. According to Sykes (1958), these principles include the following:

1. Don't interfere with inmates' interests, such as never betraying another inmate to authorities.
2. Don't lose your head and refrain from emotional displays (e.g., arguing) with other inmates.

3. Don't exploit other inmates.

4. Be tough and don't lose your dignity.

5. Don't be sucker, don't make a fool of yourself or support guards or prison administrators over the interests of the inmates.

The major theme of the inmate social code was identified by Sykes and Messinger as prison or group solidarity. The greater the number of inmates who follow the inmate code, the greater the stability of the prison population, resulting in less prison violence.

Cooley (1992) conducted research into prison victimization in part to find out if the inmate social code existed in five Canadian institutions. After interviewing 117 inmates, Cooley concluded that the inmate code, as traditionally defined, did not exist in the five institutions studied. What he did find, instead, was a set of informal rules of social control. The most important informal rules of social control are:

1. *Do your own time.* These rules define the public and private realms of prison life. They encourage group cohesion by defining proper prison behaviour, which promotes order and minimizes friction. They also discourage prisoners from asking for help from others.

2. *Avoid the prison economy.* These rules warn inmates of the consequences of conducting business in the informal prison economy. High interest rates exist in this economy, and if debts aren't paid off, physical violence may occur. These rules promote social cohesion by warning inmates of the consequences of not paying debts.

3. *Don't trust anyone.* These rules, which caution inmates to be wary of who they associate with, are a consequence of the existing informant, or "rat," system. The fewer people to whom a prisoner divulges personal information, the better. But, if you find some other inmates you can trust, support and help them, so they will respond in kind to you.

4. *Show respect.* This set of rules prescribes how inmates should interact with each other during their daily activities. These rules contribute to the social cohesion in the prison by defining appropriate and inappropriate conduct between prisoners. They also determine a prisoner's status within the prison hierarchy, and those who follow the rules are respected. Those who violate the rules may be physically assaulted. (Cooley 1992:33–34)

According to Cooley, these rules can bring the inmate population closer together or isolate them. The resulting environment can best be described as partially unstable in the sense that the prison is neither in conflict nor consensus.

The informal social control system described by Cooley creates an inmate's status within the prison. Lifers and serious violent offenders usually maintain a high status, unless an inmate loses by engaging in behaviour not accepted by the other inmates. For example, while Donald Marshall (see Chapter 1) was imprisoned at the medium-security federal institution located at Springhill, Nova Scotia, he was told that another inmate, a "greenhorn," hadn't delivered some MDA, a powerful hallucinogenic drug, to him. When Marshall confronted the other inmate, it became obvious that the new inmate didn't know about "the code that applied when a greenhorn had a 'beef' with a lifer" (Harris 1986:279). When the other inmate refused to admit he hadn't delivered the drug, Marshall knocked him unconscious.

Special Handling Units

In 1977, the Correctional Service of Canada opened two Special Handling Units (SHUs) to house male inmates "who could not be managed adequately in a maximum-security institution because of the high level of risk and danger they posed to staff and other inmates" (O'Brien 1992:11). These units were housed in two sections of existing federal correctional institutions, one in Millhaven, Ontario, and the other the Correctional Development Centre in Quebec. Two institutions built specifically as SHUs were opened in 1989 in Prince Albert, Saskatchewan, and Ste-Anne-des-Plaines, Quebec.

A new policy on the control of dangerous inmates in the federal system was introduced in 1990. SHUs became more program-oriented, and only those inmates whose needs could not be met in a less secure institution were sent to these new facilities. The formal objective of these new SHUs was to safely reintegrate prisoners into a maximum security prison. In addition, by sending inmates considered to be at risk to SHUs, other institutions became safer, thus enabling them to reintegrate larger numbers of offenders back into society (O'Brien 1992).

In 1991–92, 50 to 60 inmates with an average age of 31.5 years (ranging from 24 to 52 years) entered the Prince Albert SHU. The most common offence for those admitted was first-degree murder (21.1 percent), and the most common sentence was life imprisonment (42.1 percent). At the other SHU, in Quebec, the average age of inmates was 33 years, with a range of 22 to 55 years; their common offence was second-degree murder and robbery (20.6 percent each), while 26.5 percent were serving a life sentence. For those admitted to the Quebec SHU, 32.4 percent were serving their first federal sentence.

Prison Violence

Conflict leading to violence is an ever-present reality of prison life. Violence can involve different sets of actors: inmate versus inmate, staff versus inmate, inmate versus staff. According to official data, major assaults on inmates declined yearly from 1983–84 until 1988–89, but started to increase dramatically during 1989–90, a trend that continued through 1990–91. According to statistics collected by the Correctional Service of Canada 42 major assaults were recorded during the first three quarters of 1991–92. Of these assaults, the most common violent act was stabbing (40.5 percent), followed by punching or kicking (33 percent), clubbing (19 percent), sexual assaults (4.7 percent), and burning (2.4 percent). Over one-half of the 42 major assaults (55 percent) occurred in maximum-security institutions, followed by medium-security institutions (36 percent), and minimum-security facilities (9 percent). Just over 50 percent took place either in the inmate's cell or on the range. Most of the motives for physically assaulting another inmate were for drug-related activities (29 percent), retaliation (19 percent), attacking an informant (10 percent), and sexual (7 percent); in 2.4 percent of the cases, the victim was identified as a cell thief (Forum on Corrections Research 1992a:3–4).

Attacks on staff members varied between one and 10 annually between 1984–85 and 1991–92. On average, there are two to four major assaults on staff each year, but it is rare for a staff member to be murdered in a federal institution. Two staff members were murdered in 1984–85, but none have lost their lives since then (*Forum on Corrections Research* 1992:4).

Violence can also involve all the inmates in a correctional facility. Culhane (1985) documents nine examples of prison violence in Canada between 1975 and 1985. She describes the degradation of inmates by prison officials, and the resulting prisoner violence. One such incident occurred at Archambault Prison, north of Montreal, in 1972. Although 50 inmates were identified as having actively participated in the riot, between 75 and 150 were sent to solitary confinement. These inmates were accused of "participating passively" and therefore "had to pay the social price." Complaints about this treatment reached the attention of federal politicians; a federal inquiry failed to materialize because the guards allegedly involved denied they participated and there was a lack of corroborating evidence (Culhane 1985; Ruby 1985).

Prison Suicide

Inmate suicide is the leading cause of death in Canadian prisons. Burtch and Ericson (1979) report that between 1959 and 1975, the suicide rate of inmates in Canada's federal institutions was 95.9 per 100 000 inmates compared with 14.2 per 100 000 nonprison males in Canada. Between 1983 and 1992, 128 of the 265 offenders who died while in federal custody committed suicide (Fogel 1992). And during 1991–92, six aboriginal women committed suicide at the Prison for Women in Kingston, Ontario. As Grossmann (1992) notes, in an institution that houses approximately 110 individuals, this is an alarmingly high rate.

Concern over these suicide rates led to the creation of a suicide prevention program by the Correctional Service of Canada. In order to gain as much information as possible about male and female inmates who committed suicide, Green et al. (1992) studied 133 suicides that occurred between 1977 and 1988. They discovered most were male (129, or 97 percent) and 115 (or 80 percent) were white. The study also revealed that suicide was distributed among all age groups. In terms of marital status, one-half were single, 38 percent were married or living in common-law relationships, and 12 percent were divorced. Sixty percent had no children, 14 percent had one child, and the rest had two or more children.

The researchers report that hanging was the most common method (80 percent) of inmate suicide. Almost all of the suicides occurred within an inmate's own cell. In terms of offence and sentence characteristics, 51 individuals had committed a nonsexual offence of violence as their most recent offence, 34 had a robbery or weapons offence, 25 had a property offence, and only one individual was a first-time offender. Green and colleagues discovered that a high number of suicides occurred early on in a sentence—25 percent within 90 days of sentencing and 50 percent within a year of sentencing.

Certain factors have been deemed important in predicting and preventing suicide. The Correctional Service of Canada developed a National Strategy for the Prevention of Suicide and Reduction of Self-Injury. The goals of this strategy were to reduce the incidence of suicide and self-injury among prisoners, staff, and their relatives. To achieve these goals, the Correctional Service of Canada developed a "comprehensive" approach for assessment, prevention, intervention, treatment, support, evaluation, research, and training of staff. Specific actions included:

1. providing a safe, secure, and humane environment for those who suffer from mental illness and for those who must cope with the stresses of life in a correctional environment

2. increasing the awareness and understanding of both management and staff concerning suicide and self-injury

3. developing staff skills to prevent suicide and self-harm, including identifying suicide risk, monitoring pre-indicators and providing crisis intervention and support services

4. developing and implementing support services for survivors, as well as affected staff and inmates

While these measures may be appropriate for males, Grossmann (1992) argues that they are not applicable to aboriginal women. She argues that correctional officials should better understand the needs of these women in the context of their socioeconomic position and victimization experiences. Responses to these needs should include a variety of culturally sensitive methods of assistance that would focus on their "violent pasts and various forms of personal victimization, as well as opportunities to redress their education and employment deficiencies" (Grossmann 1992:412). The Task Force on Federally Sentenced Women (1990) recommended assistance to abused women, improved counselling services, more culturally sensitive spiritual supports, and the maintenance of relationships between offenders and their families and communities.

Prisoners' Rights, Due Process, and Discipline

Before the introduction of the Charter of Rights and Freedoms in 1982, inmates had limited legal rights. It was difficult for them to question prison rules and regulations or the decisions of prison officials. Perhaps the most important reason why inmates lacked legal rights was because provincial and federal courts were hesitant to intervene in the administration of prisons unless there were obvious, excessive, and indiscriminate abuses of power by prison officials. This policy is referred to as the "hands-off doctrine" and consists of three observations:

1. Correctional administration was a technical matter best left to experts rather than to courts ill-equipped to make appropriate evaluations.

2. Society as a whole was apathetic to what went on in prisons, and most individuals preferred not to associate with or know about the offender.

3. Prisoners' complaints involved privileges rather than rights. (National Advisory Commission on Criminal Justice Standards and Goals 1973)

Before the 1970s, Penitentiary Service Regulations insisted that prison officials provide inmates with certain basic minimum standards, such as the right to be adequately fed and clothed, essential dental and medical services, and time to exercise. These rights represented only the basic core of the Standard Minimum Rules for the Treatment of Prisoners (1957) adopted by the United Nations, covering such issues as religion, transfers, and disciplinary procedures (MacKay 1986).

At the end of the 1960s, this hands-off doctrine was challenged in the courts over the issue of due process rights within correctional facilities by prisoners and prisoner-rights advocates. In the first such case, *R. v. Beaver Creek Correctional Camps* (1969), an inmate challenged the prison's authority to make disciplinary decisions without providing inmates with due process protections, such as the right to a fair hearing and the right of having legal counsel. Also challenged were the arbitrary powers found within Section 229 of the Penitentiary Regulations, which outlined a number of activities for which inmates could be disciplined.

The Ontario Court of Appeal ruled that while natural justice also applied to inmates, there were situations in which prison officials had the right to place an inmate in segregation without proper due process safeguards and the possibility of a review of the administrative decision in question. However, while the court ruled that administrative decisions were reviewable when they involved questions about the civil rights of inmates, this case involved a decision purely administrative in nature and therefore wasn't reviewable by the courts.

The first case to significantly challenge the administrative power of prison officials was *McCann v. The Queen* (1975). Jack McCann was placed in solitary confinement in the B.C. Penitentiary for 754 days under the authority of Section 2.30(1)(a) of the Penitentiary Service Regulations, which states: "Where the institutional head is satisfied that for the good maintenance of good order and discipline in the institution . . . it is necessary that the inmate should be kept from associating with other inmates." McCann argued that his period in solitary confinement infringed on his right to freedom from cruel and unusual treatment or punishment under Section 2(b) of the Canadian Bill of Rights (Jackson 1983). The court held that prison administrators had the right to place inmates in solitary confinement with no prior hearing, unless their civil rights were in jeopardy. But it ruled that the use of solitary confinement in this case did, in fact, constitute "cruel and unusual punishment" (Jackson 1983:101–33).

However, the Supreme Court of Canada, in *Martineau v. Matsqui Institution Inmate Disciplinary Board* (1980), formally recognized that "the rule of law must run within penitentiary walls." They also stated that although prison officials are making administrative decisions, they are still subject to the duty to act fairly. In this case, two inmates at the Matsqui Institution in British Columbia were found guilty of being in a cell where they shouldn't have been. They argued that "they were not provided with a summary of evidence against them; that the evidence of each was taken in the absence of the other; that the conviction was for an offence unknown to law; and that Martineau was never given an opportunity to give evidence with respect to the charge" (Jackson 1983:126–27).

As a result of this ruling, all those who make administrative decisions concerning the rights or liberties of inmates have a duty to act fairly (Pelletier 1990).

The Duty to Act Fairly

What does it mean to "act fairly," especially for inmates in a correctional facility? The duty to act fairly involves two basic rights: (1) the right to be heard and (2) the right to have an impartial hearing. As Pelletier (1990:26) notes, the right to be heard means that all citizens have

Reporter Peter Moon on assignment in the segregation cell. A camera watches an inmate's every move. Federal convicts in some institutions can be segregated for years, but at other institutions the longest stay is about ten days. (Photo: Tibor Kolley/*The Globe and Mail*)

the right "to be informed of the allegations made against them and to respond to those allegations." The right to an impartial hearing means that "a decision must not be rendered against a person for discriminatory or arbitrary reasons."

In Canada, three areas of legal concern are related to the duty to act fairly: (1) administrative segregation (or solitary confinement); (2) involuntary transfers of inmates; and (3) discipline of inmates.

What are the powers of prison officials to place inmates into administrative segregation? Obviously, some situations, such as prison riots, may require immediate segregation. But what about other situations? In *McCann v. The Queen* (1975), which was the first case to argue the fairness of the decision to segregate, Mr. Justice Heald ruled that the decision to place an inmate in solitary confinement was "purely administrative" and therefore not subject to legal review.

This interpretation was reinforced by the decision in *Kosobook and Aelick v. The Queen and The Solicitor-General of Canada* (1976). In this case, the complainants had been told that they were placed into solitary confinement after an administrative inquiry into the stabbing of an inmate, but no charges had been laid against them. They argued that their segregation was a denial of natural justice and their right to an unbiased tribunal, the result of a decision made in an arbitrary manner, and an infringement of the Canadian Bill of Rights. They claimed that they had not been provided with due process projections and that, as a result, they had been held in arbitrary detention. The judge ruled that the prison authorities did not have any judicial or quasi-judicial functions, but rather performed the role of an administrative body. As a result, they could not violate the Canadian Bill of Rights.

However, in *Martineau v. Matsqui Institution Inmate Disciplinary Board* (1980) the Supreme Court of Canada ruled that correctional officials are under a duty to act fairly when making disciplinary decisions. In essence, the Supreme Court concluded that the rule of law must be upheld within correctional facilities. As a result of the ruling in the *Martineau* case, the Correctional Service of Canada changed its policies to fit more closely with the fairness doctrine. For example, in terms of administrative segregation, inmates now had the right to be heard within the correctional context, and prison authorities were obliged to (1) inform an inmate, in writing, of the reasons for the placement in segregation within 24 hours following this placement; (2) notify an inmate in advance of each review of the placement into segregation, in order to permit the inmate to present his or her case at a hearing in prison; and (3) advise the inmate, in writing, of decisions concerning his or her status.

Private Prisons

Some countries, including Great Britain, Australia, and France, have experimented with privatizing prisons, However, the only country to have implemented such prisons is the United States, where it is estimated that 3 percent

EXHIBIT 10.1

Inmate Participation in Treatment Programs: *R. v. Rogers* (1990)

Introduction
This case illustrates the legality of parole board officials imposing treatment on mentally ill individuals in their care. The case involves a test of Section 7 of the Charter of Rights and Freedoms, which states that "everyone has the right to life, liberty and security of the person and a right not to be deprived thereof except in accordance with the principles of fundamental justice." Furthermore, the forced treatment of an offender could constitute cruel and unusual punishment, which would be contrary to Section 12 of the Charter.

Facts of the Case
Rogers was convicted of possessing concealed weapons. At the time, a psychiatrist's report concluded that Rogers was a schizophrenic with a history of failing to take his medications, with the result that this would lead to mental disorders and hallucinations. As part of the sentence, the presiding judge imposed a probation order on Rogers, requiring him to take psychiatric treatment or medication. The probation order read as follows:

> You will take reasonable steps to maintain yourself in such condition that:

(a) your chronic schizophrenia would not cause you to conduct yourself in a manner dangerous to yourself or anyone else; and
(b) it is not likely you will commit further offenses . . . You will thereafter attend as directed from time to time at the interministerial project for the purpose of receiving such medical counselling and treatment as may be recommended except that you shall not be required to submit to any treatment or medication to which you do not consent.

Although Rogers was voluntarily taking the medication at the time of his sentencing, the court questioned the compulsory probation order.

The Decision
The court recognized that the protection of the public was the objective of the probation order compelling Rogers to submit to mandatory treatment. However, it concluded that the order placed an unreasonable restraint on Rogers's liberty and security of person, and that only in exceptional cases should this be accepted. In addition, the court stated that incarceration was a proper alternative should an individual refuse to take the treatment. While Rogers could not be required to submit to mandatory treatment to which he did not consent, the court varied the probation order to ensure that he would not engage in dangerous behaviour.

Significance of the Case
This case shows that even when the protection of society is given as the justification for mandatory treatment, the courts are reluctant to approve such an order. Alternative ways of controlling an offender, including incarceration, have to be used before the imposition of involuntary treatment or procedures. This means that people, including inmates, can refuse any treatment imposed on them; this right will be limited only in rare cases in which it is determined that the collective rights of society take precedence over individual rights. Instead, "the consequences of the refusal must be explained to the inmate and, unless persuaded to change his or her mind, he or she will have the right to live the consequences."

The National Parole Board can, however, require an offender to consent to treatment in order to qualify for conditional release. This is not considered forced treatment because the offender obtains a benefit in exchange for his or her compliance.

Source: *R. v. Rogers* (1990) 61 C.C.C. (3d) 481; Claire McKinnon and Lisa Hitch, "Selected Legal Aspects of Effective Correctional Programming: Access to Programming and Mandatory Programming," *Forum on Corrections Research* 4, no. 2 (June 1992); Claire McKinnon, "The Legal Right of Offenders to Refuse Treatment," *Forum on Corrections Research* 7, no. 3 (September 1995).

of American prisons and jails are now privately run. For example, in 1991, the Corrections Corporation of America, considered the "leader" among private prisons, operated 14 secure adult facilities and three juvenile facilities, totalling about 48 000 beds. Wackenhutt operated eight adult facilities and 3200 beds. The private sector is also involved with the design and construction of correctional facilities. Private corporations maintain they can build a facility twice as fast and 20 percent cheaper than a state government. The private sector is also involved with the financing of new construction. Traditionally, prisons and jails are owned by government and funded by taxpayers, but because of fiscal

Field Practice 10.1
Disciplinary Hearings

Refusal to Work

A 22-year-old inmate appeared at a prison disciplinary hearing charged with refusing to work in the prison kitchen. In addition, he was charged with disobeying the orders of a correctional officer as well as talking back to those in authority. His defence was that he was ill at the time, although he had not reported to the prison infirmary. He informed the members of the disciplinary hearing board that he was also worried about the failing health of his father. The board ordered the inmate lose all privileges for three days.

Fighting

A 30-year-old inmate was charged with fighting with another inmate and breaking his nose. The inmate explained to the disciplinary board that the other inmate had started the fight by referring to his ethnicity in a derogatory manner. Prior to this incident, the inmate had an exemplary record. The disciplinary board decided to place an official reprimand in his file.

Racist Comments

A 45-year-old inmate appeared before a prison disciplinary board charged with making racist remarks against two members of a religious minority group. These comments had continued over a five-month period, even after correctional guards, prison officials, and other inmates told him to stop. He had also recently threatened to kill these two individuals in the recreation area. The board sentenced the inmate to spend 30 days in solitary confinement and to apologize to the individuals he had threatened.

strategies during the 1980s, private corporations became involved with the financial construction of facilities.

In all other countries that are experimenting with private prisons, such as Great Britain and Canada, citizen approval of debt for capital projects is not required. As a result, private financial support of prisons is "less attractive . . . because the cost of raising capital is higher when the debt instruments are not backed by the full faith and credit of the government" (McDonald 1992:391).

In terms of cost-effectiveness, advocates of privatization believe that such prisons have distinct advantages. First, they are more productive because they are private and not caught in public sector bureaucracy and "red tape." Second, there is a strong belief that private prisons are efficient, which encourages greater productivity among employees. There is greater risk-taking in terms of productivity and implementing cost-cutting measures. In addition, these institutions are able "to buy in larger quantities of discounts and from a wider range of possible suppliers," thereby reducing the costs of supplies (McDonald 1992:399).

Critics of privately operated prisons argue that prisons are not institutions that can be operated on a balance sheet. They believe that the labour-intensive nature of prisons does not allow for significant amounts of technological innovations that will reduce costs. Instead, they argue that cost savings will come at the expense of reliable and well-trained employees. Any advantage private corporations may hold over their public-sector counterparts may be reduced if their employees unionize.

Furthermore, critics argue that privately run prisons will not be committed to providing quality programs for inmates. Charging that the private sector is more interested in "doing well" instead of "doing good," an American Bar Association committee wrote that "conditions of confinement will be kept to the minimum that the law requires" (American Bar Association 1986:6).

Evaluations of existing privately run correctional facilities have concluded that they may provide better services, at lower cost, than those operated by the public sector (Logan and McGriff 1989). In his study comparing costs, programs, and facilities of three privately run prisons and three comparable public-sector facilities, Sellers (1989) found that, on average, the private prisons operated at a lower cost per inmate per day ($46.17 vs. $73.76) than the public correctional facilities. He also found that each private prison had more programs, and that the overall condition of two of these three facilities was "notably better than the condition of the comparable public facilities" (Sellers 1989:18). After analyzing all the various criteria, he concluded that public prison facilities "operate less efficiently" than do private prisons. A similar conclusion was reached by Logan in his analysis of private and federal women's prisons in the United States. Logan compared these facilities on the basis of eight criteria: security, safety, order, care, activity, justice, conditions, and management. He found that private prisons were better than their public counterparts in all criteria, with the exception of care and justice. In his inmate survey, however, the state prison was considered better on all criteria except activity.

All researchers who have studied both institutions have commented on the difficulty of making direct comparisons. Even advocates of privatization believe that private prisons will not always be cheaper than public-sector facilities, but that their strength resides in their ability to be more innovative and implement changes faster and more efficiently.

Summary

The ideas underlying our contemporary correctional institutions have their origins in the United States during the 19th century. Two competing systems emerged: the Pennsylvania system and the Auburn system. While both approaches treated their inmates with great discipline and rigidly enforced rules, the Auburn system, which allowed groups of inmates to work together and then isolated them at night, formed the basis of the Canadian correctional system.

Canada's federal and provincial correctional populations have traditionally increased at a slow rate, but during the past five years they have grown by a phenomenal 31 percent. In addition to those serving a sentence in a correctional facility, there are in excess of 120 000 offenders serving a sentence in the community.

At present, over 40 federal correctional facilities operate in Canada today. They are classified according to security level, and significant differences exist between them when it comes to their physical appearance and the amount of freedom given to inmates. Five new regional facilities for federally sentenced women are close to operational. These centres will introduce new and innovative programs designed specifically for women. Many of the programs will take place in the community.

Until recently, very little information was available about prison society. Certain codes or rules exist for inmates to follow, but the prison environment is very unstable since changes are always occurring. There is much violence in Canadian prisons. Suicides, murder, and assaults occur on a daily basis, and many inmates attempt to isolate themselves from other inmates and situations they feel may lead to violence.

Today, inmates have significant, although limited, legal rights. Inmates can take their grievances to various officials and request a hearing. Various courts, including the Supreme Court of Canada, have recognized that inmates possess these rights, and have ruled in their favour in many cases.

Discussion Questions

1. Should private companies be allowed to operate Canadian federal and provincial correctional facilities? Why or why not?

2. Discuss the issue of prisoners' rights and the evolution of law concerning such rights in Canada.

3. How can we alleviate the problem of prison overcrowding without building more prisons?

4. Describe the classification of inmates and correctional facilities.

5. Discuss the special issues concerning the needs of women offenders.

6. Should women be allowed to have their children with them while serving their sentence in a correctional facility?

7. Discuss the process of "socialization" in prison. What are the negative aspects of this process? Can we change it?

8. Can prison violence ever be eliminated?

Suggested Readings

Eckstedt, J.W., and C.T. Griffiths. *Corrections in Canada: Policy and Practice*, 2nd ed. Vancouver: Butterworths, 1988.

Faith, K. *Unruly Women: The Politics of Confinement and Resistance*. Vancouver: Press Gang Publishers, 1995.

Jackson, M. *Prisoners of Isolation: Solitary Confinement in Canada*. Toronto: University of Toronto Press, 1983.

McMahon, M.W. *The Persistent Prison? Rethinking Decarceration and Penal Reform*. Toronto: University of Toronto Press, 1992.

CHAPTER 11

Community Corrections: Probation and Conditional Release Programs

Although many people would like to see most criminals put away in prison forever, the reality is that over 90 percent of offenders will be released back into society. Some offenders will be placed on probation as soon as they are sentenced or shortly thereafter, while many others will be released on conditional release programs such as parole because they are considered good risks not to reoffend.

This chapter discusses the ways in which inmates are released from prison—by parole and other conditional release programs. It looks at the issues of who makes the release decision, how the decision is made, and what the release criteria are. It also discusses the success rate of parolees.

During 1992–93, the National Parole Board, with just over 100 full-time and part-time members, made 34 555 decisions on applications for conditional release, as well as hearings concerning revocation of parole,

CHAPTER OBJECTIVES

- understand the different community sanction programs that exist today in Canada

- understand what recidivism rates mean

- examine the rates of recidivism for the community sanction programs

- look at the relationship between recidivism rates and the race, gender, marital, and employment status of offenders released on community sanction programs

conditions of release, and detention. On almost every day of the working week parole hearings take place at correctional institutions in Canada. A board panel, usually consisting of two or three individuals, listens to three or four parole applicants on average each day. Their job is to read all of the offenders' files, court files, the reasons given by the judge for the sentence, as well as police and Crown prosecutor files. In addition, they question the applicant directly as well as the prison official in charge of the offender's treatment. If an applicant refuses to answer a question, the application will probably be rejected.

The purpose of the parole hearing is to determine two seemingly contradictory issues: (1) how to protect the public by rejecting the applications of those offenders they consider to be a threat to the public, and (2) how to help those offenders whom they consider to be good risks by placing them in the community under supervision. The parole board has the authority, when they consider public safety to be at risk, to reject any application or to release the offender with some limitations on his freedom, e.g., to a halfway house. Contrary to public perception, it is not easy to get parole. Just 36 percent of the applicants for parole during 1992–93 were successful, and of those, 75 percent would complete their terms in the community without having their parole revoked.

Community Release under Attack

Starting in the early the 1970s, all forms of community sanctions, but particularly parole, came under attack by an outraged public who felt that any program whose goal was to place offenders into the community as part of their sentence was "too soft" on criminals. These criticisms were soon followed by a series of policy changes developed by criminal justice practitioners who argued that all forms of community sanction were too discretionary and failed to protect the due process rights of the offenders. These critics also asserted that the rehabilitation ideal and its various related treatment programs that were designed to reintegrate offenders back into the community were misplaced. For the following reasons, parole was abolished in a number of American states, starting with Maine in 1975. By 1984, the number of states without parole had increased to 11, although in the following year Colorado reinstated parole after having removed the parole board in 1979.

'Nothing Works'

In 1974, Robert Martinson published an article that was to have a tremendous impact on the way in which community sanctions were to operate in the following decades. This article, entitled "What Works?—Questions and Answers about Prison Reform," questioned the very existence of rehabilitation. This essay was drawn from a larger work (Lipton, Martinson, and Wilks 1975) that assessed 231 evaluation studies of treatment programs operating between 1945 and 1967. At the end of his article, Martinson (1974:25) commented that with "few and isolated exceptions the rehabilitative efforts that have been reported so far have had no appreciable effect on recidivism." Yet, in his last section, entitled "Does Nothing Work?" he pointed out that the studies reviewed were no doubt flawed in many ways, which led to the inability to find any significant treatment successes. Martinson reasoned that their failure to discover any successful treatments was grounded in large part from the lack of sophistication of both the methods and statistics used in the studies. As a result, it was almost impossible for researchers to detect any positive effects as well as problems concerning the internal quality of the programs, such as therapeutic integrity. Despite these caveats, Martinson (1974:49) wrote that it may be impossible for rehabilitation-based programs to overcome or reduce "the powerful tendencies of offenders to continue in criminal behavior" (1974:49).

Most people who read Martinson's article failed to heed his acknowledgment that there may indeed be positive effects of rehabilitation in the future. Instead, the phrase "nothing works," as Walker (1984:168) notes, became an instant cliché for critics and exerted an enormous influence on both popular and professional thinking. Five years later, Martinson (1979:244, 252) clarified his position:

> Contrary to my previous position, some treatment programs do have an appreciable effect on recidivism ... some programs are indeed beneficial. New evidence from our current study leads me to reject my original conclusion ... I have hesitated up to now, but the evidence in our surveys is simply too overwhelming to ignore.

But, while his original article is one of the most cited articles in the field of criminology, his second remains virtually ignored (Cullen and Gendreau 1989). By the time his second article appeared, the critique of rehabilitation was too powerful and entrenched. In particular, after reviewing the few research projects on parole, Martinson concluded that when parolees and nonparolees were compared, parole at best had only a delaying effect on recidivism (Waller 1974). This led to questions concerning the grounding of parole in rehabilitation (Canadian Sentencing Commission 1987).

Discretion and Disparity

Another issue raised by the critics of community sanctions was the immense discretionary power held by parole boards. Their concern was based not only on the arbitrariness of many of their decisions, but also their inability to develop a list of criteria that could conclusively predict which offenders were ready to be released back into the community. This led to numerous charges that parole authorities knew little about the criminal personality, and that they made contradictory decisions (Frankel 1972). In addition, parole boards often shortened the sentences of offenders to such a degree by releasing them on parole that they became, in essence, the main sentencing force within the criminal justice system. For example, the Canadian Sentencing Commission (1987:240), after examining statistics on both the original sentence and later parole board decisions across Canada, came to the conclusion that "there is a substantial difference between the sentence a judge hands down and the length of time an offender actually serves in prison."

This discretion, critics argue, leads to a disparity in time served by offenders. More specifically, the Canadian Sentencing Commission (1987:240) noted that "offenders serving longer sentences are more likely to get released on parole than are offenders sentenced to shorter terms." Harman and Hann (1986:27–29), for example, reported in their study that parole release dates for the offence of manslaughter from 1975–76 to 1981–82 varied each year, between 51 percent and 64 percent. Yet, when they compared these percentages with those convicted of robbery and break and enter, approximately 10 percent more manslaughter offenders were released compared with those released for robbery and 20 to 30 percent more for those convicted of break and enter.

Justice and Due Process

Other critics have focused on the lack of explicit criteria used in the decisions to grant parole. This led to confusion on the part of inmates concerning the criteria needed to improve themselves and subsequently to be granted parole. In addition, there were concerns over the fairness of parole hearings, in particular "the absence from parole of due process requisites such as the right to a hearing, to know the nature of complaints against one, and to be informed of the reasons for adverse decisions" (Bottomley 1990:339). These issues led to what has been referred to as the "pains of parole," a term used to describe the "anxiety, fear, loss of dignity, excessively limited freedom, (and) uncertainty of one's future" (Mandel 1975:520–26). In 1977, the Sub-Committee on the Penitentiary System in Canada (1977:151) concluded that

> inmates are under the impression that the Parole Board does not, in all circumstances, treat them fairly. The records contain many examples of inmates whose parole has been revoked because they arrived a few minutes late and who were charged with being unlawfully at large ... It is, therefore, extremely disconcerting to hear of inmates having their paroles suspended and revoked for essentially trivial questions.

These concerns about the role of the National Parole Board were echoed by the late Chief Justice Laskin, who commented in the case of *Mitchell v. The Queen* (1976), a case involving the matter of parole revocation:

> The plain fact is that the Board claims a tyrannical authority that I believe is without precedent among administrative agencies empowered to deal with a person's liberty. It claims an unfettered power to deal with an inmate, almost as if he were a mere puppet on a string.

Fisheye view of a prison cell. (Photo: Tibor Kolley/*The Globe and Mail*)

In 1978, new regulations under the Parole Act guaranteed inmates serving a sentence of two years or more a series of due process safeguards: namely, a hearing, disclosure of information, and reasons for the decision of why parole was denied. These safeguards did not eliminate the perception that the decisions made by the National Parole Board were unfair and that disparity continued to exist, although in a much more subtle manner (Casey 1986). Confusion about parole board decisions continued among offenders. For example, Eckstedt (1985) found that, five years after the new regulations had come into effect, offenders who requested parole hearings continued to question the fairness of their decisions. In an attempt to rectify this situation, a variety of reforms have been recommended and legal changes made. Perhaps the most significant statement came from the Canadian Sentencing Commission (1987:244–45), which recommended that parole in Canada be abolished because it violates the principle of proportionality, introduces uncertainty into the sentencing process, and transfers the decision-making power of judges. Others are content to apply the Charter of Rights and Freedoms to specific cases as they come forward (Cole and Manson 1990).

Conditional Release in Canada

The earliest form of conditional release in Canada was **parole,** which started in 1868, when a policy of reduction of sentence as a reward for good behaviour was instituted in federal penitentiaries. While there was no supervision of these inmates, they could be returned to prison to serve the remainder of their sentence if they were convicted of an indictable offence. A program of discretionary release from federal institutions was implemented in 1899, under the title of "ticket-of-leave." The federal government hired its first full-time parole officer in 1905, and government and private agencies such as the Salvation Army joined forces, in the Remission Service, to operate the parole system (Ryan 1990; Carrington 1991).

In 1958, the Parole Act was enacted. The authority to grant release and to issue revocation orders was transferred to the newly formed National Parole Board, which operated on the premise that "interviews between Board members and inmates do not serve a sufficiently useful function ... the Board should not be required to grant inmates an opportunity for a personal interview" (Cole and Manson 1990:171). All information in support of parole applications was to be collected from a variety of sources and then submitted in written form. However, the Parole Act provided little guidance concerning the criteria that the members of the National Parole Board would consider when reviewing an application for early release.

This led to concerns about the need for due process and procedural safeguards. For example, the *Report of the Task Force on the Release of Inmates* (1973) criticized the criteria for parole release as being too vague and unclear, with the effect that "neither inmates nor members of the Board are able to articulate with any certainty or precision what positive and negative factors enter the parole decision" (*Report of the Task Force on the Release of Inmates* 1973:32) As a result, the task force recommended that offenders be allowed to appear before the parole board members, giving them "the opportunity to hear from the decision-makers themselves the reasons for their decision" *(Report of the Task Force on the Release of Inmates* 1973:34). In addition, the reasons behind any decision were now to be written down and a copy given to the applicant. As a result, additional procedural safeguards were introduced into the Parole Act: namely, the granting of a parole hearing when requested and written reasons why an application was rejected. In addition, the National Parole Board (1981) published a list of factors that parole board members could consider during a hearing. These include

- the criminal record, kinds of offences and their pattern, and the length of crime-free periods between convictions
- the nature of the current offence and how serious it was
- what understanding the inmate appears to have of the situation that brought him to prison, and what he has done about it
- what the inmate has done while in prison including training, educational and employment upgrading activities
- institutional behaviour and offences
- whether the inmate has any previous parole violations
- what plans the inmate has for employment or training and how definite they are

Risk of Recidivism

Despite the introduction of these procedural changes, the National Parole Board came under increasing public criticism about its release decisions, especially after a series of homicides in 1987–88 committed by individuals on conditional release programs. To many members of the public, offenders released into the community are all potential high-risk offenders. However, there are differences in rates of **recidivism** according to the type of conditional release program an offender is placed on. For example, a profile of readmission rates to federal correctional institutions over a six-year period (as measured by six-month intervals) illustrates the differences of recidivism rates between 26 520 offenders released on full parole and mandatory supervision between 1974 and 1980. The total number of offenders returned to a federal institution was 12 767 (or 48 percent). However, there was a substantial difference between recidivism rates for those on full parole and those on statutory supervision. Of the 8751 offenders released on full parole, 30 percent were readmitted as compared with 58 percent of the 17 769 offenders placed on statutory supervision. As Figure 11.1 reveals, the majority (63 percent) who returned to a federal institution did so within 12 months of their release. Eighty-one percent of all offenders readmitted did so within 24 months of their release date. After 24 months, however, the risk of returning to a federal institution dramatically declined. According to Correctional Services Canada (1990:12), "after the two-year follow-up point, the number of offenders returning to federal institutions dropped to 2 percent and gradually tapered off each subsequent year. At the six-year follow-up point, fewer than 1 percent of offenders were readmitted." This study revealed that for those offenders on statutory supervision, the "critical" point for being readmitted to a federal institution

FIGURE 11.1

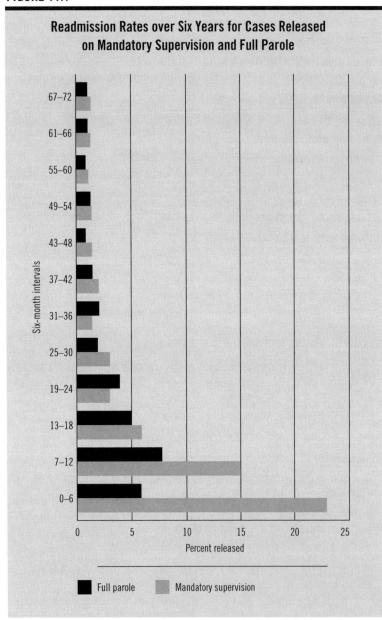

Readmission Rates over Six Years for Cases Released on Mandatory Supervision and Full Parole

Six-month intervals (vertical axis): 67–72, 61–66, 55–60, 49–54, 43–48, 37–42, 31–36, 25–30, 19–24, 13–18, 7–12, 0–6

Percent released (horizontal axis): 0, 5, 10, 15, 20, 25

■ Full parole ■ Mandatory supervision

occurs within 6 months, while, for offenders on full parole, the second six-month period is the most critical.

Due to concerns about the recidivism rate, Correctional Services Canada instructed members of the National Parole Board to shift their focus to risk factors as the prime consideration when considering release of offenders. This change was introduced in November 1986, when the National Parole Board identified its primary purpose as the protection of society. To achieve this goal, risk assessment of future crimes by offenders after release was to become its major focus (National Parole Board 1987). And, in 1988, the National Parole Board released its policy on Pre-Release Detention, which was intended to identify and clearly present the criteria for parole board decisions.

These policies utilized three key assumptions: first, risk to society is the fundamental consideration in any conditional release decision; second, the restrictions on the freedom of the offender in the community must be limited to those that are necessary and reasonable for the protection of society and for facilitating the safe reintegration of the offender; and third, supervised release increases the likelihood of reintegration and contributes to the long-term protection of society (National Parole Board 1988b; Bottomley 1990).

In 1992, the Corrections and Conditional Release Act replaced the Parole Act in the area of community corrections. This act also identified the fundamental principles that would guide corrections in the changing social and legal contexts of Canadian society. First, it is the purpose of the federal correctional system to maintain "a just, peaceful and safe society" (Haskell 1994:45). This is to be achieved by the following two criteria:

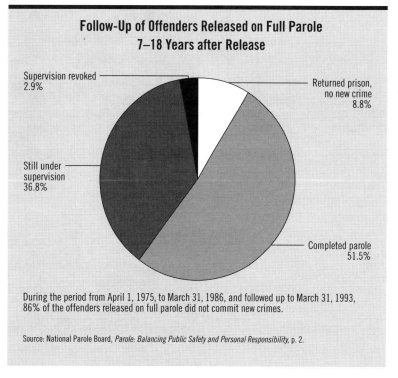

1. carrying out sentences imposed by the courts through the safe and humane custody and supervision of offenders
2. assisting the rehabilitation of offenders and their reintegration into the community as law-abiding citizens through the provision of programs in penitentiaries and in the community (Section 3, Corrections and Conditional Release Act)

FIGURE 11.2

Follow-Up of Offenders Released on Full Parole 7–18 Years after Release

Supervision revoked 2.9%

Returned prison, no new crime 8.8%

Still under supervision 36.8%

Completed parole 51.5%

During the period from April 1, 1975, to March 31, 1986, and followed up to March 31, 1993, 86% of the offenders released on full parole did not commit new crimes.

Source: National Parole Board, *Parole: Balancing Public Safety and Personal Responsibility*, p. 2.

In addition, those who drafted the Corrections and Conditional Release Act wanted to enhance for all concerned—i.e., offenders, correctional staff, and the public—an understanding and appreciation of both the principles and purposes behind correctional decision-making. As a result, there is now improved guidance to the National Parole Board in carrying out its mandate. It was hope that the board would become "more consistent and straightforward in its functioning" (Haskell 1994:46).

To achieve these ends, the Corrections and Conditional Release Act authorizes the disclosure of all relevant information to offenders (subject to certain limited exceptions) when there is an adverse decision affecting their conditional release application. In addition, the act also allows for the disclosure of some information to victims, in the hope that this will "lead to greater awareness of the legitimate reasons behind decisions that may appear arbitrary, inappropriate or even unfair" (Haskell 1994:46). The act also requires the release of all relevant information about the offender's background that could affect the conditional release decision of the parole board members. This information includes the nature of the offence(s), as well as police and prosecution files and sentencing information.

Risk Assessment

The Corrections and Conditional Release Act requires the members of the National Parole Board to distinguish different types of offenders on the basis of risk factors. All National Parole Board members are required to "specifically

Penitentiary officer Christine Grant checks refrigerator supplies with an inmate at the Frontenac Institution. (Photo: Peter Moon/*The Globe and Mail*)

assess whether an offender will commit an offence, in particular a violent offence, while on conditional release" (Sutton 1994:21) To enhance their decisions, board members are now required to have training in risk assessment and knowledge of the tools and research currently available.

National Parole Board decisions are therefore made on the basis of risk assessment, risk prediction, and risk reduction. They are based on a general knowledge of the social-psychological perspective on criminal conduct, including the assumption that criminal behaviour is, in most cases, learned behaviour.

When making decisions about conditional release, parole board members make assessments concerning five areas of an offender's situation (Sutton 1994:22):

1. behavioural history
2. the immediate situation
3. mental and emotional outlook favourable to criminal activity
4. pro-criminal social supports
5. other personal factors, including level of development, self-regulation, problem-solving skills, impulsivity, and callousness

The theory of risk assessment is based on three principles: risk, need, and responsivity. The first principle, risk, states that higher levels of service should be allocated to the higher-risk cases. However, as Andrews (1989:14) points out, "the belief persists that treatment services, if effective at all, only work for lower risk cases." Thus, high success rates of low-risk offenders on a conditional release program may be incorrectly interpreted to mean that they benefited from treatment. This may not be so because, being of low risk, they may have had high success rates even without treatment. As Andrews (1989:19) points out, "such errors involve confusing the predictive accuracy of pretreatment risk assessments with the issue of who profits from it." If high-risk offenders are improperly assessed as low-risk, they will no doubt have high recidivism rates. In his research on probation supervision programs in Ottawa, Kiessling (1989) discovered higher-risk cases in a regular supervision program had a recidivism rate of 58 percent, compared with 31 percent of high-risk cases placed in a high-risk supervision program. Therefore, it is essential to have a correct determination of risk in order to facilitate the type of programs an offender will take and benefit from.

The second principle, need, asserts "if correctional treatment services are to reduce criminal recidivism, the criminogenic needs of offenders must be targeted" (Andrews 1989:15). These needs vary, according to the individual, but the following represent some needs that can be dealt with in a rehabilitative program:

- changing antisocial attitudes
- changing antisocial feelings
- reducing antisocial peer associations
- promoting formal affection/communication
- promoting formal monitoring and supervision
- promoting identification and association with anticriminal role models
- increasing self-control, self-management and problem-solving skills (Andrews 1989:15)

Responsivity is the third principle, and it deals with the selection of the appropriate targets for change and styles of service. According to Andrews (1989), two ideas are important here: (1) what styles or types of service work for offenders, and (2) within offender groups, are there special responsivity considerations? In essence, this principle addresses effective correctional supervision and counselling.

In an effort to assess the significance of applying these principles to recidivism rates, Brown and O'Brien (1993) describe a study involving a panel of psychologists and psychiatrists and their assessments of 69 randomly selected federal offenders in a forensic unit of a Canadian hospital. The most common offences were murder (41 percent of the offences), a sexual offence (20 percent), and assault or manslaughter (19 percent). The panel used 15 recidivism risk factors—three demographic factors and 12 clinical factors—to complete their assessments. On the basis of risk scores, 26 offenders were identified to be "good risks" for release into the community and all were successful in completing their terms on parole. Recidivism risk factors therefore assisted in releasing these high-risk offenders on parole. However, much of the success of these offenders on parole, is, in part, the result of treatment services delivered in the context of risk principles within a community setting.

Contemporary Community Sanctions in Canada

Despite the fact that the law specifies offenders must receive penalties for their crimes, it also allows for the mitigation of sentences. Although some offenders do serve a period of time in either a provincial or federal provincial institution, the majority will remain in the community, at home and at work, under the supervision of probation or parole officers. During 1993–94, over 154 000 adults were under the jurisdiction of the various federal and provincial correctional agencies in Canada. Of these, approximately 80 percent of offenders were under some type of community sanction (see Figure 11.3).

Probation is a sentence imposed by a judge so that offenders can serve their sentences entirely in the community or in conjunction with another penalty, such as a fine or a period of imprisonment. While probation orders are often considered by members of the public as lenient sentences, they can and do contain strict rules and controls governing the actions of offenders.

Conditional release programs, such as parole, involve sentences after offenders have served a certain amount of time in a correctional institution. A major difference between probation and conditional release programs is that probation is imposed by a judge after an individual has been convicted of an offence. Conditional release programs, on the other hand, are not sentences imposed by the court but a release decision made by correctional authorities or a parole board after an offender has spent a part of her sentence in a correctional institution.

Probation and conditional release programs were instituted as a result of dissatisfaction with the role of prisons in our society. Prisons are considered to be too expensive to operate, have harmful effects, disrupt family relationships, and have success rates about the same as those offenders on probation and conditional release programs. The cost of operating a correctional institution, as we have pointed out, is very high. Food, medical and dental services, vocational and literacy training, 24-hour security, and escorted leaves are very expensive. Community sanctions, however, have much lower costs.

FIGURE 11.3

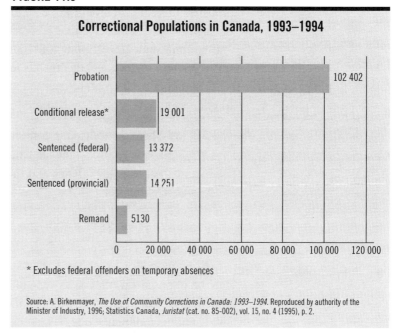

* Excludes federal offenders on temporary absences

Source: A. Birkenmayer, *The Use of Community Corrections in Canada: 1993–1994*. Reproduced by authority of the Minister of Industry, 1996; Statistics Canada, *Juristat* (cat. no. 85-002), vol. 15, no. 4 (1995), p. 2.

Guards are not needed, and capital costs are much lower since there are no expensive security devices. The offender is usually working and paying taxes, family support, and perhaps restitution to victims.

In addition, through community sanctions the harmful effects of incarceration on individuals can hopefully be avoided or reduced. Life in a correctional institution does not resemble life in society. Violence, lack of employment skills and training, and a controlled environment have led many to conclude that prisons do more harm than good. Community sanctions allow offenders to maintain connections to society, allowing them to work, be in supportive relationships, and take advantage of community resources. Finally, those who receive community sanctions usually have lower recidivism rates since they are considered lower risks. So placing these individuals in a correctional facility could be counterproductive, as it would disrupt their lives, their families, and make it much more difficult for them to reintegrate into society.

Probation

Probation is the most commonly used form of community sanction in Canada. It requires convicted offenders to serve their sentence in the community, usually under the supervision of a probation or parole officer. While under a probation order, offenders are required to conform to a number of release conditions. A breach of probation occurs when a person violates the conditions of release, a federal statute, or the Criminal Code. Currently, the maximum length of a probation order in Canada is three years.

A probation order is usually imposed at the sentencing stage, when a judge grants probation after suspending the offender's sentence. However, a judge cannot suspend a sentence for an offence that has a specified minimum punishment (Nadin-Davis 1982). A probation order can also be imposed through a "split sentence," that is, when an offender is required to complete another punishment—e.g., pay a fine or serve a period of time not exceeding two years in a correctional facility—before going on probation.

Considerable discretion is granted to a judge in determining whether or not to grant a probation order. According to Section 737 of the Criminal Code:

> 737 (1) Where an accused is convicted of an offence, the court may, having regard to the age and character of the accused, the nature of the offence and the circumstances surrounding its commission
>
> > (a) . . . suspend the passing of sentence and direct that the accused be released on the conditions prescribed in a probation order.

Every probation order has certain standard release conditions while others may be imposed on offenders, depending on their specific needs. All probationers must fulfil certain common standard conditions, according to Section 737 (2) of the Criminal Code:

> 737. (2) The following conditions shall be deemed to be prescribed in a probation order, namely, that the accused shall keep the peace and be of good behaviour and shall appear before the court when required to do so by the court and, in addition, the court may prescribe as conditions in a probation order that the accused shall do any one or more . . . things specified in the order . . .;
> (A) report to and be under the supervision of a probation officer or other person designated by the court.

Other standard conditions imposed on offenders include remaining within a particular jurisdiction, reporting to a probation officer as required, keeping authorities informed about changes of residence and employment, and refraining from contact with criminal associates (Birkenmayer 1995). Special conditions may include attending a drug counselling program or performing a specified community service order.

In 1993–94, 102 402 (or 66 percent) of all offenders under the jurisdiction of correctional authorities were on probation, a 40-percent increase in five years. This increase is not significantly related to an increase in the crime rate. As Birkenmayer (1995) notes, the use of probation exceeds the rise in the incarceration rate, which was 14 percent during the same five-year period. He suggests that the courts are increasingly using probation orders each year. Almost 90 percent of individuals placed on probation were convicted of a Criminal Code offence, while the remaining 10 percent were sentenced for violating federal statutes, such as the Narcotic Control Act. In 1993–94, the probation rate was 47 probationers per 10 000 adults in the population.

Provincial rates varied from a high of 187 probationers per 10 000 adults in the Yukon to a low of 22 probationers per 10 000 adults in Quebec.

In his analysis of those given probation during 1993–94, Birkenmayer (1995) also notes that 17 percent of probationers were female. The Yukon had the highest number of women on probation, 51 out of 10 000 females, while Quebec had the lowest number with only 3 probationers per 10 000 females. Aboriginals accounted for 12 percent of all new probationers and 17 percent of all those incarcerated during 1993–94. The four western provinces and the Yukon had the highest rates of aboriginals on probation. In the Yukon, 50 percent of all new probationers were aboriginal, followed by 45 percent in Manitoba and 41 percent in Saskatchewan.

The average age of probationers has increased from a median of 27 to 30 years between 1989–90 and 1993–94. According to Birkenmayer (1995), almost 67 percent of probationers in Canada were between 25 and 40 years of age. The median probation term has remained at 12 months since 1989–90, while the highest average lengths of probation in 1993–94 were found in Quebec (24 months), Newfoundland (19 months), Manitoba (18 months), and Nova Scotia (14 months). Finally, most males placed on probation were convicted of a violent offence while most females were convicted for a property offence. The highest number of probationers convicted of violent crimes were located in Manitoba: 56 percent of all males and 39 percent of all females given probation orders during 1993–94. These high rates are attributed to the special domestic violence programs affiliated with the Winnipeg Family Violence Court (Ursel 1994).

Conditional Release Programs

The second category of community sanctions is referred to as conditional release and includes four different programs. **Full parole** allows offenders to serve a portion of their sentence in the community until it has expired. Most inmates in the federal correctional system can apply to the National Parole Board for full parole after they have served a minimum of one-third of their total sentence, or seven years, whichever is the lesser period. Offenders who need additional eligibility requirements include those serving life sentences or sentences of preventive detention. Offenders serving a sentence of two years less a day in a provincial institution are eligible to apply for parole after serving one-third of their sentence. British Columbia, Ontario, and Quebec have provincial boards of parole for the provincial inmates held in their provincial institutions. The National Parole Board also has authority over all provincial inmates in those provinces that do not have their own boards (Eckstedt and Griffiths 1988; Birkenmayer 1995). Once offenders are released on full parole, they are placed under the supervision of a parole or probation officer and are required to follow general and specific conditions similar in nature to those granted probationers. As with all types of conditional release, offenders can be reincarcerated if they fail to fulfil the conditions of their parole or break the law.

Day parole differs from full parole in that it is only granted for short periods of time, up to a maximum of four months and renewable for a period of up to one year. Most offenders in both federal and provincial correctional facilities become eligible for day parole six months before they are eligible for full parole. The National Parole Board has the authority to grant day parole to offenders in both federal and provincial correctional institutions. Provincial parole boards do not have the power to grant day parole. The average number of offenders on day parole totalled 1622 during 1993–94, and the majority (95 percent) were federal offenders.

Temporary absences (TAs) are granted for four main reasons, namely medical, compassionate, administrative, and family and community contact. They can last from a few hours up to 15 days. TAs are granted when an offender requires medical treatment not available in a correctional facility. An example of a compassionate TA occurs when a family member is seriously ill or dies. Family and community contact TAs are granted to allow offenders to participate in community activities that will contribute in their adjustment in the community. An administrative TA is given when an offender needs to make contact with community agencies prior to his or her release (Grant and Belcourt 1992).

There are two types of TAs: escorted and unescorted. **Escorted TAs** require an offender to be accompanied by a representative of the correctional facility and may be granted any time after sentencing. These are the responsibility of the superintendent of the institution, under the authority of the Correctional Service of Canada. According to Birkenmayer (1995), during 1992–93 there were 41 493 escorted and 5432 unescorted absences granted by the Correctional Service of Canada. **Unescorted TAs** are handed out by the National Parole Board, although in practice they can also be granted by the Correctional Service of Canada. Federal inmates can apply for an unescorted TA after serving six months, or one-sixth of their sentence, whichever is longer (Eckstedt and Griffiths 1988). In 1992–93, 499 escorted and 1655 unescorted TAs were granted by the National Parole Board. According to Grant and Belcourt (1992), between 1986–87 and 1991–92, 71 percent of all unescorted TAs granted were for family and community contact purposes. Twenty-two percent were for medical reasons, followed by administrative (6 percent) and compassionate (1 percent) reasons.

Federal offenders not granted parole may be released into the community before the expiration of their sentence under **statutory release.** If provincial inmates can gain early release for earned remission (good behaviour) but are not supervised in the community, federal offenders released under statutory release are supervised in the community as if they were on parole. During 1992–93, 3164 federal inmates were released into the community under statutory release, a slight increase from the previous year (Birkenmayer 1995). Before their release, however, all inmates leaving a correctional institution on statutory supervision are reviewed by the National Parole Board. The

Corrections and Conditional Release Act allows the National Parole Board to detain an offender on statutory supervision beyond and up to the normal release date. Furthermore, they have the power to specify that an offender being released on statutory supervision live in a community residential facility if they feel the offender will be a threat to the community or will commit a crime before the termination of his sentence.

The Effectiveness of Conditional Release Programs

There is much disagreement over the effectiveness of conditional release programs in Canada today. Much of this debate has focused on the operation and administration of parole. Roberts (1988a), in his study of attitudes toward the National Parole Board, found two-thirds of Canadians considered it to be too lenient. Another study conducted by the Canadian Criminal Justice Association (1987) discovered that most members of the public felt the parole board released too many offenders. Adams (1990:11) found most Canadians were negative toward parole. Most of the people he interviewed said that offenders "get off too soon, that parole is virtually automatic after one third of the sentence and that the nature of the offender's crime and concurrent risk to society are not given proper consideration." Adams also reported that while parole is actually part of the offender's sentence, it is "not viewed generally by the public as part of the 'punishment' for a crime."

Since offenders commit different types of crimes and have different criminal backgrounds, is it fair to consider all offenders on conditional release programs as the "same"? In addition, there are different reasons why offenders may have their conditional release orders revoked: it could be for a technical violation, such as missing a curfew, or because they have been convicted of an indictable offence while under supervision of the parole board.

Recidivism Rates

A key factor in assessing the success of an offender on a conditional release program is the *recidivism rate*. In general, recidivism refers to the number of offenders who are readmitted to an institution during a particular period of time, usually when they are still under the supervision of correctional authorities. While recidivism rates can be measured in many different ways, the two most common definitions used are technical violations and convictions for new offences. A technical violation occurs when an offender breaks a condition of his release program. However, this does not mean that he has committed a new criminal offence. For example, Nouwens, Motiuk, and Boe (1993) illustrate the concept of technical violation by discussing a "fraud offender who was told to abstain from alcohol and drugs while on release (who) decides to celebrate his new-found freedom by getting drunk at a party. The police are called . . . and

FIGURE 11.4

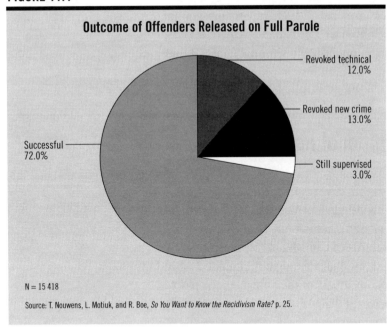

Outcome of Offenders Released on Full Parole

Revoked technical
12.0%

Revoked new crime
13.0%

Still supervised
3.0%

Successful
72.0%

N = 15 418

Source: T. Nouwens, L. Motiuk, and R. Boe, *So You Want to Know the Recidivism Rate?* p. 25.

FIGURE 11.5

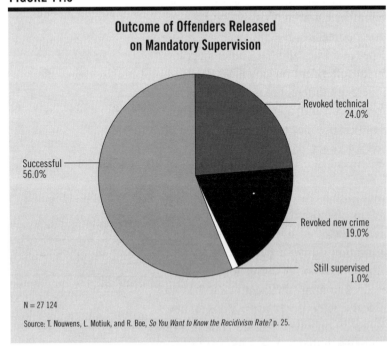

**Outcome of Offenders Released
on Mandatory Supervision**

Revoked technical
24.0%

Revoked new crime
19.0%

Still supervised
1.0%

Successful
56.0%

N = 27 124

Source: T. Nouwens, L. Motiuk, and R. Boe, *So You Want to Know the Recidivism Rate?* p. 25.

find out the offender is on parole." Other examples of technical violations include failing to stay within a specified geographical location or maintain a job.

Recidivism rates can also be measured over different lengths of time offenders are on a conditional release program. Nouwens, Motiuk, and Boe (1993) compared the short-term and long-term recidivism rates of 1000 federal offenders. Short-term recidivism was measured by looking at those offenders released over a three-year period (April 1, 1990, to March 31, 1993). The percentage of supervised offenders readmitted to a correctional facility for technical violations was 2.8 percent, while those readmitted for a new offence was 2 percent. Long-term recidivists were defined as those offenders released during a 10-year period (April 1, 1975, to March 31, 1985). During this 10-year period, 15 418 offenders were released on full parole. Of these, 72 percent (11 704 offenders) completed their sentence without being returned to custody for any reason. After these individuals had completed their parole, approximately 10 percent committed a new offence, for which they returned to the federal correctional system. During the same period, 27 124 offenders were released on mandatory supervision. Fifty-seven percent completed their sentence successfully, while 24 percent had their release revoked for technical violations and 19 percent were readmitted for a new offence. Thirty-four percent of those offenders who successfully completed their statutory supervision were readmitted to a federal institution after their sentence had finished.

Nouwens, Motiuk, and Boe (1993) also studied the readmission rate by type of conditional program release for 1000 offenders admitted to federal custody for a new offence between April 1, 1988, and March 31, 1989. By June 30, 1993, almost 92 percent of these offenders were released on some form of conditional release. During this period, the overall readmission rate was 37.1 percent. However, the highest rate of readmission was for those released on statutory supervision (46.6 percent), almost double the rate for those released on full parole (25.1 percent).

But are different types of offenders more successful on conditional release programs than others? Are those who commit a violent crime such as murder bad risks for parole, or are those convicted of a sex offence more likely to be at a higher risk of recidivism? Erwin (1992) investigated the recidivism rates of 2900 homicide offenders released between 1975 and 1990 to determine their success rate on full parole. Of these offenders 658 were convicted of first- or second-degree murder. The vast majority (77.5 percent) successfully completed their conditional release program, while 13.3 percent were incarcerated for a technical violation of their full parole and 9.2 percent for the commission of an indictable offence. Of the 69 indictable offences committed by the released offenders, 21 (30.4 percent) were narcotics offences, 12 (17.5 percent) were property offences, six (8.7 percent) involved robbery, while 17 (24.6 percent) were for other Criminal Code offences (Erwin 1992:7).

In addition, Erwin studied the full parole and supervision success rate of 2242 offenders convicted of manslaughter between January 1, 1975, and March 31, 1990. Almost all of these offenders (93 percent) were released on a conditional release program. Forty-seven percent were released on full parole and 53 percent on statutory supervision. Twenty-two percent of those released on full parole were reincarcerated: 14.6 percent for a technical violation, 6.5 percent for an indictable offence, and 0.5 percent for a summary conviction offence. Of those released on mandatory supervision, 41 percent had their full parole revoked. Thirty-one percent were revoked for a technical violation of the conditions of their parole order, 10 percent for an indictable offence, and 1 percent for a summary offence.

There is much public concern about the release of "special

FIGURE 11.6

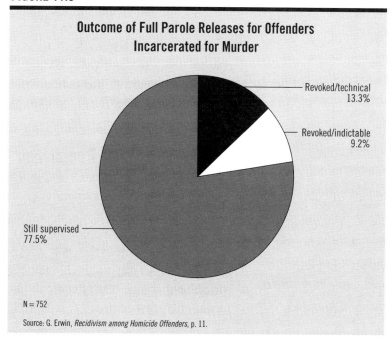

Outcome of Full Parole Releases for Offenders Incarcerated for Murder

Revoked/technical 13.3%

Revoked/indictable 9.2%

Still supervised 77.5%

N = 752

Source: G. Erwin, *Recidivism among Homicide Offenders*, p. 11.

FIGURE 11.7

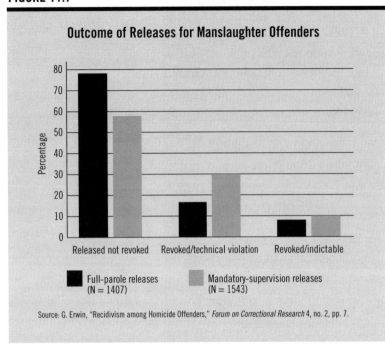

Outcome of Releases for Manslaughter Offenders

Source: G. Erwin, "Recidivism among Homicide Offenders," *Forum on Correctional Research* 4, no. 2, pp. 7.

needs" offenders, such as those identified with mental disorders, on conditional release programs. Porporino and Motiuk (1993) compared the recidivism rates of 36 male federal offenders identified as having a mental disorder with a matched group of 36 federal offenders without mental disorders. During the four-year study, almost as many offenders with mental disorders were released (67 percent) as those without mental disorders (75 percent). But offenders with mental disorders were more likely to be released on mandatory supervision (83 percent), while offenders without mental disorders (44 percent) were released more often on parole. In addition, Porporino and Motiuk (1993:17) report that there was "a tendency for mentally disordered offenders to serve more time before release and a greater proportion of their sentence." Two outcome measures were used in the study: six and 24 months. No significant differences were found concerning the recidivism rates between the two groups during the first six months of conditional release, although more offenders without mental disorders were returned to custody for a new offence or a new violent offence. After 24 months, however, those with mental disorders were more likely to have their conditional release suspended due to concern about the probability of further violent offences (Motiuk and Brown 1994:11). In contrast, offenders without mental disorders were more likely to have their conditional release revoked for the commission of a new offence.

How Inmates View Recidivism

Most criminological research uses recidivism as an indicator of the success or failure of correctional programs to prepare offenders to live a crime-free existence in the community or as a predictor of future criminal behaviour. However, Zamble and Porporino (1988) argue that both these approaches may be "incomplete because they fail to acknowledge that institutional treatment is not a one-way causal process but rather the outcome of interaction between the correctional system and offenders." Besozzi (1993) interviewed 25 offenders serving their first sentence in a federal institution, although most had prior records and had served sentences in either a juvenile or a provincial institution. At the beginning of the study, most inmates indicated that they hated prison life and, once released, did not want to return. Some even initially mentioned that their time in prison would deter them from reoffending when they returned to the outside. This attitude quickly changed for most, however, as, upon reflection, "the correctional institution became less awful and the determination not to reoffend became less resolute. The deterrent effect of prison seemed to vanish" (Besozzi 1993:37).

Besozzi (1993:35) also discovered inmates "have developed their own theories to explain why 'they always come back.'" One significant theory formulated by inmates is that the very nature of the correctional facility and parole supervision system are important "causes" of failure. By this, inmates mean that prison staff are not there to help but, rather, to ensure that they fail when they are released. Programs in the prison are simply viewed "as a way to get out sooner, not as a way to improve the odds of success on the outside" (Besozzi 1993:37). This is because they viewed prison as a place to be punished, not to be rehabilitated or to solve the problems that will likely make them reoffend when they are released.

Part of these feelings is derived from the fact that prison is a negative environment. Most inmates interviewed were unsure of how much they had changed, if at all, while in prison. As one inmate stated when contemplating the reality of leaving prison, "I think I will be more aggressive than before, when I get out. Oh yes, that's for sure, because you experience a lot of unfairness here" (Besozzi 1993:37). Another reason given is the fact that, although inmates want to change, there is a lack of both quantity and quality of resources to assist them. This was particularly true for offenders at the beginning of their sentence (Zamble and Porporino 1988). "The strongest criticisms of the correctional system came from inmates who knew they needed to change, went to prison hoping for some qualified help and think they didn't receive it" (Besozzi 1993:37).

Some offenders did indicate that they had changed, but that it was because of their own efforts and not the result of any efforts from the staff. Most of these offenders isolated themselves from the other inmates and thought about how they would live on the outside so as not to reoffend. According to one inmate, his time in prison was a "positive experience" and that he had the "opportunity to think a lot . . . to question values and attitudes to think a lot" (Besozzi 1993:37).

Overall, it was found that most inmates had vague and ambiguous feelings about their chances of surviving on the outside. According to Besozzi, this was due to the fact that they had not developed a well-defined identity, as they alternately saw themselves as law-abiding citizens and criminals. The second reason was their uncertainty caused by the indecision in the aims of the correctional system.

Risk Factors for Recidivism

Andrews (1989) reviewed the literature on recidivism and concluded that the findings from prior research were consistent in outlining characteristics that indicate an increased risk of crime. These characteristics include: having associates who have criminal tendencies or who are antisocial in nature; procriminal attitudes, values, and beliefs; generalized difficulties or trouble in relationships with others; and being male. The more risk factors present, the greater the likelihood of reoffending. According to Andrews (1989:13), research has established "beyond question, that systematic risk assessment allows the identification of lower and higher risk groups . . . offenders in higher risk groups will be responsible for a majority of the recidivistic offenses."

Of course, predictions are not always accurate: some individuals identified as high risk may never reoffend, while some identified as low risk will. In an attempt to improve risk classification of offenders, risk assessment criteria have been developed on the basis of behavioural and objective criteria. Behavioural criteria involve cognitive–behavioural and social learning models, including the modelling and reinforcement of anticriminal behaviour, graduated practice of new skills, role playing, providing resources, and concrete verbal suggestions (Andrews et al. 1990). Objective criteria, the most commonly used to compare offenders on conditional release programs, include such measures as race, drug abuse history, and employment status.

Most research on success in conditional release programs compares recidivists and nonrecidivists on a number of standard objective criteria, including gender, race, age, marital status, and employment.

Gender

Most comparisons of male and female offenders on conditional release report some differences in their recidivism rates. In general, females appear to have lower recidivism rates than do most males. Bonta, Lipinski, and Martin (1993), in their analysis of 2985 male and 81 female recidivists released from federal custody during 1983–84, report that 36 percent of the women committed a further offence within three years of their release compared with a rate of 49 percent for the males. In the case of temporary absences, Grant and Belcourt (1992) reported women were less likely to fail on this program (0.01 percent) than males (1.0 percent). However, Lefebvre (1994), in her analysis of 929 males and 44 females on day parole during 1990–91, found the overall failure rate for women was 30 percent, compared with 27 percent for male offenders. The reason for parole revocation varied among females and males: 5 percent of females committed a new offence, compared with 10 percent of males. This result supports the conclusion reported by Belcourt, Nouwens, and Lefebvre (1993), who reported that in their analysis of 968 females released from federal custody over a 10-year period, 50 percent were readmitted for a technical violation while 21 percent had their release revoked for a new offence.

Race

Racial minority group members are overrepresented in the Canadian federal prison system. In 1991, 12 percent of all admissions to federal institutions and 19 percent of those sentenced to provincial facilities were aboriginal, despite the fact that less than 3 percent of the Canadian population is aboriginal (Canadian Centre for Justice Statistics 1991). During this same period, Caucasians in this population increased from 10 315 to 10 946, an increase of 6.1 percent.

Most research reveals that aboriginals released on conditional release programs have recidivism rates higher than their Caucasian counterparts. For example, Bonta, Lipinski, and Martin (1992) reported in their analysis of 282 male aboriginal inmates an overall recidivism rate of 66 percent. They report that 84 percent of these aboriginals had been previously incarcerated. Aboriginals placed on mandatory supervision during the three-year study had a much higher recidivism rate (75 percent) than those released on full parole (33 percent).

Belcourt, Nouwens, and Lefebvre (1993) studied the success of aboriginal female offenders in all forms of conditional release programs. They report that aboriginal women were overrepresented in the group returned to a correctional facility after being released. Forty-four percent of the aboriginal women offenders were readmitted compared with approximately 19 percent of non-native female offenders.

Grant and Belcourt (1992), in their study of temporary absences, found aboriginals to be underrepresented in all TA programs except for compassionate TAs. However, they note that these differences can be explained in large part by legal variables, namely the fact that they are more likely to have been convicted of serious violent offences and to have served a greater number of multiple federal prison sentences. Given these facts, Grant and Belcourt conclude that aboriginal peoples "may therefore represent a greater risk to the community and, as with other offenders in these categories, are less likely to be granted TAs."

The reasons for these differences between aboriginal and nonaboriginal offenders have concerned the Correctional Service of Canada, various federal government committees studying conditional release programs, as well as independent researchers. For example, in its conclusion of conditional release programs in Canada, the Daubney Committee (1988:214) noted that it appears "Native inmates are often not as familiar with release preparation and the conditional release system as other inmates." Zimmerman (1992:401) reports that aboriginals "often waive the right for early release." She attributes this in part "to subtle encouragement by case management officers" (1992:409). As a result, aboriginal offenders are the least likely of all groups in the federal correctional system to be released on parole. This is in part due to certain parole criteria being "inherently weighted against aboriginal offenders"

(Zimmerman 1992:408). Aboriginals who are granted parole are more likely to find themselves returned to prison before the expiration of their conditional release program, a fact interpreted as resulting from the inappropriate conditional release requirements placed on them, more stringent enforcement of release conditions, and inadequate support upon their release.

Age, Marital Status, and Employment

Recently, Sherman et al. (1992) reported that recidivism may be higher among those who are unemployed and unmarried. Citing research from domestic violence studies, they argue that neither race nor a record of prior offences had an impact on reducing recidivism. Instead, it was their finding that "arrested persons who lacked a stake in conformity were significantly more likely to have a repeat offence than their counterparts who were not arrested" (Sherman et al. 1992:682). This suggests that those with a higher stake in conformity will be a better risk to complete their conditional release program.

Lefebvre (1994) found that the overall failure rate of her sample of day parolees was inversely related to age. For the youngest group (18–25) it was 41 percent, followed by 25 percent for those 26 to 40, and 14 percent for those over 40. The rate of failure due to the commission of a new offence was 15 percent for the youngest groups, 9 percent for those between 26 and 40, and 5 percent for the oldest group. Similar findings were discovered by Bonta, Lipinski, and Martin (1992), who found that recidivists were, on average, three years younger (26) than nonrecidivists at the time of sentencing. In their study of female offenders, Belcourt, Nouwens, and Lefebvre (1993) found a similar trend. Twenty-nine percent of those between 18 and 25 were readmitted, compared with 22 percent of those between 26 and 30, 20 percent of those between 31 and 45, 16 percent of those aged 46 to 60, and 11 percent over the age of 60.

In relation to marital status, Lefebvre (1994) found offenders who were married or involved in common-law relationships at the time of their offence had a lower failure rate (22 percent) than those divorced or separated (28 percent) or single (29 percent). Studies (e.g., Bonta, Lipinski, and Martin 1993) have consistently found recidivism rates for single, divorced, or separated offenders to be higher than for those who are married.

Frances Baines, vice-chairwoman of the National Parole Board's Ontario region, checks a file from the thousands kept by the board on federal convicts. (Photo: Peter Moon/*The Globe and Mail*)

Lefebvre (1994) studied the impact of employment and education on recidivism. She found that the overall failure rate for day parolees declined as the offender's level of education increased, from 29 percent for those with a Grade 8 education or less to 19 percent for those with postsecondary education. She also found that those who were employed at the time of their offences were twice as likely to be successful on conditional release programs than those who were unemployed (16.8 percent versus 33.9 percent respectively).

Summary

Conditional release programs can be traced back to 1868, when a formal system of parole was first implemented. Today, conditional release programs consist of various parole programs, including full parole, day parole, and temporary absences. Probation, however, is the largest conditional release program, in terms of numbers of offenders, currently practised today in Canada. During the past 20 years, largely as a result of increased legal rights for prisoners, these programs have been developed to allow better access to both probation and the various conditional release programs.

In recent years, there has been an emphasis on risk factors as the most significant consideration when considering placing offenders on these programs. Once offenders are placed on these programs, they must follow a set of rules or conditions. If they violate one of them, their release may be revoked and they will be placed back into a correctional facility. The Canadian courts have extended legal rights to all those applying for or who are on these programs. If an individual is not allowed to participate in a program, he must be told why he was rejected. In addition, if an individual's conditional release is revoked, the individual has the right to a full hearing on the issue and the right to legal counsel.

Recidivism is the measure used to evaluate the success or failure of those involved in these programs. Failures include two types: the commission of a new criminal offence or a technical violation. Recidivism rates may vary according to the type of crime for which an offender is incarcerated. Recidivism rates may vary according to the type of crime for which an offender is incarcerated and according to the type of conditional release program.

Discussion Questions

1. Discuss the use of conditional release in Canada. Should more people be placed on these programs?

2. What is the current role of the parole board? How has it changed over time?

3. Discuss the factors that influence the decision to grant parole.

4. What is the purpose of probation?

5. What are some of the problems associated with probation orders?

6. What type of offenders are most likely to reoffend?

7. Discuss the risk factors used in the decision to grant parole.

8. Should we continue our statutory supervision policy? What purposes does this policy serve?

Suggested Readings

Andrews, D., and J. Bonta. *The Psychology of Criminal Conduct*. Cincinnati: Anderson Publishing, 1994.

Caron, R. *Go-Boy!* Toronto: Hamlyn, 1983.

Cole, D.P., and A. Manson. *Release from Imprisonment: The Law of Sentencing, Parole, and Judicial Review.* Toronto: Carswell, 1990.

Culhane, C. *Still Barred from Prison*. Montreal: Black Rose Books, 1985.

Faith, K. *Unruly Women: The Politics of Confinement and Resistance*. Vancouver: Press Gang Publishers, 1993.

Gosselin, L. *Prisons in Canada*. Montreal: Black Rose Books, 1982.

Gottfredson, D.M., and M. Tonry, eds. *Prediction and Classification: Criminal Justice Decision Making*. Chicago: University of Chicago Press, 1987.

CHAPTER 12

Issues in Corrections: The Rise of Intermediate Punishments

Intermediate punishments have been used since the mid-1980s in the United States in an attempt to control prison populations, reduce the costs of prisons, and make society a safer place to live. In recent years, a few similar programs have been introduced in Canada. An outgrowth of deterrence-based policies, these programs have now been evaluated by many researchers to see if they have reached their objectives. One of the biggest problems with these programs is the fact that there are high rates of revocation and subsequent incarceration. If intermediate punishments are to be successful, more care must be taken about the quality of the programs and the type of offenders who participate in them.

CHAPTER OBJECTIVES

- outline the major forms of intermediate punishments: intensive supervision programs, home confinement and electronic monitoring, shock incarceration (boot camps), and private prisons

- evaluate whether the major goals of these programs—reducing prison populations and prison costs and increasing safety—are being achieved

- discuss whether deterrence-based programs work

- consider whether these programs would be beneficial if introduced in Canada

- discuss their negative aspects

In 1988, Judge Frances McCaffrey shocked court observers when he imposed punishment on a convicted cocaine dealer. The individual who stood before him was referred to on the campus of Middlebury College in Addison County, Vermont, as the "pharmacist." Instead of sending the drug dealer to prison, the judge sentenced the 26-year-old man to serve four months of a one-to-five-year prison term under house confinement. The media made this case front-page news, not because of the innovative nature of the sentence but because the defendant was John Zaccaro, Jr., the son of the 1984 Democratic vice-presidential candidate, Geraldine A. Ferraro.

It was soon reported that Zaccaro was serving his term of home confinement in a $1500-per-month luxury apartment in Burlington, Vermont, complete with maid services and privileges at the neighbouring YMCA. After being made aware of Zaccaro's luxury living arrangements, the prosecutor for the case, John Quinn, commented that Zaccaro was not being punished but, rather, grounded. A spokesperson for the governor of Vermont publicly announced that there was going to be an investigation and perhaps a recommendation to change the sentence. Despite these comments, Zaccaro completed his "punishment" without incident (*Los Angeles Times* 1988).

Two years later, a reporter for the *National Law Journal* (Cheever 1990) wrote a news story entitled "House Arrest Seen as Solution for Crowding Hard Time." The "solution" concerned the case of arms dealer Adnan Khashoggi, who was given the sentence of home confinement after posting bail of $10 million following an indictment on charges of mail fraud and obstructing justice in New York City. It had been alleged that Khashoggi had assisted Ferdinand and Imelda Marcos when they plundered the Philippine Treasury. The judge "confined" him to his 30 000-square-foot luxury Fifth Avenue apartment, complete with swimming pool in downtown New York City. The judicial order stated that Khashoggi had to be home between the hours of 1 a.m. and 8 a.m. In addition, he received the court's permission to holiday in Aspen, Colorado, and visit one of his twelve residences in Fort Lauderdale, Florida.

Despite the apparent inequity of these home confinement sentences, they both fit within the rationale of such programs, which according to a draft report published by the Administrative Office of the United States Courts is to

> provide ... an alternative to detention for those persons whose non-appearance or danger to the community safety cannot be controlled by less restrictive release conditions. Punishment is not appropriate for persons presumed innocent; therefore, home confinement is not used to punish, only to assure appearance and community safety.
> (Administrative Office 1991:51)

This chapter reviews the main types of intermediate punishments that have been implemented to date, namely intensive supervision probation, and home confinement and electronic monitoring. In addition, it reviews two new popular correctional programs: shock incarceration (boot camps) and private prisons. While the bulk of the evaluation literature has been published on U.S. programs, an increasing number of these intermediate punishments are appearing in Canada. For example, most provinces have started some form of intensive supervision probation: British Columbia has published the results of a pilot project on home confinement and electronic monitoring; New Brunswick has announced that a new, privately operated correctional facility will be built in the near future; and Manitoba introduced its "Made in Manitoba" boot camps on September 1, 1994. With estimates that the federal and provincial prison populations will reach 20 000 by the year 2000, these programs will no doubt come under increasing scrutiny by Canadian authorities in the next few years. Reviewing these programs in the United States provides us with some basis on which to judge them and decide if they are appropriate for the Canadian context.

Intermediate Punishments

Intermediate punishments (IP), which attempt to control offenders "between prison and probation," usually within the community, were originally introduced in the belief that they would reduce prison overcrowding and substantially reduce the costs of the correctional system. The original advocates also believed such programs would protect the community by exerting more control than traditional probation services. It was hoped that the overall effect of these new forms of punishment would also deter potential offenders from committing crimes and assist in the rehabilitation of offenders by using mandatory treatment requirements, reinforced by mandatory substance-abuse testing and the firm revocation of violators (Petersilia, Lurigio, and Byrne 1992).

Critics argue that the benefits of intermediate punishments have not been achieved. Instead, they have ushered in a new era of punitive punishments that will simply incarcerate more offenders than before (Morris and Tonry 1990). Clear (1994) has stated that these new punishments reflect the "penal harm movement," a series of seven interrelated components based on the assumption that high crime rates can be reduced if more offenders receive punishment. These components, when combined, create what is known as the *punishment paradigm*. The seven components are as follows:

1. The "root causes" of crime, such as social inequality, racism, and poverty, cannot be changed or have no relevance to the causes of crime.

2. Any programs developed and implemented to combat the root causes of crime are misplaced and will not reduce the crime rate.

3. Criminals will only be deterred if the criminal justice system ensures that they receive enough pain for their wrongs.

4. Prisons are an effective means of reducing crime because they keep criminals off the street.

Field Practice 12.1

Intermediate Punishments

A. House Confinement/Electronic Monitoring

A wealthy businessman was sentenced to 30 days to house confinement after being convicted of over 100 health, fire, safety, and building code violations in one of the apartment buildings he owned in a poverty-stricken area of the city. The judge, noting that the businessman owned a mansion, decided it would be appropriate to sentence him to serve his punishment in one of his own apartment buildings. He was not allowed to leave the building for the duration of his sentence. To make sure he stayed in the building, an electronic monitoring system was used to ensure that he did not violate his punishment.

B. Sexual Offender

A 35-year-old male was convicted of unlawful sexual intercourse with a minor. In addition, he had a lengthy record of violence and burglary. The prosecutor argued at the sentencing hearing that he was a threat to community safety. The judge sentenced the defendant to six years' imprisonment, to be followed by two years of electronic monitoring as well as intensive supervision. According to the judge, this would allow the offender to be integrated back into the community.

C. Shoplifter

A 22-year-old woman was convicted of shoplifting an article of clothing valued at $50. She had one prior conviction for a similar offence. According to her lawyer, she did not pose a threat to society and should be sentenced to the county's one-year intensive supervision program. The judge agreed, and sentenced her to one to eight hours of direct supervision a week, in which she was subject to curfew checks, employment checks, and close monitoring of her involvement in a treatment program. This enabled the defendant to keep her job as a teacher's aide and to support her two young children.

5. Society will be much safer with large numbers of criminals in prison.

6. Offenders in the community should be controlled, not incarcerated, through a variety of programs known as intermediate punishments, such as house confinement, electronic monitoring, and intensive probation supervision.

7. If crime rates do not decrease, more punishment, community control, and prisons will be needed.

Walker (1993) points out that, as a result of the wide-scale acceptance of this punishment paradigm, the number of individuals under the control of the correctional system escalated dramatically in the United States. During the early 1970s, the number of inmates in federal and state prisons totalled approximately 200 000, with an incarceration rate of 96 per 100 000 citizens. By 1989, the prison population totalled almost 800 000 inmates, with the incarceration rate increasing to 271 per 100 000 individuals. In California, for example, the state prison population increased from 20 000 in 1980 to over 100 000 in 1992 while the county jail population tripled, from 25 000 to 76 000 (Petersilia 1992).

To house these increasing numbers of prisoners, more prisons had to be built. But as soon as a new facility was built, it reached its maximum limit of prisoners in just a few years. The result was twofold: first, increasing fiscal resources went to the maintenance of existing prisons and the building of new ones; and, second, there was no apparent reduction in the crime rate. In fact, the vast majority of research on the effect of this increasing prison population on crime has found that states that imprison the most individuals do not necessarily have the lowest crime rates (Currie 1986; Steffensmeier and Harer 1993).

If prisons are too expensive and ineffective in deterring crime, and traditional programs that place offenders in the community threaten the public safety, then, the supporters of intermediate punishments argue, new policies are needed. The solution, they argue, is intermediate sanctions: by closely supervising, monitoring, and testing offenders in the community, it would be possible to control offenders both effectively and inexpensively (Cullen et al. 1995).

Today, most U.S. jurisdictions have at least one form of intermediate punishment. For example, over 70 percent of states use intensive probation supervision, with a caseload exceeding 60 000 offenders; over 50 percent have electronic monitoring programs and boot camp programs; and approximately 50 percent test probationers for drugs, with the average number of tests per jurisdiction in excess of 50 000, and the number of drug tests for parolees per jurisdiction exceeding 75 000 (Pearson 1987b; Camp and Camp 1993; Langan 1994).

Why do intermediate punishments remain so popular, especially when the United States still has overcrowded prisons, increasing crime rates, huge costs for correctional facilities, and high rates of recidivism? First, there remains the strong belief that the costs of these programs are somehow cheaper. The direct cost of administering and supervising an intermediate punishment program is generally thought to be much less than running a prison. For example, the intensive supervision probation program in New Jersey saved the state approximately $7000 for each offender yearly. Indirect cost savings result when offenders on intermediate sanctions are required to be employed, thereby generating income, paying taxes, and participating in community service projects and other such activities that would not be possible if they were imprisoned (Rackmill 1994).

Second, some states require participants to help pay for the costs of the program. Byrne, Lurigio, and Baird (1989) point out that intensive supervision probationers in Georgia have to pay a probation supervision fee of $10 to $50 per month, as well as any court-ordered fines and restitution payments. Intermediate punishments also save money by diverting large numbers of offenders away from prison. Collectively, this would save millions of dollars per year, provided a substantial number of intermediate punishment programs are in place.

Third, intermediate punishments can also result in sentences that are seen as fair, equitable, and proportional (Morris and Tonry 1990). Sending violent criminals to prison makes perfect sense, but shouldn't those convicted of fraudulent offences be given a lighter punishment, although still be under some degree of control? Such a system, Tonry and Will (1990) argue, establishes fairness and equity to sentences not involving incarceration as it can increase the punishment for those reconvicted of an offence but for whom a prison sentence would be inappropriate. Intermediate punishments also provide stronger control than normal community supervision. Hopefully they will lead to greater deterrence because anyone violating the terms of the program is likely to be caught and punished due to the greater amount of surveillance. In addition, under intermediate punishment, offenders should also commit fewer offences because the conditions of the program limit their opportunities to engage in such activities. According to Petersilia and Turner (1993), closer surveillance will likely uncover more technical rule violations.

Intensive Supervision Probation

Intensive supervision probation (ISP) is the most common form of intermediate punishment today. Between 1980 and 1990, every jurisdiction in the United States introduced some form of ISP, and by the end of the decade some 50 000 clients were involved with these programs per year. The popularity of ISPs stems from their perceived ability to reduce prison populations, eliminate the need for building costly new prisons, and prevent the negative impact of imprisonment on offenders. As well, they are seen as promoting public safety by ensuring that all offenders are subject to intensive surveillance, thereby reducing the opportunities for involvement in criminal activities (Petersilia 1987b).

What makes ISP so different from regular probation? The most commonly cited advantage is the small probation officer–client ratios, usually 15 to 40 clients per probation officer. According to Thompson (1985) other elements that characterize ISP programs include the following:

1. Supervision is *extensive*. Probation officers have multiple, weekly face-to-face contacts with offenders, as well as collateral contacts with employers and family members and frequent arrest checks.
2. Supervision is *focused*. Monitoring activities concentrate on specific behavioral regulations governing curfews, drug use, travel, employment, and community service.
3. Supervision is *ubiquitous*. Offenders are frequently subjected to random drug tests and unannounced curfew checks.
4. Supervision is *graduated*. Offenders commonly proceed through ISP programs in a series of progressive phases—each of which repre-

sents a gradual tempering of the proscriptions and requirements of ISP—until they are committed to regular supervision as the final leg of their statutory time on probation.

5. Supervision is *strictly enforced*. Penalties for new arrest and noncompliance with program conditions are generally swift and severe.

6. Supervision is *coordinated.* ISP offenders are usually monitored by specially selected and trained officers who are part of a larger specialized, autonomous unit.

ISP programs are not designed for leniency but rather as punishment. As one policy-maker in Georgia stated in reference to these programs, "we are in the business of increasing the heat on probationers . . . to satisfy the public's demand for just punishment . . . Criminals must be punished for their misdeeds" (Erwin 1986:24).

ISP programs are not easy, because they usually involve several contacts with a probation officer every week, residence only in approved locations, random drug and alcohol tests, and one year's minimum involvement. In fact, due to the intrusive nature of these programs, many offenders choose not to participate when given the chance, even if the alternative is prison. Petersilia and Turner (1993) report that 25 percent of the Oregon offenders they studied who were eligible for an ISP program preferred prison instead.

ISP in Operation

One of the first ISP programs was developed in Georgia, and it became so popular that it was duplicated in many other jurisdictions (Petersilia 1987b). This model includes five weekly contacts between an offender and a probation officer, mandatory curfew, and weekly arrest checks. Other features of the Georgia model include:

- 132 hours of mandatory community service
- mandatory employment
- automatic notification of arrest elsewhere via the state Crime Information Network Listing
- routine and unannounced alcohol and drug testing (Erwin and Bennett 1987)

Initial evaluations of Georgia's program reported that offenders had extremely low recidivism rates (16 percent) and that there was a 10 percent drop in the number of criminals sentenced to prison. It was estimated that the ISP program cost approximately $16 per day, while prison cost $60. However, there were important methodological problems with these studies, including the fact that the experimental (ISP) and control groups were not comparable.

Another criticism of Georgia's program is that due to the high incarceration rate in the state, a large number of low-risk, easily manageable offenders are available. As a result, the generalizability of these results to other jurisdictions with different prisoner profiles and levels of risk is open to question.

Another early ISP program was instituted in New Jersey, specifically in an attempt to reduce prison overcrowding. Offenders must serve from 30 to 60 days in state prison before they are eligible for the ISP program. All applicants must go before an ISP officer, and present a personal living plan that details their goals, needs, and employment and financial arrangements. If this application is approved, a sentencing panel evaluates the application and, if accepted, the inmate is placed on a six-month probationary period. If the offender successfully completes this trial period, a sentencing hearing is held to change the original sentence. This procedure is extremely rigorous, and is designed to eliminate all high-risk offenders.

The program is similar to Georgia's, with high levels of surveillance, mandatory curfews, mandatory and unannounced drug tests, and a minimum of 20 contacts per month between the client and probation officers during the first 14 months. An evaluation of this program discovered that, after three years, the ISP group had rearrest rates 10 percent lower than those who were on regular probation (24.7 percent versus 34.6 percent respectively). However, when rearrest and revocations for technical violations (e.g., failure of drug tests) were combined, 40 percent of the ISP clients were sent back to prison within the first year compared with only 32 percent of the control group (Pearson 1987a).

Some studies have found that ISPs that utilize a treatment approach do, in fact, reduce recidivism. In their study of ISPs in Massachusetts, for example, Byrne and Kelly (1989:37) found that "58 percent of the offenders who demonstrated improvement in the area of substance abuse successfully completed the one-year at risk, as compared with only 38 percent of those who did not improve." The researchers found crime control could be achieved, but through the use of rehabilitation measures.

Similar findings have been made by other researchers. For example, in their study of treatment for drug offenders within a community control program in Oregon, Jolin and Stipak (1992) report that drug treatment led to a significant reduction in offenders' drug use (from 95 percent at the time they started the program to 32 percent at the completion of the program). Latessa (1995) discovered that high-risk clients did no worse, and sometimes better, than random samples of regular probationers when they participated in ISPs with a treatment component. And finally, a study of a treatment-based ISP in New Jersey designed for high-risk offenders was found to have a lower rate of recidivism to a matched group of regular probationers (21 percent versus 29 percent), a finding attributed to the fact that ISP participants received "significantly more treatment services" (Gendreau et al. 1993:34).

Home Confinement and Electronic Monitoring

Home confinement (HC) and **electronic monitoring** (EM) are designed to restrict offenders to their place of residence. In home confinement offenders stay at their place of residence instead of in a correctional facility. In addition, the offender maintains family ties, continues employment, and can take advantage of community programs and resources.

A significant concern about HC is the issue of surveillance. How can correctional officials guarantee that offenders are following their probation orders and remaining at home during the designated times? This issue was solved by electronic monitoring, which informs officials at a central location if the offender is not following their home confinement agreement by violating a curfew order. By increasing the certainty of detection, it is hoped that EM will deter those sentenced to HC from reoffending.

As with the case of ISP, HC and EM started slowly but quickly became popular within a few years. In 1986, a total of 95 offenders were on EM programs; in one year, this number increased to 2300. By 1992 over 45 000 monitorees were being controlled by approximately 1200 different agencies (Maxfield and Baumer 1990).

Until recently, the most common form of EM technology did not involve any interaction or communication between those being monitored and those controlling the equipment. The offender wears a transmitter that constantly emits a signal that is monitored by personnel in a central office. A printer records the absence or presence of an offender in his or her home during a designated time period (Ball, Huff, and Lilly 1988).

Table 12.1 indicates EM's success rate on a sample of offenders on EM programs during 1989. The table reveals that the main reason (18 percent) for failure was technical violations, such as curfew violation or failure to make restitution payments on time. Only 48 (2 percent) of the program participants were rearrested for committing a new offence. The highest failure rates occurred during the early periods of the program. This rate was highest during the first few months of operation—28 percent for the first month, 27 percent for the second month, and 22 percent for the third. But, over time, technical violations declined dramatically while new offence violations continued, but at a very low rate.

Low-risk offenders have been the traditional target group of HC and EM programs (Brown and Roy 1995). When these programs were first instituted, they were almost exclusively used for cases of driving while impaired (DWI) and driving under suspension (DUS). Successful program completion rates were high, with rates of 80 percent to 90 percent quite common. For example, in their analysis of EM programs for DWI and DUS offenders over a seven-year period, Lilly et al. (1993) found that the successful completion rate exceeded 97 percent. According to the researchers, this rate of success is impressive, given the higher rates of EM violations during the early months and the increased surveillance of program participants. Research has consistently found a positive relationship between the age of traffic offenders and their success rates. In the Lilly et al. (1993) study, for example, the success rate for individuals 17–40 ranged between 74 and 84 percent, while the rate for those over 40 was between 85 and 92 percent.

In a pilot project conducted in British Columbia by the Ministry of the Solicitor General (1989), 92 individuals in the Vancouver region were placed on an EM program. Only nonviolent offenders were allowed to participate: three participants were convicted of drug trafficking, two for property offences, and one for a crime against a person. The vast majority of offenders, 83 (or 90 percent), were convicted for DWI and DUS, and all had at least one prior conviction. While the EM sentences varied between seven and 90 days, almost 50 percent of the program participants were placed on the program for 10 to 15 days; others were on the program for 70 to 90 days. All offenders completed their EM sentence successfully.

These success rates have led policy-makers to experiment with placing more serious offenders on HC and EM programs. An example of an EM program that works with higher-risk offenders is the Florida Community Control Plan (FCCP). According to Baird and Wagner (1990), this program involves individuals convicted of felonies who would otherwise be incarcerated in prison for a period of 12 to 30 months. During 1991–92, over 16 000 convicted felons were sentenced to this program. The degree of control and surveillance for high-risk offenders is significant, as all offenders are confined to their residences during nonworking hours, unless special permission is granted. The offender's location is monitored through 28 contacts each month, involving a combination of home visits, telephone contacts, and collateral visits. All program participants must be employed or attending school, pay program supervision fees, undergo random drug tests, and record their daily activities. In addition, there may be additional sanctions, such as community service work.

Recidivism rates (defined as rearrest, reconviction, and imprisonment/ reimprisonment) were compared to find if the FCCP is more effective than prison. The researchers found that there was very little difference between the two groups in terms of overall recidivism rates, and that those rates were high, involving approximately four out of every five program participants during the 54-month study. Ultimately, 61 percent of the FCCP group were reconvicted, while 60 percent of the prison group received a reconviction. Thus, being sentenced to the FCCP or prison made no difference for either rearrest or reconviction. However, it was noted that technical violations were considered as arrests, and a sizable number of rearrests (41 percent) were technical violations under the FCCP while only 8 percent of the rearrests of the prison group classified as parole violations. In addition, the data revealed that members of both groups reoffended quickly after they were released (Smith and Akers 1993).

EXHIBIT 12.1

Electronic Monitoring of Drug Offenders: Is It Really Successful? A Case Study

With more provincial governments in Canada deciding to use electronic monitoring of offenders as an alternative to other community-based sanctions, many people are wondering about the effectiveness of these new programs. Do they really work in terms of reducing the recidivism of offenders, or are they another "experiment" doomed to fail? This exhibit attempts to answer these questions by focusing on a case study of an electronic monitoring program for substance abusers conducted in Los Angeles.

Electronic monitoring is thought to provide an economical method of community supervision. Offenders are required to wear an anklet or bracelet equipped with an electronic device that informs the probation office if the wearer is not at home as specified in the probation order. The cost for placing an offender in jail for one day is estimated to be $40, compared to half that amount for an electronic monitoring program.

The Los Angeles Study

This research involves three high-crime areas of Los Angeles and compares 1990–91 post-release records of 126 drug offenders sentenced to house arrest with 200 drug offenders from the same areas and time period sentenced to ordinary probation. Both groups were abusers of illegal drugs (although not all were convicted of charges involving drugs), and their sentences included random tests for illegal drugs at least twice a month. Most drug charges were for possession rather than sale, and nondrug charges usually were for theft, auto theft, or burglary.

The two groups had similar personal traits:

- about 80 percent were male

- 40 percent were white, 35 percent were Hispanic, 25 percent were African American (but each group predominated in one of the three neighbourhoods involved in the study)

- the average age was 30, while the age at first recorded adult arrest was 21

- the average number of prior arrests was five, and prior convictions totalled three

- the duration of the electronic monitoring program was 90 days for 117 of the 126 cases, while two program participants received 60 days, five received 120 days, two had two successive 90-day terms (due to violations during the first term)

- interviews were conducted with 70 of the monitored offenders

- interviews were also conducted with probation officers who supervised the electronically monitored offenders as well as those who were not on the program

Record on Probation

During the first six months of their sentences:

- 43 percent of nonmonitored and 34 percent of the monitored group had their probation revoked for serious rule violations

- 45 percent of monitored compared with 28 percent of nonmonitored had no reports of rule violation

Findings

- serious probation violations began much sooner after probation began for the nonmonitored than for the monitored group

- most rule violations recorded for nonmonitored probationers were for missed or positive drug tests, whereas most violations by monitored offenders were curfew violations

- 6 percent of both groups of probationers were arrested for new offences

- of those tested, about 40 percent of both groups had at least one test positive for drugs

Other Major Findings

- those who were employed at sentencing had better outcome rates

- benefits were found with monitoring those classified in their pre-sentence report as "poor" (i.e., of lower social class origin)

- more than 90 percent of offenders from both groups were fined as a condition of probation

Reasons for Outcome Differences

- three-quarters of the monitored offenders reported more time spent at home with family during a week of the monitoring period than during a week of pre-monitoring

- monitoring fostered home life both during and after monitoring

Source: D. Glaser and R. Watts, "Electronic Monitoring of Drug Offenders on Probation," *Judicature* 76, no. 3 (1992); J. Byrne, A. Lurigio, J. Petersilia, "Introduction: The Emergence of Intermediate Sanctions," in Byrne, Lurigio, and Petersilia, eds., *Smart Sentencing* (Newbury Park, Calif.: Sage), pp. ix–xv.

A study conducted by Baumer, Mendelsohn, and Rhine (1990) found no significant differences in recidivism rates of high-risk probationers supervised by EM and those under "manual" supervision (20.5 percent for EM and 18.3 percent for the manual supervision program). In addition, 42 percent of both groups were found to have violated the terms of their programs by being absent when they should have been at home. This led the researchers to conclude that EM programs do not guarantee reduced recidivism rates compared with manual programs. In another study comparing EM program participants with manual supervision, Brown and Roy (1995) found the experimental group to be more likely to complete their home confinement sentence, although the rate of failures (18 vs. 22 percent) was not substantial. In addition, they concluded EM was a better program with a specific type of offender, namely those who were unemployed and unmarried.

According to Clear and Hardyman (1990), early supporters of intermediate punishment (IP) programs like ISP have exaggerated claims that such programs brought about a revolution in corrections—i.e., better crime control, reduced prison populations, fiscal savings, and greater public safety. Of course, more modest claims—for example, that there are little, if any, cost savings, and only a minimal increase in public safety— would lead to diminished support for these programs, and thus the implementation of these programs would be in question.

Because intermediate punishments have been viewed as the solution to so many problems, little attention was initially placed on the clarity of these programs' goals, making it difficult for researchers to state whether a program has been successful in reaching its goals. As Tonry (1990:180) has commented, ISP programs have succeeded, not in terms of achieving their stated goals, but rather in serving "latent bureaucratic, organizational, political, professional, and psychological goals of probation departments and officers."

Boot Camps

The increased interest in boot camps reflects the pattern of development for other intermediate punishments described by Morris and Tonry (1990). As with other IPs, a few advocates were able to establish experimental boot camps, and the initial evaluations reported low recidivism rates. As a result, in the 10 years following the first boot camp in Georgia in 1983, 36 states had boot camps by 1994 (Mackenzie 1994:1).

A number of criteria separate boot camps from traditional institutions. First, they are highly structured and include military drill, physical training, and hard labour. Second, the program includes a rigorous daily schedule of physical activity. Participants are usually young males convicted of nonviolent offences who did not have an extensive criminal history. Third, the length of time served by offenders ranges from three to six months, with the average stay being approximately 4.5 months (Camp and Camp 1993).

Boot camp participants are awakened as early as 4 a.m. They dress in uniform and exercise for an hour before breakfast. They attend classes until 11 a.m., when lunch is served. More physical training follows, then dormitory clean-up and counselling sessions. After a 4:30 p.m. supper, more counselling is provided. At 7 p.m. a variety of organized sports are played. An hour is reserved for personal activities such as washing and writing letters. Television is available at this time, but only educational programs. Lights are out at 9:30 p.m. The same routine is followed all week, except that on Sunday inmates are allowed visitors for three hours in the afternoon.

Although these programs are similar in the sense that they follow a military model of discipline, they vary widely in their other program components. These variations are based on different ideas about how the program can achieve the desired goals. Mackenzie and Ballow (1995) studied 11 different programs and found variations in size, number of days served, placement authority, type of program entry and exit (voluntary or coerced), as well as the type and amount of counselling offered to program participants.

Teenage inmates at Shunda Creek Youth Corrections Camp chop fallen poplar, clearing the way for a new drilling rig in the Central Alberta Rockies. (Photo: Brian Michel/*The Globe and Mail*)

Other variations were in terms of location (i.e., whether they were housed as part of a larger prison or in a separate facility), intensity of release supervision, as well as the type of aftercare during community supervision. Therefore, no unified "model" boot camp program exists.

Boot camps were introduced to lower recidivism rates and to reduce prison overcrowding. A few studies have found the recidivism rates of those who successfully completed boot camp were similar to those who were placed on regular probation or diversion programs. Mackenzie and Souryal (1995) found regular probationers in Georgia less likely than boot camp graduates to be rearrested for a crime and that they were more likely to be reincarcerated for new offences at a higher rate than regular probationers in Florida. In addition, they reported no significant differences for revocation of technical violations between both groups in Florida.

There is evidence, however, that boot camps influence offenders' behaviour more positively than those on regular probation. First, after release, but still under supervision in the community, graduates of boot camps were involved in more positive activities (e.g., community activities). The key element appears to be the amount of community supervision, with the more intensive programs having the lowest recidivism rates. In addition, boot camps have a strong focus on rehabilitation, voluntary participation, and longer program duration. Second, unlike those individuals incarcerated in traditional prisons or placed on regular probation, boot camp participants felt their experience had been positive and that they had changed for the better. The benefits of boot camps included improved physical health and educational opportunities. These effects were greatest for those individuals who spent time in boot camps that were both voluntary and provided more time for therapeutic activities (Mackenzie, Shaw, and Souryal 1992).

Research indicates that boot camps are successful in changing antisocial attitudes. It has been found that those individuals who successfully complete boot camp are more prosocial before their entry into the program than those who drop out. Second, from the time of entry until the completion of boot camp, participants have slightly higher reductions in antisocial attitudes than those incarcerated in prison. In addition, greater prosocial attitudes are discovered among boot camp graduates than among regular prisoners or probationers (Mackenzie and Shaw 1990).

Another main goal of boot camp programs is to reduce prison crowding. Some observers believe that the lower recidivism rates of boot camp graduates will result in fewer individuals going into prison, thereby reducing the need for prison space. A second way in which boot camps may affect prison overcrowding is through the reduction of time offenders spend in prison. Participants who graduate from boot camps are usually returned into the community much earlier than those incarcerated.

Studies have found that boot camps reduce the prison population only if the program focuses on prison-bound offenders. Mackenzie and Souryal discovered that program design was critical to the successful reduction of prison crowding. Programs that permitted correctional officials to select participants for the boot camp program were most likely to alleviate prison crowding because they maximized the probability of selecting offenders who would otherwise have been sent to prison. Other factors they discovered that affected the ability of boot camp programs to reduce prison crowding were the restrictiveness of eligibility and suitability criteria (i.e., stricter criteria divert fewer prison-bound offenders); length of the program (i.e., programs that keep participants in boot camp longer are less likely to reduce prison crowding); and size of the program and graduation rates (smaller programs and those that graduate fewer offenders keep fewer offenders out of prison). If boot camps are to reduce prison crowding, Mackenzie and Piquero (1994) note that the program must be carefully designed and controlled with this goal in mind.

Intermediate Punishments: How Well Do They Work?

In 1985, intermediate punishments were called the future of corrections (Sawyer 1985). But have they lived up to this original potential? Over ten years later, we have the ability to assess whether or not they have reached their goals, particularly in the areas of reducing prison populations, saving money, and deterring crime. The results of a several U.S evaluations are reviewed below in order to assess the success or failure of these programs.

Do Intermediate Punishments Reduce Prison Crowding?

This issue is perhaps the most critical for introducing IPs, as advocates argue that the number of offenders incarcerated into prison will decrease. However, as Morris and Tonry (1990:223–34) point out, this position is based on the belief that most individuals convicted of a serious crime are sent to prison, an assumption they point out is incorrect because "most felonies never were or are not now punished by imprisonment." They also claim that offenders placed on IPs would usually be placed on regular probation programs or on suspended sentence rather than those individuals who have been sentenced to prison. In addition, evaluations of IPs have discovered high rearrest rates for offenders, with the result that some states only report at best a 50 percent success rate of offenders completing the program (Erwin and Bennett 1987). Those who have found some effect of an IP on the total prison population have reported very low numbers. For example, in his evaluation of Georgia's ISP, Pearson (1987a) found there was a "saving" of 186 prison beds for a year, a number Tonry (1990) estimates would be unlikely to significantly reduce prison crowding. Tonry (1990:178) also argues that some IP programs may "fill more prison beds than they empty" because so few offenders from prison are actually placed into these programs. Instead, IP programs are filled by offenders who normally would have been placed on regular probation programs because they are low-risk offenders.

Petersilia (1987a), in her review of five electronic monitoring programs, discovered the majority of the individuals who ended up on them were not from prison, but rather offenders who were on regular probation programs. With few exceptions, "participants in the program had only been convicted of misdemeanors" (Johnson et al. 1989:156–57). As the U.S. General Accounting Office (1990:29) noted in its assessment of IPs:

> It is clear that existing programs have had little effect and are unlikely to have a sizeable one on prison populations. This is because most

programs have served a relatively small population of offenders. Programs that include *hundreds* of offenders cannot significantly affect prison populations that run into *tens of thousands.*

Are Intermediate Punishments a Cost-Saving Alternative?

One of the most common arguments for implementing IP programs is that they cost less than incarceration programs. Most of these arguments are based on average per-offender costs, which many have pointed out is a misleading unit of analysis on which to evaluate the financial savings of an IP program. One reason for this is the length of time offenders are sentenced to prison or to an IP. Morris and Tonry (1990) point out that a direct comparison of the costs is misleading because if the average IP offender serves 12 months at a total cost of $3000 but would otherwise have served three months in prison at a final cost of $4000, the intensive supervision program costs more, not less.

Another reason why this comparison is misleading is because there is an assumption that all offenders are diverted into IP from prison. However, many IP participants (a figure that varies from 50 percent to 80 percent depending on the type and location of the program) are diverted from regular probation programs. According to Tonry (1990:182), for those on ISP instead of regular probation, "ISP costs per day are six times higher than the cost of ordinary probation." Also, many offenders on IP programs may be caught for technical violations or new crimes and be sent to prison. So, if 30 percent of IP offenders are sent to prison, the additional time incarcerated has to be included into any comparison of costs.

Furthermore, most cost comparisons only look at the costs of building a new prison but ignore the cost of operating an IP, which is labour-intensive. If 25 offenders on an IP require the hiring and training of four to eight new employees, this "increases direct outlays in the form of salaries and expanded overhead expenses, but also produces longer-term financial commitments in the form of employment benefits and pensions" (U.S. General Accounting Office 1990:27).

When all costs, both direct and marginal, are factored in, any savings may be limited. For example, in their study of 14 ISPs, Petersilia and Turner (1993:309) reported that in "no site did ISP result in cost-savings during the one year follow-up period." This was due mainly to the large number of technical violations, revocations, and incarcerations and the cost of court appearances, resulting in costs up to twice as high as those for routine probation and parole supervision.

In their study of home confinement in Arizona, Palumbo et al. (1992) discovered that, due to organizational operating problems, the actual cost of the program exceeded the cost of prison. They determined that the key factor in the higher rate of costs was that while the IP programs were increasing the number of program participants, so were the prisons. As Palumbo et al.

(1992:238) report, if "an alternative is not used as a way of reducing the total number of prison beds in use, or to eliminate some of these institutions, then alternatives to incarceration cannot be cost-effective." This reasoning is supported by Tonry (1990:180), who, after analyzing the full potential of the cost-saving measures of IP programs, came to the conclusion that "only when the numbers of people diverted from prison by a new program permit the closing of all or a major part of an institution or the cancellation of construction plans will there be substantial savings."

Another reason why intermediate punishments are thought to be cost-effective is because many of them charge a fee to the offenders participating on them. Renzema and Skelton (1990:14) point out that, in the programs they reviewed, approximately 67 percent of all offenders pay fees. The average cost is $200 a month, with probationers paying "an average of $155 a month while inmates pay an average of $228 a month. A few programs charge clients as much as $15 a day for monitoring."

Tonry (1990) also points out a significant error made by those who evaluate the cost savings of IP programs: specifically, they fail to include the cost of recidivists in their analysis. With recidivism rates of about 40 to 50 percent, including this number in the cost-benefit analysis would substantially increase the costs of these programs. In addition, not all program participants come from prison. As a result, the higher the number of individuals placed onto an IP program directly from the courts, the lesser the savings because less people are being taken out of prison.

Can Intermediate Punishments Control Crime?

The third major issue concerning intermediate punishment programs is their effectiveness in controlling crime. Advocates of these programs argue that more intensive supervision will, of necessity, reduce crime. Basing their arguments on the recidivism rates reported in early evaluation studies, they stress that IPs have the potential both to "control offenders in the community and to facilitate their growth to crime-free lives (Morris and Tonry 1990). However, some studies have discovered that many offenders released from IPs committed serious crimes once they are released into the community. Even low-risk offenders on IPs have been found to reoffend at a high rate once released. For example, 40 percent of low-risk offenders on Georgia's ISP reoffend, a figure approximately the same for medium- and high-risk offenders (Erwin 1987). Numerous studies (Petersilia and Turner 1986; Wallerstedt 1984) have found that those individuals released from IP programs often have high recidivism rates, many of their offences being serious crimes. In addition, many researchers have reported that these programs fail to result in any reduction in crime rates. Pearson (1986:443–44), for example, concluded that "we can be confident that ISP at least did not increase recidivism rates." Other researchers have reported high recidivism rates, including a 40 percent recidivism rate in Georgia (Erwin 1987).

In one of the most comprehensive analyses of its kind, Petersilia and Turner (1993) reported that in the 14 ISP programs they studied, no participants were rearrested less often, had a longer time before they were rearrested, or were arrested for less serious offences than those individuals on regular probation. When they included technical violations in their recidivism measure, "the record for ISP looks somewhat grimmer" (Petersilia and Turner 1993: 310–11). Approximately 65 percent of the ISP offenders recorded a technical violation in comparison with 38 percent of those offenders on regular probation. They also found no support for the argument that offenders arrested for technical violations reduced the incidence of any future criminal acts.

Will Intermediate Punishments Work?

The concerns raised about alternative sanctions do not mean that they should be abandoned as another failed experiment. Perhaps there was too great an expectation that these programs would somehow "save" the current correctional crisis by reducing prison populations and recidivism as well as making communities safer. As Finckenhauer (1982) has noted, the history of corrections is filled with great expectations but, at the same time, littered with one failed panacea after another. New programs are attractive because they always promise to do so much, at a minimal cost. When programs are poorly conceived and implemented, and the resulting programs fail to reach their goals, it is not surprising they are labelled as another program that "didn't work."

Yet a number of important lessons can be learned by examining the rise and growth of alternative correctional programs, particularly the rapid growth in intermediate punishments. The first is that the number of offenders entering the correctional system is beyond the control of criminal justice officials. The political demands for tougher penalties and a "war on crime" can have a significant impact on the operation of all facets of our criminal justice system. The police are under more pressure to arrest and charge more alleged criminals; the courts are under more pressure to deal with these alleged offenders more speedily. But when offenders enter the correctional system, often with long sentences, correctional officials have a hard time knowing where to put them.

Underlying these intermediate punishment programs is the theory of deterrence. The results to date have revealed not only that specific programs do not reach their objectives, but also that the theory of deterrence is open to question. However, there is emerging evidence that some intermediate punishment programs, when merged with rehabilitation-based principles, achieve more favourable results (Gendreau et al. 1994). For example, the inclusion of rehabilitation programs has been recommended by researchers who have evaluated programs based on deterrence and who have seen the high rates of recidivism in these programs. For example, in their study of the Florida Community Control Program, Smith and Akers (1993:228) noted that "a more persuasive model might move back in the direction of community reintegration and propose that occupation skill enhancement, education, substance abuse treatment, behavior modification and other practices be added to the principle of closely supervising home confinement." And in their analysis of the 14 sites experimenting with intermediate supervision probation, Petersilia and Turner (1993:321) report that in the three California locations included in their study, offenders who "received counselling, held jobs, paid restitution, and did community service were arrested 10–20 percent less often than were other offenders." These comments are consistent with a growing literature on the potential effectiveness of intermediate punishment programs. Any such program would have to identify which offenders would receive treatment. This means that the risk, need, and responsivity principles have to be introduced (Andrews et al. 1990). As Petersilia and Turner (1993:320) point out, placing drug-dependent offenders into an ISP program that "forbids drug use, provides frequent drug testing, and provides no assured access to drug treatment virtually guarantees high violation rates." The potential for intermediate punishments with a strong rehabilitative component exists, but only if they "provide the opportunity to channel offenders into treatments that address criminogenic needs—sources of criminality that are not targeted and affected by surveillance and punishment" (Cullen, Wright, and Applegate 1995).

Summary

Intermediate punishments have developed rapidly to service the needs of both the social control system and offenders. These types of punishments fall between incarceration and probation, filling a need for the state to have a significant amount of control over offenders, but, at the same time, for offenders to live in the community. This allows governments to save money, open up spaces in prison for more violent offenders, and give the appearance that sentences are more fair.

The most common form of intermediate punishment is intensive supervision probation, which is characterized by close contact between probation officers and their clients. Home confinement is increasing in popularity, and it is usually accompanied by an electronic monitoring device. Boot camps are another alternative, usually directed toward young adults and youths and developed on the basis that a short-term "shock" will help them avoid future offences.

To date, advocates say that these programs have successfully met their goals. Researchers are much more cautious in their conclusions, although many program components have been identified as being crucial factors in reducing future criminality. Despite their successes or failures to date, these programs continue to flourish in the hope they are low-cost, high-security alternatives to traditional approaches of punishment.

Discussion Questions

1. Is home confinement a "real" punishment? Explain your answer.
2. Compare and contrast "regular" probation with intensive supervision probation.
3. Do boot camps reduce crime? Give reasons for your answer.
4. What are the most successful aspects of intermediate punishment programs?
5. Why do you think Canada has been slower to introduce intermediate punishments than the United States?
6. Compare and contrast active and passive electronic monitoring programs.
7. Do intermediate punishments really assist in reintegrating offenders back into society? Explain.
8. Discuss the goals of intermediate punishments. Why were they introduced?

Suggested Readings

Ball, Richard A., C. Ronald Huff, and J. Robert Lilly. *House Arrest and Correctional Policy: Doing Time at Home*. Newbury Park, Sage, 1988.

Byrne, J.M., A.J. Lurigio, and J. Petersilia, eds. *Smart Sentencing: The Emergence of Intermediate Sanctions*. Newbury Park, Calif.: Sage, 1992.

Feeley, M., and J. Simon. "The New Penology: Notes on the Emerging Strategy of Corrections and Its Implications." *Criminology* 30 (1992):449–74.

Finckenhauer, J. *Scared Straight! and the Panacea Phenomenon*. Englewood Cliffs, N.J.: Prentice-Hall, 1982.

Gordon, D.R. *The Justice Juggernaut: Fighting Street Crime, Controlling Citizens*. New Brunswick, N.J.: Rutgers University Press, 1990.

Hartland, A.T., ed. *The Search for Effective Correctional Interventions*. Newbury Park, Calif.: Sage, 1995.

McCarthy, Belinda R., ed. *Intermediate Punishments: Intensive Supervision, Home Confinement, and Electronic Surveillance*. Monsey, N.Y.: Criminal Justice Press, 1987.

Morris, N., and M. Tonry. *Beyond Prison and Probation: Intermediate Punishments in a Rational Sentencing System*. New York: Oxford University Press, 1990.

Glossary

Absolute jurisdiction indictable offence. Offences for which the accused has to be tried by a provincial court judge unless the judge determines it has to be tried by another way. These offences are found in p. 553 of the Criminal Code.

Actus reus. The illegal act. It involves either the commission of an act, such as an assault, or the failure to act, such as failing to take proper safety measures.

Adjudication. The determination of guilt or innocence of the accused by a judge.

Adversarial system. The procedure used to determine truth in a criminal court system. According to this system, the burden is on the state to prove the charges against the accused beyond a reasonable doubt.

Appeal. A review of lower court decisions or proceedings by a higher court.

Appearance notice. Issued to the accused requiring him to appear in court on a specific date and time. It is issued to the accused instead of arresting him.

Arraignment. The process in which the accused hears the formal charges laid against him and pleads either guilty or innocent.

Arrest. The taking into custody of a person thought to have committed a crime. The legal requirement for an arrest is "reasonable and probable grounds."

Auburn prison system. The prison system developed in New York in the 19th century that favoured a tier-based prison facility and congregate working conditions for inmates.

To charge a jury. The judge informs a jury of the relevant evidence of a case and the types of decisions the jury can reach about the accused.

Charge bargaining. A prosecutor's decision to reduce the number of charges against the accused in return for a plea of guilty and for information.

Classical approach. An approach to the study of criminology that emphasizes reforming laws and improving the criminal justice system as the best way to resolve the crime problem.

Common law. Early English law, developed by judges, based on local customs and feudal rules and practices. Common law formed the basis of the standardized criminal law system in England.

Community policing. A police strategy that emphasizes the reduction of fear, community involvement, decentralization of the police force, neighbourhood police stations, and order maintenance as an alternative approach to fighting crime.

Concurrence. Forms the legal relationship between the guilty mind and the illegal act.

Deterrence. The prevention of crime before it occurs by threatening individuals with criminal sanctions.

Deterrence, general. A crime-control policy that aims to stop potential law violators from engaging in illegal behaviour. It favours certain policies—such as long prison sentences—that underscore the fact that the pain associated with crime outweighs the gain.

Deterrence, specific. A crime-control policy that advocates punishment severe enough to convince convicted offenders never again to engage in criminal behaviour.

Deterrence model. One of the four main models of criminal justice. It envisions a criminal justice system with no discretion, more police, and longer prison terms. It is related to the crime control model and classical school of criminology.

Directed patrol. A police patrol strategy. Police officers are told to spend much of their patrol time in certain areas, to use certain tactics, and to watch for certain types of offences.

Discretion. The use of individual decision-making and choice to influence the operation of the criminal justice system. All the major institutions of the criminal justice system—police, courts, corrections—make decisions that influence the outcome of cases.

Disparity. The lack of uniformity in sentencing, which leads to concern about discrimination against particular groups in society. Disparity involves arbitrary differences between sentences against offenders convicted of the same crime.

Election indictable offence. An offence in which the accused (or his lawyer) may decide on what type of criminal court he wishes to to be tried in.

Electronic monitoring (EM). A system designed to insure an offender completes the terms of a court order. EM is the regulatory aspect of home confinement.

Employment equity. The federal government policy that stresses that minorities should be represented in the work force.

Fact bargaining. A type of plea bargaining in which the prosecutor decides not to introduce certain facts about the offence or offender into the court record.

Fine. One of the most common sentences in Canada. Failure to pay a fine is one of the most common reasons for the incarceration of offenders.

First-degree murder. Planned and deliberate murder—though it does not have to be planned or deliberate when the victim is a police officer, a prison guard, an individual working in a prison, or a similar individual acting in the course of duty.

Foot patrol. A type of police patrol linked to community policing. It takes police officers out of cars and places them on a beat, which allows them to strengthen ties with community residents.

Full parole. The early release of an inmate from prison subject to conditions established by a parole board. Full parole can be granted to inmates after they serve one-third of their sentence, unless their sentence specifies otherwise.

Haebus corpus. A judicial order that requests that an individual detaining another give reasons for the capture and detention. It is a legal device used to request a judicial review of the reasons for an individual's detention and the conditions of detention.

Home confinement. A type of intermediate punishment. It allows offenders to live at home while serving their sentence.

Hybrid offence. An offence that may proceed either as an indictable or summary conviction offence. The decision on how to proceed is usually made by the Crown prosecutor.

Incarceration. Occurs when an offender receives a sentence that stipulates that he spend time in either a provincial or federal correctional institution.

Indictable offence. An offence which the accused must, or has the right to, choose between a trial by judge and a trial by jury, with the exception of a few minor offences.

Infanticide. One of the four types of murder. It was introduced in 1948, and only a woman can be charged. The Criminal Code defines an infant as a child under one year of age.

Information, to lay an. The presentation to a judge of a sworn written allegation alleging the individual named in the document has committed an offence. Informations are also used to obtain search warrants.

Judicare. A type of legal aid practised in Canada. It combines elements of the public defender and judicare models.

Jury. A group of individuals whose function is to determine guilt or innocence of the accused. A jury consists of 12 citizens.

Justice model. A model of criminal justice that emphasizes legal rights, justice, and fairness. A main feature of this model is that any punishment should be proportional to the seriousness of the crime.

Legal aid. A government-supported system that allows individuals who are earning below a certain amount to receive free legal services.

Legalistic. An approach that stresses the type of crime committed as opposed to any extraneous factors such as the race or social class of the offender.

Lower court. A general term used to describe those courts that have jurisdiction over summary conviction offences. Most pleas are made in these courts.

Management of demand. A police organizational strategy that categorizes requests for service and analyzes them as to their priority, resulting in differential police responses.

Manslaughter. Unintentional homicide requiring either criminal negligence or an unlawful act.

Mens rea. A prerequisite of criminal conduct is the "guilty mind." Mens rea is based on the belief that people can control their behaviour and choose between right and wrong. It commonly is used to refer to the intent to commit a crime.

Parole. The conditional release of an inmate from his unfinished sentence of incarceration into the community. The decision to parole an individual is made by a parole board, which determines the conditions of the release.

Pennsylvania system. A prison system developed in the 19th century that emphasized solitary confinement for all inmates so they could reflect on individual penitence.

Positivist approach. A group of theories that stresses the scientific study of the criminal offender.

Preliminary inquiry. An inquiry made by a provincial court judge in a case involving an indictable offence in order to determine if there is enough evidence to order the accused to stand trial.

Pre-sentence report. An investigation usually conducted by a probation officer before the sentencing of a convicted offender. The report typically contains information about the offender's personal background, education, previous employment, and family as well as interviews with family members, neighbours, and employer.

Probation. A sentence that allows a convicted offender to serve his sentence in the community, subject to certain conditions for a designated time period.

Problem-oriented policing. A style of policing that emphasizes a focus on a specific crime problem. It features a proactive rather than reactive approach to fighting crime.

Procedural law. The rules that define the operation of criminal proceedings. It specifies the methods that are to be followed in obtaining warrants, conducting trials, sentencing convicted offenders, and reviewing cases by appeal courts. Its main purpose is to describe how substantive offences are to be enforced.

Public defender. A type of legal aid. Legal aid lawyers are employed by a provincial government to help with the legal defence of an accused.

Recidivism rate. The repetition of criminal behaviour. It is measured by criminal acts committed by persons under correctional supervision or technical violations of individuals on probation or parole and lead to a change in legal status.

Rehabilitation. A correctional philosophy that emphasizes the treatment of conditional offenders and their reintegration into the community.

Rehabilitation model. One of the four criminal justice models. It differs from the other models in its support of discretion in the system and the treatment of the offender. It is related to the positive school of criminology.

Revised Uniform Crime Reports. Reports that record incident-based criminal events. Each crime incident is analyzed for a number of individual characteristics, e.g., the relationship between offender and victim. (See also Uniform Crime Reporting.)

Revocation. The withdrawal of probation or parole orders due to the commission of a new offence or the violation of any condition set out in a parole or probation order.

Search warrant. An authorization granted to police officers by a judge that authorizes officers to search a specific place.

Second-degree murder. Any murder that is not first degree is second degree. The maximum punishment for second-degree murder is life imprisonment.

Selective incapacitation. The incarceration for long periods of time of a select group of "chronic" offenders who commit numerous violent offences.

Selective incapacitation model. One of the four criminal justice models. It emphasizes long prison sentences for the small number of individuals who chronically commit violent crimes. It rejects any type of favourable discretionary actions for those offenders.

Sentence bargaining. A form of plea bargaining that involves the reduction of a sentence in return for a plea of guilty or information.

Sexual assault. Classified as a violent crime. Legislation introduced in 1983 created three levels of sexual assault, which emphasize that these offences involve physical violence directed against an individual.

Social service. A view held by some police officers that their prime function is to assist the public in as many ways as possible. A purely legalistic approach is rejected except in extreme cases.

Statute law. Laws created by legislatures in a response to changing social conditions and public opinion.

Statutory release. A program designed to release most incarcerated offenders who have not been able to obtain full parole and have served two-thirds of their sentence.

Summary conviction. Minor offences tried on the basis of the information without other pre-trial formalities.

Summons. An order by the court requiring the appearance of the accused or a witness before it.

Superior court. The court where most indictable offences are tried, either by judge or by judge and jury.

Suspended sentence. A prison term that is delayed by a judge's order while the convicted offender is involved in community treatment. If this treatment is successful, the individual is allowed to remain in the community.

Supreme Court exclusive indictable offence. Involves those individuals who are charged with first- or second-degree murder. The case is tried by a federally appointed judge and jury.

Temporary absence. Permits the release of offenders from federal institutions so that that can access programs and various services within the community.

TA, escorted. An offender's permitted temporary absence, for a brief period, from a correctional facility, on the basis of having an escort.

TA, unescorted. An offender's permitted temporary absence, for a relatively long period of time, from a correctional facility, in order to integrate that individual into the outside community.

Total institution. Institutions that eliminate all daily and normal inmate contact with the outside world.

Uniform Crime Reporting System. National crime statistics maintained by the RCMP in Ottawa. Offences are grouped into three categories: crimes against the person, crimes against property, and "other" crimes. (See also Revised Uniform Crime Reports.)

Venir. The group of citizens called for jury duty, from which all juries are selected. This is also referred to as jury array. The purpose of the venir is to eliminate persons who are unqualified to be jurors.

Victim Impact Statement. The option given to the victim of a crime to complete a form and detail what has happened to that victim as a result of the crime. If the victim decides to fill out the form, it is placed in the case file and may have an impact on the case, particularly at the sentencing stage.

Victimless crime. Crimes for which there are no complainants or victims. It refers to consensual social exchanges punished by criminal law, e.g., selling sex and drug use.

Warrant. An authorization that grants an individual, usually a police officer, to do what is specified in the warrant, e.g., to arrest someone.

Warrantless search. Those conditions that allow an individual, usually a police officer, to search a place without a warrant, e.g., doctrine of plain view.

Watchman. A style of policing that emphasizes a reactive style of policing rather than a proactive or preventative style.

References

Abbate, G. 1995. "Native Sentences Require Review." *The Globe and Mail.* August 26: A3.

Abell, J., and E. Sheehy, eds. 1993. *Criminal Law and Procedure: Cases, Context, Critique.* North York, Ont.: Captus Press.

Abella, R.S. (1984). *Report of the Commission on Equality in Employment.* Ottawa: Supply and Services Canada.

Abraham, J.D., J.C. Feld, R.W. Harding, and S. Skura. 1981. "Police Use of Lethal Force: A Toronto Perspective." *Osgoode Hall Law Journal* 19, no. 2: 199–236.

Adams, M. 1990. "Canadian Attitudes toward Crime and Justice." *Forum of Correctional Research* 2, no. 1: 10–13.

Adler, L. 1985. "Is Plea-Bargaining So Bad?" *The Globe and Mail.* January 5: 7.

Administrative Office of the U.S. Courts, Probation and Pretrial Services Division. 1991. *Home Confinement Policies and Procedures for Pretrial Defendants.* Draft report.

Advisory Committee on Multicultural Police Recruitment and Selection. 1989. *Interim Policy Recommendations to the Ottawa Board of Commissioners of Police on Multicultural Police Recruitment and Selection.* Ottawa: Ottawa Board of Commissioners of Police.

Allen, F. 1981. *The Decline of the Rehabilitative Ideal: Penal Purpose and Social Purpose.* New Haven, Conn.: Yale University Press.

Allen, R.A. 1992. "Selective Prosecution: A Viable Criminal Defence in Canada?" *Criminal Law Quarterly* 34: 414–42.

Alschuler, A.W. 1980. "Sentencing Reform and Parole Release Guidelines." *University of Colorado Law Review* 51: 237–45.

American Bar Association. 1986. *Standards Relating to Sentencing Alternatives and Procedures.* Chicago: American Bar Association.

American Friends Service Committee. 1971. *Struggle for Justice.* New York: Hill and Wang.

Anderson, P.R., and D.J. Newman. 1993. *Introduction to Criminal Justice,* 5th ed. Toronto: McGraw-Hill Ryerson.

Andrews, D.A. 1989. "Recidivism Is Predictable and Can Be Influenced: Using Risk Assessments to Reduce Recidivism." *Forum on Corrections Research* 1, no. 2: 11–17.

———, and J. Bonta. 1994. *The Psychology of Criminal Conduct.* Cincinnati: Anderson.

———, J. Bonta, and R.D. Hoge. 1990. "Classification for Effective Rehabilitation: Rediscovering Psychology." *Criminal Justice and Behavior* 17, no. 1: 19–52.

———, I. Zinger, R.D. Hoge, J. Bonta, P. Gendreau, and F.T. Cullen. 1990. "Does Correctional Treatment Work? A Clinically Relevant and Psychologically Informed Meta-Analysis." *Criminology* 28, no. 3: 369–404.

Asbury, K.E. 1989. "Innovative Policing: Foot Patrol in 31 Division, Metropolitan Toronto." *Canadian Police College Journal* 13, no. 3: 165–81.

Avison, D. 1994. "Clearing Space: Diversion Projects, Sentencing Circles, and Restorative Justice." In R. Gosse, J.Y. Henderson, and R. Carter, eds., *Continuing Poundmaker and Riel's Request.* Saskatoon: Purich, pp. 235–40.

Baird, S.C., and D. Wagner. 1990. "Measuring Diversion: The Florida Community Control Project." *Crime and Delinquency* 36: 112–25.

Balkin, J. 1988. "Why Policemen Don't Like Policewomen." *Journal of Police Science and Administration* 16, 29–38.

Ball, R.A., C.R. Huff, and J.R. Lilly. 1988. *House Arrest and Correctional Policy: Doing Time at Home.* Newbury Park, Calif.: Sage.

Barker, T., and D.L. Carter. 1986. *Police Deviance.* Cincinnati: Anderson.

Barnhorst, R., S. Barnhorst, and K.L. Clarke. 1992. *Criminal Law and the Canadian Criminal Code,* 2nd ed. Toronto: McGraw-Hill Ryerson.

Baumer, T.L., R.I. Mendelsohn, and C. Rhine. 1990. *Executive Summary—The Electronic Monitoring of Non-Violent Convicted Felons: An Experiment in Home Detention.* Washington, D.C.: National Institute of Justice.

Baunach, P.J., and N.H. Rafter. 1982. "Sex Role Operations: Strategies for Women Working in the Criminal Justice System." In N.H. Rafter and E.A. Stanko, eds., *Judge, Lawyer, Victim, Thief.* Boston: Northeastern University Press.

Bayley, D.H. 1993. "Strategy." In J. Chacko and S.E. Nancoo, eds., *Community Policing in Canada.* Toronto: Canadian Scholars' Press, pp. 39–46.

———, and J. Garofalo. 1989. "The Management of Violence by Police Patrol Officers." *Criminology* 27: 1–21.

Becker, G. 1968. "Crime and Punishment: An Economic Approach." *Journal of Political Economy* 76: 169–217.

Beirne, P., and J. Messerschmidt. 1991. *Criminology.* San Diego, Calif.: Harcourt Brace Jovanovich.

Belcourt, R., T. Nouwens, and L. Lefebvre. 1993. "Examining the Unexamined: Recidivism among Female Offenders." *Forum on Corrections Research* 5, no. 3: 10–14.

Berg, B., E. True, and M. Gertz. 1984. "Police, Riots, and Alienation." *Journal of Police Science and Administration* 12: 186–90.

Besozzi, C. 1993. "Recidivism: How Inmates See It." *Forum on Corrections Research* 5, no. 3: 35–38.

Besserer, S., and R. Craig Grimes. 1996. "The Courts." In L.W. Kennedy and V.F. Sacco, eds., *Crime Counts: A Criminal Event Analysis.* Scarborough, Ont.: Nelson Canada, pp. 271–92.

Bienvenue, R., and A.H. Latif. 1974. "Arrests, Dispositions, and Recidivism: A Comparison of Indians and Whites." *Canadian Journal of Criminology and Corrections* 16: 105–16.

Birkenmayer, A. 1995. *The Use of Community Corrections in Canada: 1993–1994.* Ottawa: Juristat.

Birkenmayer, A.C., and S. Jolly. 1981. *The Native Inmate in Ontario.* Toronto: Ontario Native Council on Justice.

Birnie, L.H. 1987. "The Bizarre Case of Charles Ng." *Influence,* June/July.

Bittner, E. 1980. *The Function of Police in Modern Society.* Weston, Mass.: Oelschlager, Gunn and Hain.

Bloch, P., and O. Anderson. 1974. *Policewomen on Patrol: Find Report.* Washington, D.C.: Police Foundation.

Blumberg, M. 1981. "Race and Police Shootings: An Analysis in Two Cities." In J. Fyfe, ed., *Contemporary Issues in Law Enforcement.* Beverly Hills, Calif.: Sage, pp. 152–66.

Blumstein, A.J., J. Cohen, S.E. Martin, and M. Tonry. 1983. *Research on Sentencing: The Search for Reform.* Washington, D.C.: National Academy Press.

Boldt, E., L. Hursh, S. Johnson, and W. Taylor. 1983. "Presentence Reports and the Incarceration of Natives." *Canadian Journal of Criminology* 25: 269–76.

Bonta, J., S. Lipinski, and M. Martin. 1992. "The Characteristics of Aboriginal Recidivists." *Canadian Journal of Criminology* 34, nos. 3–4: 517–22.

———. 1993. "Recidivists Tend to Be ..." *Forum on Correctional Research* 5, no. 3: 14–16.

Bottomley, A.K. 1990. "Parole in Transition: A Comparative Study of Origins, Developments, and Prospects for the 1990s." *Crime and Justice: A Review of Research,* Vol. 12. Chicago: University of Chicago.

Bowie, B.W. 1988a. *An Examination of Bill C-61: Proceeds of Crime Legislative Proposals.* Unpublished manuscript.

———. 1988b. *Asset Forfeiture: The Third Dimension to Drug Enforcement.* Ottawa: Royal Canadian Mounted Police.

Boyd, N. 1995. *Canadian Law: An Introduction.* Toronto: Harcourt Brace Canada.

Braiden, C. 1993. "Community-Based Policing: A Process for Change." In J. Chacko and S.E. Nancoo, eds., *Community Policing in Canada.* Toronto: Canadian Scholars' Press, pp. 211–32.

Brannigan, A. 1984. *Crimes, Courts, and Corrections: An Introduction to Crime and Social Control in Canada.* Toronto: Holt, Rinehart, and Winston.

Brantingham, P. 1985. "Judicare Counsel and Public Defenders: Case Outcome Differences." *Canadian Journal of Criminology* 27: 67–81.

Breckenridge, J. 1992. "New Police Policy on Domestic Violence Praised." *The Globe and Mail.* September 12: A9.

Brooks, L.W. 1989. "Police Discretionary Behavior: A Study of Style." In R.G. Dunham and G.P. Alpert, eds., *Critical Issues in Policing: Contemporary Readings.* Prospect Heights, Ill.: Waveland Press, pp. 121–45.

Brown, L., and C. Brown. 1978. *An Unauthorized History of the RCMP,* 2nd ed. Toronto: Lewis and Samuel.

Brown, M.P., and S. Roy. 1995. "Manual and Electronic House Arrest: An Evaluation of Factors Related to Failure." In J. Smyka and W.L. Selke, eds., *Intermediate Sanctions: Sentencing in the 1990s.* Cincinnati: Anderson.

Brown, R.J., and K.P. O'Brien. 1993. "How Do Experts Make Parole Recommendations and Are They Accurate?" *Forum on Corrections Research* 5, no. 2: 3–4.

Brown, S., F. Esbensen, and G. Geis. 1991. *Criminology: Explaining Crime and Its Context.* Cincinnati: Anderson.

Brucker, T.M. 1992. "Disclosure and the Role of the Police in the Criminal Justice System." *Criminal Law Quarterly* 35, 57–76.

Brydges v. R. (1990), 1 S.C.R. 190.

Burns, P., and R.S. Reid. 1981. "Delivery of Criminal Legal Aid Services in Canada: An Overview of the Continuing 'Judicature versus Public Defender' Debate." *UBC Law Review* 15, 403–29.

Burris, C.A., and P. Jaffe. 1982. "Wife Abuse as a Crime: The Impact of Police Laying Charges." *Canadian Journal of Criminology* 25, no. 3: 309–18.

Burtch, B.E., and R.V. Ericson. 1979. *The Silent System: An Inquiry into Prisoners Who Suicide/and Annotated Bibliography.* Toronto: Centre for Criminology, University of Toronto.

Byrne, J.M. 1990. "The Future of Intensive Probation Supervision and the New Intermediate Sanctions." *Crime and Delinquency* 36: 6-41.

———, and L. Kelly. 1989. *Restructuring Probation as an Intermediate Punishment: An Evaluation of the Implementation and Impact of the Massachusetts Intensive Probation Supervision Program: Final Report.* Washington, D.C.: National Institute of Justice.

————, A.J. Lurigio, and C. Baird. 1989. "The Effectiveness of the New Intensive Supervision Programs." *Research in Corrections* 2, no. 2: 1–48.

————, and Pattavina. 1992. "The Effectiveness Issue: Assessing What Works in the Adult Community Corrections Program." In J.M. Byrne, A.J. Lurigio, and J. Petersilia, eds., *Smart Sentencing: The Emergence of Intermediate Punishment.* Newbury Park, Calif.: Sage, pp. 281–303.

Cahn, M.F., and J. Tien. 1981. *An Alternative Approach in Police Response: Wilmington Management of Demand Program.* Cambridge, Mass.: Public Systems Evaluation.

Camp, G., and C.G. Camp. 1993. *The Corrections Yearbook: Probation and Parole.* South Salem, N.Y.: Criminal Justice Institute.

Campbell, A.K. 1990. "Sentencing Reform in Canada." *Canadian Journal of Criminology* 32: 387–95.

Campbell Research Associates. 1992. *Review and Monitoring of Child Sexual Abuse Cases in Hamilton-Wentworth, Ontario.* Ottawa: Department of Justice.

Canada. 1984. *Report of the Commission on Equality in Employment.* Ottawa: Supply and Services Canada.

————. 1988. *Action on Drug Abuse: Making a Difference.* Ottawa: Minister of Supply and Services.

Canadian Centre for Justice Statistics. 1992. *Legal Aid in Canada: 1990–91.* Ottawa: Canadian Centre for Justice Statistics.

————. 1982. *Homicides of Police Officers in Canada.* Ottawa: Statistics Canada.

————. 1991. *Adult Correctional Services in Canada.* Ottawa: Statistics Canada.

————. 1993. *Longitudinal Court Outcome Study of Individuals Accused of Homicide Reported in 1988.* Ottawa: Statistics Canada.

————. 1994. *Canadian Crime Statistics, 1992.* Ottawa: Statistics Canada.

Canadian Criminal Justice Association. 1987. *Attitudes toward Parole.* Ottawa: Canadian Criminal Justice Association.

Canadian Sentencing Commission. 1987. *Sentencing Reform: A Canadian Approach.* Ottawa: Minister of Supply and Services.

Canfield, C., and L. Drinan. 1981. Comparative Statistics Native and Non-Native Federal Inmates—A Five-Year History. Ottawa: Correctional Service of Canada.

Caron, R. 1982. *Go-Boy!* Toronto: Hamlyn.

Carrington, D.O. 1991. *Crime and Punishment in Canada: A History.* Toronto: McClelland and Stewart.

Casey, M. 1986. "Parole—A Purely Personal View." *The Correctional Review* 1, no. 1: 19–20.

Chappell, D., and L. Graham. 1985. *Police Use of Deadly Force: Canadian Perspectives.* Toronto: Centre of Criminology.

Chard, J. 1995a. *Factfinder on Crime and the Administration of Justice in Canada.* Ottawa: Juristat.

————. 1995b. *Breaking and Entering in Canada.* Ottawa: Juristat.

Cheever, J. 1990. "House Arrest Seen as Solution for Crowding Hard Time." *National Law Journal.* March 26: 51.

Clairmont, D. 1990. *To the Forefront: Community-Based Zone Policing in Halifax.* Ottawa: Canadian Police College.

Clark, S. 1989. *Sentencing Patterns and Sentencing Options Relating to Aboriginal Offenders.* Ottawa: Department of Justice, Research and Development Directorate.

Clear, T. 1994. *Harm in American Penology: Offenders, Victims, and Their Communities.* Albany, N.Y.: SUNY.

————. 1995. "Correction beyond Prison Walls." In J.F. Sheley, ed., *Criminology,* 2nd ed. Belmont, Calif.: Wadsworth, pp. 453–75.

————, and P. Hardyman. 1990. "The New Intensive Supervision Movement." *Crime and Delinquency* 36: 42–60.

Clemmer, D. 1958. *The Prison Community.* New York: Holt, Rinehart, and Winston.

Clouthier v. Langlois (1990), 53 C.C.C. (3d) 257.

Cohen, M., and J.T. McEwen. 1984. *Handling Calls for Service: Alternatives to Traditional Policing.* Washington, D.C.: National Institute of Justice.

Cole, D.P., and A. Manson. 1990. *Release from Imprisonment: The Law of Sentencing, Parole, and Judicial Review.* Toronto: Carswell.

Committee for the Study of Incarceration. 1975. *Doing Justice.* New York: Hill and Wang.

Cooley, D. 1992. "Prison Rules and the Informal Rules of Social Control." *Forum on Corrections Research* 4, no. 3: 31–36.

Corbett, R., and G. Marx. 1992. "Emerging Technofallacies in the Electronic Monitoring Movement." In J.M. Byrne, A.J. Lurigio, and J. Petersilia, eds., *Smart Sentencing: The Emergence of Intermediate Sanctions.* Newbury Park, Calif.: Sage, pp. 85–100.

Cordner, G.W., 1981. "The Effects of Directed Patrol." In J.J. Fyfe, ed., *Contemporary Issues in Law Enforcement.* Beverly Hills, Calif.: Sage, pp. 37–58.

————, and D.C. Hale. 1992. *What Works in Policing? Operations and Administration Examined.* Cincinnati: Anderson.

————, and R.C. Trojanowicz. 1992. "Patrol." In G.W. Cordner and D.C. Hale, eds., *What Works in Policing? Operations and Administration Examined.* Cincinnati: Anderson, pp. 14–25.

Correctional Service of Canada. 1990a. "A Profile of Federal Community Corrections." *Forum on Corrections Research* 2, no. 2: 8–13.

————. 1990b. *Creating Choices: Report of the Task Force on Federally Sentenced Women.* Ottawa: Correctional Service of Canada.

————. 1994. *Corrections in Canada.* Ottawa: Correctional Services Canada.

Cox, K. 1995. "Canada Putting Private Jails on Trial." *The Globe and Mail.* May 8: A4.

Crawford, B., and C. Stark-Adamec. 1994. "Women in Canadian Urban Policing: Why Are They Leaving?" In N. Larsen, ed., *The Canadian Criminal Justice System: An Issues Approach to the Administration of Justice.* Toronto: Canadian Scholars' Press.

Criminal Justice Newsletter. 1993. "California Passes a Tough Three-Strikes-You're-Out Law." 24, April 4: 6.

Crow, C. 1994. "Patterns of Discrimination: Aboriginal Justice in Canada." In N. Larsen, ed., *The Canadian Criminal Justice System: An Issues Approach to the Administration of Justice.* Toronto: Canadian Scholars' Press, pp. 431–52.

Culhane, C. 1985. *Still Barred from Prison: Social Injustice in Canada.* Montreal: Black Rose.

Cullen, F.T., and P. Gendreau. 1989. "The Effectiveness of Correctional Rehabilitation: Reconsidering the 'Nothing Works' Debate." In L. Goodstein and D. MacKenzie, eds., *American Prisons: Issues in Research and Policy.* New York: Plenum, pp. 23–44.

————, and K. Gilbert. 1982. *Reaffirming Rehabilitation.* Cincinnati: Anderson.

————, E.J. Latessa, V.S. Burton, and L.X. Lombardo. 1993. "The Correctional Orientation of Prison Wardens: Is the Rehabilitative Ideal Supported?" *Criminology* 31, no. 1: 69–92.

————, B.G. Link, and C.W. Poulanzi. 1982. "The Seriousness of Crime Revisited: Have Attitudes toward White-Collar Crime Changed?" *Criminology* 20: 83–102.

————, W.J. Maakestad, and G. Cavender. 1987. *Corporate Crime under Attack: The Ford Pinto Case and Beyond.* Cincinnati: Anderson.

————, J.P. Wright, and B.K. Applegate. 1995. "Control in the Community: The Limits of Reform?" In A.J. Hartland, ed., *The Search for Effective Correctional Interventions.* Newbury Park, Calif.: Sage.

Currie, E. 1986. *Confronting Crime: An American Challenge.* New York: Pantheon.

D'Alessio, S.J., and L. Stolzenberg. 1995. "The Impact of Sentencing Guidelines on Jail Incarceration in Minnesota." *Criminology* 33, no. 2: 283–302.

Daubney Committee. 1988. *Taking Responsibility: Report of Standing Committee on Justice and Solicitor-General on Its Review of Sentencing, Conditional Release and Related Aspects of Corrections.* D. Daubney, chair. Ottawa: Queen's Printer.

Davis, T. 1995. "For Sale: Justice for All?" *Winnipeg Free Press.* February 7: B3.

Depew, R. 1992. "Policing Native Communities: Some Principles and Issues in Organizational Theory." *Canadian Journal of Criminology* 34, nos. 3–4: 461–78.

Desroches, F.J. 1995. *Force and Fear: Robbery in Canada.* Scarborough, Ont.: Nelson Canada.

Dickson-Gilmore, J. 1992. "Finding the Ways of the Ancestors: Cultural Change and the Invention of Separate Legal Systems." *Canadian Journal of Criminology* 34, nos. 3–4: 479–502.

Donald, P.J. 1992. *Proceeds of Crime Legislation.* Vancouver: n.p.

Doob, A.N., and A. Cavouklian. 1977. "The Effect of Revoking Bail: *R. v. Demeter.*" *Criminal Law Quarterly* 19: 196–202.

————, and J.V. Roberts. 1982. *Crime and the Official Response to Crime: The Views of the Canadian Public.* Ottawa: Department of Justice.

————. 1983. *An Analysis of the Public's View of Sentencing.* Ottawa: Department of Justice.

————. 1989. "Sentencing and Public Opinion: Taking False Shadows for True Substances." *Osgoode Hall Law Journal* 27: 491–515.

————. 1992. "Community Sanctions and Imprisonment: Hoping for a Miracle but Not Bothering Even to Pray for It." *Canadian Journal of Criminology* 32, no. 3: 415–28.

Drucker, T.M. 1992. "Disclosure and the Role of the Police in the Criminal Justice System." *Criminal Law Quarterly* 35: 57–76.

Dubienski, I., and S. Skelly. 1970. "Analysis of Arrests for the Year 1969 in the City of Winnipeg with Particular Reference to Arrests of Persons of Indian Descent." Cited in C. LaPrairie, "The Role of Sentencing in the Over-Representation of Aboriginal People in Correctional Institutions." *Canadian Journal of Criminology* 32: 429–40.

DuWors, R. 1992. *Robbery in Canada.* Ottawa: Juristat.

Eck, J.E. 1983. *Solving Crimes: The Investigation of Burglary and Robbery.* Washington, D.C.: Police Executive Research Forum.

————. 1992. "Criminal Investigation." In G.W. Cordner and D.C. Hale, eds., *What Works in Policing? Operations and Administration Examined.* Cincinnati: Anderson, pp. 26–33.

————, and W. Spelman. 1987. "Problem-Solving: Problem-Oriented Policing in Newport News." *Research in Brief.* Washington, D.C.: National Institute of Justice.

Eckstedt, J.W. 1985. *Justice in Sentencing: Offenders' Perceptions.* Ottawa: Canadian Sentencing Commission.

————, and C.T. Griffiths. 1988. *Corrections in Canada: Policy and Practice,* 2nd ed. Toronto: Butterworths.

Ellerby, L. 1994. "Community-Based Treatment of Aboriginal Offenders: Facing Realities and Exploring Realities." *Forum on Corrections Research* 6, no. 3: 23–25.

Elliot, D., 1989. "Criminal Justice Procedures in Family Violence Cases." In L. Ohlin and M. Tonry, eds., *Crime and Justice: A Review of Research,* Vol. 11. Chicago: University of Chicago, pp. 427–80.

Ellis, D., and W. DeKeseredy. 1996. *The Wrong Stuff: An Introduction to the Sociological Study of Deviance,* 2nd ed. Scarborough, Ont.: Allyn and Bacon.

Erez, E., and P. Tontodonato. 1990. "The Effect of Victim Participation in Sentencing on Sentence Outcome." *Criminology* 28, no. 3: 451–74.

———. 1992. "Victim Participation in Sentencing and Satisfaction with Justice." *Justice Quarterly* 9, no. 3: 393–417.

Ericson, R. 1981. *Making Crime: A Study of Detective Work.* Toronto: University of Toronto.

———. 1982. *Reproducing Order: A Study of Police Patrol Work.* Toronto: University of Toronto.

———, and P.M. Baranek. 1982. *The Ordering of Justice: A Study of Accused Persons as Dependants in the Criminal Process.* Toronto: University of Toronto.

Erwin, B.S. 1986. "Turning up the Heat on Probationers in Georgia." *Federal Probation* 50, no. 2: 17–24.

———. 1987. *Final Evaluation Report: Intensive Probation Supervision in Georgia.* Atlanta, Ga.: Georgia Department of Corrections.

———, and L.A. Bennett. 1987. "New Dimensions in Probation: Georgia's Experience with Intensive Probation Supervision (ISP)." *Research in Brief.* Washington, D.C.: U.S. Government Printing Office.

Erwin, G. 1992. "Recidivism among Homicide Offenders." *Forum on Correctional Research* 4, no. 2: 7–9.

Eskridge, C.W. 1985. "Sentencing Guidelines: To Be or Not to Be?" *Federal Probation* 50: 70–76.

Fagan, J. 1989. "Cessation of Family Violence: Deterrence and Dissuasion." In L. Ohlin and M. Tonry, eds., *Crime and Justice: A Review of Research,* Vol. 11. Chicago: University of Chicago Press, pp. 100–51.

Farrington, D.P. 1993. "Understanding and Preventing Bullying." In M. Tonry, ed., *Crime and Justice: A Review of Research,* Vol. 17. Chicago: University of Chicago Press, pp. 381–458.

Farrington, K. 1992. "The Modern Prison as Total Institution? Public Perception versus Objective Reality." *Crime and Delinquency* 38: 6–26.

Fedorowycz, O. 1995. *Homicide in Canada—1994.* Ottawa: Juristat.

Feeley, M., and J. Simon. 1992. "The New Penology: Notes on the Emerging Strategy of Corrections and Its Implications." *Criminology* 30, no. 4: 449–75.

Felknes, G.T. 1991. "Affirmative Action in the Los Angeles Police Department." *Criminal Justice Research Bulletin* 6: 1–9.

Finckenhauer, J.Q. 1982. *Scared Straight! and the Panacea Phenomenon.* Englewood Cliffs, N.J.

Fine, S. 1994a. "Lawyers Object to Changes in Legal Aid." *The Globe and Mail.* September 24: A1, A5.

———. 1994b. "Jury Had Right to Acquit Farmer of Murder, Experts Say." *The Globe and Mail.* November 18: A6.

Finkler, H. 1992. "Community Participation in Socio-Legal Control: The Northern Context." *Canadian Journal of Criminology* 34, nos. 3–4: 503–12.

First Nations Policing Policy. 1992. Ottawa: Solicitor General of Canada.

Flanagan, T.J., and K. Maguire, eds. 1990. *Sourcebook of Criminal Justice Statistics— 1989.* Washington, D.C.: U.S. Department of Justice.

Fleming, T. 1981. "The Bawdy House 'Boys': Some Notes on Media, Sporadic Moral Crusades, and Selective Law Enforcement." *Canadian Criminology Forum:* 101–15.

Fogel, M. 1992. "Investigating Suicide." *Forum on Corrections Research* 4, no. 3: 8–9.

Foran, T., and M. Reed. 1996. "The Correctional System." In L.W. Kennedy and V.F. Sacco, eds., *Crime Counts: A Criminal Event Analysis.* Scarborough, Ont.: Nelson Canada, pp. 293–311.

Forcese, D. 1992. *Policing Canadian Society.* Scarborough, Ont.: Prentice Hall.

Forst, B.F., and J.C. Hernon. 1985. *The Criminal Justice Response to Victim Harm.* Washington, D.C.: U.S. Department of Justice.

Forum on Corrections Research. 1992a. "Violence and Suicide in Canadian Institutions: Some Recent Statistics." *Forum on Corrections Research* 4, no. 3: 3–5.

———. 1992b. "Inmate Suicide: What Do We Know?" *Forum on Corrections Research* 4, no. 3: 5–7.

———. 1991. Vol. 3, no. 2.

Frankel, M.F. 1972. *Criminal Sentences: Law without Order.* New York: Hill and Wang.

Frase, R.S. 1991. "Sentencing Reform in Minnesota, Ten Years After." *Minnesota Law Review* 75: 727–54.

———. 1995. "State Sentencing Guidelines: Still Going Strong." *Judicature* 78, no. 4: 173–79.

Freiberg, P. 1990. "Rehabilitation Is Effective if Done Well, Studies Say." *American Psychological Association Monitor.* September.

Friedland, M.L. 1965. *Detention before Trial.* Toronto: University Toronto Press.

Fyfe, J. 1982. "Blind Justice." *Journal of Criminal Law and Criminology* 73, 707–22.

Fyfe, J.J. 1988. "Police Use of Deadly Force: Research and Reform." *Justice Quarterly* 5, no. 2: 165–205.

Gall, G.L. 1990. *The Canadian Legal System,* 3rd ed. Toronto: Carswell.

Galt, V. 1996. "Stemming the Tide of School Violence." *The Globe and Mail,* February 2: A1, A6.

Gartner, R., and A.N. Doob. 1994. *Trends in Criminal Victimization: 1988–1993.* Ottawa: Juristat.

Geis, G. 1974. *Not the Law's Business.* New York: Schocken.

———, and A. Binder. 1991. "Sins of Their Children: Parental Responsibility for Juvenile Delinquency." *Notre Dame Journal of Law, Ethics and Public Policy* 5: 303–22.

Geller, W.A., and M.S. Scott. 1991. "Deadly Force: What We Know." In C.B. Klockars and S.D. Mastrofoski, eds., *Thinking about Police.* New York: McGraw-Hill, pp. 446–76.

Gendreau, P., F.T. Cullen, and J. Bonta. 1994. "Intensive Rehabilitation Supervision: The Next Generation in Community Corrections?" *Federal Probation* 58, no. 1: 72–78.

———, M. Papparozzi, T. Little, and M. Goddard. 1993. "Does Punishing Smarter Work? An Assessment of the New Generation of Alternative Sanctions in Probation." *Forum on Corrections Research* 5, no. 3: 31–34.

Gibb-Clark, M. 1985. "Has the Justice System Gone Askew in Ontario?" *The Globe and Mail.* August 15: A7.

————. 1995. "Ontario Lawyers Postpone Legal Aid Work." *The Globe and Mail.* September 12: B1.

Gibbon, A. 1994. "RCMP Ran Phony Exchange House in Drug Sting." *The Globe and Mail.* September 1: A4.

Gibbs, J. 1975. *Crime, Punishment, and Deterrence.* New York: Elseviser.

Gideon v. Wainwright, 372 U.S. 335 (1963).

Giliberti, C. 1990. "Study Probes Effectiveness of Victim Impact Statements." *Justice Research Notes* 1: 1–8.

Globe and Mail, The. 1994. "Lawyers Have a Big Stake in Legal-Aid System." September 29: A6.

Goff, C., and N. Nason-Clark. 1989. "The Seriousness of Crime in Fredericton, New Brunswick: Perceptions toward White-Collar Crime." *Canadian Journal of Criminology* 31: 19–34.

Goffman, E. 1961. *Asylums.* New York: Doubleday.

Goldstein, H. 1979. "Improving Policing: A Problem-Oriented Approach." *Crime and Delinquency* 25: 236–58.

Goldstein, J. 1960. "Police Discretion Not to Invoke the Criminal Justice Process: Low Visibility Decisions in the Administration of Justice." *Yale Law Journal* 69 (March):543–94.

Grant, B.A., and R.L. Belcourt. 1992. *An Analysis of Temporary Absences and the People Who Receive Them.* Ottawa: Correctional Services Canada.

Green, C., G. Andre, K. Kendall, T. Looman, and N. Potovi. 1992. "A Study of 133 Suicides among Canadian Federal Prisoners." *Forum on Corrections Research* 4, no. 3: 20–22.

Greenwood, P. 1982. *Selective Incapacitation.* Santa Monica, Calif.: Rand Corp.

————, and J. Petersilia. 1975. *The Criminal Investigation Process. Vol. III: Observations and Analysis.* Santa Monica, Calif.: Rand Corp.

Griffiths, C.T., J. Klein, and S.N. Verdun-Jones. 1980. *Criminal Justice in Canada.* Vancouver: Butterworths.

————, and S.N. Verdun-Jones. 1994. *Canadian Criminal Justice,* 2nd ed. Toronto: Harcourt Brace.

Griset, P.L. 1991. *Determinate Sentencing: The Promise and the Reality of Retributive Justice.* Albany, N.Y.: State University of New York Press.

Grosman, B. 1969. *The Prosecutor: An Inquiry into the Exercise of Discretion.* Toronto: University of Toronto.

Grossmann, M. 1992. "Two Perspectives on Aboriginal Female Suicides in Custody. *Canadian Journal of Criminology* 34, nos. 3–4: 403–16.

Gunn, R., and R. Linden. 1994. "The Processing of Child Sexual Assault Cases." In J.V. Roberts and R.M. Mohr, eds., *Confronting Sexual Assault: A Decade of Legal and Social Change.* Toronto: University of Toronto Press, pp. 84–112.

————, and C. Minch. 1988. *Sexual Assault: The Dilemma of Disclosure and the Question of Conviction.* Winnipeg: University of Manitoba.

Hagan, J. 1977. *The Disreputable Pleasures.* Toronto: McGraw-Hill Ryerson.

————, and C. Morden. 1981. "The Police Decision to Detain: A Study of Legal Labelling and Police Deviance." In C.D. Shearing, ed., *Organizational Police Deviance: Its Structure and Control.* Toronto: Butterworths, pp. 9–28.

Hale, D.C., and S.M. Wyland. 1993. "Dragons and Dinosaurs: The Plight of Patrol Women." *Police Forum* 3, no. 2: 1–6.

Hall, J. 1947. *Theft, Law and Society,* 2nd ed. Indianapolis: Bobbs-Merrill.

Hamparian, D.M., R.S. Schuster, S. Dinitz, and J.P. Conrad. 1978. *The Violent Few: A Study of Dangerous Juvenile Offenders*. Lexington, Mass.: Lexington Books.

Hann, R.G. 1973. *Decision Making in the Criminal Court System: A Systems Analysis*. Toronto: Centre of Criminology.

Harman, W.G., and R.G. Hann. 1986. *Release Risk Assessment: An Historical Descriptive Analysis*. Ottawa: Solicitor General of Canada.

Harris, M. 1986. *Justice Denied: The Law versus Donald Marshall*. Toronto: Totem.

Haskell, C. 1994. "The Impact of the Corrections and Conditional Release Act on Community Corrections." *Forum on Corrections Research* 6, no. 3: 45–46.

Havemann, P. 1986. "From Child Saving to Child Blaming: The Political Economy of the Young Offenders Act, 1908–1984." In S. Brickey and E. Comack, eds., *The Social Basis of Law*. Toronto: Garamond Press, pp. 225–42.

Hendrick, D. 1995. *Canadian Crime Statistics, 1994*. Ottawa: Juristat.

Hess, H. 1995. "The Cost of Crime." *The Globe and Mail*. March 17: A3.

Hogarth, J. 1971. *Sentencing as a Human Process*. Toronto: University of Toronto Press.

Hornick, J.P., B.A. Burrows, D.M. Phillips, and B. Leighton. 1993. "An Impact Evaluation of the Edmonton Neighborhood Foot-Patrol Program." In J. Chacko and S.E. Nancoo, eds., *Community Policing in Canada*. Toronto: Canadian Scholars' Press, pp. 311–32.

House of Commons Debates. May 26, 1966. *Hansard* VI: 62.

———, May 6, 1993. *Hansard* 132 (247): 19015–24.

Howard, R. 1996. "Cost of Crime Put at $16-Billion." *The Globe and Mail*. March 9: A1, A7.

Hudson, B. 1987. *Justice through Punishment: A Critique of the "Justice" Model of Corrections*. London: Macmillan.

Hung, K., and S. Bowles. 1995. *Public Perceptions of Crime*. Ottawa: Juristat.

Hunt, J.C. 1990. "The Logic of Sexism among the Police." *Women and Criminal Justice* 1, no. 2: 3–30.

Hunter v. Southam Inc. (1984), 14 C.C.C. (3d) 97.

Hyde, M. 1992. "Servicing Indian Reserves: The Amerindian Police." *Canadian Journal of Criminology* 34, nos. 3–4: 369–86.

Indermaur, D. 1987. "Public Perception of Sentencing in Perth, Western Australia." *Australian and New Zealand Journal of Criminology* 20: 163–83.

Irwin, J. 1974. "Adaptation to Being Corrected: Corrections from the Convict's Perspective." In D. Glazer, ed., *Handbook of Criminology*. Chicago: Rand-McNally, pp. 971–93.

Jackson, M. 1983. *Prisoners of Isolation: Solitary Confinement in Canada*. Toronto: University of Toronto.

Jacoby, J.E., and C.S. Dunn. 1987. "National Survey on Punishment for Criminal Offenses." Paper presented at the National Conference on Punishment for Criminal Offenses, Ann Arbor, Mich.

Jaffe, P., D. Reitzel, E. Hastings, and G. Austin. 1991. *Wife Assault as a Crime: The Perspectives of Victims and Police Officers on a Changing Policy in London, Ontario from 1989–1990*. London, Ont.: London Family Court.

———, D.A. Wolfe, A. Telford, and G. Austin. 1986. "The Impact of Police Charges in Incidents of Wife Abuse." *Journal of Family Violence* 1: 37–49.

Jain, H.C. 1994. "An Assessment of Strategies of Recruiting Visible-Minority Police Officers in Canada: 1985–1990." In R.C. Macleod and D. Schneiderman, eds., *Police Powers in Canada: The Evolution and Practice of Authority*, pp. 138–64.

Jamieson, K., and T. Flanagan, eds. 1989. *Sourcebook of Criminal Justice Statistics— 1988.* Washington, D.C.: U.S. Department of Justice.

Jamieson, S. 1973. *Industrial Relations in Canada,* 2nd ed. Toronto: Macmillan.

Jayewardene, C.H.S., and C.K. Talbot. 1990. *Police Recruitment of Ethnic Monirities.* Canadian Police College.

Jensen, H. 1989. "Hiding the Drug Money." *Maclean's.* October 23.

Johnson, B.R., L. Haugen, J.W. Maness, and P.P. Ross. 1989. "Attitudes towards Electronic Monitoring of Offenders: A Study of Probation Officers and Prosecutors." *Journal of Contemporary Criminal Justice* 5, no. 3: 153–64.

Johnson, H. 1991. *Public Perceptions of Crime and the Criminal Justice System.* Ottawa: Juristat.

———. 1995. *Children and Youths as Victims of Violent Crimes.* Ottawa: Juristat.

———. 1996. *Dangerous Domains.* Scarborough, Ont.: Nelson Canada.

———, and K. Rodgers. 1987. "Getting the Facts Straight: A Statistical Overview." In E. Adelberg and C. Currie, eds., *Too Few to Count: Canadian Women in Conflict with the Law,* 2nd ed. Vancouver: Press Gang.

Jolin, A., and B. Stipak. 1992. "Drug Treatment and Electronically Monitored Home Confinement: An Evaluation of the Community-Based Sentencing Option." *Crime and Delinquency* 38: 158–70.

Juristat. 1996. *Police Personnel and Expenditures in Canada—1994.* Ottawa: Canadian Centre for Justice Statistics.

Justice Report. 1990. Vol. 7, no. 3. Ottawa: Canadian Criminal Justice Association.

Kania, R.R.E., and W.C. Mackey. 1977. "Police Violence as a Function of Community Characteristics." *Criminology:* 27–48.

Karp, C., and C. Rosner. 1991. *When Justice Fails: The David Milgaard Story.* Toronto: McClelland and Stewart.

Kelling, G.L., T. Pate, D. Dieckman, and C. Brown. 1974. *The Kansas City Preventive Patrol Experiment: A Summary Report.* Washington, D.C.: Police Foundation Report.

———, and J.Q. Wilson. 1982. "Broken Windows: The Police and Neighborhood Safety." *Atlantic Monthly* 249.

———, and M.H. Moore. 1988. *Perspectives on Policing.* Washington, D.C.: National Institute of Justice.

Kelly, D.P. 1984. "Victims' Perceptions of Criminal Justice." *Pepperdine Law Review* 11: 15–22.

Kennedy, L.W., and V.F. Sacco, eds. 1996. *Crime Counts: A Crime Event Analysis.* Scarborough, Ont.: Nelson Canada.

Kiessling, J. 1989. Cited in D.A. Andrews, "Recidivism Is Predictable and Can Be Influenced: Using Risk Assessments to Reduce Recidivism." *Forum on Corrections Research* 1: 11–17.

Kingsley, B. 1993. *Common Assault in Canada.* Ottawa: Juristat.

Klein, J. 1976. *Let's Make a Deal: Negotiating Justice.* Toronto: D.C. Heath.

Klockars, C. 1971. *The Idea of the Police.* Beverly Hills, Calif.: Sage.

———, and S. Mastrofski, eds. 1991. *Thinking about Police: Contemporary Readings.* New York: McGraw-Hill.

Koller, K. 1990. *Working the Beat: The Edmonton Neighborhood Foot Patrol.* Edmonton: Edmonton Police Service.

Kong, R. 1994. *Urban/Rural Criminal Victimization in Canada.* Ottawa: Juristat.

Kosobook and Aelick v. The Solicitor-General of Canada (1976), 1 FC 540.

Koza, P., and A.N. Doob. 1975. "The Relationship of Pre-Trial Custody to the Outcome of a Trial." *Criminal Law Quarterly* 17: 391–400.

Kramer, J.H., R.L. Lubitz, and C.A. Kempinen. 1989. "Sentencing Guidelines: A Quantitative Comparison of Sentencing Policy in Minnesota, Pennsylvania, and Washington." *Justice Quarterly* 6, no. 4: 565–88.

Kruttschnitt, C. 1984. "Sex and Criminal Court Dispositions: The Unresolved Controversy." *Journal of Research in Crime and Delinquency* 20, no. 3: 213–32.

Landau, T. 1994. *Public Complaints against the Police: A View from Complainants.* Toronto: Centre of Criminology, University of Toronto.

Langan, R. 1994. "Between Prison and Probation: Intermediate Sanctions." *Science* 264: 791–93.

Langworthy, R.H., and L.F. Travis. 1994. *Policing in America: A Balance of Forces.* Don Mills, Ont.: Macmillan.

LaPrairie, C., 1994. *Seen but Not Heard. Report 1: The Inner City Sample, Social Strata, and the Criminal Justice System.* Ottawa: Department of Justice.

———. 1990. "The Role of Sentencing in the Over-Representation of Aboriginal Offenders in Correctional Institutions." *Canadian Journal of Criminology* 32: 429–40.

———, and E. Diamond. 1992. "Who Owns the Problem? Crime and Disorder in James Bay Cree Communities." *Canadian Journal of Criminology* 34, nos. 3–4: 417–34.

Latessa, E. 1995. "An Evaluation of the Lucas County Adult Probation Departments ISP and High Risk Groups." In A.T. Hartland, ed., *The Search for Effective Correctional Interventions.* Newbury Park, Calif.: Sage.

Law Reform Commission of Canada. 1974a. *Studies on Sentencing—Working Paper 3.* Ottawa: Information Canada.

———. 1974b. *Discovery in Criminal Cases.* Ottawa: Information Canada.

———. 1975. *Criminal Procedure: Control of the Process.* Ottawa: Minister of Supply and Services Canada.

———. 1983. *Police Powers: Search and Seizure in Criminal Law Enforcement—Working Paper 30.* Ottawa: Law Reform Commission of Canada.

———. 1984. *Questioning Suspects.* Ottawa: Minister of Supply and Services Canada.

———. 1984a. *Disclosure by the Prosecution.* Ottawa: Minister of Supply and Services.

———. 1984b. *Questioning Suspects—Working Paper 32.* Ottawa: Minister of Supply and Services.

———. 1985. *Arrest—Working Paper 41.* Ottawa: Law Reform Commission of Canada.

———. 1986. *Classification of Offenses—Working Paper 54.* Ottawa: Law Reform Commission of Canada.

———. 1987. *The Charge Document in Criminal Cases—Working Paper 55.* Ottawa: Law Reform Commission of Canada.

———. 1988a. *Compelling Appearance, Interim Release, and the Pre-Trial Detention.* Ottawa: Law Reform Commission of Canada.

———. 1988b. *Our Criminal Procedure—Report 32.* Ottawa: Law Reform Commission of Canada.

———. 1989. *Plea Discussions and Agreements.* Ottawa: Law Reform Commission of Canada.

———. 1990a. *Disclosure of the Prosecution—Report No. 22.* Ottawa: Law Reform Commission of Canada.

———. 1990b. *Controlling Criminal Prosecutions: The Attorney General and the Crown Prosecutor.* Ottawa: Law Reform Commission of Canada.

———. 1991a. *Police Powers—Report 33.* Ottawa: Law Reform Commission of Canada.

———. 1991b. *Aboriginal Peoples and Criminal Justice.* Ottawa: Law Reform Commision of Canada.

LeBlanc, T. 1994. "Redesigning Corrections for Federally Sentenced Women in Canada." *Forum on Corrections Research* 6, no. 1: 11–12.

LeFave, W., 1965. *Arrest: The Decision to Take a Suspect into Custody.* Boston: Little, Brown.

Lefebvre, L. 1994. "The Demographic Characteristics of Offenders on Day Parole." *Forum on Corrections Research* 6: 11–13.

Lewis, C. 1991. "Police Complaints in Metropolitan Toronto." In A.J. Goldsmith, ed., *Complaints against the Police: The Trend to External Review.* Oxford: Clarendon Press, pp. 153–75.

Lewis, D. 1992. *An Exploratory Study into Sentencing Practices in Summary Convictions Court in British Columbia.* Vancouver: Legal Services Society of British Columbia.

Lilly, J.R., R.A. Ball, G.D. Curry, and J. McMullen. 1993. "Electronic Monitoring of the Drunk Driver: A Seven-Year Study of the Home Confinement Alternative." *Crime and Delinquency* 39: 462–84.

Linden, R., and C. Fillmore. 1993. "An Evaluation Study of Women in Policing." In J. Hudson and J. Roberts, eds., *Evaluating Justice: Canadian Policies and Programs.* Toronto: Thompson Educational Publishing, pp. 93–116.

Linden, R., and C. Minch. 1982. *Women in Policing: A Review.* Ottawa: Solicitor-General of Canada.

Lipinski, S. 1991. *Adult Female Offenders in the Provincial/Territorial Corrections Systems, 1989–90.* Ottawa: Juristat.

Lipton, D., R. Martinson, and J. Wilks. 1975. *The Effectiveness of Correctional Treatment.* New York: Praeger.

Logan, C. 1993. *Criminal Justice Performance Measures for Prison.* Washington, D.C.: Bureau of Justice Statistics.

———, and B.W. McGriff. 1989. "Comparing Costs of Public and Private Prisons: A Case Study." *NIJ Reports* 216: 2–8.

Loree, D.J. 1993. "Innovation and Change in a Regional Police Force." In J. Chacko and S.E. Nancoo, eds., *Community Policing in Canada.* Toronto: Canadian Scholars' Press, pp. 139–82.

Los, M. 1994. "The Struggle to Redefine Rape in the Early 1980s." In J.V. Roberts and R.M. Mohr, eds., *Confronting Sexual Assault: A Decade of Legal and Social Change.* Toronto: University of Toronto, pp. 20–56.

Los Angeles Times. 1988. "Posh Zaccaro 'Jail' Quarters Upset Government." August 15: 2.

McCann v. The Queen (1975), 29 C.C.C. (2d) 377.

McCorkle, R.C. 1992. "Personal Precautions to Violence in Prison." *Criminal Justice and Behavior* 19, no. 2: 160–73.

McDonald, D.C. 1992. "Private Penal Institutions." In M. Tonry, ed., *Crime and Justice: A Review of Research,* Vol. 16. Chicago: University of Chicago, pp. 361–419.

MacDougall, D.V. 1979. "The Crown Election." *Criminal Reports* (3d) 5: 315–25.

McGahan, P. 1984. *Police Images of a City.* New York: Peter Lang.

MacKay, A.W. 1986. "Inmates' Rights: Lost in the Maze of Prison Bureaucracy?" *The Correctional Review* 1: 8–14.

Mackenzie, D. 1994. *Multi-Site Evaluation of Shock Incarceration: Executive Summary.* Washington, D.C.: National Institute of Justice.

Mackenzie, D.L., and D.B. Ballow. 1995. "Shock Incarceration and Recidivism: An Examination of Boot Camps in Four States." In J.O. Smylka and W.L. Selke, eds., *Intermediate Sanctions—Sentencing in the 1990s.* Cincinnati: Anderson.

———, and A. Piquero. 1994. "The Impact of Shock Incarceration Programs on Prison Crowding." *Crime and Delinquency* 40, no. 2: 250–61.

———, and J.W. Shaw. 1990. "Inmate Adjustment and Change during Shock Incarceration: The Impact of Correctional Boot Camp Programs." *Justice Quarterly* 7, no.1: 125–50.

———, J.W. Shaw, and C.C. Souryal. 1992. "Characteristics Associated with Successful Adjustment to Supervision." *Criminal Justice and Behavior* 19.

———, J.W. Shaw, and V.B. Gowdy. 1993. "An Evaluation of Shock Incarceration Programs in Louisiana." *Research in Brief.* Washington, D.C.: National Institute of Justice.

———, and C. Souryal. 1995. "Inmates' Attitude Change during Incarceration: A Comparison of Boot Camp and Traditional Prison." *Justice Quarterly* 12: 325–54.

McMahon, M. 1988. "Police Accountability: The Situation of Complaints in Toronto." *Contemporary Crisis* 12: 301–27.

Majury, D. 1994. "Seaboyer and Gayme: A Study InEquality." In J.V. Roberts and R.M. Mohr, eds., *Confronting Sexual Assault: A Decade of Legal and Social Change.* Toronto: University of Toronto, pp. 268–92.

Makin, K. 1995. "A Lawsuit Nearly Impossible to Win." *The Globe and Mail.* November 16: A8.

———. 1992. *Redrum the Innocent.* Toronto: Penguin.

Mandel, M. 1975. "Rethinking Parole." *Osgoode Hall Law Journal* 13: 501–46.

Mannette, J., ed. 1992. *Elusive Justice: Beyond the Marshall Inquiry.* Halifax: Fernwood.

Manning, P.K. 1971. "The Police Mandate, Strategies, and Appearances." In J.D. Douglas, ed., *Crime and Justice in American Society.* Indianapolis: Bobbs-Merrill.

———. 1989. "The Occupational Culture of the Police." In L. Hoover, ed., *The Encyclopedia of Police Science.* Dallas: Garland.

Martin, D. 1995. "Tracy's Right Was Taken from Her." *The Winnipeg Free Press.* August 3: A7.

Martin, J. 1970. "The Role and Responsibility of the Defence Advocate." *Criminal Law Quarterly* 12.

Martin, M., and L. Orgrodnik. 1996. "Canadian Crime Trends." In L.W. Kennedy and V.F. Sacco, eds., *Crime Counts: A Criminal Events Analysis.* Scarborough, Ont.: Nelson Canada, pp. 43–58.

Martin, S.E. 1991. "The Effectiveness of Affirmative Action: The Case of Women in Policing." *Justice Quarterly* 8, no. 4: 489–504.

———. 1990. *On the Move: The Status of Women in Policing.* Washington, D.C.: Police Foundation.

Martineau v. Matsqui Institution Disciplinary Board (1980), 1 S.C.R. 602.

Martinson, R. 1974. "What Works? Questions and Answers about Prison Reform." *Public Interest* 35: 22–54.

———. 1979. "Symposium on Sentencing: Part II." *Hofstra Law Review* 7: 243–58.

Mauer, M. 1994. "Testimony before the U.S. Congress House Judiciary Committee on 'Three Strikes and You're Out.'" Washington, D.C.: The Sentencing Project.

Maxfield, M.G., and T.L. Baumer. 1990. "Home Detention with Electronic Monitoring." *Crime and Delinquency* 36: 521–36.

———. 1979. "New Findings, New Views: A Note of Caution Regarding Sentencing Reform." *Hofstra Law Reform* 7: 243–58.

Mewett, A.W. 1996. *An Introduction to the Criminal Process in Canada,* 3rd ed. Scarborough, Ont.: Carswell.

Miethe, T.D., and C.A. Moore. 1986. "Racial Differences in Criminal Processing: The Consequences of Model Selection on Conclusion about Differential Treatment." *Sociological Quarterly* 27: 217–37.

———. 1985. "Socioeconomic Disparities under Determinate Sentencing Systems: A Comparison of Preguideline and Postguideline Practices in Minnesota." *Criminology* 23, no. 2: 337–64.

Miller, F.W. 1970. *Prosecution: The Decision to Charge a Suspect with a Crime.* Boston: Little, Brown.

Ministry of the Solicitor General. 1989. *Electronic Monitoring System for Offender Supervision: Pilot Project Evaluation.* Victoria: Province of British Columbia.

Mitchell, A. 1994. "Murder Sentence Stirs Angry Reaction across Nation." *The Globe and Mail.* November 18: A7.

———. 1995. "Latimer Murder Appeal Denied." *The Globe and Mail.* July 19: A1, A2.

Mitchell v. The Queen. 1976. 2. S.C.R. 577.

Mittelstaedt, M., and D. Downey. 1995. "Tories Withdraw Legal-Aid Threats." *The Globe and Mail.* September 14: A3.

Moon, P. 1994. "Native Self-Policing a Growing Force." *The Globe and Mail.* May 11: A4.

———. 1995. "Parole Hearings Mix of Hope, Fear, Nerves." *The Globe and Mail.* April 15: A1, A5.

Moore, C.A., and T.D. Miethe. 1986. "Regulated and Unregulated Sentencing Decisions: An Analysis of First-Year Practices under Minnesota's Felony Sentencing Guidelines." *Law and Society Review* 20: 254–77.

Moore, M.H. 1992. "Problem-Solving and Community Policing." In M. Tonry and N. Morris, eds., *Crime and Justice: A Review of Research,* Vol. 15. Chicago: University of Chicago, pp. 99–158.

———, and R.C. Trojanowicz. 1988. *Corporate Strategies for Policing.* Washington, D.C.: National Institute of Justice.

Morash, M., and L.B. Myers. 1995. "Gender, Workplace Problems, and Stress in Policing." *Justice Quarterly* 12, no. 1: 113–40.

Morgan, D.C. 1986. "Controlling Prosecutorial Powers—Judicial Review, Abuse of Process and Section 7 of the Charter." *Criminal Law Quarterly* 29: 15–65.

Morris, N., and M. Tonry. 1990. *Between Prison and Probation: Intermediate Punishments in a Rational Sentencing System.* New York: Oxford University Press.

Morrison, P., and R. Kong. 1996. *Motor Vehicle Crimes.* Ottawa: Juristat.

Morse, B., and L. Lock. 1988. *Native Offenders' Perceptions of the Criminal Justice System.* Ottawa: Minister of Supply and Services.

Motiuk, L.L., and S.L. Brown. 1994. "Sex Offenders and Their Survival Time on Conditional Release." *Forum on Corrections Research* 6, 14–17.

Moyer, S. 1987. *Homicides Involving Adult Suspects 1962–1984: A Comparison of Natives and Non-Natives.* Ottawa: Solicitor-General.

———, F. Kopelman, C. LaPrairie, and B. Billingsley. 1985. *Native and Non-Native Admissions to Provincial and Territorial Correctional Institutions.* Ottawa: Solicitor General of Canada.

Myers, M.A. 1995. "The Courts: Prosecution and Sentencing." In J.F. Sheley, ed., *Criminology,* 2nd ed. Belmont, Calif.: Wadsworth, pp. 407–27.

Nadin-Davis, R.P. 1982. *Sentencing in Canada.* Toronto: Carswell.

National Parole Board. 1981. *A Guide to Conditional Release for Penitentiary Inmates.* Ottawa: National Parole Board.

———. 1987. *Briefing Book for Members of the Standing Committee on Justice and Solicitor General.* Ottawa: National Parole Board.

———. 1988a. *Final Report—Task Force on Aboriginal Peoples in Federal Corrections.* Ottawa: Supply and Services.

———. 1988b. *National Parole Board Pre-Release Decision Policies.* Ottawa: Ministry of Supply and Services.

Normandeau, A. 1990. "The Police and Ethnic Minorities." *Canadian Police College Journal* 14: 215–29.

———. 1968. *Trends and Patterns in Crimes of Robbery.* Ph.D. dissertation. Philadelphia: University of Pennsylvania.

———, and B. Leighton. 1990. *A View of the Future of Policing in Canada.* Ottawa: Solicitor General of Canada.

Nouwens, T., L. Motiuk, and R. Boe. 1993. "So You Want to Know the Recidivism Rate." *Forum on Corrections Research* 5, no. 3: 22–26.

O'Brien, R.L. 1992. "Special Handling Units." *Forum on Corrections Research* 4, no. 3: 11–13.

Ogrodnik, L. 1993. *Canadian Crime Statistics, 1993.* Ottawa: Juristat.

———, and R. Paiement. 1992. *Motor Vehicle Theft.* Ottawa: Juristat.

Ontario. 1989. *The Report of the Race Relations and Policing Task Force:* Toronto: Province of Ontario.

Ontario Ministry of Corrections. 1991. *Annual Report 1990–1991.*

Osborne, J.A. 1983. "The Prosecutor's Discretion to Withdraw Criminal Cases in the Lower Courts." *Canadian Journal of Criminology* 25, no. 1: 55–78.

Ouimet, R. 1969. *Report of the Canadian Committee on Corrections—Toward Unity: Criminal Justice and Corrections.* Ottawa: Information Canada.

Packer, H.L. 1968. *The Limits of the Criminal Sanction.* Stanford: Stanford University.

Padavic, I., and B.F. Reskin. 1990. "Men's Behavior and Women's Interest in Blue-Collar Jobs." *Social Problems* 37, no. 4: 613–27.

Palumbo, D.J., M. Clifford, and Z.D. Snyder-Joy. 1992. "From Net-Widening to Intermediate Sanctions: The Transformation of Alternatives to Incarceration from Benevolence to Malevolence." In J.M. Byrne, A.J. Lurigio, and J. Petersilia, eds., *Smart Sentencing: The Emergence of Intermediate Sanctions.* Newbury Park, Calif.: Sage, pp. 229–44.

Palys, T.S., and S. Divorski. 1986. "Explaining Sentencing Disparity." *Canadian Journal of Criminology* 28: 347–62.

Pearson, F. 1986. *Research on New Jersey's Intensive Supervision Program: Final Report.* Washington, D.C.: National Institute of Justice.

Pearson, F.S. 1987a. "Evaluation of New Jersey's Intensive Supervision Program. *Crime and Delinquency* 34: 437–48.

———. 1987b. *Preliminary Findings of Research on New Jersey's Intensive Supervision Program.* New Brunswick, N.J.: Rutgers University Press.

Pelletier, B. 1990. "The Duty to Act Fairly in Penitentiaries." *Forum on Corrections Research* 2: 25–28.

Petersen, C. 1993. "A Queer Response to Bashing: Legislating against Hate." In J. Abell and E. Sheehy, eds., *Criminal Law and Procedure: Cases, Context, Critique.* North York, Ont.: Captus Press, pp. 225–26.

———. 1982. "Doing Time with the Boys: An Analysis of Women Correctional Officers in All-Male Facilities." In B.R. Price and N.J. Sokoloff, eds., *The Criminal Justice System and Women.* New York: Clark Boardman.

Petersilia, J. 1987a. *Expanding Options for Criminal Sentencing.* Santa Monica, Calif.: Rand Corp.

———. 1987b. "Georgia's Intensive Probation: Will the Model Work Elsewhere?" In B. McCarthy, ed., *Intermediate Punishments: Intensive Supervision, Home Confinement and Electronic Monitoring.* Monsey, N.Y.: Criminal Justice Press, pp. 15–30.

———. 1992. "California's Prison Policy: Causes, Costs, and Consequences." *The Prison Journal* 72: 8–36.

———, A. Abrahamse, and J.Q. Wilson. 1990. "The Relationship between Police Practice, Community Characteristics, and Case Attrition." *Police Studies* 1, no. 1: 23–38.

———, and E.P. Descheres. 1994. "What Punishes? Inmates Rank the Severity of Prison vs. Intermediate Sanctions." *Federal Probation* 58, no. 1: 3–8.

———, A.J. Lurigio, and J.M. Byrne. 1992. "Introduction: The Emergence of Intermediate Sanctions." In J.M. Byrne, A.J. Lurigio, and J. Petersilia, eds., *Smart Sentencing: The Emergence of Intermediate Sanctions.* Newbury Park, Calif.: Sage, pp. ix–xv.

———, and S. Turner. 1993. "Intensive Probation and Parole." In M. Tonry, ed., *Crime and Justice: A Review of Research,* Vol. 17. Chicago: University of Chicago, pp. 281–336.

———, and S. Turner. 1986. *Prison versus Probation in California: Implications for Crime and Offender Recidivism.* Santa Monica, Calif.: Rand.

Picard, A. 1995. "Police Get Weekend Jail Terms in Beating." *The Globe and Mail.* July 14: A1, A2.

Platiel, R. 1995. "One Question on Compensation: How Much?" *The Globe and Mail.* January 28: A6.

Porporino, F.J., and L.L. Motiuk. 1993. "Conditional Release and Offenders with Mental Disorders." *Forum on Correctional Research* 5, no. 3: 17–19.

Posner, C. 1991. "An Historical Overview of the Construction of Canadian Federal Prisons." *Forum on Corrections Research* 3, no. 2: 3–5.

Price, A.C., and B.G. Stitt. 1986. "Consistent Crime Control Philosophy and Policy: A Theoretical Analysis." *Criminal Justice Review* 11, no. 2: 23–30.

Quigley, T. 1994. "Some Issues in the Sentencing of Aboriginal Offenders." In R. Gosse, J.Y. Henderson, and R. Carter, eds., *Continuing Poundmaker and Riel's Request.* Saskatoon: Purich, pp. 269–98.

Rackmill, S.J. 1994. "An Analysis of Home Confinement as a Sanction." *Federal Probation* 58, no. 1: 45–52.

Rand Research Brief. 1994. *California's New Three-Strikes Law: Benefits, Costs, and Alternatives.* Santa Monica, Calif.: Rand Research Corp.

Reed, M. 1995. *Correctional Services in Canada: Highlights for 1993–94.* Ottawa: Juristat.

R. v. Askov (1990), 59 C.C.C. (3d) 449.

R. v. B.(A.) (15 May 1989), Barrie DC 988, Ontario District Court (unreported).

R. v. Barnes (1991), 63 C.C.C. (3d) 1.

R. v. Bazinet (1986), 25 C.C.C. (3d) 273.

R. v. Beaver Creek (1969), 2 D.L.R. (3d) 545.

R. v. Bickford (18 January 1989), Ontario Court of Appeal.

R. v. Black (1989), 50 C.C.C. (3d) 1.

R. v. Charles (1987), 36 C.C.C. (3d) 286.

R. v. Clarkson (1986), 25 C.C.C. (3d) 207.

R. v. Collins (1987), 1 S.C.R. 265.

R. v. D.(E.) (1990), 57 C.C.C. (3d) 151.

R. v. D.(S.) (1992), 72 C.C.C. (3d) 575.

R. v. Duarte (1990), 1 S.C.R. 30.

R. v. Ducharme (1990), Unreported, British Columbia Court of Appeal.

R. v. Jacoy (1988), 45 C.C.C. (3d) 46.

R. v. Joey Smith (1989), 50 C.C.C. (3d) 308.

R. v. Hansen (1977), 37 C.C. (2d) 371.

R. v. Harris (1987), 57 C.R. (3d) 356.

R. v. Heisler (1984), 11 C.C.C. (3d) 97.

R. v. Khan (25 August 1988), 59 C.C.C. (3d) 92 (S.C.C.).

R. v. L (W.K.) (1991), 64 C.C.C. (3d) 321.

R. v. Lyons (1987), 37 C.C.C. (3d) 1.

R. v. Manninen (1983), 34 C.C.C. (3d) 385.

R. v. Meddoui (1990), 61 C.C.C. (3d) 345.

R. v. Mellenthin (1992), 76 C.C.C. (3d) 481.

R. v. M.E.R. (1989), 49 C.C.C. (3d) 475.

R. v. Moses (1992), 71 C.C.C. (3d).

R. v. Oakes (1986), 24 C.C.C. (3d) 321.

R. v. Preston (1990), 79 C.C.C. (3d) 61.

R. v. Rickett (1975), 28 C.C.C. (2d) 297.

R. v. Ross 49 C.C.C. (3d) 475, 1989.

R. v. St. Jean (1970), 15 C.R.N.S. 194.

R. v. Singh (1983), 8 C.C.C. (3d) 38.

R. v. Smith (1989), 50 C.C.C. (3d) 97.

R. v. Storey (1990), 53 C.C.C. (3d) 316.

R. v. Therens (1985), 18 C.C.C. (3d) 481.

R. v. Thompson (1989), 50 C.C.C. (3d) 126.

R. v. Tomaso (1989), 70 C.R. (3d) 152.

R. v. Willis (1987), 37 C.C.C. (3d) 184.

Reiss, A. 1967. *The Police and the Public.* New Haven, Conn.: Yale University Press.

———. 1992. "Police Organization in the Twentieth Century." In M. Tonry and N. Morris, eds., *Crime and Justice: A Review of Research,* Vol. 15. Chicago: University of Chicago Press, pp. 51–98.

Reiss, A.J. 1974. "Discretionary Justice." In D. Glaser, ed., *Handbook of Criminology.* Chicago: Rand McNally.

Renner, K.E., and A.H. Warner. 1981. "The Standard of Social Justice Applied to an Evaluation of Criminal Cases Appearing before the Halifax Courts." *Windsor Yearbook of Access to Justice* 1: 62–80.

Renzema, M., and D. Skelton. 1990. "Trends in the Use of Electronic Monitoring: 1989." *Journal of Offender Monitoring* 3, no. 3: 12, 14–19.

Report of the Aboriginal Justice Inquiry. 1991. *The Justice System and Aboriginal People.* Winnipeg: Province of Manitoba.

Report of the Task Force on the Release of Inmates. 1973. Ottawa: Information Canada.

Report to Parliament by the Sub-Committee on the Penitentiary System in Canada. 1977. Ottawa: Minister of Supply and Services.

Richards, B. 1992. "Burden of Proof." *The Wall Street Journal.* December 8: A1, A8.

Roberg, R.R., and J. Kuykendall. 1993. *Police and Society.* Belmont, Calif.: Wadsworth.

Roberts, J.V. 1988a. "Early Release from Prison: What Do the Canadian Public Really Think?" *Canadian Journal of Criminology* 30: 231–49.

———. 1988b. "Public Opinion about Sentencing: Some Popular Myths." *Justice Report* 5: 7–9.

———. 1994. *Criminal Justice Processing of Sexual Assault Cases.* Ottawa: Juristat.

———, and A.N. Doob. 1989. "Sentencing and Public Opinion: Taking False Shadows for True Substances." *Osgoode Hall Law Journal* 27: 491–515.

———, and R.M. Mohr, eds., 1994. *Confronting Sexual Assault: A Decade of Legal and Social Change.* Toronto: University of Toronto Press.

———. 1994. "Sexual Assault in Canada: Recent Developments." In J.V. Roberts and R.M. Mohr, eds., *Confronting Sexual Assault: A Decade of Legal and Social Change.* Toronto: University of Toronto, pp. 3–19.

Roberts, T. 1992. *Assessment of the Victim Impact Statement Program in British Columbia.* Ottawa: Department of Justice, Research and Sentencing Directorate.

Rodgers, K. 1994. "Wife Assault in Canada." *Canadian Social Trends.* Ottawa: Statistics Canada: 3–8.

Ross, R. 1994. "Duelling Paradigms? Western Criminal Justice versus Aboriginal Community Healing." In R. Gosse, Y. Youngblood Henderson, and R. Carter, *Continuing Poundmaker and Riel's Request.* Saskatoon: Purich, pp. 241–68.

Rossi, P.H., E. Waite, C.E. Bose, and R.E. Berk. 1974. "The Seriousness of Crimes: Normative Structure and Individual Differences." *American Sociological Review* 39: 224–37.

Rothman, D.J. 1971. *The Discovery of the Asylum.* Boston: Little, Brown.

Royal Canadian Mounted Police. n.d. *RCMP First Nations Community Policing Service.* Ottawa: RCMP.

Rubenstein, M.L., S.H. Clarke, and T.J. White. 1980. *Alaska Bans Plea Bargaining.* Washington, D.C.: Government Printing Office.

Ruby, C.C. 1985. "Violence in and out of Prison." *The Globe and Mail.* June 29: E6.

Ruby Collins v. The Queen (1987) 1 S.C.R. 265.

Rudwick, E. 1962. *The Unequal Badge: Negro Policemen in the South: Report of the Southern Regional Council.* Atlanta: Southern Regional Council.

Russell, P. 1987. *The Judiciary in Canada: The Third Branch of Government.* Toronto: McGraw-Hill Ryerson.

Ryan, H.R.S. 1990. "Foreword." In D.P. Cole and A. Manson, *Release from Imprisonment: The Law of Sentencing, Parole, and Judicial Review.* Toronto: Carswell, pp. v–x.

Sacco, V.F. 1995. *Fear and Personal Safety.* Ottawa: Juristat.

Salhany, R.E. 1986. *Arrest, Seizure, and Interrogation,* 3rd ed. Toronto: Carswell.

Sawyer, K. 1985. "Tougher Probation May Help Georgia Clear Crowded Prisons." *Washington Post.* August 16: A1.

Schmidt, A.K. 1989. "Electronic Monitoring." *Journal of Contemporary Criminal Justice* 5: 133–40.

Schmolka, V. 1992. *Studies on the Sexual Abuse of Children in Canada. Is Bill C-15 Working? An Overview of the Research on the Effects of the 1988 Child Sexual Assault Amendments.* Ottawa: Ministry of Supply and Services.

Sellers, M. 1989. "Private and Public Prisons: A Comparison of Costs, Programs, and Facilities." *International Journal of Offender Therapy and Comparative Criminology.*

Senna, J.J., and L.J. Siegel. 1995. *Essentials of Criminal Justice.* Minneapolis/St. Paul: West.

Shannon, E. 1991. "New Kings of Coke." *Time.* July 1.

Shannon, L. 1988. *Criminal Career Continuity: Its Social Context.* New York: Human Sciences Press.

Shapland, J., J. Willmoew, and P. Duff. 1985. *The Victim in the Criminal Justice System.* Brookfield, Vt.: Gower.

Shaw, M. 1994. "Women in Prison: A Literature Review." *Forum on Corrections Research* 6, no. 1: 13–18.

Shearing, C.D. 1984. *Dial-a-Cop: A Study of Police Mobilisation.* Toronto: Centre of Criminology.

———. 1992. "The Relation between Public and Private Policing." In M. Tonry and N. Morris, eds., *Crime and Justice: A Review of Research,* Vol. 15. Chicago: University of Chicago, pp. 399–434.

Sherman, L.J. 1975. "Evaluation of Policewomen on Patrol in a Suburban Police Department." *Journal of Police Science and Administration* 3: 434–38.

Sherman, L.W. 1986. "Policing Communities: What Works?" In A.J. Reiss and M. Tonry, eds., *Crime and Justice: A Review of Research,* Vol. 8, pp. 343–86.

———. 1985. "Causes of Police Behavior. The Current State of Quantitative Research." In A.S. Blumberg and E. Nieferhoffer, eds., *The Ambivalent Force*, 3rd ed. New York: Holt, Rinehart and Winston, pp. 183–95.

———. 1980. "Causes of Police Behavior: The Current State of Quantitative Behavior." *Journal of Research in Crime and Delinquency* 17: 80–87.

———, and R. Berk. 1984. "The Specific Deterrent Effects of Arrest for Domestic Assault." *American Sociological Review* 49: 261–72.

———, and E.G. Cohen. 1986. *Citizens Killed by Big-City Police: 1974–1984.* Washington, D.C.: Crime Control Institute.

———, P.R. Gartin, and M.E. Buerger. 1989. "Hot Spots of Predatory Crime: Routine Activities and the Criminology of Place." *Criminology* 27, no. 1: 27–56.

———, and R.H. Langworthy. 1979. "Measuring Homicide by Police Officers." *Journal of Criminal Law and Criminology* 70: 546–60.

———, D.A. Smith, J.D. Schmidt, and D.P. Rogan. 1992. "Crime, Punishment, and Stake in Conformity: Legal and Informal Control of Domestic Control." *American Sociological Review* 57: 680–90.

Sichel, J.L., L.N. Friedman, J.C. Quint, and M.E. Smith. 1978. *Women on Patrol: A Pilot Study of Police Performance in New York City.* New York: Vera Institute of Justice.

Silverman, R., and L.W. Kennedy. 1993. *Deadly Deeds: Murder in Canada.* Scarborough, Ont.: Nelson Canada.

Silverman, R.A., J.J. Teevan, and V.F. Sacco, eds., 1991. *Crime in Canadian Society,* 4th ed. Toronto: Butterworths.

Singer, S. 1988. "The Fear of Reprisal and the Failure of Victims to Report a Personal Crime." *Journal of Quantitative Criminology* 4: 289–302.

Skolnick, J. 1966. *Justice without Trial.* New York: Wiley.

Smith, D., C. Visher, and L. Davidson. 1984. "Equity and Discretionary Justice: The Influence of Race on Police Arrest Decision." *Journal of Criminal Law and Criminology* 75: 234–49.

Smith, L.G., and R.L. Akers. 1993. "A Comparison of Recidivism of Florida's Community Control and Prison: A Five-Year Survival Analysis." *Journal of Research in Crime and Deliquency* 30: 267–92.

Solicitor General of Canada. 1991. *Annual Report on Electronic Surveillance as Required under Subsection 195 (1) of the Criminal Code 1989.* Ottawa: Minister of Supply and Services Canada.

———. 1985. *Victims of Crime.* Canadian Urban Victimization Survey. Ottawa: Solicitor General of Canada.

Sparks, R. 1981. "Surveys of Victimization—An Optimistic Assessment." In M. Tonry, ed., *Crime and Justice—An Annual Review of Research.* Chicago: University of Chicago Press, pp. 1–60.

Stansfield, R.T. 1996. *Issues in Policing: A Canadian Perspective.* Toronto: Thompson Educational Publishing.

Statistics Canada. 1982. *Canadian Urban Victimization Survey.* Ottawa.

———. 1991. *Public Perceptions of Crime and the Criminal Justice System.* Ottawa.

———. 1994. *Violence against Women Survey.* Ottawa.

Steffensmeier, D., and M.D. Harer. 1993. "Bulging Prisons, An Aging U.S. Population, and the Nation's Crime Rate." *Federal Probation* 57, no. 2: 3–10.

Stenning, P. 1983. *Legal Status of the Police.* Ottawa: Law Reform Commission of Canada.

Stinchcombe v. R. (1991), 68 C.C.C. (3d) 1.

Stolzenberg, L., and S.J. D'Alessio. 1994. "Sentencing and Unwarranted Disparity: An Empirical Assessment of the Long-Term Impact of the Sentencing Guidelines in Minnesota." *Criminology* 32, no. 2: 301–10.

Strauss, M. 1985. "Judge Indicts Biased Sentencing Practice." *The Globe and Mail.* October 18: A1, A2.

Stuart, D. 1994. "Policing under the Charter." In R.C. Macleod and D. Schneiderman, eds., *Police Powers in Canada: The Evolution and Practice of Authority.* Toronto: University of Toronto Press, pp. 75–99.

———, and R.J. Delisle. 1995. *Learning Canadian Criminal Law,* 5th ed. Carswell: Toronto.

Sub-Committee on the Penitentiary System in Canada. 1977. Ottawa: Supply and Services Canada.

Suriya, S.K. 1993. "The Representation of Visible Minorities in Canadian Police: Employment Equity Beyond Rhetoric." *Police Studies* 16, no. 2: 44–62.

Sutton, J. 1994. "Learning to Better Predict the Future: National Parole Board Risk-Assessment Training." *Forum on Corrections Research* 6, no. 3: 20–22.

Swartz, M.A. 1973. Quoted in J. Caplan, *Criminal Justice.* Mineola, N.Y.: Foundation Press.

Sykes, G. 1958. *The Society of Captives.* Princeton, N.J.: Princeton University Press.

———, and S. Messinger. 1960. "The Inmate Social Code." In R. Cloward et al., eds., *Theoretical Studies in the Social Organization of the Prison.* New York: Social Science Research Council, pp. 6–9.

————, and E.E. Brent. 1983. *Policing: A Social Behaviorist Perspective.* New Brunswick, N.J.: Rutgers University Press.

————, and F. T. Cullen. 1992. *Criminology,* 2nd ed. Fort Worth, Tex.: Harcourt Brace Jovanovich.

Takagi, P. 1974. "A Garrison State in a 'Democratic' Society." *Crime and Social Justice* 5, 34–43.

Taking Responsibility: Report of the Standing Committee on Justice and the Solicitor General on Its Review of Sentencing. 1988. Ottawa: Supply and Services.

Tappan, P. 1966. "Who Is the Criminal?" *American Sociological Review* 12: 96–102.

Taylor, C.J. 1979. "The Kingston, Ontario Penitentiary and Moral Architecture." *Histoire Sociale/Social History* 12, no. 24: 385–408.

Territo, L., J.B. Halsted, and M.L. Bromley. 1995. *Crime and Justice in America,* 4th ed. Minneapolis/St. Paul: West Publishing.

Then, E. 1990. *An Introduction to Part XII.2 of the Proceeds of Crime.* Edmonton: University of Alberta.

Thomas, C., and C. Logan. 1992. "The Development, Present Status, and Future Potential of Correctional Privatization." In P. Seidenstat, ed., *Privatizing Correctional Institutions.* New Brunswick, N.J.: Transaction.

Thompson, D. 1985. *Intensive Probation Supervision in Illinois.* Chicago: Center for Research in Law and Justice.

Toch, H. 1977. *Living in Prison.* New York: Free Press.

Tonry, M. 1990. "Stated and Latent Functions of ISP." *Crime and Delinquency* 36: 174–91.

————. 1991. "The Politics and Processes of Sentencing Commissions." *Crime and Delinquency* 37: 307–29.

————, and R. Will. 1990. *Intermediate Sanctions.* Washington, D.C.: National Institute of Justice.

Tracy, P., M.E. Wolfgang, and R.M. Figlio. 1990. *Delinquency in Two Birth Cohorts.* New York: Plenum.

Travis, F.T. 1990. *Introduction to Criminal Justice.* Cincinnati: Anderson.

Trojanowicz, R.C., 1982. *An Evaluation of the Neighborhood Foot Patrol Program in Flint, Michigan.* East Lansing, Mich.: Michigan State University.

————, and B. Bucqueroux. 1990. *Community Policing: A Contemporary Perspective.* Cincinnati: Anderson.

Tso, T. 1992. "Moral Principles, Traditions, and Fairness in the Navajo Nation Code of Judicial Conduct." *Judicature* 76, 1.

Tunnell, K.D. 1990. "Choosing Crime: Close Your Eyes and Take Your Chances." *Justice Quarterly* 7, no. 4: 691–710.

Tyler, T. 1992. "Police Trials: Is Justice Being Served?" *The Toronto Star.* May.

United States Department of Justice (Bureau of Justice Statistics). 1985. *Pretrial Release and Misconduct.* Washington, D.C.: U.S. Government Printing Office.

United States General Accounting Office. 1990. *Intermediate Sanctions: Their Impacts on Prison Overcrowding, Costs, and Recidivism Are Still Unclear.* Washington, D.C.: United States General Accounting Office.

Ursel, J. 1994. *The Winnipeg Family Violence Court.* Ottawa: Juristat.

Vallee, B. 1986. *Life with Billy.* Toronto: Seal.

Van Den Haag, E. 1982. "The Criminal Law as a Threat System." *Journal of Criminal Law and Criminology* 73: 709–85.

Vera Institute of Justice. 1972. *Programs in Criminal Justice Reform.* New York: Vera Institute of Justice.

Verdun-Jones, S. 1989. *Criminal Law in Canada: Cases, Questions, and the Code.* Toronto: Harcourt Brace Jovanovich.

Vinglis, E., H. Blefgen, D. Colbourne, P. Culver, B. Farmer, D. Hackett, J. Treleaven, and R. Solomon. 1990. "The Adjudication of Alcohol-Related Criminal Driving Cases in Ontario: A Survey of Crown Attorneys." *Canadian Journal of Criminology* 32, no. 4: 639–50.

Visher, C. 1987. "Incapacitation and Crime Control: Does a 'Lock 'Em Up' Strategy Reduce Crime?" *Justice Quarterly* 4, no. 4: 513–44.

———. 1995. "Career Offenders and Crime Control." In J.F. Sheley, ed., *Criminology,* 2nd ed. Belmont, Calif.: Wadsworth, pp. 515–33.

Von Hirsch, A. 1976. *Doing Justice.* New York: Hill and Wang.

Walker, S. 1984. *Sense and Nonsense about Crime.* Belmont, Calif.: Wadsworth.

———. 1993. *Taming the System.* New York: Oxford University Press.

———. 1994. *Sense and Nonsense about Crime,* 3rd ed. Belmont, Calif.: Wadsworth.

Waller, I. 1974. *Men Released from Prison.* Toronto: University of Toronto.

———. 1994. *Sense and Nonsense about Crime: A Policy Guide,* 2nd ed. Pacific Grove, Calif.: Brooks/Cole.

Wallerstedt, J. 1984. *Returning to Prison.* Washington, D.C.: National Institute of Justice.

Warden, A.P. 1993. "The Attitudes of Women and Men in Policing: Testing Conventional and Contemporary Wisdom." *Criminology* 31, no. 2: 203–43.

Welch, S., J. Gruhl, and C. Spohn. 1984. "Sentencing: The Influences of Alternative Measures of Prior Record." *Criminology* 22: 215–27.

———, and C. Spohn. 1986. "Evaluating the Impact of Prior Record of Judges' Sentencing Decisions: A Seven-City Comparison." *Justice Quarterly* 3: 389–407.

Wexler, J.G., and D.D. Logan. 1983. "Sources of Stress among Women Police Officers." *Journal of Police Science and Administration* 11: 46–53.

Wheatley, J.R. 1974. "Plea Bargaining—A Case for Its Continuance." *Masssachusetts Law Quarterly* 59: 31–41.

Wheeler, G. 1987. "The Police, the Crowns, and the Courts: Who's Running the Show?" *Canadian Lawyer.* February.

———, and R. Hissong. 1988. "Effects of Sanctions on Drunk Drivers: Beyond Incarceration." *Crime and Delinquency* 34: 29–42.

Williams, J., and D. Rodeheaver. 1991. "Processing of Criminal Homicide Cases in a Large Southern City." *Sociology and Social Research* 75: 80–88.

Wilson, J.Q. 1968. *Varieties of Criminal Behavior.* Cambridge, Mass.: Harvard University.

———. 1975. *Thinking about Crime.* New York: Basic Books.

———, and A. Abrahamse. 1992. "Does Crime Pay?" *Justice Quarterly* 9, no. 3: 359–78.

Wilson, M. 1994. *Spousal Homicide.* Ottawa: Juristat.

———, and M. Daly. 1994. *Spousal Homicide.* Ottawa: Juristat.

Wilson, O.W., and R.C. McLaren. 1977. *Police Administration.* New York: McGraw-Hill.

Winnipeg Police Department. 1990. *Statistical Report.*

Wolff, L. 1992. *Arson in Canada.* Ottawa: Juristat.

Wolfgang, M.E., R.M. Figlio, and T. Sellin. 1972. *Delinquency in a Birth Cohort.* Chicago: University of Chicago Press.

Wood, C. 1989. "Police: A Call for Racial Balance." *The Toronto Star.* April 12: A22.

Worden, A.P. 1993. "The Attitudes of Men and Women in Policing: Testing Conventional and Contemporary Wisdom." *Criminology* 31, no. 2: 203–42.

Wright, C. 1995. *Risk of Personal and Household Victimization.* Ottawa: Juristat.

———. 1993. *Longitudinal Court Outcome Study of Individuals Accused of Homicide Reported in 1988.* Ottawa: Canadian Centre for Justice Statistics.

Young, G. 1995. *Risk of Personal and Household Victimization.* Ottawa: Juristat.

———. 1995. *Police Personnel and Expenditures in Canada—1993.* Ottawa: Juristat.

———. 1994. *Trends in Justice Spending—1988/89 to 1992/93.* Ottawa: Juristat.

———. 1993. *Police Personnel and Expenditures in Canada.* Ottawa: Juristat.

Yuile, J.C., M.A. King, and D. MacDougall. 1988. *Child Victims and Witnesses: The Social Science and Legal Literatures.* Ottawa: Department of Justice.

Zamble, E., and F. Porporino. 1988. *Coping, Behavior and Adaptation in Prison Inmates.* New York: Springer-Verlag.

———. 1990. "Public Support for Criminal Justice Policies: Some Specific Findings." *Forum on Corrections Research* 2: 14–19.

———, and K. Kalm. 1990. "General and Specific Measures of Public Attitudes toward Sentencing." *Canadian Journal of Behavioral Science* 22: 327–37.

Zedlewski, E. 1987. *Making Confinement Decisions.* Washington, D.C.: Government Printing Office.

Zimmerman, S. 1992. "'The Revolving Door of Despair': Aboriginal Involvement in the Criminal Justice System." *University of British Columbia Law Review:* 367–426.

Zimring, F.E., and G. Hawkins. 1988. "The New Mathematics of Imprisonment." *Crime and Delinquency* 34: 425–36.

Index

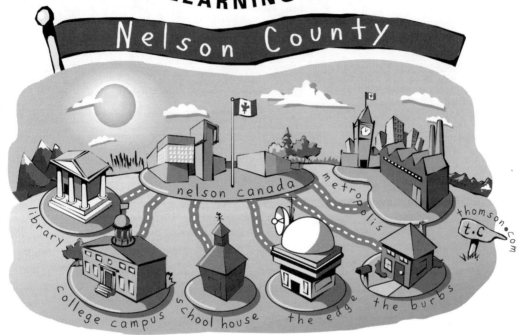

A COMMUNITY OF LEARNING SOLUTIONS

Nelson County

library

college campus

school house

the edge

the burbs

nelson canada

metropolis

thomson.com

t.c

Visit us on the Web at **http://www.nelson.com/nelson.html**.
You can also send us your comments via e-mail at **college_arts_hum@nelson.com**.

To the owner of this book

We hope that you have enjoyed *Criminal Justice in Canada,* and we would like to know as much about your experiences with this text as you would care to offer. Only through your comments and those of others can we learn how to make this a better text for future readers.

School _____ Your instructor's name _____

Course _____ Was the text required? _____ Recommended? _____

1. What did you like the most about *Criminal Justice in Canada?*

_____

_____

_____

2. How useful was this text for your course?

_____

_____

_____

3. Do you have any recommendations for ways to improve the next edition of this text?

_____

_____

_____

4. In the space below or in a separate letter, please write any other comments you have about the book. (For example, please feel free to comment on reading level, writing style, terminology, design features, and learning aids.)

_____

_____

_____

_____

Optional

Your name _____ Date _____

May ITP Nelson quote you, either in promotion for *Criminal Justice in Canada* or in future publishing ventures?

Yes _____ No _____

Thanks!

You can also send your comments to us via e-mail at
college_arts_hum@nelson.com

PLEASE TAPE SHUT. DO NOT STAPLE.

TAPE SHUT

TAPE SHUT

- - - - - - - - - - - - - FOLD HERE - - - - - - - - - - - - -

TAPE SHUT

TAPE SHUT

MAIL⤳POSTE

Canada Post Corporation
Société canadienne des postes

Postage paid   Port payé
if mailed in Canada si posté au Canada
Business Reply   **Réponse d'affaires**

0066102399   01

Nelson

0066102399-M1K5G4-BR01

ITP NELSON
MARKET AND PRODUCT DEVELOPMENT
PO BOX 60225 STN BRM B
TORONTO ON M7Y 2H1